Adventure Guide

British Columbia

Adventure Guide

British Columbia

Ed & Lynn Readicker-Henderson

HUNTER

HUNTER PUBLISHING, INC,
130 Campus Drive, Edison, NJ 08818
☎ 732-225-1900; ☎ 800-255-0343; Fax 732-417-1744
www.hunterpublishing.com

Ulysses Travel Publications
4176 Saint-Denis, Montréal, Québec
Canada H2W 2M5
☎ 514-843-9882, ext. 2232; fax 514-843-9448

Windsor Books
The Boundary, Wheatley Road, Garsington
Oxford, OX44 9EJ England
☎ 01865-361122; Fax 01865-361133

ISBN 1-58843-366-8

This and other Hunter travel guides are also
available as e-books in a variety of digital formats
through our online partners, including
Amazon.com and Netlibrary.com.

Cover photo: Canoe Reach © Airphoto - Jim Wark
Interior photos provided by the authors unless otherwise specified.
Index by Nancy Wolff

Base maps provided by Lynn Readicker-Henderson
Maps by Kim André © 2004 Hunter Publishing, Inc.

www.hunterpublishing.com

Hunter's full range of guides to all corners of the globe is featured on our website. You'll find guidebooks to suit every type of traveler, no matter what their budget, lifestyle, or idea of fun.

Adventure Guides – There are now over 40 titles in this series, covering destinations from Costa Rica and the Yucatán to Tampa Bay & Florida's West Coast and Belize. Complete with information on what to do, as well as where to stay and eat, *Adventure Guides* are tailor-made for the active traveler, with all the practical travel information you need, as well as details of the best places for hiking, biking, canoeing, horseback riding, trekking, skiing, watersports, and all other kinds of fun.

Alive Guides – This ever-popular line of books takes a unique look at the best each destination offers: fine dining, jazz clubs, first-class hotels and resorts. In-margin icons direct the reader at a glance. Top-sellers include *The US Virgin Islands, The Cayman Islands* and *Aruba, Bonaire & Curaçao.*

Our **Romantic Weekends** guidebooks provide escapes for couples of all ages and lifestyles. Unlike most "romantic" travel books, ours cover more than charming hotels and delightful restaurants, with a host of activities that you and your partner will remember forever.

One-of-a-kind travel books available from Hunter include *The Best Dives of the Bahamas; Golf Resorts; Cruising Alaska* and many more.

Full descriptions are given for each book at www.hunterpublishing.com, along with reviewers' comments and a cover image. You can also view pages and the table of contents. Books may be purchased on-line via our secure transaction facility.

Contents

Introduction

British Columbia, plain and simple, has everything. If you're looking for the pleasures of civilization, there's Victoria and Vancouver, two of the most popular cities in North America. If you're after the wild, there's the almost untouched Stikine wilderness.

British Columbia is the most diverse province in Canada: from the central plains to the coastal mountains and the Rockies, from the dry Okanagan Valley to the rainforests of the Pacific islands, it's like the rest of the world in miniature.

There's great history, too – the early HBC traders, and the First Nations villages that are coming back strong, keeping their traditions alive. There's also wildlife: bears, moose, whales. You can have high tea in Victoria and be out watching killer whales jump within an hour.

BC is also as easy a place in which to travel as you'll ever find. People are friendly, with that famed Canadian politeness. They speak good French and better English. There's a tourism infrastructure that's among the most organized in the world, ready to get you out and help you have fun.

Best of all is the land. It's so spectacular that it makes you want to pull over the car so you can gawk. There's something new and different around every corner.

Who We Are, What We Do & What You're in For

We've been writing guidebooks that deal with British Columbia for more than a dozen years; over that time, we've been lucky enough to get to see and do an astounding range of stuff in the province. We've sat with bears and kayaked with whales. We've ridden boats on pristine rivers and hiked trails that led to truly the middle of nowhere. We've stayed in hotel rooms that make us burn to win the lottery so we can move in permanently.

The goal of this book is to take advantage of that experience – hey, it's a rough job, but somehow we slug through it – to introduce you to the places and things that we think you're going to love.

However, let's admit to a few biases up front: you travel to see the wild, to be outside, to see the best that this great spinning globe of ours has to offer; you travel to find out what's different in cities and towns – gravy on french fries, an entire nation bemoaning its coinage. You don't go out there to eat or sleep at the same places you can find at home. Chain stores, in all their many permutations, make for mediocre experiences. We believe that you get the best trip when you deal with the people who live, work and make a place their home. If you're planning to spend your trip eating two meals a day at McDonald's, this book isn't for you.

We also believe the best travelers, the happiest travelers, are the ones who know what they're looking at. That's why we spend so much time on history and culture. There's a whole different country out there. It ain't just like it is back home.

And we hope it never is.

Geography

■ Land

 British Columbia is defined by the chains of mountains that line the land: to the north are the **Cassiar** and **Omineca Mountains**; to the southeast, the **Columbia Mountains**; and to the east, the **Coast Mountains** and the mighty **Rockies**. These mountains divide the province into sections of plateaus and valleys, rich for agriculture and animal husbandry, while blocking off huge tracts of land that are left to wilderness.

The **Coast Mountains** separate the rainforests of the coast from the drier interior; farther north, the **Fairweather Range** includes the highest point in British Columbia, Mt. Fairweather – one of the biggest massifs in the world. You can see it from 50 miles off, and it still looks huge.

At the far side of the province are the **Rockies**, dropping down to parallel the Alaska Highway, and then moving over towards the next province, Alberta, and one of the great park systems of the world. Here, Jasper, Banff, Kootenay and Yoho parks combine to form a UNESCO World Heritage Site.

■ Water

 The rivers of the province are no less impressive. The largest of them, the **Fraser River**, is 850 miles long and is fed by the Nechako, Quesnel, Chilcotin and Thompson rivers. The **Kootenay** flows down to the Columbia River in Washington State, and westward to the Pacific, weaving a tortuous path between mountain ranges. More than a quarter of a billion birds stop along the **Stikine** – the fastest free-flowing river left on the continent – during the height of the migration season.

■ The Coast

 If all that wasn't enough, British Columbia has a long chain of islands, including **Vancouver Island**, biggest on the west coast – almost the size of England, in fact. There are the delightful little **Gulf Islands** – Salt Spring issues its own currency – and farther north, the islands of BC mesh with those of Alaska, forming the **Inside Passage**. **Princess Royale Island** has Kermodie bears. A rare subspecies of black bear, Kermodies are white. Off the beaten track are the **Queen Charlotte Islands**, home to some of the richest First Nations cultures in Canada. "First Nations" is an accepted term throughout Canada used to refer to all groups that were here before the arrival of Europeans.

Along the coast, there is the single greatest glory of the north, the **Western red cedar** (*Thuja plicata*). The cones are oval, as opposed to the round yellow cedar cones. This tree was the department store for First Nations peoples. They made their canoes from it, their houses, their clothes. The tree also provided medicine. The biggest Western red cedar trees are around Vancouver Island – stop at Cathedral Grove, or from Tofino, go over to Meares Island, where there's a tree trunk more than 60 feet in circumference. These trees can live over a thousand years; they rot from the inside, so a perfectly healthy tree may have a hollow space in it that's 10 or 15 feet across and 30 feet high. Red cedars also provide a base for other forest growth: the biggest trees on Meares Island have more than 50 species of plants growing on them. You can't understand life on the coast until you've taken a good look at these giants.

When William H. Seward bought Alaska from the Russians, his grand plan was actually to use it as leverage to allow the United States to annex British Columbia. The man knew a good thing when he saw it.

History

The land that is now British Columbia was first brought to European attention by Juan Perez in 1774; **Captain Cook** was the first European to land in the area, near Vancouver Island, in 1778, and he was quickly followed by **George Vancouver**. But the early explorers weren't really interested in British Columbia itself. They were actually just out there in search of a Northwest Passage.

So what finally got people interested in the territory? **Fur**. Plain and simple. Europe needed beavers to make felt for hats, and Canada had a lot of beavers. Prices were ridiculously high, and so traders and *voyageurs* headed into the interior, looking for fur sources.

From the official standpoint, it was **Alexander Mackenzie** who opened the territory, when his 1793 expedition reached the Pacific Coast by land – a decade before Lewis and Clark ever turned their sights west. Mackenzie was not only the first to cross the continent, he was one of the greatest explorers the North has ever seen. After dipping his toes in the Pacific Ocean, he headed north, following what is now the Mackenzie River system to the Great Slave Lake and eventually to the coast of the Arctic Ocean. He kept hearing stories about a big river to the west (the Yukon, no doubt), and in his search to find it, he created the foundations for Canada's western provinces, mapping endless stretches of land that see few visitors even today.

Where explorers first trod, tradesmen soon followed. After Mackenzie opened the West, **Simon Fraser** and **George Thompson** – names common to Canada's landscape today – followed in his footsteps. They took the trade out of the disorganized hands of the independent trader and opened a series of fur-trading posts for the **Northwest Company**, which was later absorbed by the **Hudson's Bay Company**. The HBC, expanding as quickly as it could, sent out men to solidify the company's hold on trade and to fend off territorial encroachment by upstart fur traders.

The first whites to settle permanently in British Columbia were a ragged group of hunters and trappers, who either lived with the Indians (the term currently in use through much of Canada is First Nations peoples) or took advantage of them, seeking their fortune in furs.

From this beginning grew the modern province of British Columbia.

Actually, in the beginning, it looked as if there were going to be three provinces, or at least three territories. The islands, including Vancouver Island, were not incorporated into the larger area until the middle of the 1800s. The Stikine River was also an independent administrative district, left to its own devices until the influx of gold miners made some kind of central control necessary.

Date modern BC to the territory joining the Dominion of Canada in 1871, and to the first railroad in the province, which joined BC to points east in 1875.

BC today is the best of Canada, with the best landscape, unparalleled scenery and plenty of open space. You can travel for days and not see another human, or you can hang out on the corner of Robson Street in Vancouver, and feel as if, sooner or later, the entire world will walk by. BC has found its niche in a diverse economy and vast natural beauty.

▪ The Gold Rushes

 Even a brief look at the history of the North shows that if it weren't for gold, there still might not be anybody north of Seattle. The Russians stuck pretty much to the coastline while Alaska was theirs – move 100 miles inland and it's almost impossible to find a Russian place name – perhaps because they had their own great North, and crossing Siberia had dimmed their ardor for Arctic land crossings. And while there were certainly explorers in the North, and the HBC built fort after fort in British Columbia, the truth is, sooner or later the fur trade was going to dry up.

MAD AS A HATTER

The fur trade tumbled about the time someone in England figured out a way to make imitation beaver felt out of rabbit fur. The process involved a mercury bath. Those involved quickly got sick with mercury poisoning, hence the term, "mad as a hatter."

The basic and inglorious truth is that the land was opened up by prospectors with nothing on their minds but gold.

Gold made people crazy; it made them perform superhuman feats of strength and endurance. Long after anyone sane had turned around and headed south, would-be miners were standing knee-deep in snow, frozen and half-starved, thinking the next trip to the stream might be the lucky one. And if not this stream, then the next. Maps became hot commodities, trading for several thousand dollars each at a time when that much money could provide you a reasonable living for several years. Exploration became a by-product of the search for gold.

The **Klondike rush** is the most famous and it conjures up the most vivid images – miners heading north over the Chilkoot Pass in winter, dragging their gear behind them; trails littered with dead horses; a mad rush to build boats to float the Yukon to the goldfields.

 Rent Charlie Chaplin's movie, *The Goldrush*, for a taste of how the search for gold turned into legend.

But there were actually hundreds of gold rushes. Moving north through British Columbia is to move along the history of gold strikes. From the southern Fraser, up to the Cariboo rush, BC was the place to be. Nobody would have ever found gold in the Yukon if all the good land in BC hadn't already been staked out. It's pretty safe to assume that nearly every creek in the North has been panned, mined, prodded and poked by people looking for gold; and any time one person got lucky, everyone else within shouting distance came running. Throughout the North there are places named for their distance from the last big strike: Sixtymile, Fortymile.

These miners were not, for the most part, having a good time. They were freezing their butts off a long way from home, and, more often than not, coming up empty. Even their equipment, which should have made their lives easier, made things worse. Some early advice to would-be miners said that their most important bit of clothing would be "a good pair of well-nailed boots. They may be high or low, but should be over eighteen inches." The same writer goes on to suggest a "nine-pound eiderdown sleeping bag" for summer. What these guys would have done for a chance to shop at REI.

GOLD CLAIMS

The tradition of mining claims continues, and much of the North has been staked out by miners who will be quite displeased if they catch you looking for gold on their claim. They'll probably let it pass if you're just standing in a stream for a few minutes, swishing your gold pan around – most miners today are well past that method, working with high-tech and expensive equipment – but you do need to be cautious and courteous. The Natural Resources flyer says, "The gold you pan probably won't concern them as much as the possible vandalism of equipment, liability, or interruption of their operations." Then again, it might. Technically, you must have permission to be on someone's claim. The days when claim-jumpers were routinely shot are still not so far in the past. Claims should be marked off by highly visible stakes, so watch for them.

Most streams coming out of the mountains have some kind of gold flake in them and, by working the stream gravels, you might find a few. There's still gold out there, at least in trace amounts.

There's still a lot of land that's not claimed, and many commercial operators will let you pan gold in their claims for a small fee.

> **AUTHOR TIP:** If you're in a stream, the best place to look for gold is where turbulence changes slow water to fast. Put a bit of gravel from the stream into your pan, add some water, and swish gently, allowing water and rocks to swish over the sides of the pan. Gold is heavier than gravel and, as you eliminate rocks and dirt from the pan, the gold stays behind.

You've got to try panning for gold at least once – this is what brought people up North to begin with.

Climate

Because BC's terrain is so varied, about all we can tell you is to expect the unexpected. You can roast on a summer day in the Okanagan Valley, or nearly freeze your butt off over the mountains near Whistler. Those averages and trends compiled by the weather bureaus on the climate of the North rarely mean anything to travelers.

As a general guideline, summers are mild and beautiful, with temperatures in the 50°-80°F range – usually in the lower end of that range – throughout most of BC. However, it might rain at any time, and snow storms are not unknown at higher elevations in June and July. The Okanagan can hit 100°F.

The mountains cool down quickly, and the larger mountains and big northern lakes create their own highly unpredictable weather patterns. You can find an area suffering from full flood conditions, facing a forecast with nothing but rain, while on the other side of the nearest mountain range people are fearing drought.

Overall, expect long summer days – northern reaches of the province can get upwards of 16 hours of daylight in midsummer – and yes, it is very, very easy to get sunburned up there, particularly on your face and head. The weather is warm and sunny, punctuated regularly by rain and cold – how regularly is mostly a matter of luck. Nights tend to be quite cool.

For summer travelers, not much special clothing is needed. It is best to bring a light jacket and a sweater or two. If the temperature drops, it's better to have on several layers of light clothes, rather than one layer of heavy clothing, since layers trap warm air and keep you toasty. You'll need them, and there's no telling when. Don't skimp on your rain shell. A good lightweight Gore-Tex or similar shell will get you through almost any summer weather, especially if you layer it with a sweatshirt. If you're planning to get really wet – by flyfishing or whitewater rafting – skip the Gore-Tex and go for Gumby clothes. Only rubber rain gear can keep you completely dry in the wettest conditions.

In the winter, things are quite a bit harsher. Workers on the Alaska Highway faced temperatures of -50°F in BC. Do not venture out into a Northern winter without appropriate clothing and preparation. The days are short and the nights are incredibly cold.

■ The Aurora Borealis

 There's a little quirk of the climate that's worth keeping an eye out for. In fact, a lot of people visit the North for no reason other than the hope of seeing the *Aurora borealis*, or Northern Lights.

As most people travel in the summer, of course, it's too light to see the display unless you find yourself wide awake at 2 am or so.

The aurora is produced by a high-vacuum electrical discharge, created by interactions between sun and earth. What you see – the glowing curtain of lights – is charged electrons and protons formed by the sun hitting gas molecules in the upper atmosphere. The aurora can be compared to a TV picture. Electrons strike the screen (or the air), getting excited and making a glow. The most common color for the aurora is a yellow-green, caused by oxygen atoms roughly 60 miles above the earth.

The lights get more intense the farther north you go. People in Montana occasionally see a display; around Muncho Lake, you've got a really good chance of seeing lights on clear, dark nights. There are those who say they can hear the aurora make crackling sounds, but scientists haven't been able to prove it.

Head outside after dark and look north. You never know.

Wildlife

Keep your camera ready, because this is where BC really shines. Traveling around the province, you've got an excellent chance of seeing moose, black bear, grizzly bear, Dall's sheep, stone sheep, mountain goats, wolves, fox, beaver, deer, elk and caribou, not to mention a host of smaller mammals, without ever leaving your car. The streams and lakes are teeming with king salmon, sockeye, Dolly Varden, grayling, char and trout. In the sky are hundreds of species of birds: sandhill cranes, endless varieties of ducks and geese, the ubiquitous raven and the near-legendary yellow-bellied sapsucker. Any time you stop for a picnic, a magpie is likely to land on the table and steal food. Bald eagles are everywhere along the coast – there are more bald eagles on Vancouver Island than in all the continental United States – along with murres, rhinoceros auklets and puffins.

Throughout this book, we note areas where you stand a good chance of seeing wildlife, be it mountain goats, eagles, bears, moose, whatever. But it's best to be ready anywhere; animals go where they want to go. That's part of the fun of being a wild animal.

■ Catching A Glimpse

 What you will see of this amazing variety of fauna is largely a matter of luck, partly a matter of timing and partly a matter of looking in the right places and being able to see the moose hiding in the brush. But keep in mind that no matter where an animal is supposed to be, it's always going to be where it wants to be.

Traditional wisdom says that the bigger animals come out in the early morning and late evening. In the far North in the summertime, 5 to 8 am and 7 to 10 pm are prime animal-spotting hours. Along the roadsides, these times are good because there are fewer cars to scare off the animals.

A baby mountain goat grazes along the Icefields Parkway.

Also keep a close eye out by water, where animals go to drink and feed. The banks of ponds, streams and lakes are great spots to see bears.

> **WARNING:** *The best way to see animals is from the comfort of your car. The signs saying "Moose Area" or "Caribou Area" are not jokes. In a confrontation with a moose, both the moose and your car will lose, so drive with caution. The car is your safest viewing place.*

The number one rule for safe animal viewing is this: *Never get out of your car to follow an animal*. There are three simple reasons.

- As long as you're in your car, the animal isn't going to think you are food. Get out on foot, and guess what? You're back in the food chain, and you're a whole lot lower down on it than you're used to being. Even if they don't want you for food, you might set off their defensive mode. Every year people are attacked by moose. Invariably, the moose wins. Bambi does not live in British Columbia.

- Even opening your car door might cause the animal to flee. Should you follow, you are endangering the animal's survival by taking it from its food source and possibly from its young, and by making it burn valuable calories. This is a crime, subject to arrest and fines. If you see someone hassling wildlife, take down the plate numbers and report them at the next ranger station.

- Finally, you are depriving others of a chance to see the animal.

Never forget that these animals are wild and interested only in their own survival. When you spot an animal, pull your car slowly to the side of the road. A Canadian Park Ranger told us that the biggest danger on the Alaska Highway is from people who do not follow this advice, thus causing accidents. Yeah, sure, park your car dead center in the road to gawk. The animals might get a kick out of watching a serious collision. It's more exciting for everybody to see a bear than to come around a corner and find someone stopped in the road trying to watch a bear. So get your car off the road, and then shut off the engine – although sometimes this sudden change of sound can startle an animal, so opinions are divided on this. Make no sudden moves or sounds. Remember that you are invading the animal's home, and that its rights are foremost. The quieter you are, the more likely it is that the animal will look you over for a moment and then go back about its business, leaving you plenty of time for photos.

Never feed an animal (except the mosquitoes; there isn't much you can do about that), and keep all food at your campsite in scent-proof containers to discourage the curious. At all times, treat animals with respect; they, in turn, will treat you to a look at the beauty and the power of nature.

■ Land Animals

Other than birds, the three most common animals along the BC roadsides are the moose, the bear and the mosquito. Perhaps the most sought-after is the wolf.

Moose

Moose are the largest members of the deer family, standing from five to seven feet high at the shoulder. The antlers, which grow only on the male, can measure six feet from tip to tip. Covered in thick, coarse brown fur, moose are ungainly animals, but they can move with surprising grace and speed, and we think they have a kind of Zen dignity.

Moose are grazing animals, eating twigs, bark, grasses, moss and water lilies. Willow is one of their favorite foods. Sometimes you can see where moose have been through because there will be a "hedge line" – all the plants cropped off at an even height.

Although moose live in small groups in the winter, during the summer months they tend to live alone, and the males are rarely sighted down from the mountains.

Moose breed in the fall. The males go through a fairly elaborate jousting routine, putting their antlers to good use while they try to establish dominance. Gestation period is about 240 days, with the calves born in May and June. Twin calves are not uncommon, and sometimes there are even triplets.

More people are injured by moose than by any other wild mammal in the Americas. The only other large mammals in the world that can cause as much damage (besides people themselves) are the hippos of Africa. Moose are very territorial and protective, especially of their young. They are larger than you think, and their hooves are very sharp. They can kick both forwards and backwards. Never think of a moose as a big, harmless galoot. Sit and watch them all you want, but do it from a safe distance. Only an idiot with a death wish tries to sneak up on a moose.

If the moose comes at you, run. This is the exact opposite of the advice for bear encounters. Moose just want you out of their territory. If they see you running away, they'll likely give up the chase and go back about their business.

We had a moose charge us once when we were on a motorcycle. We came around a corner, and she was eating willows by the side of the road. She didn't know what a motorcycle was, but she was protecting her calf, and she was sure we were a threat; on our part, we were desperately trying to get the bike turned around and get out of there before she killed us. Seeing a moose, hackles raised, coming at you is not something you want to experience. Do not wait to hear what the moose breath feels like. Run.

 For the best batch of moose photos you'll ever see, pick up a copy of Michio Hoshino's book, ***Moose***.

Bears

There's nothing quite like seeing a grizzly or a black bear walking in the woods or along the shore of a lake or stream hunting for fish. Or better yet, leaping into the water and coming up soaking wet, shaking itself.

Brown Bears

Brown bears, or grizzlies, are rarer and considerably larger than their cousins, the blacks. Your odds of seeing a grizzly along the roadside are minimal, but we've seen them along the Cassiar quite a few times, as well as on some back roads. The Khutzemateen Sanctuary (see page 249), near Prince Rupert, is BC's prime grizzly spot.

Grizzlies average seven to nine feet long, with males ranging from 400 to 1,100 pounds. Females run about 20% smaller. Brown bears can range from dark brown to blonde in color; the easiest way to distinguish them is by the hump on their back, just behind the head. Brown bears have a life expectancy of about 20 years in the wild.

These bears are bigger and faster and more dexterous than you can imagine. There is no thrill quite like watching a grizzly eat a fish, its claws moving as delicately as a pair of chopsticks. T-shirts in some of the roadside shops show a grizzly paw the size of a dinner plate; the caption says "Actual Size," and it's not a joke. The biggest grizzly track we've found, on the Stikine River, near Telegraph Creek, was 17 inches long, heel to pug. And that was in a place where there weren't really big bears.

Black Bears

More common are black bears. You're almost sure to see at least one black bear (if not a lot more) somewhere along the roadside. They range from three to five feet in length and weigh from 150 to 400 pounds. A good-sized black bear is easily mistaken for a brown bear because a black bear can range in color from black to very light brown. In fact, British Columbia has a kind of black bear that is actually white: the Kermodie, found around Princess Royal Island in British Columbia and around the junction of the Cassiar and the Yellowhead highways near Kitwanga. Kermodies are incredibly rare; if you spot one, run to the nearest lottery ticket vendor. Your luck has never been better.

The life cycle of browns and blacks is similar. Cubs (one or two, very occasionally three) are born during the mother's hibernation. Black bear cubs weigh only a few ounces at birth, and their birth may not even wake the mother. They attach themselves to a teat, and the mother keeps sleeping.

In his 1555 book, *A Description of the Northern Peoples*, Olaus Magnus wrote that the "she-bear, a creature full of wiles, gives birth to shapeless cubs, which she licks with her tongue into a form like her own." Imagine a world that full of marvels.

A black bear caught on film near Stewart-Hyder.

Rising from hibernation, the bears spend the first week or two not quite awake. Their metabolism, shut down during the winter, is still pretty slow. They come out of their dens, dig up a few skunk cabbage tubers (which act as a laxative, helping to get things running again after the long sleep), and then go back to sleep for a while longer.

The bulk of the summer is spent eating, exploring and teaching the young bears what they need to know. Bears are very playful and, while not particularly social, cubs can have a great time with each other.

Come fall and the first touch of colder weather, the bears seem to enter a kind of frantic mood, as they try to pack on enough fat to last them through the winter. Bears along the coast move down to salmon streams and start to gorge themselves on the return. A bear may eat part of 50 fish a day. They eat the stomach, brains, some skin and the roe, the parts with the most fat, leaving the rest behind for birds to scavenge.

Come winter, the bears hole up in their dens. One of the last things they do before hibernating is eat some clay if it's available – sometimes you'll see scratch marks in clay banks, where a bear has tried to find some better tasting clay. This is thought to help plug up the digestive tract for the winter.

Bears are omnivorous – they eat anything. They are also highly intelligent and extremely curious. When threatened, surprised or angered, they are extremely dangerous.

Bear Encounters

While virtually every story you've ever heard about bear attacks is likely to be untrue, you do not want to mess with bears in the wild. They are not like Yogi waiting to steal a picnic basket. They're animals with jaws strong enough to take off your leg, and if you provoke one, it will react.

However, bears really have no interest in you at all. In fact, they're usually appalled that you're even there, and they'll do anything they can to get away from you. This makes it fairly easy to stay safe. All you have to do is make sure the bear sees you first. To avoid untoward encounters with bears, there are a few simple precautions you should take.

- The easiest thing to do is **avoid contact**. Never get out of your car when you spot a bear. When hiking, make some noise to alert bears of your presence. Talk loudly, bang a stick against trees, or drop a few pebbles into an empty soft drink can and tie it around your waist so it clanks, or wear a small bell (locals call these Grizzly Dinner Bells). Problem is, it's incredibly annoying to hike with all that noise. A bit less intrusive is to sing or simply talk loudly. We tend to just call out, "Hey, Bear," when walking around blind corners in places where bears might be, and that seems to work. The bears don't want to see you – they just want to eat and get on with their business.

- **Never smell interesting**. Try not to walk into the wind; bears don't see well, but they do have an excellent sense of smell. They are both curious and hungry. Bears are omnivores, like humans, and they'll eat pretty much anything – berries, fish, squirrels, whatever looks good.

  They are also known to eat camping gear if the right mood hits them. Cooking inside a tent is an invitation to disaster, as are strong perfumes or soaps. Keep all smells away from your campsite, and keep your food in a bearproof container or up in a tree, hanging from a rope. If you're keeping food in the car, the trunk is safer than the interior – at least that way they won't tear up your upholstery if they want at your pretzels. Bears have only about six months to get fat enough to make it through hibernation, and so they get touchy about their food supply. When you consider a squirrel is only about 2,000 calories, you know it takes a lot of eating to fill a bear.

- If you see a **bear cub**, head back the way you came, away from the cub, as quickly as possible, without showing signs of distress. Get out of there, because where there's a cub, there's a protective mother nearby. There are more stupid people/bear altercations because of people wanting to pet the cute bear cub than all other causes combined. People see a cub out playing, and seem to forget that Mom has claws big enough to whack off a human head in a single blow. Stay away from cubs. Period.

- Bears like to leave their dinner and then come back to it again later. If you see a lot of **carrion birds** – ravens, eagles, hawks – circling, that could mean there's a kill nearby; go another direction.

- Bears always have the rights to berry bushes and **fishing streams**. A single bear can eat 2,000 or more berries in a single day (and you have to wonder who counted seeds in bear scat, and for how long, to come up with that number), so a loaded bush is always tempting for a bear. Stay out of thick patches of bush.

- Never let a **dog** loose in the forest; it's generally better to leave your dog at home. Dogs and bears don't get along. Dogs suddenly think they're Superdog when faced by a bear. Even pampered weiner dogs have been known to go out after grizzlies. Guess who won.

If you see a bear, don't run and don't panic. Food runs, and you will lose any race you have with a bear. On a dirt road, we once startled a bear. We were driving maybe 25 mph; the bear passed us, and ran straight up a hill and out of sight faster than we could put on the brakes. This speed is not unusual; bears have been clocked at well over 30 mph, and browns at 41 mph – that's 100 meters in under six seconds. You don't stand a chance if you run and the bear feels like chasing you.

In closer quarters, the advice of bear experts is to stand your ground and speak to the bear in a firm tone of voice. If the bear stands, it is not necessarily a threat sign (since bears have lousy eyesight, they stand to get a better look). Keep talking to the bear. Let it know you're there and not interesting. Do not turn your back to the bear. Do not, under any circumstances, run. Back away slowly, but if the bear starts to follow, hold your ground. If you can, back up to a tree and start to climb. Climb high, though, because grizzlies can reach quite a ways. Climbing won't work against black bears, who can climb better than you.

If you're facing a bear and the bear woofs and runs, even in your direction, that's okay. Hold your ground. But if it holds its own ground and woofs, or pops its teeth together, it's time for you to back up. Keep facing the bear, don't run, don't panic, but give the bear some room.

If the bear turns sideways, that's not a good sign. It's a threat posture. Just like you wave your arms to show the bear you're big, the bear is showing you its flanks to prove how big it is. Take this as a sign to start backing up, slowly. If the bear follows you, drop your hat or jacket, something that smells like you but doesn't smell like food. Most bears will investigate what you drop, and be satisfied.

Absolutely do not imitate the bear's sounds or postures. This is the number two stupid thing people do, next to trying to pet cubs. If the bear is in a threat pose, you want to submit, not mirror it back.

Look big. If you're in a group, everybody stand together. If you've got a coat on, spread it out. Hold your arms out.

Play dead only as an absolutely last resort. Curl into a fetal position, keep your pack on for extra protection, and cross your arms behind your neck. Reports vary on which attacks are worse. Grizzlies tend to maul and get it over with. Black bears hang out and nibble, and are more likely to think you're food, or at least a really fun toy that they can swat around for a while. If you're attacked, hold still for as long as possible. Something that doesn't move loses its entertainment value, and the bear will probably get bored and leave pretty quickly.

Guns are pretty much useless against bears. Unless you're either very lucky or a crack shot with an ice cool head, calm enough to make Clint Eastwood look like he needs Ritalin, you'll just piss off the bear. Pepper sprays can work from about 20 feet, but it's best not to get that close in the first place. These sprays are the choice of locals. However, it's not a good idea to go merrily tromping off into the bush figuring the pepper spray will protect you. Use it as a last resort, at best.

PEPPER SPRAY FOR DINNER?

Recently, there have been a number of cases of people figuring that pepper spray, since it deters bears when sprayed in their faces, would also act as a kind of bear repellent. These people have sprayed pepper spray all over their backpacks and tents. The problem is, old pepper spray smells like dinner. Bears come running for it.

If you're going to carry pepper spray, remember it works only when fresh – and not always then. Buy a spray that has 1-2% capsaicin in it, and that has at least 225 grams of power. A can will run you about forty bucks. Spray in the direction of the bear while it's still a ways off; sometimes, just walking into the mist will deter it. If the bear is closer than 25 feet, adjust for the wind and aim for the face. Read the label before you need to know how it works, and follow the directions carefully. Like a recent article in *Backpacker* magazine said, "This stuff isn't brains in a can." If you follow the rules above, you'll never need the stuff.

You cannot take pepper spray with you on an airplane. And one more caveat: sooner or later, everybody – and we mean everybody – who carries bear spray ends up blasting themselves with it.

THE FUN SIDE OF PEPPER SPRAY

Once you've blasted yourself with pepper spray, you have two immediate problems to deal with. The first is that anything strong enough to stop a bear is not going to be that much fun on you. If it's in your eyes, head for the nearest stream and wash your eyes out with clear water for at least 15 minutes. If you've got contacts in, toss them; you'll never want them in your eyes again. On your skin, there are two schools of thought: one says that washing just spreads that capsaicin, the ingredient that stings; the other says try to get the damn stuff off you by rinsing until you can rinse no more. If you've got some cooking oil or vegetable oil with you, rub that on; it will dissolve the capsaicin, and then you can wash the oil off so you don't smell like lunch.

Which brings up problem two, mentioned above: loose pepper spray to a bear is like the smell of bacon to a truck driver. You now smell like a good snack. Leave. Go find a hotel. Take a long shower. Toss your clothes in the garbage.

Pepper spray is good stuff; it's what people who spend their time in the woods all carry. Just make sure where you're aiming it.

Here's an old-timer story of what to do as the last resort, when you're being attacked by a bear: jam your fist down its throat and block the airway. Maybe before the bear finishes chewing off your arm, it will suffocate. Maybe.

All of these precautions work in theory, but still depend upon the bear's mood. If the bear doesn't feel like being placated, it won't be. The bear doesn't know and doesn't care about the rules.

Finally, do not ever, for any reason, feed a bear. Bears are very, very smart. If they get food from a person once, they're likely to think it can happen again, and that's how you end up with bears in garbage cans and rummaging around houses. When that happens, sooner or later, forestry officials will have to kill the bear. Why don't they just relocate them, you ask? Because bears are smart, and they know where home is. Relocated bears will do just about anything to get back home. They've been known to swim hundreds of miles, just to get back to that trash can. A fed bear is a dead bear.

 The best bear pictures ever were taken by Michio Hoshino; they're in his book *Grizzly*.

The one true, cautionary bear tale we will tell is that Hoshino, an extremely cautious man who spent his life around bears and knew the rules as well as he knew his cameras, was killed by a grizzly, somewhere in Siberia. Hoshino was sleeping. Perhaps the bear took offense at the color of his tent – it's impossible to know. The point is that, in the end, a bear will do exactly what he wants to do.

Nevertheless, bear attacks are extremely rare. Take proper care and don't worry too much. We hiked in bear country for four years before we had even the most mild confrontation. Now, after so long doing this, we've had bears sneak up and smell our feet. We're still here to tell the story. Obey the rules, and remember the bear is boss.

Wolves

You're not likely to see one, but keep your eyes peeled. A wolf sighting is more exciting than just about any other thing you'll see in the North.

The first wolf we ever saw chased us. We were on a motorcycle, and the wolf was crossing the highway. It heard us, its ears twitched, and it was off. The only sad part was that we were going too fast to enjoy watching the wolf.

The first thing you have to be sure of when you spot a wolf is that it isn't a coyote. There are a lot more coyotes in the North than wolves. Coyotes are smaller in both body and head. Wolves have short, rounded ears, while coyote ears tend to be longer and pointed. If you're tracking, you'll see a wolf has front paws larger than its rear paws; it's the other way around on a coyote.

Wolves have suffered from massive negative publicity ever since Little Red Riding Hood went home and lied her fool head off. There is legal wolf hunting, and you can bet even more are killed illegally. The population is barely holding its own, and it's likely to slip fast if there's a bad year for the food supply.

It wasn't always like this. The wolf was considered a powerful animal by Northern Native Americans. The Kwakiutl believed that if a bow or gun was used to kill a wolf, the weapon became unlucky and had to be given away. Wolves were guiding spirits and companions.

They are simply beautiful animals to watch.

The **gray wolf**, *Canis lupus*, averages between 40 and 80 inches long, nose to tail. They can be three feet high at the shoulder, and weigh up to

130 pounds. We have a plaster cast of a wolf track, taken off the Stikine River, that's over six inches long. Wolves can get big. They are a mixture of browns, tans and grays; usually the muzzle is a lighter color than the rest of the body.

Wolves are quintessential pack animals, feeding on caribou, deer, sheep, goat, moose and whatever else they can hunt. In hard times, they go after squirrels, marmots and other small game.

Wolves stick to their own territory. They are so territorial, in fact, that it is believed prey animals are often able to find the "no man's land" between two wolf packs and so travel through an area safely. For the wolves, being so territorial makes them easier to hunt.

The gray wolf once ranged over nearly all the land north of what's now the Canadian border. They are reduced to pockets now.

 For a great movie with some of the best wolf photography ever, try *Never Cry Wolf*, based on the book by Farley Mowat.

You may also be interested to contact Friends of the Wolf, a conservation group devoted exclusively to the protection of wolves and wolf habitat. Write them at PO Box 21032, Glebe Postal Outlet, Ottawa, Ontario, Canada K1S 5N1.

Other Mammals

The coastal regions are host to a variety of smaller mammals: voles, beaver, weasels, mink, squirrels, mice, marten, porcupines and so on. Most of these live quite deep in the forest and you're unlikely to spot them, although you might get a mouse or a vole wandering into your campsite.

■ Marine Life

Whales

 Spend some time on the coast and you're going to see whales. They might be just the little beluga whales, the stately humpback or the incredible grey whales, but if you're on the water, you're going to come across something. Your best bets are around Victoria for orca, Prince Rupert for humpback, and Tofino for greys.

Humpbacks

Humpbacks (*Megaptera novoeanglioe*) are most commonly seen in the northern coastal area. Humpback whales grow to 50 feet, but most are closer to 40. They are distinguished by the way they swim and their shape at the waterline: their back forms a right angle as they dive.

Whales do not generally show their tails above water unless they are sounding or diving deep – when you see the tail, that's usually the last you'll see of the whale.

Humpback tails are as distinctive as human fingerprints, and scientists use the patterns on their huge, broad tails as means of identification.

One of the main points of study with humpbacks is their **song**. Scientists all over the coast are dropping hydrophones in the water to record whale song, which has definite rhythms and repetitions. Whales have been known to stop a song when leaving the North for warmer waters, and then pick it up on exactly the same note when they return the following year.

The fluke of a humpback whale, Prince Rupert.

The premier animal sighting is a **breaching** whale. Humpbacks come all the way out of the water. It's an amazingly slow move – the whale just keeps moving up and up and up before falling back down on its side. Whales like to flop back and forth, beating the water with their flukes. Some of the reasons for this behavior are unknown, but often it's seen when the animals are feeding. Breach behavior is also thought to be simply for the fun of it, and sometimes as a sign of agitation. There are less scrupulous whale-watching tour operators who will take out a dozen small boats, surround a group of whales from a legal distance, and thrill their clients with the whales coming up out of the water – which the whales are doing because they're seriously pissed off and feeling threatened by the boats.

Humpbacks **feed** only in British Columbia and Alaska; they fast during the winter months in Hawaii. In the rich waters of the northern coast, whales create a "bubble net" by swimming around a school of krill and trapping them in exhalation. The whales then lunge up through the krill, mouths open, scooping up tons of krill and sea water. The water gets squeezed out through the baleen, long spiny plates that take the place of teeth in many species of whale.

When watching the sea, look for the spout, the whale's breath, which is visible from quite a distance. It looks like a small palm tree of water and, from a distance, is much easier to spot than the body of the whale.

Minke

Minke whales (*Balaenoptera acuturostrata*), also common along the coast, have an almost invisible spout, and they don't stay on the surface for very long when they breathe, making them very difficult to spot; they're also likely to stay up only for a couple of breaths at most. Minkes are often mistaken for large porpoises, very small humpbacks or, occasionally, orca. The smallest of the rorqual whales, minke whales run up to 31 feet for females, 27 feet for males, weighing up to perhaps 10 tons. They are characterized by a triangular snout. Their body color is black above and white below, and many have a band of white in the middle of their flippers. Their dorsal fin is considerably back of the center, giving them an oddly sleek, racy look. Minke are not particularly endangered: there are estimated to be more than 500,000 of them. They mostly travel alone.

Gray Whales

Off the west coast of Vancouver Island – particularly around Tofino – you have a good chance of seeing gray whales (*Eschrichtius robustus*). These are, like the name says, mostly gray, with white mottling. They have a narrow, tapered head, and although they don't have a dorsal fin, they do have a dorsal hump, about two thirds of the way back on the body. This is followed by a series of six-12 knuckles along the dorsal ridge that extend to the fluke (tail). Its flippers are paddle shaped and pointed at the tips. Its fluke is about 10-12 feet across, pointed at the tips, and deeply notched in the center. A full-grown gray male measures about 45 feet, with the females a little bigger. An adult gray whale weighs 30-40 tons.

Gray whales are baleen whales, eating small crustaceans and tube worms. Like humpbacks, they feed primarily during the summer months, but they travel farther north, moving into the Bering and Chukchi seas.

A gray whale has between 130 and 180 baleen plates hanging from each side of its upper jaw. Each piece is anywhere from two to 10 inches long, and kind of a dirty white color.

Grays reach sexual maturity at five-11 years of age, or when they reach 36-39 feet in length. Females bear a single calf, at intervals of two or more years. Courtship and mating behavior are complex, and frequently involve three or more whales of mixed sexes. Mating and calving both occur primarily in the lagoons of Baja California, Mexico, although both have been observed during the migration. Gestation is 12-13 months. Calves weigh 1,100-1,500 pounds and are about 15 feet long at birth. They nurse for seven or eight months on milk that is 53% fat (human milk is 2% fat).

Gray whales are fairly easy to spot. They generally blow three to five times in 15- to 30-second intervals, and then raise fluke and head down. They can stay underwater for up to 15 minutes.

There used to be three major gray whale populations. The Asian and North Atlantic groups have been pretty much cleaned out from hunting, so only the North Pacific population has any kind of numbers, with somewhere around 20,000 whales. The International Whaling Commission has listed the gray whale as a fully protected species since 1947.

HOW TO KILL A WHALE

Killing whales isn't as difficult as it once was. If you're a Norwegian with no recriminations, or a Japanese hiding behind the façade of scientific research (but that doesn't explain the whale meat stores all over Japan, does it?), you chase them down in a large ship and shoot a harpoon at them from a cannon. When the harpoon hits the whale, the tip explodes, hopefully killing it before you have to waste another couple hundred bucks on a second harpoon.

But it wasn't always like this, and there's no real way to look at the history of the North without looking at the history of whaling. From the 1600s into the 1900s, whales provided lamp oil, corset stays, perfume bases and a hundred other must-have items.

The best account of traditional whaling is, of course, *Moby Dick*. Melville had done his time on a whaling ship, and he knew what he was talking about. When a sailing ship spotted a whale or a group of whales, they lowered whaleboats – about 20 feet long – and gave chase. They drew close enough to lance the whale and harpoon it. This meant, really, getting right on top of the whale. Then the crew held on for the ride, trying to stick more lances in the whale and injure it enough to slow it down. It was incredibly dangerous, bloody work, and a whaling ship that didn't lose a few crew members to accidents was a miracle ship.

Let Melville tell it: *A short rushing sound leaped out of the boat; it was the darted iron of Queequeg. Then, all in one wild commotion, came an invisible push from astern, while forward the boat seemed striking on a ledge. The sail collapsed and exploded; a gush of scalding vapor shot up nearby; something rolled and tumbled like an earthquake beneath us. The whole crew were half suffocated as they were tossed helter-skelter into the white curdling cream of the squall. Squall, whale and harpoon had all blended together, and the whale, merely grazed by the iron, escaped.*

European and American hunters set out in ships 100 feet or longer, only getting near the whales in the small boats at the last moment. Eskimo and Inuit hunters paddled out after whales in their kayaks. The killing technique was essentially the same: lance it, wear it out. But the Native hunters were doing this in boats not much bigger than your couch at home.

By the way, if you're wondering, whale meat tastes kind of like greasy, rubbery tuna fish.

Orca & Porpoise

Orca

Orca (*Orcinus orca*), or killer whales, are not actually whales; rather, they're the largest member of the porpoise family. Orca can be more than 30 feet long, and the dorsal fin on a male can be as much as six feet high. At birth, orca weigh roughly 400 pounds. A full-grown orca can weigh as much as nine tons, and can swim 34 miles per hour.

Orca travel in pods, with anywhere from three to 25 animals moving together. There are no accurate estimates for the total orca population, as the animals move very quickly and scientists are never sure if they've counted the same one twice. There's also the complication that orca have two distinct cultures: resident pods and transients. Residents tend to eat salmon and stick pretty close to one place; transients eat marine mammals, and can range over thousands of miles of territory. The two do not mix.

The most distinctive feature of the orca is the black and white coloration. Dall's porpoise, which are similarly marked, are often mistaken for orca. However, the Dall's porpoise grows to only six or eight feet. There are a couple of other differences in the coloring: an orca has a white patch behind each eye, which is not usually present on a Dall's, and their flukes are white on the underside, whereas a Dall's is usually white at the edges.

The best place to see orca is in Victoria, which is near three resident pods. Nearly 80 animals are in the waters here during the summer months.

Dall's Porpoise

Dall's porpoise, which grow to a maximum size of 300-450 pounds and five to seven feet long travel in groups of 10-20 animals. They forage at all levels of the ocean, and are known to dive to depths of more than 1,600 feet. These are highly playful animals; if you see porpoise swimming alongside a ship, they'll be Dall's. Extremely fast swimmers, able to top 35 miles per hour, these porpoise will happily chase boats and play in the wake unless the boat drops below 12 miles an hour or so; then the porpoise seem to lose interest and drop away, looking for something more fun to do.

Harbor Porpoise

Harbor porpoise are also a fairly common sight, but you don't see them for long. They are darker, more sedate in their movements, and more shy in their approaches than Dall's porpoise. They are much smaller, too, growing to only 125-145 pounds, and perhaps four to six feet in length. They travel in small groups of no more than five animals, and come up only briefly to breathe, making sightings fairly short-lived.

Seals, Sea Lions & Otters

Harbor Seals

Harbor seals, like harbor porpoise, are shy and difficult to spot. They come up quietly, take a quick look around with only their head and nose protruding above the water – and the black color can make them almost impossible to spot – then they disappear. And since a harbor seal can dive to 600 feet and stay down for over 30 minutes, you might be wasting your time hoping one pops back up. When the seal dives, its heart rate slows to 15-20 beats per minute, about a quarter of its heart rate when at the surface.

Harbor seals grow to weigh about 180 pounds. They're covered with short hair, and are usually colored either with a dark background and light rings, or light sides and a belly with dark splotches.

They generally stay within about 150 miles of the place they were born. They do not migrate, but they will wander about to find food – walleye, cod, herring, salmon, squid and octopus, among other sea life. You'll sometimes see them surprisingly far upstream on bigger rivers, as they follow the salmon. We've seen harbor seals 100 miles up the Stikine River.

SEA LION OR SEAL?

How do you know if what you're looking at is a seal or a sea lion? It's really pretty easy.

- Seals have short, clawed front legs; sea lions have long, broad front flippers.
- Seals don't have visible ears; you can see the ears on a sea lion.
- When they're out of water, seals lie down; sea lions sit up.

Sea Lions & Otters

While harbor seals disappear when you spot them, sea lions and otters, on the other hand, are showmen. Sea lions jump, splash and play constantly, as do the otters. Steller sea lions can grow to 1,200 pounds or more, and there's nothing quite like watching them at a haul out. They aren't as shy as seals. A diver told us of a few sea lions coming up behind them on a dive and repeatedly swimming in fast circles around the divers while occasionally giving someone a playful nudge. Both seals and sea lions like to pull themselves out of the water and bask in the sun at rocks. Another good place to watch for them is on channel markers and buoys.

The Russians killed whatever seals and sea lions they came across – why not, they're were out hunting anyway – but what they were really after were sea otters. Sea otters were once hunted almost to extinction as fur traders made fortunes on their rich, luxurious pelts – the first sealing expedition, in 1741, brought back 900 pelts; in 1800, Alexander Baranov estimated that in the previous 10 years, more than 100,000 pelts had been taken. It was noticed quite early on that this couldn't continue – already by 1818, it was reported that "along the whole expanse of coast from Cape Ommaney to Kenai Bay, only two places remain where we can still hunt, namely, Lituya Bay and Yakutat; but even there, they are no longer native, but hide someplace farther along the coast to the southeast where they are more protected." The Russians were letting the locals do all the killing, and contemporary reports show that they were really, really good at it, even without threats of violence from the Russians. "The Aleuts are the only people born with a passion for hunting sea otters. When they spot a sea otter, they surround it, and the person closest... gets to shoot him with a dart and has the right to claim the kill."

 For more on Russian sea otter hunting, see K.T. Khelbnikov's, ***Notes on Russian America***, beautifully translated by Serge LeComte and Richard Pierce.

Why were the Russians killing off the otters? So they could sell the pelts to China and trade for tea. The English had their opium trade for the exact same reason.

Now sea otters, quite well protected by law, are back, and there's a healthy population that stretches from Seattle to the Aleutians. This in itself has brought up controversy, with fishermen in both Canada and Alaska saying that the otters are interfering with their catches. It's one of those debates that will never be settled.

Sea otters grow to six feet and live, somewhat communally, in kelp beds. Rather odd is that while they live in groups, they don't really interact with each other; there may be some play fights and mating behavior, but other than that, they pretty much pretend the other otters aren't there. Their diet consists largely of fish, marine bivalves and sea urchins, and they're famous for using rocks to bash open tough shells. There's a flap of skin under their forelegs in which they can stash food or rocks.

FURRY FACTS

The fur of a sea otter is a miraculous thing. Otters have up to 125,000 hairs per square inch, more than double just about any other mammal. This high-density fur makes otters the prime target for coats, hats, boots and anything else for which a dead animal might be useful.

The thickness of the hair is an evolutionary development in lieu of layers of subcutaneous fat. Most marine mammals have thick fat layers to keep them warm in the cold waters. Hair is all the otters have, and this is part of why they were so susceptible during the oil spill in Prince William Sound: the fur, matted with oil, lost its insulating capabilities and the oiled otters literally froze to death.

Even when it's working well, the thick fur has some drawbacks. A sea otter has a metabolic rate two times higher than most animals its size, so the body is working overtime to maintain its core temperature. You'll see that sea otters generally keep their feet lifted out of the water – this helps keep the wet surface area to a minimum, and keeps the otter warmer. Should the otter get overheated, there is a solution: like polar bears, sea otters have extra blood veins in their feet. They can send blood through these veins, close to the surface of the skin, and cool off. It's estimated that 80% of the excess heat can be shed this way.

Although sea otters are very unpopular with local fishermen, they're actually a very important species for the maintenance of a healthy environment along the coast. Sea otters eat urchins, abalone and other animals that feed on kelp. Without the otter predation, the kelp beds, which shelter numerous schools of young fish, would quickly be gone.

Fish

British Columbia has more lakes, streams and rivers than you could fish in 10 lifetimes. The diversity of finny things is truly staggering.

But what you're after is salmon, right?

Salmon

There are five types of salmon in BC: pink, chum, coho, sockeye (or red) and, the prize of them all, the king, or chinook.

Now that we've said that, we're going to list a sixth type of salmon, the steelhead. Steelhead, long classified as a trout, was officially moved into the salmon category in 2000. For reasons that require explaining more about fish biology than you're interested in, there are a lot of fish experts who aren't real happy with this decision. Yes, steelhead move from freshwater to saltwater and back, but that's about all they have in common with salmon. Right now, there are lots of Ph.D. candidates getting dissertation material out of the debate, even though there aren't enough steelhead to make them important commercially.

All salmon share the trait of returning to the waters in which they were born to spawn and die. During the summer months, this means rivers clogged with dying fish, and a lot of very happy bears.

But it's the **chinook** that anglers fuss over. Chinook salmon grow up to 100 pounds, and 30-pound catches are common. The fish also also fight.

A few years ago, a man had a chinook on the line for over 24 hours. He lost it when his guide used the wrong sized net and snapped the line.

Chinook run usually from May through July. The chinook is rather astounding in its run, traveling more than 2,000 miles in only two months. Once returning to the site of its birth, the female lays up to 14,000 eggs. The fish in the run may be anywhere from three to seven years old; there is not a clear cycle for chinook.

A full-grown fish has black spotting on its back and dorsal fin, and a line of black along the gum line.

Trolling is your best bet for catching chinook, using herring as bait.

While the chinook is the trophy fish, a lot of people prefer **coho salmon** for eating. Coho, which grow from eight to 12 pounds, don't have the tail spots that kings do. Their fins are usually tinted with orange, and the male has a hooked snout.

Coho spend a fair amount of their lives in freshwater; after hatching, the fish may hang out in estuaries through the summer and then move back into freshwater for the fall. They spend as much as five years in freshwater before their saltwater period, which averages about 18 months.

Again, your best bet at a coho catch is trolling with herring for bait. The run lasts from July into September, and coho fight enough to make chinook seem like logs.

Sockeye, or red salmon, are probably the biggest part of the fishery, and they have been for thousands of years. They spend one to four years in the ocean, and then do the run home. Average weight is four to eight pounds at maturity, but they can get bigger; some 15-pounders have been caught.

There are a few places where there are landlocked species of sockeye, called "**kokanee**." These stay pretty small, and you're not that likely to run into them. It's the ocean-going type that everybody's after, and they find them in abundance. Most of them are caught with gill nets, which are a small step up from the drift nets you read about.

If you're fishing for sockeye, troll like you would for any other salmon.

The other two species of salmon are caught more on a commercial than a sport basis. The **pink salmon**, or humpback, grow to about four pounds. They're steel blue on top and silver on the side. They get their nickname, humpie or humpback, from the hump that develops (along with hooked jaws) when they enter freshwater. Pink salmon mature in only two years, and they do not survive spawning. These are the primo fish for commercial fishermen; more than 45 million fish a year are taken.

Chum salmon, which are green-blue on top with small black dots, mature at about four years. They spend most of that time at sea, primarily in the Bering Sea or the Gulf of Alaska. A full-grown chum will weigh between seven and 15 pounds. There is a huge commercial fishery for chum in Alaska, primarily through gill netting or seining; about 11 million fish a year are taken.

Dolly Varden are part of that steelhead/salmon debate. Right now, they're still classified as an ocean-going trout. They are a mottled olive-brown, with dark marks. Mature males are bright red on their lower body, while the fins are red-black with white edges. They also develop a strongly hooked lower jaw.

The Dolly Varden run is from mid-August into November. They actually move in and out of freshwater for most of their lives, not migrating into the sea until they are three or four years old. They're still quite small at this time, only about five inches long. Spawning generally happens when the fish is five or six years old and, unlike other salmon, roughly 50% of Dolly Varden live to spawn a second time. The fish can live as long as 16 years.

Dolly Varden never reach the size of coho or chinook – a full-grown fish is only about four pounds – but they are around all year.

AN UPHILL STRUGGLE

There is a bit of salmon behavior you're bound to see if you're traveling during the run months: salmon, gathered near a stream mouth, jumping. You'll hear various explanations for this behavior, ranging from "they're trying to catch bugs to eat" to "they're trying to shed scale parasites." The jumpers are actually female fish, loosening their eggs before heading upstream.

Salmon populations are declining rapidly. Some of this is due to over fishing, some to climate changes. Over the past hundred years, 232 genetically distinct strains of salmon (that's strains, not species) have gone extinct. Due to decreasing runs, the value of the salmon catch almost dropped in half between 1994 and 2000. Having an oil tanker worth of poison spilled into the ecosystem didn't do anybody any favors, either.

That said, there is some hope. The return of pinks was so large in 2001 that most canneries stopped taking them; there were too many to process. Fish returns run in cycles; there's hope that this huge return is a marker of the end of the bad years.

The **life cycles** of all the types of salmon are more or less similar – it's a matter of how long they stay in a particular phase of the cycle that really changes.

At hatching, baby fish are called alevin. This is a tiny little bit of a fish, with a yolk sack (that is being used for nutrition), remaining attached. Alevin live in the gravel where they are born, six to 12 inches down in the streambed.

The next stage is the **fry** stage, where they start to look like real fish. They are about an inch or two long at this point, and they start to get vertical bar marks – like they'll get later when they're packaged and barcoded in the supermarket – to help them hide in the streambed. This stage lasts a couple of months.

Next, they turn into **fingerlings**, or parr. They've gotten bigger now – a couple of inches or so – and they may stay in this stage for anywhere from a couple of months (pink and chum) up to a couple years (sockeye and chinook). The bar lines have gotten darker, and they're really just building up strength for their final freshwater stage.

That's the **smolt**. At this point they are more than six inches long , and they've lost the bar marks as they become silver for better camouflage in the open ocean. They undergo a massive physical change, getting ready for the change from freshwater to saltwater: their gills essentially reverse, and their hemoglobin changes to cope with the lower amount of oxygen that comes with saltwater living.

As soon as the fish hits saltwater, it changes from a smolt into an adult salmon. It's time to go out in the open water.

Walt Disney taught you in all those nature films that samon always come back to the stream where they were born. That's mostly true – salmon navigate by a sense of smell so sensitive that it could detect one drop of vermouth in a 500,000-gallon martini. They know where they're going. However, there are always a few that don't want to go along with the crowd. About 8% decide that home ain't good enough, so they head out for other streams. This is good, as it can help populate new areas; it's bad, because, as we'll explain below, it gives alien fish a chance to move in where they don't belong.

WHY HATCHERIES & FISH FARMS SUCK

So, what to do about this overall decline in fish population? Screw with nature, of course.

You can see hatcheries at work in a lot of towns along the coast. The idea here is that, if nature lets about one out of a thousand eggs actually grow into salmon and return to spawn, why not scoop some eggs up and increase the odds?

Hatcheries raise the fish in controlled environments. This makes sure that the salmon don't have any chance to develop the wild smarts they'll need to survive. It's a lovely way to dilute a gene pool, particularly when the hatchery-raised salmon breed with wild. Think how smart chickens are after centuries of domestication, how well they'd do in the wild. Same thing with hatchery fish.

Once a hatchery is up and running, it gets its own return of salmon. The fish are imprinted with marks, so they can be tracked. Once they make it up to the home hatchery, they're pulled out of the water, gutted and the roe and smelt are mixed by hand. Oh, and all that valuable protein, the fish that once was, is discarded. It's the rule.

The salmon at various life stages are then held in tanks, rather than the stream. Rather than having anything to do with Darwinism – which works for most species – survival becomes a matter of luck. A big part of the luck is surviving the diseases that tend to thrive in hatcheries.

The next bright idea is fish farm, which are common in Canada. The first problem here is that most fish farms stocked with Atlantic salmon, a species alien to the region. Farms are built in streams, again with holding pens for different life stages. The fish are packed in so tightly that they can hardly swim, and the concentration of fish in one batch of step ponds means there's a whole lot of fish waste churning out into the ocean – as much as from a town of 10,000 people. The fish themselves are more susceptible to disease and pollution in this cradle-to-the-table captive cycle. Of course, that means they get antibiotics pumped into their food.

Canadian fish farms are allowed to shoot any marine mammals that might come by and see these pens as a free lunch – about 900 seals and sea lions are shot a year.

There's also the little detail that farm-raised fish are eating fish-meal pellets – ground up bits of other fish. The Worldwatch Institute looked into this and discovered that for every gram of farm-raised salmon that hits your dinner table, five grams of other fish were turned into salmon food. This really helps the part of the worldwide fishing industry that's out to strip the oceans bare. Estimates are that in British Columbia alone, this means a waste of 90,000 tons of edible protein.

Because the fish are eating unnatural food, they don't come out looking nice and healthy and pink. But dyes fix that.

The increase of fish farms has devastated the traditional culture of the coasts. Towns that used to support 40 or 50 fishermen now support only two or three.

Shall we talk about Frankenfish? Genetic engineering is turning out salmon that mature in a fraction of the time it takes in nature. We have no idea what the long-range effects of this might be. And if you think the fish are confined to pens, forget it: Fish escape. Aliens enter the gene pool and the wild streams – Atlantic salmon have been found in quite a few Alaskan rivers. In 1997, a single fish farm in Washington State "lost" over 350,000 Atlantic salmon in one whack. Try and think of any way this is a good thing.

In 1980, 1% of the salmon market was comprised of farmed salmon; today that number is 56%.

Salmon aren't just out making salmon dinners. They're a vital part of the entire ecosystem, almost the base level, the cornerstone of the Pacific Northwest's economy, ecology and culture. You can't understand the Northwest coast without taking salmon into account.

Besides yourself, there are 137 other animal species that depend on salmon at some stage of their life for animal protein – everything from bald eagles to bears, seals, sea lions and everything in-between.

The forest also depends on salmon. The rotting fish that die in streams after the spawn provide 17% of the nutrients found on the rainforest floor along a stream. About 60% of the nutrients that freshly hatched salmon depend on comes from their spawned-out parents.

Disappear the fish, you disappear the forest; and that disappears it all.

Cooking Your Catch

Once you've made your catch, it's time for dinner. We offer here two superb recipes, courtesy of Wrangell's Alaska Vistas outfitters (see the Stikine River section, page 281, for their details).

FOR SALMON:

Mix up a marinade of ½ cup of soy sauce, ½ cup of brown sugar and ½ teaspoon of liquid smoke seasoning. Marinate fillets for at least six hours, turning them a couple of times.

Grill on a low fire. Slide the fish back and forth in the pan, and use olive oil to prevent sticking. Turn over only once.

Cook until the fish is no longer transparent – about five minutes per side, maximum.

This recipe also works well for steelhead trout.

FOR HALIBUT:

Mix ½ cup of butter, ½ cup of soy sauce, ¼ cup of lemon juice and two tablespoons of Worcestershire sauce. Coat an aluminum tray with olive oil or nonstick cooking spray. Place halibut on the tray and cover with the sauce mix.

Cook until the meat is no longer transparent (shouldn't take more than 10 minutes, tops). Use very low heat – halibut is very easy to overcook.

CATCH & RELEASE

If you're not hungry, follow these basic steps to release the fish:

- Land the fish quickly and carefully.
- Don't lift the fish entirely out of the water.
- Use only a soft or knotless mesh net, and keep your hands wet while handling the fish.
- Use barbless hooks, and keep the fish underwater while you're pulling at the hook. If you can't get the hook out, cut the line off the hook – sooner or later, the hook will rust out.
- Stick the fish into the current, or swish it back and forth in the water to revive it. Make sure the gills are working, and let the fish swim out of your hands.

A lot of catch and release fish still end up dying, due to improper release techniques. Some basic care keeps them out there and alive.

■ Birds

Eagles

 There are more bald eagles on Vancouver Island than in all the continental US. Just south of Whistler, Squamish and Brackendale have the second-biggest winter population of bald eagles in the world. It may be the national bird of the US, but for the most part, a bald eagle is a lot happier in Canada.

Eagles build the largest bird nests in the world, weighing up to 1,000 pounds. A pair of eagles will return to the same tree year after year, making the nest a little bigger each time. The nest is abandoned only when the tree threatens to give way. Most nests are close to the water's edge.

Adults are distinguished by the trademark white head; adolescent eagles are a dull brown and are harder to spot. Eagles themselves are easy to spot, once you get the hang of it: look at the tops of trees and keep looking for a white patch. Eagles are amazingly patient and can sit, almost unmoving, for hours on end. They do not generally hunt by circling around, looking for prey, the way you're probably used to seeing hawks. They're more likely to sit until something catches their eye – and they have great eyes, with vision roughly 20 times better than 20-20, and the ability to filter glare off water so they can see fish moving beneath the surface.

Eagles dive for fish. An eagle's talons lock when they are under pressure and cannot be released until the pressure is alleviated (this is a commonly accepted fact, but it's getting to be a little controversial now; what it comes down to is nobody's quite sure). Bald eagles can put as much as 6,000 pounds of pressure into each talon. All this means if the eagle grabs a fish that weighs more than it can lift, the eagle goes face first into the water. It doesn't happen often, but it's a memorable sight. After the face plant, if the eagle is unable to swim to shore with the prey, it is entirely possible that the weight of the would-be victim can actually exhaust and drag the eagle down, drowning it. Eagles are good swimmers, though, using their wings like arms to swim. Young eagles get a lot of swimming practice, because they have to learn to keep their wings up when they hit the water; wings down, they don't have the necessary strength or lift to get back up in the air, and they have to swim to dry land to take off. When you see an adult eagle hit, the wings are up and extended fully, ready for the powerful thrusts needed to get airborne again.

EAGLE-SPOTTING TIPS

- Look for white spots in the tops of trees. Eagles like to find the highest point they can, then sit there endlessly, doing a remarkable impression of life after taxidermy. Young eagles don't have the white heads that help you to pick them out against the dark backdrop, but they'll head for high points, too.

- If you come across an eagle on the ground, stay back. As with all wild animals, if you make the bird move, you're endangering it and making it burn calories it has better uses for.

- If you want good bird shots, you'll need a telephoto lens, fast film, and some luck.

- Find out when fishing boats are dumping leftover bait (usually in the late evening) and head down to the docks. There's nothing quite like watching a full-grown, 30-pound eagle hit the water at full speed.

Other Birds

British Columbia is a birder's delight. You can watch **brown creepers** at campsites in the southern part of the province, or along the coast, check out the alcids: the **auks** and auklets, **murres** and particularly the **puffins**. Alcids are birds that can "fly" underwater. The Audubon Society describes them as "chunky, penguin-like seabirds, chiefly dark above and white below, with short wings and large webbed feet located far back on the body." This doesn't quite do them justice.

Puffins are kind of a symbol of the North. Their colorful beaks and the way they fly – flailing their wings like whirligigs – makes them seem a kind of clown of the sea. And there are some oddities about them: for instance, their jaws are not hinged, but rather open and close something like a crescent wrench. This means they can stuff a lot of fish in their mouths at one time. A puffin biologist we know counted 42 fish in one bird's beak at a single time. The problem with this is that sometimes they eat so much they become too heavy to get airborne. If, say, the wake of a boat disturbs them, they try to get airborne, but just end up smacking face-first into the first wave they hit.

This does not mean that they're not amazing birds. A tufted puffin can dive a lot deeper than you can; and while it's down there, air squeezing out of the space between its feathers, it's as graceful as a seal.

Still along the coast, **great blue herons** stand in shallows, **rhinoceros auklets** fly past even though they look too chunky to ever get off the ground. When the tide is out, shorebirds appear in full force, feeding off the exposed marine life. **Sand pipers**, **plovers**, several types of **gulls** and **ducks**, **ravens** and more swoop down at low tide to feed on blue bay mussels, steamer clams, wrinkled whelk, file dogwinkle, sea urchins and even the occasional starfish left high and dry by the receding waters.

Even if you're not a birder, it's useful to have a field guide for the trip. When that barred owl swoops your car, you're going to wonder what it is.

■ Other Beasts

 Guess what? Once you're in the North, you're quite a few steps further down the food chain than you're used to being. Meet your new friends.

Flying Bugs

A much bigger threat to your health and sanity than bears or moose are **mosquitoes**. They are bigger, meaner and more abundant than you ever imagined. During the summer months, the biomass of mosquitoes in the North outweighs that of the caribou – there can actually be swarms of mosquitoes that cover an area bigger than Rhode Island, and we're talking mosquitoes with bites powerful enough to raise welts on a moose. There are many stories of animals going insane from mosquito bites; and there are reputable reports of caribou so drained of blood after a trip through bad mosquito country that they died. They're big, they're mean and they're everywhere. And, as if the mosquitoes weren't enough, there are **black flies**, **no-see-ums**, **snipe flies** and **moose flies**.

Anywhere you go in the BC, something small and highly annoying will want to eat you. So what chance do you have against them? Simple measures are the best protection.

Mosquito repellents are quite effective, especially those that include the chemical DEET. The more DEET the better, but if putting serious toxins on your skin doesn't thrill you, there are people – you can usually recognize them because they're busy scratching – who swear by Skin So Soft lotion.

Wear long-sleeved clothing, and tuck the cuffs of your pants into your socks.

Try to camp where there is a breeze – a wind of five mph will keep the mosquitoes away. In your RV, camper or tent, make sure the screens are made of the smallest netting money can buy.

In hotels, check the window screens before opening the window. Mosquito coils are popular, but they're not going to work outside of an enclosed area, and who knows what that smoke is doing to you?

Where the mosquitoes leave off, the no-see-ums start in. The same precautions work against these huge clouds of biting bugs. If you're camping, check all screens: they can get through the tiniest opening.

 If you're interested in knowing your enemy, get a copy of *The Mosquito Book*, by Scott Anderson and Tony Dierckins. The subtitle says it all: "More than you'll ever need to know about... the most annoying little bloodsuckers on the planet."

You will get bit. Hydrocortisone cream can help stop the itching, and there are a variety of specialized products designed to do the same. Pick up a tube or two, and then prepare to accept the mosquitoes. They're as much a part of life as the coming and going of the tides.

Economy & Government

Something like 90% of the population of Canada lives within in a hundred miles of the US border. Because of this – and because so much of Canada's media and culture is dominated by imports from the south, and except for that "eh" business, they speak English just like back home – all too many people forget that when they cross the border, they're in a different country. Really.

But Canada is its own country, and quite an impressive one at that. For starters, it has a higher literacy rate than the US, as well as better health care and safer streets.

Canada is part of the **British Commonwealth**. That means, at a fundamental level that nobody takes very seriously, the Queen of England is boss. Just a boss with absolutely no power. She's still much respected – on a recent visit to BC, she was sent out to a hockey game for the ceremonial puck drop (which, once the costs were toted up, turns out to have run over CAN $100,000, once all the extra security, etc., was figured in).

Canada is run by a **prime minister** – who, like whoever happens to be US president, is widely disparaged – and a **parliament**. Each province has its own legislative assembly and capitol – in British Columbia, the seat of power is in Victoria, in the quite lovely Parliament Building, designed by Rattenbury.

Politics are dominated by two parties – the **New Democrats** and the **Liberals**. Again, it doesn't particularly matter who's in charge, nobody likes them.

What Canada does well is take care of its people. Yes, taxes are very high, but so is the standard of living. Unemployment isn't too horrible a problem – although you will see a lot of panhandlers on the streets of Vancouver – and even with the current economic troubles, the economy is diverse enough to keep ticking. And there's this weird idea that the people who live in the country should all have health insurance. The government actually provides it, and the system works. Imagine.

BC's economy is dominated by three things: **lumber**, **fishing** and **tourism**. It's also got good, healthy mining industries, and extensive agriculture, particularly in the Okanagan Valley, where there are fine wineries.

Vancouver is actually the fourth-largest **film production** center in the world now, behind Mumbai, Hollywood and New York. If you watch a show on US television that has forest backdrop, odds are it was shot in Vancouver – *The X-Files*, for example, or *Stargate SG-1*. On our last visit to town, Robin Williams was hanging out at the Virgin Records shop, and Uma Thurman was in one of the restaurants, hoping nobody would recognize her.

People & Culture

B ack at the beginning of this chapter, we told the BC story as one of fur and gold. But that's the European history of British Columbia. The First Nations people would tell something of a different story.

About 15,000 years ago, the first people came into what is now British Columbia. They moved over the Bering Sea Ice Bridge, and kept heading south. The migration took maybe as much as 3,000 years before there was a decent population in BC, but by then, local characteristics were starting to show "characteristics" determined by climate.

You can divide BC's **First Nations** population into two main groups: coastal and interior. The two had little culture in common and completely different lifestyles.

On the coast, the **Haida**, the **Tsimshian**, the **Kwakiutl** and the **Salish** held potlaches, carved totem poles (see below) and lived a pretty rich lifestyle, thanks to the natural wealth of the ocean.

Things were a little rougher in the interior. These people had more in common with the Plains Indians in the United States, chasing bison and moving when the food supply required it. The **Athabascans** – this is the same group that inhabits much of interior Alaska – adopted a few customs from their coastal neighbors, but this was an interior lifestyle. The **Beaver**, the **Slavey**, the **Dene** and the **Carriers** were hunters, and they were highly practical people. When the HBC (Hudson's Bay Company) moved in, they had no trouble getting the best of any deal.

Negotiations continue over tribal status in British Columbia. Quite a few groups have signed off on it; others are still holding out. There have never been reservations, at least not quite as they existed in the US, but there are reserves, areas that are tribally owned and operated.

The past few decades have seen a strong resurgence of First Nations culture in BC – totem carving is alive and well, as are many other traditional art forms. First Nations people are looking for that balance between integrating with the modern world and maintaining their culture and traditional lifestyles. You'll see this tension as you travel in BC; it's making everybody stronger.

■ Totem Poles

 Totem poles are a coastal thing; First Nations peoples in the interior never made them. In fact, if you look at a map of British Columbia, you face two highly distinct Native cultures: inland and coastal, divided mostly by the Coast Mountains. Get more than a hundred miles inland, and you're completely out of totem pole culture.

And what a rich culture it was. Stretching from the southern reaches of the Fraser River, well into Alaska, totems are the faces of the landscape.

Contrary to popular opinion, totem poles were never objects of worship. They were a heraldic emblem as well as a method of storytelling, a means of keeping a community memory. Although the poles used common elements and figures, any attempt to "read" a totem is possible only if you know the family and the story the pole commemorates. Usually this is only feasible if there were written records of the pole raising, or if a member of the family that commissioned the pole still exists.

Poles were usually erected after a family had achieved some measure of economic success. Part of the fun of raising a pole was to show off to the neighbors. The largest poles were reserved for chiefs of extended family groups and those of higher social ranks.

Totem pole carvers were among the highest-status residents of the coastal regions. They were tested on their knowledge of mythology and religion, as well as their carving experience, before being retained to carve a pole. They were welcomed in every village, enjoyed unrestricted freedom to travel, and were often wealthier and more famous than tribal chiefs. The down side of being a carver was that, if you made a mistake, you could be put to death.

Carvers were apprenticed when young, and they were expected to have the spiritual abilities of a shaman. Although poles were not religious in nature, their impor-

Traditional totem pole at K'san.

tance to the community required a great deal of sensitivity and stamina. Larger memorial poles could take over a year to carve.

Poles were invariably carved of cedar wood; larger poles were often hollowed first to make them more manageable. Tools, before European contact, were made of stone or bone. In the farther northern reaches of the pole-carving cultures, hammered copper was used.

Poles were not brightly colored. Because of the nature of cedar wood, which must be able to breathe, painting the pole was the first step to destroying it. Native carvers used simple pigments made of plant materials, charcoal and some oxides. Few colors other than black, red and blue were used, and poles were seldom entirely painted. Instead, the colors were used as accents, and many poles were not painted at all.

Poles fall into seven basic types.

- ■ **Memorial poles** were erected to honor a deceased chief. These were heraldic in nature and were considered the finest of all poles. Very few examples remain in a well-preserved state.

- **Grave figures** are the most numerous of poles. Smaller than memorial poles, they showed the totemic figure of the deceased, identifying the grave site as that of a certain branch of a clan.

- **House posts and pillars** were probably the first type of pole developed, springing from the design of the long houses used along the Pacific Coast. The houses in this area were heavily decorated inside and out, and the posts and pillars were part of the adornments. Most of these disappeared with the houses, but they were once probably more numerous than grave poles. The only limit to the use of house posts was the wealth of the owner and the space available.

- Similar to the house post was the **house front**, or **portal pole**. This was purely a measure of status, fronting a house to show who lived there by incorporating the family's crest or totemic figures.

- **Welcoming poles** were erected by the waterfront. These were usually unpainted, and in old pictures of villages in Southeast you'll see these standing in pairs. They were often constructed just for the occasion of a potlatch, or a large tribal gathering (see below).

- **Mortuary poles** are related to the grave figures, but are considerably rarer. Only the Haida made general use of these poles, which were erected at a memorial potlatch.

- There were the special poles that didn't fit into the above categories. These could tell stories of a successful hunt, but more often they were erected by chiefs out for revenge. The poles were designed to ridicule a specific person or group; considering the cost and difficulties of creating a pole, it's easy to imagine just how mad you'd have to be to put up a ridicule pole.

Poles were a vital part of coastal culture. A single village might have a hundred poles, and the raising of one was always a cause for celebration. A singer was hired to relate the history of the family and to narrate its accomplishments. The singer also hired and trained dancers to perform at the pole raising. Despite stories to the contrary, slaves were not sacrificed to the pole, nor buried beneath the base. Only a single skeleton has ever been found under a pole.

Despite the joy at their raising, poles were not necessarily meant to last; when their function was done, poles were allowed to fall into disrepair. With increasing European settlement, many native villages were forced to move and the poles were left behind to rot. When hiking in remote areas, one sometimes encounters a moss-covered tree with a face – it's an old pole, turning into forest mulch.

Archeologists and anthropologists have done a remarkable job finding and preserving poles, but taken out of context they lose some of their beauty and become nothing more than museum pieces. Many such pieces suffer from the fact that early European efforts to preserve poles involved painting them, and so hastened the destruction.

After decades of neglect, totem carving is making a comeback. There are trained carvers working in several communities in BC, and the tradition is being revitalized with the incorporation of modern elements into standard designs.

■ Potlach

 Pole raising often coincided with a potlatch. This term is a corruption of the Nootka word *patshatl*, meaning gift. Potlatches are famous in story as an opportunity for a family to give away all its possessions, showing its wealth, but they were a lot more complicated than that. A potlatch was given only with extreme protocol. Guests arrived on the shore in order, according to their status and rank. They were greeted by their hosts with great display. Then the feasting, which could last for several days, began. The pole raising was the height of the celebration. After the pole's story was told and the singing and the dancing finished, the gift-giving began. Gifts were carefully selected. An improper gift could be given as a purposeful insult and could lead to war. The generous spirit of the potlatch was not well understood by Europeans and the qualities of the poles were not generally appreciated. In 1884, Canadian law forbade potlatch ceremonies. This was merely another nail in the coffin for local villages.

 Christopher Braken's ***The Potlach Papers***, although it can get very annoyingly postmodern at times, is a good look at what happened when the Canadian government came in and tried to rip the heart out of a culture.

The problem started in 1763, when a royal proclamation noted that aboriginal people in what's now Canada retained title to lands they had not surrendered by treaty to agents of the crown.

According to King George III, who was about to get his butt kicked by the annoying colonists south of Canada's domains, "It is just and reasonable, and essential to our Interest and the Security of our Colonies, that the several Nations or Tribes of Indians with whom We are connected and who live under our protection should not be molested or disturbed in the provision of such Parts of Our Dominions and Territories as, not having been ceded to or purchased by Us, are reserved to them, or any of them, as their Hunting Grounds."

Yeah, that worked really well. There were a few attempts in the early 1850s to buy land – James Douglas of the HBC signed treaties giving him the lands for Ft. Victoria, Nanaimo and Rupert, among others – but by 1878, this had pretty much stopped.

Once the government decided it owned the land (whether it did or not), a decision had to be made as to what should be done with it. There was so much of it, just ready for fun. The only problem were those pesky people already living there, and those pesky people had a habit that the staunch Protestant establishment simply couldn't grasp or cope with: the Natives of Canada, particularly along the coast, liked to give stuff away. Not just little presents here and there. They held something that came to be known as the potlach, when they gave absolutely everything they owned away.

Bracken quotes a British source: "The collection of property for the purpose of distribution is the constant aim of many of the natives who, to the common observer, seems listless and idle. The Indian who stands by your side in a tattered blanket, may have 20 new blankets and yards of calico in his box at home. Whatever he acquires beyond immediate necessaries goes to increase this stock, until his high day comes in the winter season, when he spreads his feast and distributes gifts among the guests, according to their rank."

Clearly, that simply couldn't be allowed to continue. If the government had known what communism was – Marx hadn't come up with it quite yet – they would have declared the Natives commies and wiped them out.

Instead, they just passed laws to make them stop giving stuff away. They set up missions with the express purpose of teaching the joy of hoarding goods, like proper Europeans.

According to one territorial official, those groups who rejected the European system by continuing to give away all their possessions "should be rebuked, warned and instructed, and gradually trained for responsible management of their own little affairs."

Aren't colonialists fun?

The official went on to point out that the potlach, the cornerstone of coastal society – which had been running pretty well for a few thousand years – produced "negligence, thriftlessness, and a habit of roaming about which prevents home associations and is inconsistent with progress."

On February 12, 1884, legislation was brought before the House of Commons to outlaw the potlach. It read like this:

> Every Indian or person who engages in or assists in celebrating the Indian festival known as the "Potlach" or the Indian dance known as the "Tamanawas," is guilty of a misdemeanor, and liable to imprisonment for a term not exceeding six months and not less than two months.
>
> Every Indian or person who encourages, either directly or indirectly, an Indian to get up such a festival or dance, or to celebrate the same, or who assists in the celebration of the same, is guilty of a like offence, and shall be liable to the same punishment."

The Natives responded quite quickly to this new law: they completely ignored it. To obey would have, in many ways, simply been capitulating to the complete loss of freedom and tradition. When, in 1885, an elder of the Cowichan village of Comeakin petitioned to hold a potlach, he made it clear that this was a legal matter, a way of repaying both his own debts and those of his recently deceased son. Breaking down the potlach meant destroying the very fine fibers that held society together.

According to George Shaw's 1909 book, *Chinook Jargon and How to Use It*, "The *potlach* was the greatest institution of the Indian, and is to this day. From far and near assembled the invited guests and tribes and with feasting, singing, chanting and dancing, the bounteous collection was distributed: a chief was made penniless. The wealth of a lifetime was dissipated in an hour, but his head ever after was crowned with the glory of a satisfied ambition: he had won the honor and reverence of his people. It was a beautiful custom; beautiful in the eyes of the natives of high or low degree, confined to no particular tribe, but met with everywhere along the coast."

In 1885, three potlachers were prosecuted: their sentence was confinement to their villages and compulsory school attendance. But modernization was killing off the potlach without government intervention. "For the old time Indians it might be harmless enough, but for the young men and women of the present generation it is the shortest and easiest imaginable way of going to the bad." Who was helping kill out the tradition? Not the government, which really had more things to worry about, but the missionaries, who absolutely could not believe that generosity was a good thing. Every chance they got, they were running back to Victoria to complain that this open spirit was ruining their chances of converting the Natives. While the government didn't really care that much what the Indians themselves were doing – they could see the handwriting on the wall that the time of the Natives was quickly ending – they did care about the whining of these White meddlers. The sporadic enforcement of potlach regulations almost always comes down to a missionary getting pissed off and forcing the local magistrate to act.

According to Franz Boas, the greatest of anthropologists who ever worked along the BC coast, "Potlaches are celebrated at all important events," including marriages, deaths, and the taking of a name. "When a chief has to give a great potlach to a neighbouring tribe, he announces his intention, and the tribe resolve in council when the festival is to be given." Invitations are sent out, and when all is ready, a messenger goes out to get the guests, who arrive "dress up at their nicest," and in their canoes "proceed to the village in grand procession." They're met by the chief's son or daughter, who performs a dance in the honor of the guests. The guests are given a few blankets on the beach, and finally, "after a number of feasts have been given, the chief prepares for the potlach, and under great ceremonies and dances, the blankets are distributed among the guests, each receiving according to his rank." According to Boas, the underlying principle of potlach was "that of the interest-bearing investment of property." When you gave, you knew exactly what you'd get back, later down the road.

Christopher Bracken quotes Horatio Hale, who wrote, "We may imagine the consternation which would be caused in England if the decree of a superior power should require that all benefit societies and loan companies should be suppressed, and that all deposits should remain the property of those who hold them in trust."

One of the most important items of exchange during the potlach was coppers. These were flat copper plates, built around a frame in the shape of a T. There are several good ones on display in the museum in K'san; you can also see them in Victoria, Vancouver, and a few other places.

According to Boas, "These coppers have the same function which bank notes of high denomination have with us. The actual value of the piece of copper is small, but it is made to represent a large number of blankets and can always be sold for blankets. The value is not arbitrarily set, but depends upon the amount of property given away in the festival at which the copper is sold. On the whole, the oftener a copper is sold the higher its value, as every new buyer tries to invest more blankets in it. Therefore the purchase of a copper also brings distinction, because it proves that the buyer is able to bring together a vast amount of property."

Bracken elaborates: "Coppers are always sold to rivals, often to a rival tribe, and the purchaser is under pressure to pay whatever price is asked for it. "If it is not accepted," adds Boas, "it is an acknowledgment that nobody in the tribe has money enough to buy it, and the name of the tribe or clan would consequently lose in weight. Therefore, if a man is willing to accept the offer, all the members of the tribe must assist him in this undertaking with a loan of blankets."

Canadian officials made a half-hearted effort to enforce the potlach ban, but they knew a lost cause when they saw one. It was easier to wait for the cultures to completely die off, which, much to everyone's surprise, they stubbornly refused to do.

By the 1920s, missionaries describing the revival of potlach tradition as "a fall from whiteness."

In January 1920, at the insistence of the missionaries, eight men were charged with potlaching. Seven of them were sentenced to two months in jail. In March 1921, another man was sentenced to three months, and in December 1921, five men were sentenced to two months in prison for taking part in the sale of a copper.

In February 1922, there were charges laid against 34 people; 32 were finally charged. The court gave them a month to renounce potlaching and get a suspended sentence. Ten did, 22 did not, and so went to jail. Items from the potlach were seized, and many were sent to museums; they weren't returned to the proper owners until 1979.

There are still potlaches today, and they're still modeled after the old ways: we met a Kwakiutal man who was putting off assuming chieftainship for as long as possible, simply because he didn't have the $100,000 or so necessary to do a potlach up right.

BC's Top 20 Destinations

It's hard to narrow BC's best to just 20 attractions. Lists always fall short. But here, in no particular order, are some of our greatest hits.

1. Victoria, the most British city in Canada.

2. Vancouver, where the wild is never more than a few minutes away from a fine restaurant.

3. Tofino, an artist colony on the west coast of Vancouver Island where you can watch gray whales or paddle out to see some of the largest trees in the world.

4. The **Okanagan Valley**: wine country, farmer's markets and the best honey you'll ever taste.

5. Ski Whistler. It's reason enough to learn how to ski.

6. Animal watch. Whether you're after land animals – bear, moose – or those in the ocean, BC has them all.

7. The **Stikine River**. It's the last great undammed river in North America.

8. The **Alaska Highway**. Every year, thousands of people head north on the Alaska Highway. The single biggest stretch of it is in British Columbia.

9. Whitewater raft on the Fraser River, which has Class V rapids and no waiting.

10. Hike the Coast Trail, along the Strait of Juan de Fuca. It offers anywhere from four days to a week of scenery where the ocean is on one side of you, and old-growth rainforest is on the other.

11. Soak in a hot spring: Liard, along the Alaska Highway, is maybe the best known, but Canada's largest hot spring is Fairmont, in the BC Rockies.

12. Fish for salmon along the coast.

13. Take a ferry to the **Gulf Islands** and see what life would be like if you could live it more slowly, and with a whole lot more money.

14. Take a train. VIA Rail has connections to points east, or the Rocky Mountaineer Railtour can take you on one of the great train trips of the hemisphere, from the coast to the high Rockies.

15. Check out the weirdest **fossils** anywhere at the **Burgess Shale** – it's like evolution was high on helium.

16. Golf. There are more than 250 courses in the province.

17. Windsurf. Squamish has the best windsurfing in Canada, second only to the Columbia River Gorge. Best of all, you'll get the place to yourself.

18. Go to the **rodeo** in **Cloverdale** and see how the cowboys live.

19. Take in the fantastic **Royal Canadian Museum** in Victoria, or the collection of **First Nations masks** at the University of BC in Vancouver.

20. Canoe the Bowron Lakes circuit. A week that will stand out in your memory for the rest of your life.

Practicalities

Transportation

British Columbia is roughly the size of California. It can be a long way between points out there, and transportation can become a real issue if you're not in a car.

Anybody **driving** into British Columbia should read the *Customs* section on page 60. With the current state of international paranoia, delays can happen at the borders.

If you're going to **fly** into BC, you'll end up using Vancouver as a hub. The only other city with regular

flights is Victoria and, except for connections from Seattle, most of those go through Vancouver as well. Several dozen airlines fly into Vancouver, Canada's second-busiest airport. Of course, with the current state of the airline industry, services can change fast. Your best bet is to check online at www.yvr.ca for current flight offerings and services.

VIA Rail, ☎ 800-561-8630, www.viarail.com, has service to some towns along the coast, but it's not particularly convenient and the stops are limited; BC Rail stopped its passenger trains in 2002.

Greyhound Bus, ☎ 800-661-8747, www.greyhound.ca, has service to southern towns but, again, schedules can be inconvenient and the number of towns serviced is limited.

On the good side, **BC Ferries**, ☎ 888-223-3779, www.bcferries.com, runs a fleet of more than 30 ships, from huge flagship boats that ply the Inside Passage to small ships that make short hops between the Gulf Islands. This is your best way from Vancouver to Vancouver Island, via the terminals at Tsawassen (south of town) or Horseshoe Bay (north of town). You can also get on a longer jump, from Port Hardy, at the northern tip of Vancouver Island, to Prince Rupert, which connects with the Alaska Marine Highway (☎ 800-642-0066, http://alaska.gov/ferry). Prince Rupert is also the terminus for BC Ferries ships to the Queen Charlotte Islands.

For detailed information on the AMH, see our book, *Adventure Guide to the Inside Passage & Coastal Alaska*, also by Hunter Publishing.

There are a couple of ferries that connect BC with the mainland US; see the Victoria section, page 86, for more details.

When to Go, For How Long

Considering the climate, most people – except for skiers – travel between the months of June and September. However, Victoria has milder weather than Seattle, and can be a great destination any time of year. Vancouver gets a little rainy, but you won't be sorry if you show up in January.

If you're thinking about traveling in the northern reaches of the province, the Alaska Highway is most crowded in July and August, but people who go in the shoulder seasons of May to June or September to early October find the land just as hospitable and quite a bit emptier. Most seasonal businesses shut down somewhere between the beginning and end of September, and remain closed until mid-May or the beginning of June. This makes it more difficult to find needed services during those times, but there's always something open. With patience and careful planning, you can make a successful and enjoyable trip at any time of year. If you're looking to avoid crowds, there's no better time than the middle of winter. Pack your long johns and cross-country skis. You'll have a great time.

If you're in a rush, you can do the province in two weeks. That gives you a few days on Vancouver Island, a few in Vancouver and a quick trip north. You could also do a loop, up the Cassiar Highway and down the Alcan (the Alaska Highway), using Vancouver as a starting and stopping point, in a week. Ten days lets you get over to the great parks of Banff, Jasper, Kootenay and Yoho. But again, that's a long haul.

If you've got only a week, stick to the southern reaches: Vancouver City and the island pleasures of Victoria, with side trips out to Strathcona, or Tofino, or Whistler. With two weeks, add on the Okanagan Valley and the parks. With three weeks, you can start to have some real fun.

Costs

All prices in this book are listed in Canadian dollars. At press time, US $1 was equal to CAN $1.33, but over the months we were working on this book, the Canadian dollar fluctuated by about 15%. Any way you cut it, though, things are cheaper here than they are south of the border. You can find a perfectly nice hotel for under CAN $60, and most campsites run only CAN $12; a good meal is an easy find for under CAN $15. Expeditions are a fraction of what they'd cost in Alaska: whale-watching for CAN $80 or so, river rafting for under CAN $75.

In the cities – okay, there aren't that many of them – things are still pretty reasonable. You can get a suite in downtown Victoria for under CAN $150. Staying downtown in Vancouver can be very expensive, but if you've got transport and can get out of the city center to sleep, prices drop dramatically.

The only real expensive thing in BC is gas: figure it's going to run at least double the US price.

If you've still got to cut costs, pack sandwiches for lunch, eat donuts or fruit (depending on your health ideas) for breakfast, and save the eating out money for dinner. People with tents can reasonably camp virtually anywhere that's not private land. This means you can just head off into the bush and pitch a tent for free – just remember the bear precautions.

Those who are able to splurge are in luck, too. We list some very expensive expeditions in this book – and they're worth it, and will give you memories that will last a lifetime.

One place not to skimp is on your gear. We've seen a lot of trips ruined because people weren't properly outfitted. This doesn't mean you should spend a fortune on the same gear climbers use on Everest. But you'll be a lot happier in waterproof boots than in tennis shoes, and there's a simple reason why everyone you meet in the North has a closet full of Gore-Tex: it works, and it's comfortable, and it works.

Tourist Information

Nearly every city, town, village and hamlet in BC has a tourist information booth. These vary from tiny, empty offices to huge buildings stocked with free literature. The staff of these centers are uniformly friendly and usually offer a wealth of information. They also can steer you in the right direction in the event of an emergency. Don't fail to make use of these treasure troves – and don't neglect to sign their guest books; the government looks at those when deciding on continued funding.

Tourist bureaus can be helpful even before you leave home. Call or write (e-mail or snail mail both work) and tell them where you are going and what you want to see. They'll soon fill your mailbox with flyers. **Tourism Department of British Columbia**, 1130 W Pender St., Suite 600, Vancouver, BC, V6E 4A4, Canada, ☎ 800-663-6000, www.hellobc.com. This is one of the most organized tourism outfits in the world. They'll even make hotel reservations for you, and they have a wide variety of special packages and programs. Talk to these people. We know people who work for BC Tourism who'll call this number when they're planning their own vacation.

If you're going to be going beyond BC, **Tourism North** is a consortium of BC, Alaska, Yukon and Alberta tourism. They put out some nice brochures and booklets that give you an idea of how to link a long trip together. See them on the Web at www.northtoalaska.com.

Tourism Yukon, 100 Hanson St., Whitehorse, YT, Y1A 2C6, Canada, ☎ 867-667-5340, www.touryukon.com.

Alaska Division of Tourism, PO Box 1180, Juneau, AK 99811-0801, USA, ☎ 907-465-2010, www.travelalaska.com.

For info about Alberta – which we include part of in this book, because that's where the killer parks are located – visit www.travelalberta.com, ☎ 800-661-8888.

For information on the Northwest Territories, contact **Economic Development and Tourism**, PO Box 1320, Yellowknife, NWT, X1A 2L9, Canada, ☎ 800-661-0788.

The booklet, *Guide to First Nations Tourism in British Columbia*, is available at most general info centers. Or go online to learn more about aboriginal tourism at www.atbc.bc.ca. Aboriginals were here first. Make sure you leave some of your travel dollars with them.

Lodging

Whatever your luxury scale, BC can keep you happy. There are resorts that run more than a grand a night, and there are campgrounds where you can pitch a tent for a few bucks.

As mentioned above, Tourism BC will help you make hotel reservations – ☎ 800-hello-bc, www.hellobc.com. They also publish the indispensable *BC Accommodations Guide*, which lists quality hotels and campgrounds all over the province. Pick up a copy of this – it's free – at the first Tourist Info Centre you hit when you get to BC. You'll use it a lot.

For campground reservations, contact **BC Parks**, ☎ 800-689-9025, www.discovercamping.ca. (There is some upheaval going on with a lot of the government-run campgrounds in BC, so this contact information could change over the life of this book.) Except for very popular locations – close to Victoria, Vancouver or Whistler, and in the Rockies Parks – you're not likely to need a reservation. Only a couple of times during the research for this book did we ever hit a full campground – and then all we had to do was move a few miles down the road to the next one.

Shopping

You'll find no shortage of ways to spend your money. The majority of shops carry identical items, but there are a few unique places.

If you're looking for First Nations crafts, find co-ops. For ivory and whalebone articles, co-ops are generally cheaper and the quality considerably higher than you'll find at tourist shops. Plus, if you do make a co-op purchase, you can be sure that your money is getting back to the artist. Often you meet the artisan him- or herself. Sometimes, you meet the hunter.

Besides whalebone and ivory, watch for exquisite soapstone and jade carvings done by First Nations people. In the southern areas of the region, you'll find the highly geometric art of the Haida and Kwakiutl, usually carved and painted on wood, although artists are adapting traditional methods to modern means, producing stunning lithographs and prints. Several tribes specialize in beadwork.

> **IT'S THE LAW:** Goods made from endangered species cannot be imported into the US or Canada. Goods made from non-endangered wildlife are subject to special regulations. There are also some very odd restrictions that you must not forget. See the *Customs* section, below, for details.

■ Ethical Issues

Although many of the products for sale in First Nations art co-ops are made from endangered species, strict controls are enforced. The bone, ivory and baleen (a kind of strainer that replaces teeth in some kinds of whales; pieces of it can be 10 feet long) must come from animals that were hunted under subsistence regulations and used for food by villagers. This rule is sometimes abused. There's also the question of what defines subsistence. In theory, it's an animal killed for your own use, but the law also allows kills to be used for trade. And here's where the gray area comes in.

First Nations cultures, quite unlike Western cultures, traditionally believed that waste was a bad thing; it was an insult to the land and the animals. Interpret this however you want, but it's a commonsense idea: when one bad salmon run can mean your whole village starves, it's in your best interest to keep the salmon coming back.

Now, of course, you can just run out to the grocery store.

As you shop in BC, just be aware of what you're buying if you buy a product made from animal hide or bone or ivory. When all's said and done, the abusers are not as many as those using the law and their traditional rights correctly. For the most part, when you buy these products, you are supporting a traditional way of life, one that predates European civilization by thousands of years.

Getting Out

The whole point of coming up here is to see the incredible wilderness. The road system opens only the tiniest portion of the province. To really enjoy BC, you've got to get out.

■ Boating

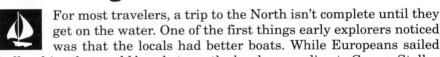

For most travelers, a trip to the North isn't complete until they get on the water. One of the first things early explorers noticed was that the locals had better boats. While Europeans sailed bulky ships that could barely turn, the locals, according to George Stellar (after whom so many Northern animal species are named, including the Steller sea lion, the incredibly common Steller jay and the now-extinct Steller sea cow – and yes, it usually is spelled differently), were in boats "about two fathoms long, two feet high, and two feet wide on the deck, pointed toward the nose but truncated and smooth in the rear.... On the outside [the] frame is covered with skins, perhaps of seals, and colored a dark brown." Stellar had spotted a kayak, and it didn't take the Europeans long to figure out that these tiny boats could do just about anything. Meanwhile, in the interior, explorers and trappers were heading up the rivers in bark and skin canoes, some 30 feet long.

Precautions

The water up North is still great – perfect for paddling. But whether you canoe one of the wild rivers, head for the fjords to watch glaciers calve, head out fishing or cruising, or just want to sit in a boat and watch the sky overhead, there are things you have to keep in mind. Many of the Northern lakes remain wild and remote, so excursions onto the water require a high degree of planning and self-sufficiency.

Always **file a float plan and itinerary** with an agency, authority, relative or friend. Should you end up late, stranded or in need of rescue, a search can be underway a lot more quickly if someone knows where to start. Details of the float plan should include the type, color and length of your boat, the number of people in your group and even the color of clothes everybody's wearing when they head out (remember, it's a lot easier to spot a red jacket than a green one).

Get an accurate **weather forecast** before you set off and watch for any signs that conditions are deteriorating. Keep your eyes on the horizon and peaks for clouds coming in. Carry an emergency supply of food, clothing and essentials separate from your other gear, in a waterproof container. This can save your life if you have to weather a storm.

Have PFDs (personal floatation devices – life jackets) and wear them at all times.

Be aware of the dangers, conditions, symptoms and treatment of **hypothermia** – see the *Health* section, page 59. Northern waters are always cold, and getting wet in them can kill you.

Watch out for **bears, marine mammals and other wildlife**. Salmon-spawning streams and berry bushes are prime bear spots. Marine mammals should be viewed only from a distance. It's illegal and dangerous to chase after an animal, and an angry seal can easily capsize a boat. Remember, to most marine mammals, a guy in a kayak looks just like a killer whale. Respect the animals.

If you're going on the ocean, be aware of **tidal races** and fluctuations. Have – and know how to use – charts and tables to ensure safe boating. The tides can move very fast in some spots, and the tidal variations are often extreme. Remember this when you're pitching your camp – stay well above the high-water mark, high enough so that wakes and unusual waves won't bother you.

Boil and purify all drinking water, no matter where you land, and practice eco-sensitive rules of waste and sewage disposal. No-trace camping is the only way to go.

Take some kind of **signaling device** to use in case of an emergency. This can be a VHF radio, an EPIRM (emergency position indicating radio beacon), flares and mirrors. More than one person in your group should know how to use these.

Have a **contingency plan** in case anyone in your party gets separated. Pick a spot to meet and choose regular times to check in by walkie talkie; don't count on your cell phone signal working everywhere.

Finally, you need to plan a rational approach to threatening situations. **Remaining calm** is the first thing to do. Then you can make a clear assessment of the emergency and take proper corrective measures. Find shelter, food and water and keep a level head. That will just about ensure survival and rescue.

The odds of an emergency are remote – more likely, you will enjoy peace and safety on the water. But the more prepared you are for an emergency, the more relaxed your days on the water will be.

If you haven't brought your own boat, they are easy to rent and run about CAN $40 a day for a single kayak. You will have to prove that you know

Practicalities

what you're doing with one; it's annoying for the outfitters to have to hunt down yahoos who got in over their heads. If you can't do a water re-entry, forget renting and stick with guided trips.

All time spent on the water is good time.

WHITEWATER CLASSIFICATIONS	
Class I	Almost flat water, with maybe a few riffles. No obstructions or real waves.
Class II	Easy rapids, with waves up to three feet high. Not a real problem for those who understand their boat.
Class III	Rapids with irregular waves; may need some serious maneuvering skills.
Class IV	Long, difficult rapids and possible need for very precise maneuvering. You may need to scout the route from shore before you do the rapid, and only experts have any business in a canoe in Class IV. Kayakers had better know how to Eskimo roll. Anybody going through a Class IV had better know how to swim, just in case.
Class V	Think Class IV, but a whole lot worse. You have no business being out here unless you've done a lot of rivers already in your life.
Class VI	Forget it. A cold and wet way to commit suicide.

■ Charters/Outfitters

Once you get out of the car, you're probably going to end up hiring a charter operator or two to take you farther into the bush. There are hundreds of operators anxious and ready to take you fishing, hiking, biking, canoeing, kayaking, parasailing, bungee jumping.... You name it, you can pay somebody to help you do it.

When chartering or booking with an outfitter, be up-front about what you want to do and what you hope to accomplish – but be reasonable. Even the most experienced boat captain can't guarantee you'll catch a fish. But different species need different tricks and lures, and a good captain is up on where and when your chances are best. A good captain also is going to tell you this himself, without promising record catches. The same holds true for rafting trips. Maybe the last group went Class IV without anybody pitching out of the boat, but how often does someone go overboard (if they tell you never, they're lying)?

Before booking the trip, find out exactly how long a half-day or whole-day charter is. Find out how long different operators have been working the area, and ask about their licenses or affiliations. Ask what they do for you. You'll find rafting trips where you sit while other people paddle. This is great for many people, but some folks like more participation. There are fishing charters where the guides hardly let you touch a line until it's time to reel in. Others sit back and let you do everything yourself.

Find out what gear is supplied and what you need to bring. If it's an all-day trip, is lunch provided or should you pack your own PB&J? (We're developing a theory that you can gauge the quality and quantity of fishing charter operators in any city by the number of Subway sandwich shops.)

If one charter company is much more expensive – or far cheaper – than the others, find out why. At a basic level of service, boat charters should include all fishing gear, some kind of refreshments, and at least some help on processing the fish. However, some operators run cheaper trips, not because they skimp on the service, but because they run in different areas. This might mean a float trip that takes a less crowded fork in the river, a kayak operator who paddles a different stretch of coastline, or an operator who is simply trying something completely different. And you'll find out what's going on only if you take the time to ask. Hey, it's your money and your vacation.

For fishing and water sightseeing, ask what kind of boat you'll be on. Charters range from Boston Whalers with Alaska cabins – basic, serviceable and far from comfortable, but great for serious fishing – to luxury cabin cruisers.

If you're booking a kayak trip, you should find out how far from town you're going, what kind of things you're likely to see, and how long you'll be in the boat. Kayaks move slowly; five miles is about as far as most novices can paddle without beginning to hurt in the legs or hands. Also, because kayaks are slow, where you start paddling is usually a pretty good reflection of what you'll see. Most good outfitters will have pictures of trips for you to look at. We have never yet come across a kayak outfitter who wasn't very good with the beginning paddle/safety demonstration. Have no fear: even if it's your first time, you'll know what to do when you get in the boat.

The only way to ensure you get what you want out of a charter or booked trip is to let the operator know what you're after. Operators don't want to take you out if they don't have what you want – it just means you waste your money and they end up with an unhappy client, making everybody miserable. Make your expectations known, match the trip to your needs and you'll have a great time.

■ Wilderness Hiking & Camping

There is so much of British Columbia to explore beyond the highway that you could easily spend a hundred lifetimes hiking in the backcountry and still have plenty to see.

The backcountry is wonderful if you're prepared, a terror if you're not. Throughout this book, we emphasize the importance of preparation before you set off on any hike into the bush. Here are a few of the details you'll need to take care of before you lace on your (broken-in) boots.

First, get **maps**. Topographical maps are available in most cities; if you don't know how to read one, get a good explanation before you head out. All the modern global positioning systems and tricky radios won't be as useful as topo maps and an old Boy Scout compass.

For any lengthy hike, tell somebody where you're going and when you expect to be back. Nobody will search for you if no one knows you're lost.

Practice **no-trace camping**. Nothing rains on the parade of your wilderness experience faster than ending a 10-mile hike and finding old cans where you wanted to pitch the tent. Here's what you've got to do:

- **Plan ahead**. This makes sure you're not in over your head. Nothing messes up the wilderness like a good search party looking for someone where they shouldn't have been to begin with. Planning ahead also means knowing what to do when you're face-to-face with a moose, a bear, or a case of hypothermia.

- Stick to **harder surfaces** wherever you can. The forests and tundra have a very short growing season and are a lot more fragile than you might think; in tundra, it can take more than a decade for a footprint to disappear. So stay on the trails if there are any, and try to camp where somebody else has camped before you.

- If you **pack it in, pack it out**. You can make this easier on yourself by getting rid of excess packaging material before you head out. It's amazing how much garbage is simply packaging.

- **Human waste** gets buried, at least six inches deep, 200 feet or more from water. And if you're going to wash your dishes after dinner, keep your soap away from water sources.

- **Leave it as you find it.** This means no chopping down trees. Don't mess with what you find.

- Finally, skip the **campfire**. Pack in a stove and use it for cooking. If you've really got to make a fire, use only dead and down wood, and try to build the fire where someone else has already had their fire. Remember, a fire is not out until you can run your hands through the ashes and feel no heat.

Make sure to pitch your tent above the tide line if you're on the coast. Tides can raise the water dramatically, and it's not at all uncommon for novice campers to wake up right before the tent floats off. Even a mile or two up a river, the tide can change the water level by several feet.

Current thinking is that big tarps under your tent just funnel rainwater to where you're sleeping. A footprint tarp under the tent takes care of this and still protects the bottom of your gear.

Boil all water before drinking it.

Read the *Wildlife* section, page 14, and know what to do if you run into a bear or moose.

Know your limitations. It's not at all uncommon for novice hikers to get in over their heads in the bush. Know the conditions of the hike before you set off. Local ranger stations are great sources.

 It's a good idea to pack a copy of ***The Outward Bound Wilderness First-Aid Handbook.*** It will get you through most emergencies, from having to splint a break to treating beaver fever.

River Crossings

If you're hiking in the backcountry, sooner or later you're going to have to cross a river. To avoid swimming – not at all what you want to do in water that's running about 45°F – here are the basic rules:

- Cross **early in the day** and never cross after a storm. Watch for storms in the same watershed – water levels can change dramatically and rapidly.

- You're probably going to look for a narrow place to cross, but narrow usually means deep and fast. Rivers tend to be slower and more shallow in **wide spots**. You're wet for an extra few yards, but it's worthwhile. Head for the wide places.

- Keep your **boots** on. They have better traction than your feet.

- Keep your **pack** loose, so you can get it off if you need to swim. Make sure anything you can't allow to get wet – like your sleeping back and a set of dry clothes – are in dry bags. If you can't roll your pants up high enough, take them off. Hypothermia can strike just from wind hitting wet clothes.

- If you've got a **rope**, loop it around a tree. You can only cross a river that's half as wide as your rope is long – that loop lets you get it back once you're safely on the other side.

- Finally, if you do swim and the current grabs you, assume river swim position: as if you're sitting in an easy chair, feet in front of you, body upright. If you can't see your toes, your legs are too low. Taking it like this means your feet – not your head – are the first to encounter river obstacles.

■ Fishing

 In British Columbia, there are separate licenses for saltwater and freshwater fishing, and even for a few separate species of fish. For information on saltwater fishing, write to the **Department of Fisheries and Oceans**, 555 W. Hastings St., Vancouver, BC V6B 5G2, Canada.

For freshwater rules, and information on hunting, write to the **Ministry of Environment,** Fish and Wildlife Branch, 780 Blanshard St., Parliament Buildings, Victoria, BC V8V 1X4, Canada.

Health

This is Canada, one of the cleanest, safest countries in the world. There are no major health hazards involved in traveling in British Columbia, and the water coming out of the taps is a lot cleaner than whatever it is you're drinking at home. Still, there are a few things to keep in mind.

If you are currently taking any **medication**, be sure to carry an adequate supply for the length of your trip. If you have allergies, take along some antihistamines. A lot of flowers bloom along the road.

It's a good idea to pack a **first aid kit**. You can buy a perfectly good one at any camping store. It should include several sizes of bandages, disinfectant, a small pair of scissors, moleskin, pain reliever, antiseptic cream and tape. When choosing your kit, keep in mind the number of people that may be using it. Should you go far from civilization, beef up your kit accordingly. Add more bandages, a lot more moleskins and a broad-spectrum antibiotic.

For those who are hiking and camping, a means of **water purification** is a must. No matter how clear the streams may look, you really don't know where the water has been, and you should not assume it's safe to drink. Purifying drinking water is a simple precaution against a lot of possible discomfort. You can use filters, which are expensive but don't alter the water's taste, or you can buy iodine or chemical tablets, which are cheap and taste terrible. With either product, follow the manufacturer's directions carefully. The third and easiest way to purify water is to boil it. Bring the water to a full boil for five minutes. If you're in the mountains, increase the boiling time by one minute per 1,000 feet over 5,000 feet of altitude.

If you insist on trusting nature and not purifying your water, pack more of the broad spectrum antibiotic and remember that most diarrhea goes away in three or four days. If it doesn't, or if there is blood in the stool or a fever comes on, see a doctor.

Take along **sunblock**. There can be more than 20 hours of daylight per day on the highway; the farther north you go, the greater your risk of sunburn. Choose a sunblock with an SPF of 15 or higher. It's perhaps not surprisingly difficult to buy sunblock in most BC drugstores. While working on this book, we took a break and went through two weeks in Hawaii without so much a hint of a burn; a month later, in Victoria, we got boiled like lobsters. Don't underestimate the sun.

Perhaps most important is a massive supply of **mosquito repellent**. Those with the chemical DEET work best; they're more expensive (which means you can get a bottle for two bucks instead of one), but they're worth every penny. If you don't want to put such a toxic chemical on your body, there are those who swear by Skin So Soft, available in most drug stores and now jazzed up with a special repellent ingredient. If you're using DEET, remember to wash it off with warm water and soap and be sure to clean your hands before touching food.

DEET ALERTS

DEET is nasty stuff, but mosquito experts (yes, there are such people; odds are you picked on them while you were in high school, but now they're making more money than you) swear it's the only thing that truly works. There are a couple of other warnings about DEET. Children should not use a concentration higher than 10%. You should never use DEET on broken skin, nor should you apply it under your clothes (although a drop on the top of your hat brim will keep mosquitoes away without you having to put poison on your face). Don't mix DEET with any kind of skin lotion – the lotion drags the DEET down into your system through your skin, where you don't want it. If you use DEET on your clothes, wash them as soon as you take them off. Remember that DEET is highly toxic.

Whatever you do about mosquitoes and other things that bite, take along some hydrocortisone cream to soothe the itch when mosquitoes and other biting insects have no respect for modern chemistry.

■ Hypothermia

Hypothermia is the number one killer of outdoorsmen, but it can be easily avoided. Hypothermia occurs when the body is unable to maintain its core functioning temperature; to save the vital organs in the middle of the body, it begins to shut down the extremities. Wet and wind in combination are the main causes. Victims of hypothermia may display uncontrollable shivering, loss of coordination and sudden sleepiness. Often, they are unwilling to believe anything is wrong with them. Should a member of your party show signs, get him or her out of the elements immediately and into dry clothes. Hot drinks can help in a minor case of hypothermia, but in more extreme cases, they can be a choking hazard. Put the victim into a sleeping bag. If the symptoms are severe, strip both the victim and yourself and get into the sleeping bag together. Try not to let the victim fall asleep, and do not give him or her any alcohol. It's also recommended that you not rub them vigorously in hopes of restoring circulation. In a severe case, get the victim to a hospital as quickly as possible. With hypothermia, quick action saves lives. From personal experience, we can tell you that the person suffering from hypothermia has no idea what's happening. From the inside, it's actually rather peaceful. So watch out for each other.

Legalities & Customs

There are a few things to keep in mind when crossing the border between the US and Canada. How quickly or slowly you get through the border, though, may end up being more a matter of current geopolitical mood than anything you do. Overall, expect more hassle trying to come back into the US than going into Canada.

US citizens entering Canada and Canadian citizens entering the US don't need passports or visas – although showing a passport does speed up border crossings, especially in this time of rampant paranoia. Without a passport, all travelers should carry some form of positive identification, preferably more than one kind: a driver's license and a birth certificate are both good, but really, a **passport** is going to make your life a lot easier, and we're firm believers that everyone should have one anyway. Permanent residents of either country who are not citizens should carry proof of residency. Always check with your consulate or embassy as to current requirements, as security measures change daily.

Fruits and **vegetables** may be inspected or confiscated. This is especially true when you enter Canada from Washington; remember this when you're driving past the fruit stands that line the highway in the miles before the border.

Dogs and **cats** over three months old must be vaccinated for rabies; you must have a certificate from a licensed veterinarian that the shot has been given within the past three years.

You cannot take **pistols** or any firearm with a barrel length of less than 18.5 inches into Canada. "Long guns" – rifles – are allowed, at least hunting rifles and shotguns. Semi-automatic weapons are forbidden. Canadian Customs will ask if you are carrying any weapons. The penalty for bringing in an illegal firearm is stiff.

Do not even think about bringing illegal **drugs** into either country. Carry copies of your prescriptions – this speeds matters up if they want to check the pill bottles and it makes it easier if you lose your bottle and need a refill somewhere along the way.

Both countries prohibit import of products made from **endangered species**. This becomes confusing, because there are products made from whale, walrus ivory, bear, seal and wolf in gift shops everywhere. However, if you buy one of these items in Canada, you will not be allowed to transport it into the US; if you buy it in Alaska, you will not be allowed to transport it through Canada on the way home without a special permit. Avoid this hassle by not buying endangered species products in Canada. When in doubt, call the local Customs office (☎ 604-666-7042) for details before making your purchase and trying to ship it. You can buy fossilized ivory and whalebone, legally transporting it through either country. If you have any questions, contact the local Fish and Wildlife Office or its equivalent; numbers are provided throughout this book. (As for the ethical questions of buying products made from endangered species, see the section on *Shopping*, page 51.)

When you return to your home country, Customs officials will assess **duty** on items purchased abroad. For US citizens who have been out of the country for less than 48 hours, the duty-free allowance is US $25; after more than 48 hours, it's US $400. Canadian citizens are allowed CAN $20 after 24 hours, CAN $100 after 48 hours, and CAN $300 after seven days.

People who are not residents or citizens of the US or Canada should check with their country's embassies or consulates for current entry requirements.

For the latest information on Customs, write to the **Department of the Treasury**, US Customs Service, Washington, DC 20041, or your local Customs office. In Canada, write to the **Customs Office**, 1001 W. Pender St. Vancouver, BC V6E 2M8, Canada.

Electricity

Both Canada and the US run on 110-120 voltage, and the plug shape is the same, so no adapters are needed. Be aware, however, that many of the smaller towns use generators to supply their power, so there may be minor fluctuations. When charging a rechargeable battery item, such as a video camera or a personal computer, watch for unusual heat or unusual charging time. Should this occur, unplug your machine and try charging it again in a larger town.

Metric Conversion

Officially, Canada uses the metric system; however, a lot of Canadians haven't realized this yet, and if you ask most of them a weight or a distance, they'll frequently answer in pounds and miles. Speed limit signs, however, do use kilometers (90 kph equals 55 mph). In this book, we use the US system, because it is more readily recognized by people in both countries.

Going Metric?

To make your travels a little easier, we have provided the following charts that show metric equivalents for the measurements you are familiar with.

GENERAL MEASUREMENTS

1 kilometer	=	.6124 miles
1 mile	=	1.6093 kilometers
1 foot	=	.304 meters
1 inch	=	2.54 centimeters
1 square mile	=	2.59 square kilometers
1 pound	=	.4536 kilograms
1 ounce	=	28.35 grams
1 imperial gallon	=	4.5459 liters
1 US gallon	=	3.7854 liters
1 quart	=	.94635 liters

INCHES

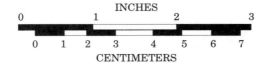

CENTIMETERS

TEMPERATURES

For Fahrenheit: Multiply Centigrade figure by 1.8 and add 32.

For Centigrade: Subtract 32 from Fahrenheit figure and divide by 1.8.

CENTIGRADE		FAHRENHEIT
40°	=	104°
35°	=	95°
30°	=	86°
25°	=	77°
20°	=	64°
15°	=	59°
10°	=	50°

Money

■ Currency & Exchange

We're in a shop in Canada, and a tourist from Des Moines whips out US dollar bills in the utter expectation that they'll be good.

Canada is not the US.

Canada has its own money – and it's not nearly as ugly as the US bills. Canada was even wise enough to simply take the $1 bills out of circulation and replace them with coins, instead of spending billions of dollars giving people a choice, as the US has done with more than one utter failure to introduce a $1 coin.

At press time, one US dollar was equivalent to $1.33 Canadian dollars.

Denominations are the same: pennies, nickels, dimes, quarters. Canada has the $1 coin – a loony, named after the loon on the coin, and a $2 coin, a tooney. Bills go $5, $10, $20, $50, etc.

Many businesses in Canada accept US dollars in payment. This is, in our opinion, a horrible thing, showing an utter lack of respect. On the other hand, the businesses get their revenge for this economic colonialism by giving really, really terrible exchange rates.

There are ATMs (actually, Canadians call them ABMs – automatic bank machines) everywhere, so it should be no problem to withdraw money from your home bank account. Doing this saves you commission at change bureaus, helps you keep closer track of what you're spending and gets you a better exchange rate.

Mastercard, VISA and American Express are pretty much universally accepted.

Practicalities

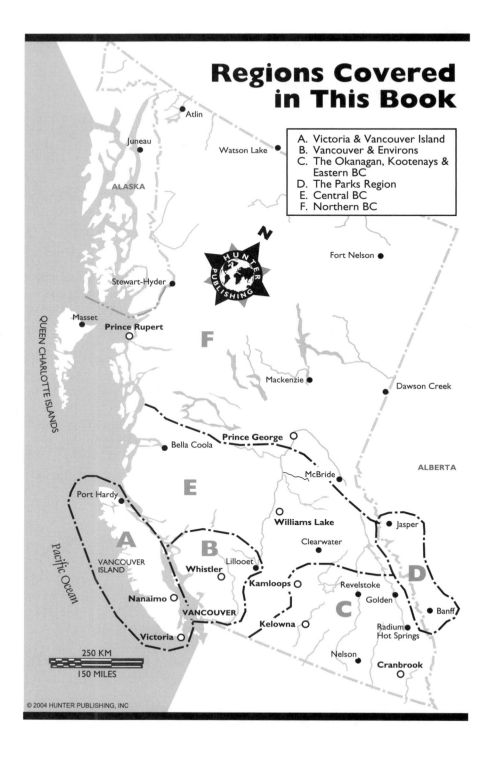

Regions Covered in This Book

A. Victoria & Vancouver Island
B. Vancouver & Environs
C. The Okanagan, Kootenays & Eastern BC
D. The Parks Region
E. Central BC
F. Northern BC

Atlin

Juneau

Watson Lake

ALASKA

N
HUNTER PUBLISHING

Fort Nelson

Stewart-Hyder

QUEEN CHARLOTTE ISLANDS

Masset
Prince Rupert O

F

Mackenzie

Dawson Creek

Bella Coola

Prince George O

ALBERTA

McBride

E

Port Hardy

O
Williams Lake

Jasper

A

Clearwater

VANCOUVER ISLAND

Pacific Ocean

B
Lillooet
Whistler O

Nanaimo O

VANCOUVER

Kamloops O

Revelstoke
Golden

C

D

Banff

Kelowna O

Radium
Hot Springs

Victoria O

250 KM

150 MILES

Nelson

Cranbrook O

Victoria & Vancouver Island

It's the largest island on the west coast, and it has not only some of the biggest trees in the world – as well as sea monsters, orca and fairly regular Bigfoot sightings – it also has the city of Victoria, recently voted the top city in North America. Once you're on the island, it'll be hard to think of a reason to leave.

Victoria

How can you not love a city that puts flower pots on all its lamp posts? Victoria is, plain and simple, one of the glory cities of the western hemisphere. It's beautiful, friendly, civilized. And it's diverse. You can go from having high tea at one of the fanciest hotels to chasing sea monsters, all in a few hours. You can tour classics of Victorian architecture, or hang out with orcas.

It doesn't get much better than Victoria. Whatever you want, it's here.

■ History

Located at the southern tip of Vancouver Island, the area that's now Victoria was first settled by the **Songhees**, the **Saanich** and the **Sooke**. Each had its territory, but there was fairly free mixing, even with groups from across the Straits of Juan de Fuca. The culture was fairly typical for the northwest coast: clan houses, totems and, thanks to the incredibly rich sea and forest, plenty of time to develop life as a form of art.

The First Nations people had their first brush with Europeans in 1790, when the Spanish explorer **Manuel Quimper** showed up and claimed the island for Spain.

But wait, say those of you who were actually paying attention in history class. By 1790, Nootka Sound, on the western edge of the island, was already the most important trade port in the Pacific Ocean, where untold numbers of furs were being shipped off to China and traded for tea. In fact, you can go back even further than that: Captain Cook himself had been in Nootka Sound – he's the one who put the name on the maps, after all. (By the time he'd gotten this far north, Cook had pretty much run out of the names of people to suck up to, and so he was keeping local names when naming new places.) Cook sailed into Nootka Sound in 1778, fully 12 years before Quimper had his little ceremony on the beach.

Cook liked Nootka Sound; he liked the looks of the land around it, and he especially liked the people, who had "a very agreeable air, with a degree of softness and melody."

SECOND COMING

Cook also found out that he wasn't the first one here. During the usual show-and-tell that followed landing, the Nootka men brought out some silver spoons, which were clearly Spanish. Cook figured they must have belonged to the *Santiago*, which had been this way in 1774, before its scurvy-ridden crew turned south once more.

Nootka Sound was ground zero for the fur trade, and with the rich forests of huge cedar trees, also the perfect place for ship repair. However, Quimper's claim on Victoria's area still held, for the simple reason that nobody knew the land he was standing on was in any way attached to Nootka Sound. For all anybody knew at that time, the two places could have been separated by 10 different islands. Or one could have been an island, the other part of the continent. The maps were blank.

It was a member of Vancouver's party, **James Johnstone** (for whom the nearby Johnstone Strait is named) who first circumnavigated the island. This was, actually, part of a long series of one-upsmanship shows between Vancouver and the Spanish, with both trying to map more of the newly discovered land first, and so strengthen their claim. This was all, in the manner of the time, quite civilized. Vancouver's man Puget (yeah, the Puget Sound guy) wrote, "As I had no Orders from Captain Vancouver respecting the Spanish Survey in case of meeting their Boats; their Determination of this Inlet [Toba Inlet] proved of no Service to us, for we were under the Necessity of following it up to its Source; We therefore took our Leave."

In other words, the Spanish were going hard and fast, not worrying about the details. Vancouver, trained in the art of mapping by the greatest explorer the world has ever seen, Captain James Cook, took the time to do things right.

But the crews got along fine. Vancouver and the Spanish captain Juan Franciso de la Bodega y Quadra got along famously, hanging out with each other and eating dinner together, rather than mixing with their rabble crews. When Johnstone came back to report that they were all on the edge of an island, Vancouver's impulse was to name the thing Quadra and Vancouver Island.

That didn't last long. The British consolidated their holdings on the Pacific northwest coast. The Spanish, who were the first to map so many areas – all the way up to Prince William Sound in Alaska – pulled out. And so Vancouver Island it was.

Once the land was clearly under **British** rule, it didn't take long for the HBC to move in. On March 14, 1843, **James Douglas** gave orders to build Fort Victoria. Actually, he gave the orders to build Fort Camosack. A bit later, he changed his mind and gave the orders to build Fort Albert. Same place, new name. Before it was all done, he changed the name again, this time to Fort Victoria. If you look carefully at the seawall of Victoria's inner harbor, you can see where Douglas had his fort.

Douglas had started off pretty simply: "Put six men to dig a well, and six others to square building timber." But the plans were a little more far-reaching. Like everything else built west of the Canadian Rockies, this was to be an outpost for the HBC, ever interested in continuing to expand the largest commercial empire the world has ever seen. They were in the midst of a corporate expansion that would have embarrassed the McDonald's corporation, setting up a string of trading posts from Ottawa to the Pacific.

The official story is that the people about to be displaced by this fort were okay with it. Douglas wrote, "Spoke to the Samose today, and informed them of our intention of building in this place, which appeared to please them very much, and they immediately offered their services in procuring pickets for the establishment, an offer which I gladly accepted, and promised to pay them a blanket for every 40 pickets which they bring."

Blankets were good things, the heart of First Nations trade. Within a few days, Douglas had more than 1,200 First Nations people bringing him anything he needed.

The British Government, or at least the part of it that existed largely to keep the two shadow governments – the HBC and the East India Company – happy, simply gave away Vancouver Island, lock, stock, barrel, and residents, in 1849. The stipulation was that the HBC had to establish settlements within five years.

Victoria & Vancouver Island

This fit right in with their plans. The line between a settlement and a trading post can be a very, very thin one.

And, to be fair, trading posts bring settlements. By 1852, there were enough people around Fort Victoria to start laying out streets, building up a proper little town. The "Fort" got dropped off the name, and what we know today as the marvelous city of Victoria got its start. Ten years later, it was incorporated.

It still wasn't part of British Columbia, though. The BC mainland became a crown colony in 1858; it wasn't until 1866 that anybody got around to including the coastal islands as part of the territory, but right away, those with power realized that Victoria was a whole lot nicer than the old capital, New Westminster. It was on the ocean. It didn't rain much. The scenery was fantastic. And so in 1868, Victoria was named capital of the territory; three years later, when the territory became a province, officially entering the confederation, the capital stayed put.

For the next 40 years, Victoria was an amalgamation of rough and tumble frontier post, and the most civilized of cities.

In 1892, a man named **Francis Mawson Rattenbury** arrived in the town. He was only 25 years old, but the guy had vision. All you have to do is look at the Inner Harbour: what you see is what Rattenbury wanted you to see. His Parliament building, opened in 1898, his Empress Hotel, built in 1905. The building that houses the Wax Museum is also his.

Maybe it's the strength of Rattenbury's vision that has made Victoria what it is today: a city that combines the best of its British heritage with a frontier, anything-is-possible ethos. About 350,000 people call the greater Victoria area home today, and they live in a clean, fairly organized city that is very, very easy to get out of, and a lot of fun to be in.

▪ Basics

 Pretty much everything you're going to want in Victoria is within walking distance of the Inner Harbour.

AUTHOR NOTE: Driving around downtown is a complete and utter nightmare. If you've got a car, find a garage and start walking. It will really help your blood pressure.

Start at the **Tourist Info Centre**, 812 Wharf St., ☎ 250-953-2033, right on the corner of the Inner Harbour, across the street from the Empress Hotel. The good staff members here are frequently jumping because there are so many people coming in. If you haven't made a hotel reservation and you're arriving in summer, stop here first. There are discount coupons for some hotels and the staff can help you if you're in a jam.

BC's Capitol building in Victoria.

■ Museums & Attractions

Victoria has one of the best museums in Canada, the **Royal British Columbia Museum**. Even if you're not a museum person, you've got to take a look at this place, if only for the First People's Gallery, one of the finest collections of northwest coast Native artifacts anywhere in the world. It's beautifully arranged, too, with a tribal house, a stunning collection of totem poles and what's probably the definitive collection of Haida argilite (a black slate found only in BC) carvings. Setting this museum apart from so many others is simply the quality of display: everything is shown to its best advantage. There's even a replica of the back end of Vancouver's ship. When you're looking at how claustrophobic the captain's quarters were, remember that the ordinary seamen got hammocks in stuffy below decks, and that was it.

The museum also has special exhibits – a recent one was on Chinese dinosaurs – kid's exhibits, a deep-water exhibit, a reconstruction of an old gold mining town, and more. Just in case that's not enough for you, there's an IMAX theater, too. It's not at all hard to spend most of a day here. If you get hungry, food at the snack bar is surprisingly good, or, for CAN $20, you can have high tea in the museum.

The museum is located next door to the Parliament Building, facing the Empress Hotel. There's no way to miss it. Admission is CAN $13 for adults, CAN $8 for students/seniors. Open every day, 9 am to 5 pm. http://rbcm1.rbcm.gov.bc.ca/.

Once you've done the museum, walk away from the water to the carving shed. There's usually somebody at work here – on nice days, one side of the shed just drops away so you can see inside. There are also good totem poles on the grounds.

Right across the street from the museum, behind the Empress, is the **Crystal Garden**, a botanical garden and butterfly habitat. It's also home to a lemur breeding program – and considering what trouble the lemurs are having on their home island of Madagascar, there's no way to emphasize how important the effort is. In addition to good jungle-like scenery and lots of butterflies, there are also tropical birds and even some good bat displays, including Madagascar fruit bats. The Crystal Garden is a very popular place with the kids. ☎ 250-381-1213. Admission CAN $9. www.bcpcc.com/crystal. It opens at 9 am every day, and closing times vary depending on season.

Coming out of the Crystal Garden, walk towards the harbor, past the Parliament Building, and you'll come to two more of Victoria's small museums, the Undersea Gardens and the Wax Museum.

The Undersea Gardens, 490 Belleville St., ☎ 250-382-5717, www.pacificunderseagardens.com, is inside what looks like an anchored yacht. It has a variety of aquariums and offers a chance to see what's under all that water out there. It's worth the look in to see a giant Pacific octopus and the wolf eel, which is probably bigger than your couch. You just don't get many chances at that. There are daily explanatory shows, or you can just hang out and look at the aquariums. Admission CAN $7.50. Open every day; call for seasonal hours.

The **Wax Museum**, ☎ 250-388-4461, www.waxworld.com, directly next door, is your usual wax museum, with plenty of displays of both Canadian and British history – there are some pretty odd juxtapositions, such as Voltaire sitting next to Robert Service – along with a pretty good chamber of horrors. Better is the Franklin Expedition display and film, which gives you a sense of what serious nutcases the early polar explorers must have been. Admission CAN $9. Open daily, 9 am until at least 5 pm (later in summer).

The **Parliament Building** is open daily for free tours. If you have an hour to kill and a serious interest in history, it's worthwhile. Unfortunately, the tour doesn't really give you much of a look at what Rattenbury created, as most of the building is closed off. Perhaps the most interesting thing on the tour are Rattenbury's original drawings, which are in the hallway next to the waiting room.

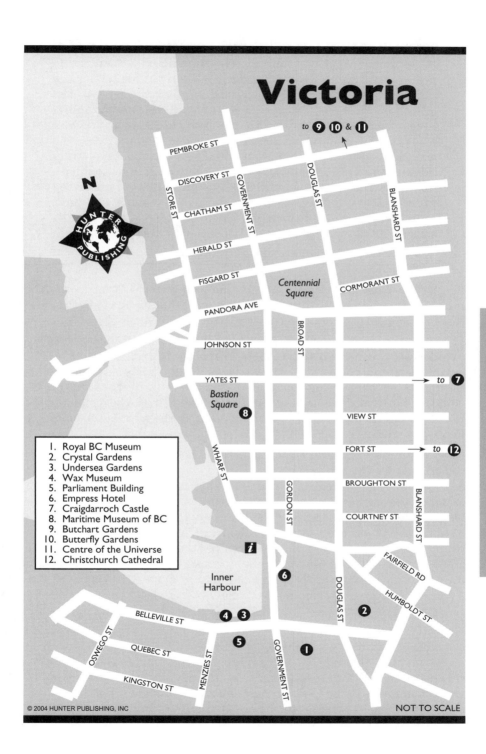

Victoria

to **9** **10** & **11**

PEMBROKE ST

DISCOVERY ST

STORE ST

CHATHAM ST

GOVERNMENT ST

DOUGLAS ST

BLANSHARD ST

HERALD ST

FISGARD ST

Centennial Square

CORMORANT ST

PANDORA AVE

JOHNSON ST

BROAD ST

YATES ST → *to* **7**

Bastion Square **8**

VIEW ST

FORT ST → *to* **12**

WHARF ST

BROUGHTON ST

GORDON ST

BLANSHARD ST

COURTNEY ST

1. Royal BC Museum
2. Crystal Gardens
3. Undersea Gardens
4. Wax Museum
5. Parliament Building
6. Empress Hotel
7. Craigdarroch Castle
8. Maritime Museum of BC
9. Butchart Gardens
10. Butterfly Gardens
11. Centre of the Universe
12. Christchurch Cathedral

FAIRFIELD RD

i

Inner Harbour **6**

HUMBOLDT ST

BELLEVILLE ST **4** **3**

OSWEGO ST

QUEBEC ST

MENZIES ST

5

GOVERNMENT ST

DOUGLAS ST

2

1

KINGSTON ST

N

HUNTER PUBLISHING

Victoria & Vancouver Island

NOT TO SCALE

THE PRIVATE LIFE OF FRANCIS M RATTENBURY

Rattenbury was just a fun guy. He came up with this utterly brilliant design for BC's Parliament Building at the tender age of 25, and had the guts to keep pushing it through gross cost overruns – the man had expensive taste in marble and no ability to compromise. Later in life – that inability to compromise again – he ran off with his mistress and returned to England, where he was clubbed to death by his mistress' new lover. The mistress killed herself after the trial, the lover ended up in prison, with his sentence to hang commuted. Although Rattenbury is buried in an unmarked grave in England, there are some who have seen Rattenbury's ghost in the Empress Hotel – the ghost is supposed to be pretty fussy and demanding, just like the man himself was.

Private life aside, Rattenbury put his stamp on Victoria. If you look at the Inner Harbour from the water, what you see is what he wanted you to see. It's his vision that gives Victoria its continental flavor.

You can take in another of Rattenbury's buildings by touring the **Empress Hotel** with **Bird's Eye View Walking Tours**, ☎ 250-389-2727. Seven bucks gets you an hour of wandering around parts of the hotel even the guests don't see. If you don't have a chance for the tour, it's still worthwhile to stop in at the hotel's tiny public museum, in the basement on the Parliament side. It's free, and you can see how the rich folk used to live while in Victoria.

Head further afield for a look at the private lives of the rich at the turn of the century at **Craigdarroch Castle**, 1050 Joan Crescent, ☎ 250-592-5323, www.craigdarrochcastle.com. Built by coal baron Robert Dunsmuir in 1889, the castle has 39 rooms spread over five floors, and was the height of upper-class comfort. Over the years the building has seen some hard times – it was used as a hospital during the war – but it's been beautifully restored, and a tour will convince you that the only way to live is in a house where the servants have their own set of stairs. This is a beautiful house on a beautiful property. Admission CAN $10. Daily, 10 am-4 pm; extended summer hours are 9 am-7 pm.

The best way to get to the castle is to walk up Yates Street from the Inner Harbour. Yates is full of antique stores, used bookshops, and more – it's the most interesting shopping street in the town. Craigdarroch is about an hour's pleasant walk, if you're taking time to windowshop. If you decide to take a taxi to the castle, get a receipt, and you'll save a buck on the admission price. By bus, get on a number 11 or 14, get off at Joan Crescent – you'll see the castle from there, a minute away.

In Bastion Square, in a building that was once the first Provincial Courthouse in BC, is the **Maritime Museum of British Columbia** (28 Bastion Square, ☎ 250-385-4222, www.mmbc.bc.ca). This is well worth a stop, simply for a chance to see what early mariners went through. You've heard of hardtack, that great ship staple? The Maritime Museum lets you know what was in it: as Joseph Banks, the naturalist on Cook's first voyage wrote, "Our bread is indeed indifferent, occasioned by the quantity of Vermin that are in it, I have often seen hundreds nay thousands shaken out of a single bisket." Hardtack, just in case you want to try the recipe at home, was mostly made out of pea flour and bone dust. Yeah, bone dust. Hardtack made in the 1850s was being served to British soldiers during World War I. Meanwhile, they were living on ships roughly 100 feet long by 30 feet wide – upwards of a hundred men, for more than three years at a time.

If all that wasn't enough fun, the complete lack of vitamin C in the typical sailor's diet caused scurvy. Cook figured out that if he forced – and it was a matter of forcing – his sailors to eat fresh vegetables whenever possible, he could maintain a pretty scurvy-free ship. He didn't know the details, but he knew what worked. Here's Banks on the glory of scurvy: "First, loose teeth, spontaneous weariness, heaviness of the body, difficulty breathing, especially after body motion; rottenness of the gums, a stinking breath, frequent bleeding of the nose, difficult of walking; sometimes a swelling, sometimes a falling away of the legs in which there are always livid, plumbeous, yellow, or violet colored spots."

Visit this museum (CAN $6), then sneer at your friends who've been on cruise ships. Open daily in summer, 9:30-5 pm.

After all that, you're going to need to get out and smell the flowers. **Butchart Gardens,** www.butchartgardens.com, ☎ 866-652-4422, is one of Victoria's prime destinations. The botanical garden covers more than 55 acres. Like most fun things of this sort, it was started by rich people with time on their hands: Mr. Robert Butchart was the man-

Butchart Gardens is a top destination.

ager of a cement company, the biggest around. His wife didn't much care for the limestone quarry her husband's company abandoned, once it stopped being productive, so she turned it into a garden. The center of Butchart Gardens is where Mrs. Butchart started, at the Sunken Garden, which includes a 70-foot fountain. Perhaps more popular is the Rose Garden, with more varieties of roses than you knew existed. Roses named after dogs, after famous people, after their colors.... There's also a Japanese Garden (skip it if you've been to Japan and know what it should really look like), and an Italian Garden, done up as if it were in front of a palazzo.

At Butchart, many of the plants are left unlabeled, so the experience is more of simply walking through a really nicely done garden than through something out to educate you. There's a free plant ID guide, and there are staff around who can answer your questions.

Basic admission to the garden is CAN $19.25. If you don't have your own car, the easiest way to get there is by way of one of the tour operators who run regular trips. **Garden Express**, ☎ 250-388-6539, offers round-trip transport and admission for CAN $27.25. You can add on the Butterfly Garden for another CAN $8. Buses leave about every half-hour from right behind the Empress.

You'll pass the **Butterfly Gardens** on the way to Butchart. Tours give you plenty of time to look inside this 12,000-square-foot greenhouse. If butterflies are your thing, this is a must-see. ☎ 877-722-0272, www. butterflygardens.com.

Another spot you'll pass on the way to Butchart is the **Centre of the Universe**. Really. That's what all the signs say. It's the name of Victoria's observatory, open for free tours from 10-6 daily, April through October (in winter, closed Mondays); in summer, it's also open until 11 pm on Saturday, Sunday and Wednesday. They offer films, tours of their six-foot telescope and, if you're here for the night shows, telescope parties, for close-up looks at the stars. The Centre of the Universe is at 5071 W. Saanich Rd., ☎ 250-363-8290.

If you've got time downtown and are looking for a quiet place to duck out for a few minutes, **Christchurch Cathedral**, 912 Vancouver St., is worth a look. Built in chunks from the turn of the century to the 1950s, it's a good, classic cathedral, open daily.

■ Tours

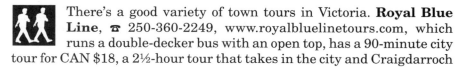

There's a good variety of town tours in Victoria. **Royal Blue Line**, ☎ 250-360-2249, www.royalbluelinetours.com, which runs a double-decker bus with an open top, has a 90-minute city tour for CAN $18, a 2½-hour tour that takes in the city and Craigdarroch

Castle for CAN $27, as well as day/evening tours of Butchart Gardens for CAN $40/$38. You get an extra hour on the cheaper evening tour, and if you go on Saturday in July and August, you'll be there for the fireworks show.

Gray Line, ☎ 250-388-5428, 800-663-8390, does Butchart for CAN $43 (add on the Butterfly Garden for an extra $9.50), or a city tour for CAN $20.75 (CAN $28 if you include Craigdarroch).

Next to the Parliament Building you'll see horse-drawn carriages. These take you around a quiet downtown neighborhood with beautiful houses and elaborately landscaped lawns. **Victorian Carriage Tours**, ☎ 250-361-1220, has an hour-long tour for CAN $105, or a 45-minute ride through Beacon Park for CAN $85. These prices are for the entire carriage, so buddy up.

There are some great walking tours. If you want to do it yourself, pick up the *James Bay Heritage Walking Tour* map from the Tourist Info Centre. James Bay is the oldest, maybe grandest, neighborhood in town, with most of the houses dating from the late 1800s to early 1900s. Walking among these buildings is a good way for architecture buffs to spend a day.

Find out where the people who built these houses ended up, with a cemetery tour. The **Old Cemeteries Society** runs Saturday tours year-round, or evenings in July and August. Check their schedule to see which cemetery they're walking through: there are tours of gold rush notables, the Chinese graveyard, women artists, and more. Standard tours are only CAN $5. Their CAN $10 July and August presentations leave every night at 9 pm from the Cherry Bank Hotel, 825 Burdett St., just a few minutes from the Inner Harbour. ☎ 250-598-8870.

If the cemeteries get you in the mood for ghosts, try **Ghostly Walks**, ☎ 250-384-6698. Meet them in front of the Visitor Info Centre (VIC) daily at 7:30 pm from late June to Labor Day for a lively look at Victoria's past. These tours are really well done: you'll hear the chains clanking long before the tour is over. Best of all, you get filled in on little bits of Victoria history that you simply won't hear anywhere else. You'll see where the Hawaiian village used to be, find out where Robert Service lived when he was a bank teller in Victoria, and find out just what ghosts can get up to with dark chocolates. Don't miss it. CAN $12. If you need more ghost stories when you're done, the guide's book *Ghosts and Legends of Bastion Square,* available in local bookstores, is well worth picking up. Mr. Adams also runs an annual Ghosts of Victoria festival in October. Check out the website at www.discoverthepast.com.

Victoria Bobby Old Town Walking Adventures, ☎ 250-953-2033, www.walkvictoria.com, departs from the VIC at 11 am. For CAN $15 you get a look at where Fort Victoria once stood, the narrowest street on the

Victoria & Vancouver Island

island, Chinatown, Market Square, and more. Again, it's a nice way to take in the history of the town.

If all that walking has made you thirsty, head to **Vancouver Island Brewery**, 2330 Government St., ☎ 250-361-0005, www.vanisland-brewery.com. It offers guided tours on Fridays and Saturdays at 3 pm.

Much farther afield, **Big Tree Forest Walks** loads you on a bus and takes you to the west edge of the island, where there are trees bigger than you'd think possible – Western red cedars with trunks 30-plus feet around. Trips leaving from Victoria are run by the **Carmanah Forestry Society**, ☎ 250-381-1141, a volunteer organization doing good work. These trips take a full day, so be prepared.

■ Adventures

 Once you've had enough of the cultured life of the city, it's time to get out and about. Luckily, there's no shortage of things to do in the wild.

On Foot

Hiking: Island Adventure Tours, ☎ 250-812-7103, www.islandadventuretours.com, has a really nice guided hike in East Sooke Wilderness Park. The trip takes about six hours, including the drive out to the park. The hike itself is six miles on a trail with old-growth rainforest on one side and the ocean on the other. Cost is CAN $95. For CAN $125, you can get in on their Juan De Fuca Marine Trail Hike, which takes eight hours. If you want to do the whole trail, their three-day expedition is CAN $349, including gear, transportation, a guide, and meals. Swank it up a little by staying in B&Bs for CAN $549.

Rock Climbing: If you're looking for more vertical walks, try **Slipstream Rock and Ice**, which guides climbing trips. Half-day programs are under CAN $50. They've also got an office in Squamish, which, frankly, has better rock climbing. ☎ 800-616-1325, www.slipstreamadventures.com.

On Water

Victoria Marine Adventure Centre, 950 Wharf St., ☎ 250-995-2211, 800-575-6700, has set itself up as a one-stop booking center. They can send you out on orca-watching trips (see below), as well as wildlife tours to look at seals, sea lions and some of the 200 or so species of birds that pass through the region. Two-hour trips are CAN $59. They also rent powerboats, kayaks and bikes, and can set you up on a fishing trip (see below). If you're looking for something different in the way of accommodation, stay in their moored yacht, available by the night.

Sailing: The *Thane*, a two-masted sailing ship, goes out three times a day for three-hour sails. Cost is only CAN $45 per person, and it gives you a nice taste of life on the water. ☎ 250-885-2311.

Paddling: Le-La-La Canoe Adventures, ☎ 250-727-7958, offers trips in a traditional 42-foot cedar canoe. This canoe was made from a single log by a 78-year-old carver who says this is it for him, he's done. Trips leave from the Inner Harbour; a two-hour paddle is only CAN $45, and there are special deals with longer trips. You go with two First Nations guides, who tell stories and legends and make sure everybody stays in rhythm. This is likely to be your only chance to paddle this kind of classic canoe. If you're serious about Pacific Northwest history, you absolutely can't miss out on this. It's a thing of beauty.

Island Adventure Tours, ☎ 250-812-7103, www.islandadventuretours. com, has a wide variety of paddles available, including a moonlight paddle in summer. They're also the best people to talk to for longer trips in the outlying islands.

Island Eco-Tours, ☎ 250-216-2389, has guided paddles near Fisgard Lighthouse for CAN $75; a longer tour at the Discovery Islands runs CAN $109.

Victoria Marine Adventure Centre, 950 Wharf St., ☎ 250-995-2211, 800-575-6700, rents kayaks for CAN $20/hour, single or double, with a two-hour minimum. They also have a two-hour guided paddle around the Inner Harbour for CAN $55, and a two-hour guided evening paddle that ends with dinner at the Blackfish Café, for CAN $79.

Vancouver Island Canoe & Kayak Centre, ☎ 250-361-9365 or 877-921-9365, 575 Pembroke St., www.canoeandkayakcentre.com, has shoreline tours for CAN $69, harbor tours for CAN $55.

Ocean River Sports, ☎ 250-381-4233, www.oceanriver.com, 1824 Store St., runs short trips around the harbor, or longer trips, including a five-day paddle through Clayquot Sound.

Fishing: A River Runs By, ☎ 250-598-3441, 1419 Lang St., www. ariverrunsby.com, offers day-long guided fly-fishing trips. If you've never fly-fished before, this is a good place to start, as they also offer private lessons, with all the necessary toys supplied.

Victoria Marine Adventure Centre, 950 Wharf St., ☎ 250-995-2211, 800-575-6700, offers a wide variety of charter boats. Four-hour trips run CAN $150/person, with a minimum of four people. They'll also charter you a whole boat, starting at CAN $80/hour, with a five-hour minimum.

In Nature

ORCAS

There are three resident pods of orca near Victoria, totaling about 80 killer whales. From May through October, with a 30-minute boat ride out of Victoria Harbour, you can be in the middle of the action. There's no easier way to see killer whales than this.

The downside is, because there are so many killer whales, and because they are reasonably predictable – some of the operators advertise a 95% success rate in finding orca each day – it can get fairly crowded out in the water, with a dozen boats surrounding a pod. The Victoria operators have a voluntary set of guidelines about how they'll act around the orca, and this keeps things from getting out of hand, but you are likely to see at certain times a bunch of boats racing towards distant fins.

As with any trip, the fewer people you're out with, the better you'll see things. For this reason, we suggest the Zodiac trips, although many people may feel more comfortable on a larger boat – and the Victoria options for these are good, too.

Victoria Marine Adventure Centre, on the waterfront at 950 Wharf St., books for several operators, so you can pretty much pick and choose when you want to go. This is a quality operation. Three-hour trips are CAN $89/adults, CAN $59 for kids under 16. You load up on a Zodiac – the kind of boat Jacques Cousteau used to use around the world. These are open-air, very fast and very safe. To keep you from freezing your butt off in the windrush, the company puts you in cruiser suits. The captains have a good knowledge of killer whale culture and behavior, so while you're watching, they'll fill you in on orca life.

Other companies offering the Zodiac experience include **Springtide**, ☎ 250-385-8433, at 45 Songhees Rd.; **Seacoast Expeditions**, ☎ 250-383-1525, at 146 Kingston St.; and **Great Pacific Adventures**, ☎ 250-386-2277, at 811 Wharf St.

If you're looking for a more substantial boat, **Orca Spirit Adventures**, ☎ 250-383-8411 or 888-672-ORCA, www.orcaspirit.com, at the Coast Victoria Harbourside Hotel, takes you out in a 50-foot ship capable of hitting 50 mph – this means you get to the whales a little faster than you would in a Zodiac. The ship has two viewing decks and is quite comfortable.

Five Star Whale Watching, ☎ 250-388-7223 or 800-364-9617, 706 Douglas St., www.5starwhales.com, has a large catamaran with plenty of observation space, as well as a couple of smaller, very fast cruisers. Finally, **Wild Cat Whale Watching**, ☎ 250-384-9998 or 800-953-3345, 1234 Wharf St., www.victoria-whale-watching.com, sends you out in an open catamaran with room for 54 people.

You'll often see orca off the coast of Victoria.

In the Air

Victoria probably offers more air tours than any other town of comparable size in the country. Whether you want to look at glaciers, islands or wineries, there's a charter flight for you.

Victoria Marine Adventure Centre, 950 Wharf St., ☎ 250-995-2211, 800-575-6700, books with **Cooper Air**, which offers a half-dozen different ent trips. Do a fly-over of the Gulf Islands for CAN $269/person (two people), which includes an hour flight and an hour-long tour of Ganges Island. An air tour of Victoria is only CAN $93. For something really different, take their Saturna Island Winery Tour, which flies you over to the island, gives you a tour of the winery, and finishes with lunch and a tasting before your flight back. Price is CAN $294/person for two passengers, CAN $254 for three or more.

Hyak Air, ☎ 250-384-2499, 1234 Wharf St., has 1½-hour glacier tours of Mt. Olympus for CAN $225/person, Gulf Island tours for CAN $199, and a Fly & Dine package at Butchart Gardens for CAN $179. They fly you out to the gardens, where you can tour the fantastic botanical attractions; then you get lunch at the Butchart restaurant and enjoy a limo ride back to town.

West Coast Air, ☎ 250-388-4521, 1000 Wharf St., www.westcoastair. com, has town fly-bys for CAN $93, a 90-minute glacier run for CAN $225, and a Gulf Island flight for CAN $199. They also have regular flights to Vancouver (CAN $99 one way/CAN $198 return).

Adventures with Monsters

Tired of the same old whale-watching tours? Feeling jaded because you've seen 80 or so killer whales? Victoria's got the solution: their very own sea monster.

The **cadborosaurus** has long been a part of Vancouver Island oral history. Europeans started reporting sightings more than a hundred years ago, but nobody believed them until 1933, when Major W.H. Langley, a pillar of the community, reported seeing the monster. The cadborosaurus has a long greenish body, with loops like those you see in pictures of the Loch Ness Monster. The head is supposed to look like a horse or a camel. Somebody sees the thing two or three times a year, most frequently in Cadboro Bay. The best times to monster-watch are dusk and early morning.

If that isn't enough, there have been plenty of **Sasquatch** sightings on Vancouver Island. Near Strathcona Park, somebody found 16-inch footprints in 1988. If you go into the island's deep forest, you'll think it's a pretty good place for a prehistoric creature to live, hiding from freaks with tape recorders and cameras. You can make a nice home in the hollow of a Western red cedar, and live it up pretty well.

The official scoop from Sasquatch scientists is that the creatures are nocturnal, making beds on piles of vegetation, much as gorillas do. They're omnivorous and live in small groups of one male and maybe four females, plus young. They figure the males to be around eight feet tall and 800 pounds; the females, six feet and 500 pounds.

One more thing: In 1967, someone reported seeing a mermaid on the rocks near Active Pass. There are photos to prove it.

> **NOTE:** Finally, if you're going alone into the deep woods of Vancouver Island to hunt monsters, keep in mind that over the past few years the cougar population has boomed. Keep a clean camp and keep an eye out.

A view of Victoria from the water.

■ Shopping

 If you're looking for the standard tourist stuff, you don't have to go very far: Government Street, right past the Info Centre, is full of t-shirts, postcards, stuff with maple leaves and more. Mixed in are also some places that are worth lingering. Regular shopping hours are 9-6, although most are open until 8 pm or later in summer.

For all your reading needs, **Munro's Books**, 1108 Government St., is a Victoria institution. There's a good selection of books on Canada, right by the front door. **Russell Books**, 734 Fort St., is the place for used books.

Fort Street is called **Antiques Row**: lots of shops with old china, books, furniture, and more.

If you're short on outdoor gear, **Valhalla Pure**, 615 Broughton, ☎ 250-360-2181, has a good selection, from hard-core climbing gear to good raincoats and heavy shoes.

Hill's Native Art, 1008 Government St., ☎ 866-685-5422, www.hillsnativeart.com, has one of the better selections of quality First Nations crafts, at quite reasonable prices. The staff is very knowledgeable, and the art is simply stunning.

Sasquatch Trading Co., 1233 Government St., ☎ 250-386-9033, offers a good mix of high-quality pieces – some really beautiful masks – and more general items. Nice people.

Eagle Feather, 904 Gordon St., ☎ 250-388-4330, is Native-run and -operated, and sometimes there's a carver at work inside. It has some good stuff.

British Columbia has quite a number of wineries – there are some on Vancouver Island and a bunch over in the Okanagan Valley. **British Columbia Wine**, 644 Broughton St., ☎ 250-388-0606, has the largest selection of local vintages you're going to find, including a good stock of ice wine – a dessert wine made from grapes that have frozen on the vine. If that's not your thing, try the Wild Goose pinot gris or Nota Bene, a red from Black Hills Winery that's so popular bottles of it have to be rationed. Locals call it the "king of reds."

If you want to see where wine gets made, head up to Cowichan Valley, or, more conveniently, drive out towards the ferry terminal at Swartz Bay. About halfway there, you'll see signs to **Victoria Estate Winery**, 1445 Benvenuto Ave., ☎ 250-652-2671, in the suburb of Brentwood Bay. It's easy to combine a stop here with a trip to Butchart Gardens, as they share the same neighborhood.

Finally, it's maybe a little odd for your shopping list, but **Utopia**, 564 Johnson St., ☎ 383-5945, has t-shirts. Not souvenir t-shirts, but pop culture t-shirts. Been looking to get Mr. T on your chest? Look here first. Bugs Bunny, Winnie the Pooh (Lynn has an "Eeyore Rules" shirt from here), nuclear bomb tests, whatever. We come here for our Tin Tin needs – sadly, Tin Tin is not well known south of the border. It's a fun place to look around.

■ Where to Eat

 There's only one restaurant in the world where we'll stand in line and wait for a table: **Pagliacci's**, 1011 Broad St., ☎ 250-386-1662. It's small, it looks like a dump, it has lengthy wait times for dinner and, once you're inside, you get some of the best Italian food you've ever had – and carrot cake that is simply not to be believed. Prices from CAN $12.

Our other must-stop on each trip to Victoria is Chinatown's **Hunan Village,** 546 Fisgard, ☎ 250-382-0661. The sesame chicken is astounding. You should get out, with some leftovers, for under CAN $20.

Willie's Bakery, 537 Johnson St., ☎ 250-381-8414, is a required stop first thing in the morning for fresh muffins and cups of coffee big enough to drown in. It has good egg dishes, and on nice days, you can sit on the patio outside.

Yates Street, just a block past Bastion Square, has lots of choice eateries, including local favorite **Ferris**, 536 Yates, ☎ 250-360-1824, with its don't-miss sweet potato fries and meals for as little as CAN $12. Just around the corner, at 1250 Wharf Street, is **Chandlers**, ☎ 250-385-3474, a good choice for a seafood night out, with some entrées under CAN $20. Across the street is the **Pita Pit**, a local choice for large portions on the cheap. Four bucks is enough to get you more lunch than you can likely handle.

Sam's Deli, on Government St., right by the Tourist Info Centre, has good ploughman's lunches for CAN $8; if you like fresh juice in the morning, this is the only place to go.

Pounders, on Yates just off Wharf, has all the exotic ingredients you need for a good Mongolian-style stir fry: ostrich, kangaroo, and more. If your dish of ingredients adds up to exactly a pound, you get it free; otherwise, you'll still get full for under CAN $10.

The cheapest – and one of the best – lunches in town is at the **hot dog cart** outside Munro's Books, on Government Street. It has the best dogs anywhere and is an easy, quick walk from the harbor. A smokey (what a hot dog wants to be when it grows up) and a drink will set you back a couple toonies (that's about four bucks).

In summer months, there's steady traffic to **Barb's Place**, on Fisherman's Wharf. Take the harbor ferry, or walk along past the wax museum to this fish-and-chip joint with a few tables that you've got to wedge yourself into. Expect a crowd. It's cheap – lunches around CAN $8 – and it's good.

If you're feeling ethnic, we have three quick recommendations. **J and J Wontons** is a noodle house on Fort that's actually gotten itself into the *Zagat Guide*. **Eugene's Greek Restaurant**, on Broad Street at Trounce Alley, is a consistent winner of the best of Victoria Greek food category and serves spanakopita for only CAN $3.50. **Niko Niko Teriyaki**, 1000 Langley St., just half a block up from Government, has great quick Korean and Japanese dishes, for about CAN $8.

Swan's Bistro, 506 Pandora St., has great lunches – try the chicken burger – and a traditional English pub menu. The dinner fare is more varied, and they have a microbrewery that has won numerous awards, including a silver for their raspberry ale and a bronze for their Riley's Scotch ale at the Canada Brewing Awards. There's a glassed-in area that's perfect on a warm day.

Hugo's Grill & Brewhouse, downstairs in the Magnolia Hotel, 625 Courtney, ☎ 250-920-4844, gets lively in the evenings despite its slightly odd décor. It serves drinks and well-above-average bar food, including lamb burgers.

Victoria & Vancouver Island

Another good night spot choice is the very popular **Spinnaker's Brew Pub**, 308 Catherine St., ☎ 250-384-6613. It has Canada's first microbrewery and the choice of pub food or pretty fancy dinners. This place can be jammed on the weekends.

If all that sounds like too much meat, **Green Cuisine**, 560 Johnson St., ☎ 250-385-1809, is 100% vegan. Everything is made fresh on the premises, and they have a nice patio area.

For a very swank night out, try **The Mark**, ☎ 250-380-4487, at the Hotel Grand Pacific. The menu, which changes weekly, includes the freshest wild game, and there's one of the better wine lists in the province.

■ Tea

 Traditional British afternoon tea is a Victoria institution.

The Empress Hotel, ☎ 250-384-8111, has a variety of tea servings – they pour upwards of a quarter million cups a year. Basic tea in the swankest setting in town will run you about CAN $50.

The **Royal BC Museum** has a CAN $20 tea, overlooking the inner harbor. ☎ 250-216-3897.

The bargain choice for locals is **Point Ellice**, 2616 Pleasant St., ☎ 250-380-6506. Tea at this classic Victorian house is only CAN $17, including a tour of the grounds, and maybe a game of croquet. To get here, take the Harbour Ferry's Gorge run, and tell them where you want to get off.

Other choices include the **James Bay Tearoom**, 332 Menzies St. (right behind the Parliament Building), ☎ 250-382-8282; and **Windsor House**, 1885 Oak Bay Ave., ☎ 250-595-8020, a 10- or 15-minute walk from the harbor.

Murchies, on Government St., just a block from the harbor, has all your British tea needs, from pots and cups to blends specially made for the queen. There's also a nice bakery.

If British tea isn't your thing, try a fantastic assortment of Chinese and Japanese varieties at **Silk Road**, 1624 Government St., ☎ 250-704-2688. This is one of the best tea shops we've ever been in.

■ Where to Stay

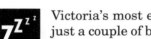 Victoria's most expensive hotels overlook the harbor, but move just a couple of blocks away and prices drop dramatically. If you show up in Victoria without reservations, stop first at the Inner Harbour Tourist Info Centre (812 Wharf St., ☎ 250-382-6539): you can get discount coupons for a wide variety of lodgings and pick up the free *British Columbia Approved Accommodation Guide*, with listings all over

the province. As we've said before, anybody traveling in BC should have one of these.

Swan's Suite Hotel, 506 Pandora, ☎ 250-361-3310, www.swanshotel. com, is a five-minute walk from the harbor. A one-bedroom suite – many with water views, all with a full kitchen and room to sleep four comfortably – start at $145 in high season. Despite the bargain price, this is a swank, luxe place, with an art collection that is not to be believed. If you're in Victoria for a special occasion, the owner's suite is probably the nicest room in the entire city – 3,000 square feet, a rooftop hot tub, a full kitchen and dining room, and more. We didn't want to leave – and you don't have to, since the bistro downstairs is one of Victoria's most popular dining spots and will deliver to the room. There are also some good packages: for art lovers – it took two years to catalog the collection in Swan's – get a suite, lunch, dinner and admission to the Art Gallery, for $300 in high season. Their Romance Package gets you champagne, a loft suite and a horse-drawn carriage ride for $289.

The Magnolia Hotel and Spa, 623 Courtney St., ☎ 250-381-0999, www.magnoliahotel.com, is a block from the Empress. Some of the rooms have water views and fireplaces, and all of them are very, very comfortable. The service is unbelievably good. If you're tired from walking around town, spend an afternoon in the on-site spa. Doubles from CAN $269.

Across the harbor, at the foot of the bridge, is the **Delta Victoria**, 45 Songhees Rd., ☎ 250-360-2999, www.deltahotels.com, which may have some of the best views in the city (you're looking back at the city). There's a spa, indoor pool and very large rooms. Doubles start at CAN $269.

The dowager queen of Victoria is, of course, the **Fairmont Empress Hotel**, 721 Government St., ☎ 250-384-8111, www.fairmont.com/empress. It's been there for a hundred years, it's the town's main landmark, and it's a thing of beauty. Doubles start at CAN $279, but water views are going to cost more.

Moving down the economic scale a bit – although not necessarily in comfort – right in the heart of downtown is the **Bedford Regency**, 1140 Government St., ☎ 250-384-6835, www.bedfordregency.com, with clean, surprisingly quiet doubles starting as low as CAN $89, even in summer. This is as convenient as it gets, right next door to Murchies. Upper-floor rooms in the back of the hotel have water views. A good choice.

The Cherry Bank Hotel, 825 Burdett Ave., ☎ 250-385-5380, is a bit farther out, but basic doubles are as low as CAN $69. The **Strathcona**, 919 Douglas St., ☎ 250-383-2739, is right behind the Empress, with high-season rates starting at CAN $89 for a double; it's a popular nightlife spot, so you might want to check the room for bar noise.

Head behind the Parliament Building for the **James Bay Inn**, 270 Government St., ☎ 250-384-7151. This converted house – which once belonged to BC's most famous artist, Emily Carr – is walking distance from the harbor, but in one of Victoria's most pleasant neighborhoods. Doubles from CAN $133 in summer.

Traveller's Inn has two locations near downtown, with basic doubles for around CAN $110 (1850 Douglas St., ☎ 250-381-1000; 1961 Douglas St., ☎ 250-953-1000).

Year-round, the **hostel**, at 516 Yates St., ☎ 250-250-4511, an easy walk from the harbor, has beds from CAN $16.50.

If you have a car, the **Accent Inn** is just a few minutes outside of downtown, towards the ferry terminal, at 3233 Maple St., ☎ 250-475-7500, 800-663-0298. It gets you out of the downtown congestion. This is a nice property run by very nice people. Like all their properties around BC, it's a quality show at a bargain price. Doubles from CAN $99.

■ Transport

 What's the number one stupid question the people at Tourist Info get? Where's the bridge back to Vancouver? They actually have people yelling at them, sure they got here by bridge.

Didn't happen. You've got two options for getting onto Vancouver Island: by plane or by ferry.

There are two ferries from the Vancouver City area. The one most convenient to Victoria leaves from Tsawessen, about 18 miles/30 km south of Vancouver, and arrives about 18 miles/30 km north of Victoria. Sailings are hourly in summer, but if you're trying to go at rush hour, you might be waiting for a while. Make reservations at ☎ 604-444-2890.

The other ferry leaves from north of Vancouver and arrives at Nanaimo. See *Nanaimo*, pages 96, for more details.

Pacific Coast Lines, ☎ 604-662-8074, www.pacificcoach.com, has daily bus service between the towns. Get on a bus, which takes you to the ferry; get off the ferry and get on another bus to head into downtown.

For travelers coming from Seattle, the **Victoria Clipper IV** makes the run in only two hours. Some sailings have stop-offs in the San Juans. The ship leaves from downtown Seattle, near Pioneer Square, and docks right by the Inner Harbour in Victoria. ☎ 800-888-2535, www.victoriaclipper. com.

Washington State Ferries, ☎ 206-464-6400 in Washington, ☎ 250-381-1551 in Victoria, has a run from the Inner Harbour to Anacortes. www. wsdot.wa.gov/ferries.

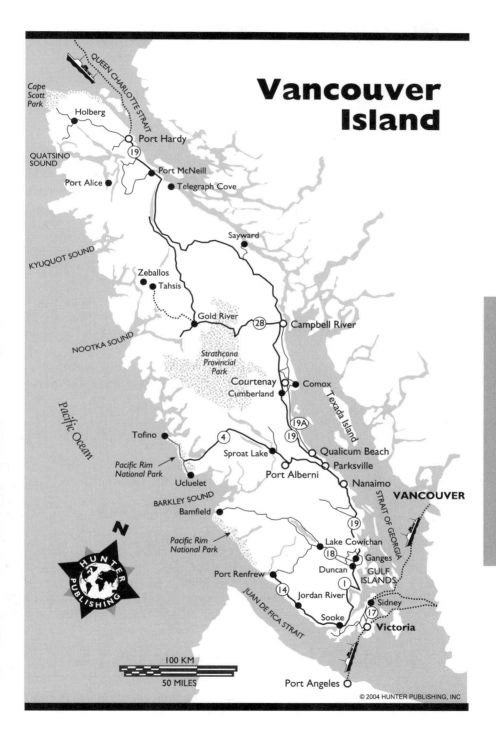

Vancouver
Island

Cape Scott Park
QUEEN CHARLOTTE STRAIT
Holberg
Port Hardy
19
QUATSINO SOUND
Port McNeill
Port Alice
Telegraph Cove
KYUQUOT SOUND
Sayward
Zeballos
Tahsis
Gold River
28
Campbell River
NOOTKA SOUND
Strathcona Provincial Park
Courtenay
Comox
Cumberland
Texada Island
Pacific Ocean
19A
Tofino
4
19
Qualicum Beach
Sproat Lake
Parksville
Pacific Rim National Park
Port Alberni
Ucluelet
Nanaimo
BARKLEY SOUND
Bamfield
VANCOUVER
Pacific Rim National Park
STRAIT OF GEORGIA
19
Lake Cowichan
18
Ganges
Duncan
GULF ISLANDS
Port Renfrew
1
14
Jordan River
Sidney
JUAN DE FUCA STRAIT
Sooke
17
Victoria
N
HUNTER PUBLISHING
100 KM
50 MILES
Port Angeles

© 2004 HUNTER PUBLISHING, INC

Victoria & Vancouver Island

More useful is the *Black Ball's* Port Angeles sailing, with four crossings daily in summer. This is a vehicle ferry, but they don't take reservations, so plan on showing up early. ☎ 250-386-2202. Once you're in Port Angeles, it's a pretty drive to Seattle.

For getting around the Gulf Islands, **BC Ferries**, ☎ 888-223-3779 or 250-386-3431, www.bcferries.bc.ca, has regular sailings of small ships; fares are as low as a few bucks.

The Victoria Airport is about 12 miles/20 km outside of town. If you're coming in on a commercial flight, the **AKAL Airporter** bus meets all planes and charges only CAN $13 to any hotel downtown. ☎ 250-386-2525. (It's a CAN $30 or more taxi ride from the airport to downtown.)

Air Canada, ☎ 888-247-2262, www.aircanada.com, and **Horizon Air**, ☎ 800-547-9308, www.horizonair.com, are the main carriers.

A couple of floatplane services connect Victoria to Vancouver and Seattle. **Harbour Air**, ☎ 250-384-2215, **West Coast Air**, ☎ 250-388-4521, and **Helijet International**, ☎ 250-382-6222, are all options.

Once you're in town, rent bikes at **Victoria Marine Adventure Centre**, 950 Wharf St., ☎ 250-995-2211, 800-575-6700, or **Island Boat Rentals**, 811 Wharf St., ☎ 250-995-1661. You can also rent boats at either spot.

Tofino makes a great side-trip out of town. The **Tofino Bus**, ☎ 866-986-3466 or 725-2871, runs trips to Tofino for CAN $50 one-way, CAN $90 return – and they can carry your surfboard, bike or kayak, too.

To get to the West Coast Trail or the Juan de Fuca trailhead, **WCTE**, ☎ 250-477-8700, makes daily runs. They also offer baggage storage and can rent you hiking gear.

Vancouver Island

You've got three choices for leaving Victoria: take one of the sea routes, detailed in the *Basics* section for the city in this book, or get in a car and drive. You can go as far north as Port Hardy, where you can pick up BC Ferries and link to Prince Rupert and even the Alaska Marine Highway, or you can head west, to where the land ends at Port Renfrew.

West Along Highway 14

Highway 14, the Sooke Road, is not quite a hundred miles of remote scenery, with a few towns and suburbs along the way, before you get to the beaches. If you look at it on the map, you'd think there would be killer ocean views along the road, but mostly there aren't, as there tends to be forest between the highway and the water. However, there are plenty of places to stop and hike, hang out on the beach, or just watch the world go by.

This can be a very busy road on summer weekends, as Victoria's residents all head out. The road is mostly narrow, and it's got a lot of curves and turns. As you get closer to Port Renfrew, there are also some steep grades, complete with switchbacks. So, although it doesn't look very far – hey, it's only 60 miles/100 km – travel along this road is going to take a while. Figure on two or more hours travel time from Victoria to the end of the line at Port Renfrew's Botanical Beach.

The first section of the highway takes you through Victoria's suburbs, with only a few stops worth mentioning. You intersect with the **Galloping Goose Trail** just past the Colwood Interchange. The trail goes from downtown Victoria more than 31 miles/50 km, and is very popular with bikers.

The other stop in this area is the **lighthouse** at Fort Rodd Hill, ☎ 250-478-5849. It's open daily from 10-5:30; look for the exit signs before Colwood Corners. The lighthouse was the first on BC's coast, and it's a nice spot to walk around and look at the ocean.

As you drive, you stay in a largely suburban area – there's even a casino at the junction where Highway 14 meets the road north, Highway 1 – until you hit the small town of Sooke, about 20 or 30 minutes from Victoria, depending on traffic.

■ Sooke

Sooke is the southernmost harbor in western Canada, but that doesn't mean a whole lot any more. It's a quiet town of about 12,000 people, many of whom make the daily commute to Victoria, many more of whom retired here after working in Victoria all their lives. There was a gold rush in 1864, but it died out almost as soon as it began.

Attractions

 Most people come to Sooke for one reason, and one reason only: **Sooke Harbor House**, a restaurant and hotel that makes pretty much every "Best Of" list out there. The hotel part of the operation is, to say the least, swank. There are only 28 rooms, with ocean views, Jacuzzi tubs, all the stuff you'd expect when you were shelling out CAN $300 or more a night.

But it's the restaurant that really draws people. They have two simple ideas here. The first is to have the best wine list in the world – and they come close. Secondly, they use only BC ingredients. Dishes change with the seasons and with what's available. Try the seafood, from clams and whelks to sea urchins and a huge variety of fish. Make sure there's plenty of room on your credit card. This is a special occasion first choice for many people who live in BC. It's that good. ☎ 800-889-9688, www.sookeharbourhouse.com.

Sooke also has a nice **museum** and **art gallery**, on Highway 14, as part of the Info Centre. There's good information on the First Nations history of the region, and the art gallery features local artists. ☎ 250-642-6351.

Adventures on Water

 Rush Adventures, ☎ 250-642-2159, 5449 Sooke Rd., www.rush-adventures.com, rents kayaks and does half-day (CAN $50) and full-day (CAN $75) trips around Sooke. If you've never paddled before, sign up for their beginner class, which will make you pretty comfortable in the water.

Let somebody else do the work of getting you onto the water with **Sooke Coastal Explorations**, ☎ 250-642-2343, www.sookewhalewatching. com. They offer daily whale watching trips in summer – you're looking for the same pods that the Victoria trips go after, but you're starting from a more remote, scenic area. CAN $65 for adults.

Sooke has a **charter boat association**, ☎ 250-642-7783, that serves as a one-call fisherman's resource. Tell them what you're after, they'll set you up with the right boat.

Adventures on Foot

 Just east of Sooke is **East Sooke Wilderness Park**, which has some great hiking trails – if you're looking for a good hike along the Straits, this is the place to come, unless you want to try the entire Coast Trail. You can drive out here yourself – the signs are obvious, just get off the main highway at East Sooke Road – and head out along the beach, or take a guided hike with **Island Adventure Tours**, ☎ 250-812-7103. The trip takes about six hours, including the drive out to the park, for a cost of CAN $95. The hike itself is six miles/10 km on a trail where you've got old-growth rainforest on one side of you, and the ocean on the other. For CAN $125, you can get in on their Juan De Fuca Marine Trail Hike, which takes eight hours. If you want to do the whole trail, their three-day expedition is CAN $349, including gear, transportation, a guide and meals.

If you're looking to hike on your own, the park has more than 31 miles/50 km of trail. Start at Aylard Farms, which can lead you to the Coast Trail for the best views.

Continue on Highway 14 out of Sooke, and you start to leave the city behind. **French Beach Provincial Park** has campsites (☎ 800-689-9025) and great views of the Straits of Juan de Fuca.

The **Juan de Fuca Marine Trail** starts (or ends, really, since most people start in Port Renfrew) at China Beach, about 23 miles/37 km west of Sooke. It's a 29-mile/47-km hike end to end, and if you can get the reservations scheduled right, you can link up with the West Coast Trail and spend two weeks straight hiking through old-growth rainforest and along the beach. For camping reservations on the Juan de Fuca Trail, ☎ 250-391-2300. You can't really get lost on the trail: keep the ocean on the same side, you'll get where you're going. But it is remote, it is prone to nasty weather, and you should go fully prepared. Depending on tides, the trail can occasionally be under a bit of water, so you might have to scramble, and you are going to get your feet wet and muddy.

If you don't want to try the entire trail, you can bail out at any of a number of spots along the way, including Sombrio Beach and Parkinson Creek, where the trailheads meet car-accessible camping.

Anybody on the hike should remember that this is wild country. There are bears and cougars who also like to use the trail, so make some noise.

If you're simply looking for a nice way to stretch your legs, you can stop at China Beach, Sombrio Beach or Parkinson Creek – they're about six miles/10 km apart – and simply walk a bit of the trail to see what it's like. Keep an eye on the ocean for orcas, gray whales and seals.

> **AUTHOR TIP:** When you're stopping at these beaches, take the paid parking very seriously. There are machines: just put your money in and put the receipt on the dashboard. Ignoring this can mean an expensive ticket.

Back on the highway, keep heading west for Port Renfrew. You'll pass the road to Lake Cowichan – don't try it unless you've got 4WD or are happy taking your car on rough logging roads. You can get to the lake more easily off Highway 1.

The road moves into thicker forest, seemingly farther and farther away from the ocean, although you will get glimpses of water through the trees. There are some one-lane bridges, and a lot of switchbacks that slow you down on this part of the trip. But the forest is beautiful, and you cross the occasional stream that looks like the world when it was factory new.

■ Port Renfrew

Port Renfrew is a tiny, end-of-the-line ("hey, we're the beginning of the road," the locals will insist) town with about 400 people. You don't see much of it coming in on the main road – the town itself is kind of hidden in the trees.

There are two reasons to come out here: to hike or to hang out on the beach. Either way, it's worth the drive.

Adventures on Foot

 Hiking: The Juan de Fuca Marine Trail (see above) ends (or begins, depending on which way you want to look at it) here. More importantly, the West Coast Trail begins here.

The **West Coast Trail** is regularly listed as one of the best hikes in the world. It's more or less the same scenery you'd get along the Juan de Fuca Trail, but much, much better. The trail is more remote and considerably less populated. The trail started off as an escape route for mariners shipwrecked along the coast.

The West Coast Trail is 47 miles/77 km from end to end, and takes anywhere from five to 10 days, depending on conditions. Be prepared, especially for rain and wetness.

You cannot get on this trail without a permit. On any given day, only 60 people are allowed to begin the hike, and it's split up, so you're not going to be seeing very many people. Of those 60, 48 will have reservations; the other 12 permits are given on a first-come basis. But why take chances? Figure out your hiking dates, and on March 1, get on the phone to **Discover British Columbia**, ☎ 800-663-6000, to make your reservation. There is a CAN $25 reservation fee, and then a CAN $70 fee for actually making the hike. There are also some short ferry crossings you'll need to pay for, and a CAN $20 fee for crossing the First Nations lands of the Huu-ay-aht.

Before you set out, you'll need to figure out how to get back. The trail is one-way, and if you start off in Port Renfrew, you end up, effectively, in the middle of nowhere. Well, actually, you're just two miles/three km outside of the town of Bamfield, but that doesn't mean much. For transport, check with **West Coast Trail Express**, ☎ 250-380-0580. They can get you to or from both Renfrew and Bamfield.

What do you get on the hike? Scenery. Ocean. Huge trees. Bogs. Waterfalls. Tide pools. A chance to put your pack down and watch orca. It's the best hike in all the Northwest. You are going to need to be in good shape for the hike: not only because of the distance, but also because of the conditions. Hiking in Pacific Northwest forests is nothing at all like hiking forests elsewhere. Things are thicker here, wetter, and you'll be scrambling over logs, crossing rivers and even working your way down cliffs.

There are several guidebooks specific to the trail; you should be sure to pick up at least one of them. Look in Munro's Books in Victoria for the best selection. Also, check online for books and maps at www. westcoasttrailbc.com, which has all the rules and regs, and a PDF guidebook. You'll also want the absolutely vital tide tables, available at most sporting goods shops that have fishing gear (coast towns tend to make them easy to find). Check for the latest conditions with the park office in Port Renfrew, ☎ 250-647-5434.

 Pick up a copy of *Hiking the West Edge: West Coast Trail and Juan de Fuca Trail*, by Ian Gill, or *West Coast Trail*, by Tim Leadem.

Beachcombing: If the hike is a little too ambitious for you, there's still fun to be had in Port Renfrew. Drive out to **Botanical Beach**, one of the best tide pool beaches you'll ever find. Stay on the main road to the T-junction, then go left. From there, it's about two miles/3.5 km up a graveled road to the parking area.

The sea gets a little wild here, so it's carved interesting shapes into the beach, including lots of pools for marine critters to gather. You'll see creepy crabs, sculpins, sea stars, star fish, limpets and more. You can easily spend a day wandering from pool to pool, just seeing who might be home.

Before you drive out this far, though, check the tide tables. There's not so much to see at high tide. You want to be here on a good minus tide.

Oh, and if you go to the beach in spring, don't forget to look up from time to time. Gray whales pass right by here on their migration.

Where to Stay

Port Renfrew has some good places to stay if you're like us and find the town a place you'd like to hang out for a while.

The **West Coast Trail Motel** is right at the trailhead, and it's one of the regular stops for hikers getting their first or last shower from the trail. ☎ 250-647-5565. Doubles from CAN $69.

The Arbutus Beach Lodge, ☎ 250-647-5458, is about the same price. It has waterview rooms and one private cabin.

You can get out of Renfrew the way you came in, or, if conditions are reasonable, there's a gravel road that leads up to Lake Cowichan. This is another logging road, so its condition can change pretty quickly. Get local information before setting out, and keep a very close eye out for logging trucks if you go.

Victoria & Vancouver Island

North Along Highway 1

Highway 1 leads from Victoria to Parksville; the road keeps going north there, it simply changes name to Highway 19. You can stay on this road all the way to Port Hardy, at the northern end of the island. Along the way, you've got a chance to see wineries, great totem poles, trees bigger than you could imagine, and a lot of logged area trying to recover.

The road is wide and good leaving Victoria. One thing to watch for, though, is that annoying Canadian habit of changing speed limits at random. The road is pretty heavily patrolled, and it only occasionally makes sense when suddenly the speed limit drops by 20 or 30 kph.

■ Duncan

The first place worth getting off the road for is the small town of Duncan, the biggest town in the Cowichan Valley. Duncan has about 5,000 residents, and it also serves as the center for the local Cowichan First Nations groups, which comprise about 3,000 people living in the area. This means that Duncan is a good place to get a look at First Nations culture. There are some wonderful totem poles scattered around the town, and the Cowichan Native Village gives you a chance to see craftsmen and more at work.

Attractions

The **Duncan Information Centre** is at 381, Trans-Canada Highway, ☎ 250-746-4636. Pick up your copy of the Totem Pole Guide, which gives you an explanation of the more than 40 poles standing in the town. There is a nice blend of old- and new-style poles here; if you're used to the more sedate poles of Southeast Alaska, or if you've already seen the poles in Ks'an or Gitanyow, these will come as a bit of a shock, as they're colorful and much more lively in style. Some of the best poles are downtown, next to the old railway station. From there, simply walk into town and you'll find more poles hidden between buildings and in courtyards. It makes a stroll through the town quite entertaining: these poles appear when you least expect them.

Once you've had your fill of poles, head out to the **Cowichan Native Village**, 200 Cowichan Way, ☎ 250-746-8119. It's open daily, 9-6 (until 5 in winter). There's a tribal house, a carving shed and regular dance performances. There are also lots of artists at work, and you can get one of the famous Cowichan sweaters – these people lived in the wet and cold for thousands of years and really knew how to dress for it. In summer, there's also a salmon bake. It's well worth stopping here. Adult admission is CAN $10.

BIGNESS: If you're collecting "biggest useless objects" around BC – you'll have plenty of chances – Duncan claims to have the world's largest hockey stick. It's in front of the Cowichan Community Centre, and it offers the same question all of these giant things do: Why?

There is one very unusual attraction in Duncan. Did you ever want to learn how to hunt with a bird? **Pacific Northwest Raptors**, 1877 Herd Road, ☎ 250-746-0372, pnwraptors@shaw.ca, can teach you how. Using trained hawks and falcons, they offer programs that teach you to fly a bird, CAN $60 for a half-day, or a full day of falconry for CAN $115. It's interesting, it's unusual and you'll be the only kid on your block who's done this.

There's not much reason to spend the night in Duncan, but if you need to, there are plenty of hotels along the main road into town. If you're southbound, though, you're almost in Victoria, and if you're headed north, you really haven't gotten very far by the time you got here. Might as well head on in to the Cowichan Valley for a quick look around.

■ Cowichan Valley

The Cowichan Valley is kind of an escape valve for Victoria. There are pretty little towns here, endless logging roads – if you have a 4WD vehicle and aren't worried about getting run over by a logging truck, there's more backcountry here than you can do in 10 vacations – and a few wineries.

The road in from Highway 1, Highway 18, runs alongside the **Cowichan Valley Demonstration Forest**, which is overseen by the BC Forestry Museum, ☎ 250-715-1113. The forest offers lots of short hikes and informative signs tell about reforestation and logging.

Camp at the beautiful **Cowichan River Provincial Park**, 10 miles/ 17 km west of Highway 1, one of the better spots in the area. You can take the 11-mile/19-km Cowichan River Footpath from the campground to the Stoltz Pool and Marie Canyon. It makes for a pleasant day of walking. For campsite reservations, ☎ 800-689-9025.

Lake Cowichan Information is at 125C South Shore Rd., ☎ 250-749-3244. Stop here to see if there are any wineries open with tastings. Next door is the **Kaatza Station Museum**, which features Vancouver Island railway history and includes a 1929 steam locomotive.

From the town of Lake Cowichan, you can follow the north or the south shore; the two roads meet up at the far end of the lake, but on both, the paving gives way to gravel long before the roads meet. From the far end of the lake, there's a reasonably good gravel road that can get you back to Huu-ay-aht First Nations territory and the town of Bamfield, the end of the Pacific Rim National Park and the West Coast Trail. The south shore is a little more traveled, and along it, you can access Gordon Bay Provincial Park and the Honeymoon Bay Wildflower Ecological Reserve. The reserve has the island's largest concentration of pink Easter lilies, along with a few dozen other flower species.

Off the south shore, you can also head south along the gravel road to **Nitinat Lake** and the **Carmanah-Walbran Provincial Parks**, which cover over 30,000 acres along Nitinat Lake and its environs. Inside the park are some of the biggest Sitka spruce in the world, some of them over 230 feet/70 meters tall, with trunks up to 13 feet/four meters in diameter. The Carmanah Giant, at 313 feet/95 meters, is probably the tallest tree in Canada and the biggest Sitka spruce anywhere.

SITKA SPRUCE

The Sitka spruce took a big hit during World War II, when it turned out to be the perfect wood for making practically anything – boats, fighter planes (Howard Hughes' massive Spruce Goose was made of Sitka spruce). The wood is strong, light and easy to work with. Today, it's the main feature of most good guitars.

If you're going to hike into these parks, know what you're doing, don't expect rescue if you screw up, and watch for floods. It's not a place for newby hikers.

Back on the main highway, you'll pass a couple of small towns, including Crofton and Chemainus. Just north of Duncan is the **Somenos Marsh Wildlife Refuge**, which has a few dozen species of nesting waterfowl. Just past that is the **BC Forest Museum**, ☎ 250-715-1113, near Somenos Lake. It's open daily in summer and offers a good chance to see how logging has really shaped the history of the Pacific Northwest. It's a serious issue: we can go with the extreme ecologists, who say no more logging, or we an admit that we all still use lumber products – from the paper this book was printed on to the frame of your house – and figure out the best way to log in a sustainable fashion. Unfortunately, the two sides are too far apart to see each other. No matter what your political stance, you'll learn something here. Besides, once you're done being educated, you can ride the narrow-gauge train, and who doesn't love a choo-choo?

■ Nanaimo

Stay on the highway past Cassidy and Cedar, until you get to Nanaimo, which is where many people get their first experience of Vancouver Island on Highway 1, when they come in from the Nanaimo ferry terminal in Horseshoe Bay, north of Vancouver. Nanaimo, while it seems like a nice place to live, just isn't the kind of place a traveler is going to find particularly attractive. If you come in to town, or are heading north from Victoria, keep going. We apologize to the Nanaimo Chamber of Commerce, but it's our job to get you out to the wild. If you do like the looks of this perfectly pleasant town, stop by the **Visitor Info Centre** at 2290 Bowen Rd., ☎ 250-756-0106.

Attractions

 One thing that's worth a look is the **Bastion**, at the corner of Bastion and Front streets, ☎ 250-753-1821. Open daily in summer, it's part of an original HBC fort, with a good collection of military stuff from the mid-1800s. There's even a gun ceremony at noon every day. If you're not going inland to see Ft. St. James or one of the other HBC posts, don't miss this. You really can't understand British Columbia until you find out what the HBC did here.

Adventures in the Air

 Bungee Jumping: The biggest attraction in Nanaimo is the **Bungy Zone**, on Nanaimo River Rd., ☎ 800-668-7771, 250-753-5867, www.bungyzone.com. It's a 164-foot/50-meter jump over the Nanaimo River Gorge. If you're planning a trip just to jump, call and find out when the next Naked Bungy Weekend is going to be held.

Once you leave Nanaimo, you're on Highway 19, and that even splits into two options: 19A follows the shoreline from Parksville to Campbell River; the faster 19 goes inland a little bit. There are regular opportunities to move from one highway to the other. If you're just trying to get north, stay on 19.

■ Qualicum

The main attraction on 19A is **Qualicum Beach**, 29 miles/47 km north of Nanaimo. If you're looking for the perfect Vancouver Island beach, this is it.

Qualicum Beach Info Centre is at 2711 W. Island Highway, ☎ 250-752-9532. You'll see the totem pole marking the turnoff from the highway. From there, simply head to the beach and start soaking up the sun. White sand, rocks, tide pools – it's all here.

From the Buckley Bay Ferry Terminal, just north of town, you can hop over to Denman Island, and from there to Hornby. Like most of the Gulf Islands, these are now weekend retreats for people who probably have more money than you do. Hornby has been drawing a lot of attention lately as the best place to see the sixgill shark, which usually inhabits much deeper waters.

The other good reason to come to Qualicum is for **Horne Lake Caves Provincial Park**. There are two caves you can explore for free – bring a flashlight and rent a helmet from one of the outfitters at the cave site. There are also guided cave walks for CAN $15. ☎ 250-757-8687. There aren't that many places where you can get underground along the Pacific Northwest coast. It's a good chance to see what holds all those trees up.

If you stay on 19 at the Parksville junction, you'll almost immediately see the turnoff for Highway 4. Don't even stop to think about it. Turn.

Highway 4: The Road to the Edge of the World

Despite the size of the island, there really aren't that many places you can easily get to. There's the main highway that runs the entire eastern edge of the island, but to get to the west is a whole lot harder. The road to Sooke gives you only a taste.

But there are two roads that cut completely across the island – paved roads, not logging roads. If you want to see the west side of the island, you've got two choices: Highway 4 to Tofino, and Highway 28 to Gold River. Gold River takes you back to remote, Alaska-like scenery. The road to Tofino takes you to one of the coolest little towns in Canada, one that just happens to have a few extra attractions, like trees big enough for a family of trolls to set up housekeeping, migratory gray whales and a beach that, in winter, kicks up the best surf in Canada.

Highway 4 is a good road, but it can be heavily traveled; once you're over the ridge of mountains, it also gets pretty twisty and curved, so if there's an RV jam on the road, this drive can take a while. It's 115 miles/187 km from the junction to the town of Tofino, but three hours is a reasonable estimate for driving time (allow longer if you get caught up in the beautiful Cathedral Grove).

There are quite a few provincial parks, including **Englishman River** (☎ 800-689-9025) and **Little Qualicum Falls** (no reservations), where you can camp or hike. Little Qualicum Falls is particularly pretty.

Cathedral Grove, the main attraction on this chunk of road, is part of MacMillan Provincial Park, 19 miles/31 km west of Parksville. You won't be able to miss it: you come around a sharp corner in the road, and suddenly there's a traffic jam and a full parking lot. It's worth the effort to stop here and look for a space, though, as Cathedral Grove has some of the largest Douglas fir trees left on the island. These are up to 800 years old, and they tower, they loom, they filter light down through their needles and make everything quite different and special.

The downside is that it's crowded. And if you stop to think about it, it's a little depressing. The whole island used to look like this. Now there's a tiny section set off for tourists.

Still, the trees are just doing their job of being trees. And they're doing it really, really well. Stop and tell them thanks.

There's one town of size along Highway 4 – Port Alberni – if you need gas or lunch. It's about nine miles/15 km west of Cathedral Grove.

▪ Port Alberni

Port Alberni has about 19,000 residents. It's mostly a mining and logging town, and it's always been an important transshipment point, with easy ocean access. If you need to get out and stretch your legs a little, you can walk around the harbor a while.

Alberni's **Info Centre** is at 2533 Redford St., ☎ 250-724-6535. If you're curious, they can set you up with tours of logging operations and the pulp mill.

Adventures on Water

 Boat Trips: If you want to get onto the water yourself, talk to the **Alberni Marine Transportation Company**, ☎ 800-663-7192, for trips to Barkley Sound, Ucluelet and into the Broken Islands. (These islands have beautiful scenery, and if you head that way without a kayak, you'll just whack yourself on the head with frustration once you're there.) **Batstar Adventure Tours** leads kayaking trips into the estuary. ☎ 877-449-1230.

There's a good unpaved road that stretches from Port Alberni to Bamfield; it's just over 61 miles/100 km long, and once you're in the tiny town of Bamfield, there's easy access to the West Coast Trail. Bamfield is a good place to simply drop off the map for a while. There's not really an info centre, but you can find a fair amount online at www.bamfield-chamber.com.

Kayakers flock here in summer to paddle the Broken Islands. We suggest you go with a good guide. Talk to **Island Adventure Tours**, ☎ 250-812-7103, back in Victoria.

▪ Bamfield

Bamfield has that end-of-the-world vibe. The main road in town is actually a boardwalk – which does, somehow, have highway status.

Adventures on Water

Take the *Lady Rose* for a spin to the Broken Islands or Ucluelet. The same folks also rent kayaks. ☎ 800-663-7192. Spend the night at **Bamfield Lodge**, ☎ 250-928-3419, or **Mills Landing**, ☎ 250-728-2300. Either one can help you book paddling or fishing trips.

■ Sproat Lake

If you stay on Highway 4, the road parallels the huge Sproat Lake, with a good campground at **Sproat Lake Provincial Park**, ☎ 250-954-4600. There are some petroglyphs near the campground, and the lake is home to Canada's squadron of Martin Mars Bombers, planes used to fight forest fires — if you were watching the news during the California fires in late 2003, you saw some of these that Canada loaned for the emergency. These planes can carry more than 25 tons of water at a whack, to dump on fires.

Adventures on Foot

Hiking: At the far end of the lake, about 28 miles/45 km west of Port Alberni, you'll see the trailhead of the **Clayoquot Valley Witness Trail**. This is a 26-mile/58-km hike through some pretty rough patches of forest, but it will lead you to Clayoquot Sound and up to Clayoquot Provincial Park, which you're not likely to see otherwise. It's a good multi-day forest hike. Check with the First Nations office in Opitsaht, ☎ 250-725-3233, for more information.

Once you're past the lake, the road starts twisting and turning, working its way to the end of the line at the Pacific Ocean. Right before you hit water, there's a junction: go left to the small town of Ucluelet — which mostly serves as an overflow for Tofino, but has a vibe all its own — or right to the Pacific Rim National Park Reserve and the Vancouver Island playground town of Tofino.

■ Ucluelet

Ucluelet is five miles/eight km from the road junction. About 2,000 people call the place home, and mostly they're making their livings off tourists who couldn't find a room in Tofino, and from logging and fishing. The waters in Barkley Sound can get so wild that the locals have just started calling January and February "storm-watching season." For those who love dramatic weather, it's a good place to be.

Tourism Info is at Government Wharf, on Main St., ☎ 250-726-4641.

It doesn't take too long to get a good look at Ucluelet; that's part of the beauty of the place. It's slow and kicked back, and if you find Tofino is just a little too much for you, this is a good base for hanging out on the western edge of the world.

Take a look at **Du Quah Gallery**, 1971 Peninsula, ☎ 250-726-7223, for quality Native art.

Adventures on Water

Paddling: Take a day-kayak trip with **Majestic Ocean**, ☎ 800-889-7644. Ucluelet is the closest you're going to get to the Broken Islands, so it's a good place to start out from. **Jamie's Whaling Station** has an office in Ucluelet, ☎ 877-470-7444, with trips for gray whales and, maybe, orca. Another good choice is **Subtidal Adventures**, ☎ 877-444-1134. They run nature trips into the Broken Islands for CAN $45, whale-watching trips for CAN $40 in March and April.

Fishermen can call **Long Beach Charters**, ☎ 250-726-2878, for full-day charters from CAN $105. They also do whale-watching/fishing trips for CAN $140 – no, you're not fishing for whales. Kayak drop-offs run about CAN $75.

Adventures on Foot

Hiking: The best hike in town is from the lighthouse to He-tin-Kis Park. It's not much of a hike, but it'll stretch your legs and let you walk along the ocean.

Where to Stay

For a different kind of place to stay, try the **Canadian Princess Resort**, ☎ 250-726-7771, www.canadianprincess.com, which is actually in an old steamship that's permanently moored in Ucluelet Harbor. You're staying in the staterooms, which does mean you'll be sharing bathrooms if you want to stay on the boat. They have more private rooms ashore. Doubles range from about CAN $125. They also run lots of trips, including whale trips for CAN $49, and fishing trips for CAN $99.

Little Beach Resort, 1187 Peninsula Rd., ☎ 250-726-4202, has cabins right by the beach. Basic rooms start at around CAN $60.

There are a bunch of motels down on Peninsula Road. If you're showing up in town without a reservation, start there – you won't have any trouble securing a bed.

Campers should head to **Island West Fishing Resort**, 1990 Bay St., ☎ 250-726-7515.

■ Pacific Rim National Park

It's 26 miles/42 km between Ucluelet and Tofino, and for almost that entire stretch you're in the Pacific Rim National Park. This is reason enough to come to the western edge of the island. You've got fantastic beach rammed right up against rainforest.

The main attraction in the park is **Long Beach**, seven miles/11 km of beige sand, with the open ocean beyond. Park your car (don't forget to pay the park fee – they're serious about this), and hang out, looking at water that stretches all the way from here to Asia. We cannot walk on this beach ourselves without thinking about the great, early explorers: Vancouver, Cook, Malaspina, Quadra. They all were in this area, looking at the dense forests of the island, looking for space, open space, where they could simply get off the ship and not be claustrophobic for a little while. You can just imagine the early explorers swarming ashore at Long Beach and running up and down the sand, screaming with joy. And you know, as you stand there today, looking at the vast ocean behind, imagining crossing it in a ship not much bigger than some of the RVs you passed on the road, that these people were serious, serious lunatics.

Stop at the Wickaninnish Bay and Centre, at the end of Long Beach Rd. The center has observation decks – this is right on the gray whale migration route, from late February into May – and displays of the local wildlife. A good hike that starts right outside the center takes you through forest into beach.

Then choose your spot of beach and hang out. The beach can be very crowded, but most people rarely venture far from their car. If you take a little bit of a hike, you'll get a place to yourself. It's a beautiful beach. A lot of the guidebooks say it's a good place for beachcombing, but we find it a little disappointing in that respect. There are lots of shorebirds to watch, though, and really, we don't need much more than a spot in the shade to watch the waves come in to keep us happy. There's a good reason why this is such a popular beach.

There is one campground in the park, at **Green Point**. Show up very, very early to claim a spot, or don't bother. ☎ 800-689-9025.

Park Information is right on the highway, land side of the road. It's open 10:30-6 daily in summer, and has good displays on the park's history and geography. ☎ 250-726-7721.

If all you're doing is driving through the park to get to Tofino, you don't need to pay the park fee. If you're going to stop, get out your wallet. Two hours runs CAN $3, all day will set you back CAN $8. Regular checks are made of all the parking lots, and if you're there without a tag, you're busted.

■ Tofino

The first time we came to Tofino was at the end of a much-too-long day of driving. In the last stretch, we'd been stuck behind a herd of RVs who'd been riding their brakes for the past 50 miles. When we got into town, it was crowded, the streets were jammed with people walking around, and the downtown looked like it should have been abandoned 20 years before.

Then we parked, walked around, and fell in love with Tofino.

That's how it goes for most people.

Attractions

 Tofino does not give the best first impression. At a quick glance, it looks like tourism gone very, very bad. But right below that, there's a laid-back town with people who come here because there's simply no way to have a bad time here. It's a glory spot, and the residents are smart enough to keep fighting big development to keep it that way.

Park wherever you can find a spot downtown, and head to Tofino's **Info Centre**, on Campbell St., ☎ 250-725-3414. Tofino is really only a few streets long, and everything is within walking distance once you're in the town center.

The **Rainforest Interpretive Centre**, 451 Main St., ☎ 250-725-2560, is a good place to get an idea of just what's going on with all those trees out there. It has good displays on the natural habitat and how the First Nations people used it.

Cultural Adventures

 To get a First Nations take on the area, book a trip with **Tlaook Cultural Adventures**, ☎ 250-725-2656, www.talook.com. They have paddling trips in traditional canoes for CAN $140, which includes a salmon bake, or a quick sunset paddle for CAN $44. They also have the very cool Cultural Mystery trip, for CAN $58, which can include anything from visiting fish traps to gathering food in the forest and from the water.

Adventures in the Air

 Flightseeing: Get up in the air and enjoy the view. Flightsee with **Tofino Air**, ☎ 866-4863247, or **Atleo River Air Service**, ☎ 250-725-2205.

Adventures on Water

 Most people come to Tofino for one of four reasons: watch whales, go kayaking, go surfing, or hang out on the beach. We've already covered the beach, back in Pacific Rim National Park. Now it's time to get onto the water.

Whale Watching: Tofino is right on the path of the gray whale migration route, so there are plenty of outfitters ready to take you to see whales. Prime season is March and April; later in the summer, the odds go down, but there are still grays around as late as October. There are also orca in the area, and lots of other marine life.

All the whale-watching outfitters keep a very close eye on each other, so prices are similar, and everybody goes to the same places. The best way to choose is to talk to a couple of offices and see who you like the most. Outfitters include **Seaside Adventures**, ☎ 888-332-4252; **The Whale Centre**, ☎ 888-474-2288, www.tofinowhalecentre.com; **Adventures Pacific**, ☎ 888-4TOFINO, and **Ocean Outfitters**, ☎ 877-906-2326. You don't really need to plan more than a few hours ahead, there are so many possibilities. Book your trip, load up on the Zodiac, and head out.

Kayaking: The waters around Tofino are very, very calm, a perfect place for a novice paddler. For more experienced paddlers, there's the Broken Island group, or simply head out, find a nice little island, and enjoy a day on the waters around it.

The best guided tours go to **Meares Island**, where you'll get out of the kayak and walk around to see the giant Western red cedars. Western red cedar is a magic wood: it's what the First Nations people made practically everything out of, and it's what much of the forest depends on for its continued life. On Meares Island, you can actually go inside a cedar that was old when Columbus first got lost.

> ## CEDAR SAVVY
> Cedars rot from the inside out, so a perfectly healthy tree can have an empty space inside that's the size of a good living room. On Meares Island, there's another tree with more than a hundred different plants growing out of it – some of them full-sized trees in their own right. It's a very, very cool place.

Tofino Sea Kayaking Company, ☎ 250-725-4222, runs a high-quality operation, with Meares trips, as well as longer paddles. They also have a small but good bookstore, and run the **Paddler's Inn B&B**, with rooms overlooking the water for only CAN $65. A Meares Island paddle is CAN $58 and it's really your best bet for a short excursion (the trip is four hours). If you're more ambitious, join them for their five-day trips into

Clayoquot Sound, some of the best paddling on the west coast. Prices start around CAN $960.

If you know what you're doing – and they'll ask and know if you're fibbing – they'll rent you kayaks for CAN $43/day for singles, CAN $74 for doubles. Because they're looking out for you, they won't rent to solo paddlers.

If the Sea Kayaking Company is all booked up, there are plenty of other operators in town. Again, everybody watches everybody, so prices stay very close. **Paddle West Kayaking**, ☎ 250-725-4253, does Meares Island trips for CAN $58, or a quick paddle in the Sound for CAN $44. **Remote Passages**, ☎ 800-666-9833, is another good choice.

Surfing: Show up on Long Beach any time of year and you'll see surfers. In fact, a lot of people make trips here in the summer just to surf; problem is, all the good waves are in the winter. If you're just learning, summer is not a bad time. Waves are low and gentle, and you'll get a feeling for this most amazing sport.

Check with **Inner Rhythm Surf Camp**, ☎ 250-726-2211, 877-393-SURF, www.innerrythm.net, for surfing lessons and equipment. A three-hour beginner lesson runs CAN $59; they also have multiple-day surf camps, if you're serious, and run their own campground, and cabins.

Once you've surfed, you'll understand. It's really how God meant us all to get around.

Shopping

Tofino thrives on having lots and lots of little shops to take your money. There's some good stuff here and, luckily, it's all so close together, making it easy to browse from shop to shop, going back to what you like after you've had a chance to compare. We're just going to point out a couple of the more unusual places.

For First Nations art, the best choice is **House of Himwitsa**, 300 Main St., ☎ 250-725-2017. It has good masks, a selection of books that will fill you in on First Nations history, a really good selection of amber, and more. Whatever your price range or interest, you're covered here.

Fiber Options, 120 Fourth St., is that rare animal, a T-shirt shop worth looking into. Shirts have great raven and bear designs.

Saltspring Soapworks, which is part of a small Canadian chain, has handmade soaps and other goods. It's at 300 Main St.

Where to Eat

Schooner on Second, 331 Campbell St., is a local favorite for its organic dishes. This is kind of a hidden treasure in Tofino: you're in and out without spending too much, you just had a delicious meal, and you haven't done anything horrible to your body. What a concept.

Common Loaf Bake Shop, 180 1st St., is the place to go for your morning fill-up. It has great baked goods and a view that will make you linger over your coffee.

Café Vincente, 441 Campbell, fills up with locals who come for the tasty burgers and fish dishes at lunchtime.

For something a little more upscale, the **Sea Shanty**, in the same building as House of Himwitsa, has fresh seafood and flat out the best water views in town.

Where to Stay

Tofino can fill up. It's a good idea to book ahead if you can.

Ever want to stay in one of the best hotels in the world? **The Wikaninnish Inn**, ☎ 250-725-3100, regularly makes the best lists. You get killer views, fireplaces, huge bathtubs and all the pampering that you expect when you're shelling out upwards of CAN $400 a night for a double. A great place for a special getaway, or if you cashed out of those Internet stocks in time.

For people with more marginal occupations (like guidebook writers, for instance), there's plenty of reasonably priced accommodation around town, although Tofino is, on average, more expensive than any other place in BC, except downtown Vancouver.

Cable Cove Inn, 201 Main St., ☎ 250-725-4236, is easy walking from downtown, and all the rooms have fireplaces and water views. Doubles from CAN $160.

The Himwitsa Lodge, right smack in the middle of downtown, ☎ 250-725-3319, 800-899-1947, has rooms with the same amazing view as the restaurant. It's pretty swank, with doubles around CAN $200.

If those are out of your price range, **Maquinna Lodge**, 120 First St., ☎ 250-725-3261, has pleasant rooms, some water views, starting around CAN $85 for a double.

The Inn at Tough City, 350 Main St., ☎ 250-725-2021, is an old inn made from salvaged bricks. It has a good, old-time feel to it and standard rooms. Doubles from CAN $140.

Red Crow on the Oceanfront, 1084 Pacific Rim Highway, puts you in a room with views of Meares Island and the Sound. There's a hot tub and they've got canoes you can use. Doubles from CAN $150.

For the bare bones, try **Whalers on the Point Guesthouse**, part of Hostelling International. They're at 81 West St., ☎ 250-725-3443. A spot in the dorm runs CAN $22, and there are some private rooms.

Campers don't have a whole lot of options. If you couldn't get space in the campground near Long Beach, try **Bella Pacifica Campground**, ☎ 250-725-3400, which has good sites right by the beach. Full hookups are available, and they have good tent sites as well.

Crystal Cove Beach Resort, 1165 Cedarwood, ☎ 250-725-4213, has RV sties, good water views and all the facilities you might need.

You can also try **MacKenzie Beach Resort**, 1101 Pacific Rim Highway. They don't take reservations, but they do have a good spot right by the water.

Back on **Highway 19**, the road stays wide and well-paved from the junction north. If you're looking for beaches, get off at Qualicum; otherwise, there's not a lot of advantage to taking the slower, seaside route if all you're doing is heading north. On the inland route, do watch out for the randomly changing speed limit signs, though.

■ Courtenay-Comox Valley

About an hour north of Nanaimo, you hit the Courtenay-Comox Valley region. This is one of those places where it's really, really great to live – some people in Victoria come up here for vacation. But it doesn't have much for the traveler. Still, there are some reasons to get off the road.

Attractions

The **Info Centre** is at the junction with Highway 19A. Look for the steam locomotive out front. It's open daily, year-round, ☎ 250-334-3234.

The town's big attraction is its **Courtenay & District Museum**, 360 Cliffe Ave., ☎ 250-334-0686, and what sets it apart from most local museums is the quality of the paleontological fossils. There were a lot of dinosaurs running around this area. The big find was back in 1988, when a couple of people discovered a nearly complete elasmosaur from about 80 million years ago. It was a very unusual find for west of the Rockies, and it set off something like a fossil rush in the area, with scientists trying to find whatever else might be here. The museum has guided fossil walks and a map to show you the best sites in the area. There are also some good First Nations displays, and a bit of railroad history.

Just outside of town are the **Royston Wrecks**, 15 ships left here to die. Included are a couple of Navy war ships, some old whaling ships, and more, all sunk here to form a breakwater. If the light is good, it's a photographer's dream for shooting scenes of decay.

The town of **Comox**, part of the valley of the same name, isn't much more than a suburb of Courtenay. Hop over to Comox to see the **Filberg Heritage Lodge & Park**, which started life as a private pleasure garden.

Now it's open to the public, with good gardens and landscaping, a totem pole and a lodge house to show you how much fun it was to be rich. It's CAN $3 to enter the lodge, but you can wander the gardens for free.

Most travelers end up in Courtenay because they took the train here. It's one of the more scenic rides in British Columbia, with daily departures from Victoria on the **E&N Railiner**, run by VIA Rail. All you have to do is sit back and watch the mountains on one side of the train, the ocean on the other. ☎ 250-383-4324, 800-561-8630.

You can also get between Comox and Powell River, over on the mainland, on **BC Ferries**. This is a good option if you want to avoid driving through Vancouver. Sailings are four times a day and take a bit more than an hour. ☎ 250-386-3431.

Where to Stay

 You won't have any trouble finding a place to stay for the night in Courtenay/Comox. There are the chains – **Coast Hotels**, ☎ 250-338-7741 and **Travelodge**, ☎ 250-334-4491, and some nice smaller properties, like the budget **Sleepy Hollow Inn**, 1190 Cliffe Ave., ☎ 250-334-4476 (doubles CAN $60), and **Bates Beach Oceanfront Resort**, 5726 Coral Rd., ☎ 250-334-4154, with doubles from CAN $70; they have full-service RV sites as well.

Highway 19: Campbell River to Port Hardy

It's less than 30 miles/50 km from Courtenay to Campbell River, but somewhere in the course of that drive, you change landscapes. Everything manmade gets a little smaller; everything natural gets a little bigger.

The area from here all the way north to Port Hardy has been heavily logged over the years. Replantings help to a large extent, but most of the forest you'll see from the highway has signs neatly tucked away that tell you the last time it was stripped bare.

However, away from that, the scenery starts to get truly wild. The drive through Strathcona Provincial Park to Gold River is gorgeous, through the wild forest into a landscape that seems as if it's made of nothing but trees and water. It's a spectacular side-trip.

Between Courtenay and Campbell River, be sure to stop at Oyster Bay Shoreline Regional Park. It's a perfect picnic site with views over to Quadra Island, and a good chance of seeing large wildlife in the water.

■ Campbell River

Some towns just feel good when you drive into them. There's no real reason to like Campbell River, but it has a laid-back feel, some nice landscape, and houses hidden in the trees. If you lived here, you'd hate it as a kid, and then would spend the rest of your life trying to figure out how to move back, because you'd gradually realize how great it is. Campbell River grew the way it did because until 20 years ago or so, it was where the pavement ended. That meant it was the end of the world, which meant it had to have everything, but on a small scale.

Even today, the Campbell River mostly serves as a crossroads. From the town, you can take Highway 28 into Strathcona Provincial Park, or you can hop on a ferry and head over to Quadra Island. Or you can just stay on Highway 19, which will lead you to the northern edge of the island. But there's plenty to do here, and if you like the conveniences of a town without the hassles, it's a good base for exploring northern Vancouver Island.

About 30,000 people call Campbell River their home, and it is still kind of the last outpost. There's a lot of land north of here, but not very many people.

The **Info Centre** is at 1235 Shoppers Row, in Tyee Plaza, ☎ 250-287-4636. Tyee Plaza shopping center also has a grocery store and post office; there's a bookstore right across the street. The Info Centre is open daily in summer, weekdays the rest of the year.

Attractions

Most of what you'll want to do in Campbell River is outside, but it's still a good idea to start off inside, at the **Campbell River Museum**, 470 Island Highway, ☎ 250-287-3103. Open daily in summer, and Tuesday- Saturday the rest of the year. The museum has good First Nations history, lots of stuff on the area's past glory as a fishing spot (it ain't what it used to be, but anglers still flock here) and they run field trips to local sites. Stop in to see what's going on while you're in town.

The **Gildas Box of Treasures Theatre**, 1370 Island Highway, ☎ 250-287-7310, has regular First Nations dance performance and culture shows. Check for current times and performances.

We've never listed a bowling alley in one of our books before, but this time we just had to: **Crystal Lanes**, 1661 16th Ave., has ninepins, something that's completely disappeared from the United States. Sometimes, you need to do these things just because you can.

If you need fishing gear, or any kind of outdoor gear, hit **River Sportsman**, 2115 Island Highway, ☎ 250-286-1017. This is also the place to get your license.

There are a couple industrial tours, if you're interested. **Quinsam Salmon Hatchery** is open from mid-August to mid-October. If you've never seen a salmon hatchery before, you really shouldn't miss it. This is the most important fish in the north, and an hour spent learning its lifecycle is well worthwhile. ☎ 250-287-9564.

Norske Skog Elk Falls Pulp & Paper Mill tour shows you what happens to trees after they cut them down: all of those intermediate stages between making shade and coming into your house as paper and such. Open in summer, with tours at 10 am. Note that you must wear walking shoes while touring the facility – no open toes allowed. ☎ 250-287-5594.

Adventures in the Air

 Flightseeing: If you're looking for an overview of northern Vancouver Island, take a flightseeing tour. **Island West**, ☎ 250-926-0222, or **Parallel Aviation**, ☎ 250-923-6233, offer glacier flights, Strathcona oversees and cross-island trips. Prices start at CAN $99.

For regularly scheduled service from Campbell River to other points on the island or to the mainland, try **Pacific Coastal Air**, ☎ 800-663-2872.

Adventures on Water

 Fishing: Campbell River used to be called the salmon capital of the north. The really big fish are gone, but it's still a good place to drop a line, and there are plenty of outfitters ready to get you on the water.

Tyee Marine, ☎ 250-287-2641, www.tyeemarine.com, has been outfitting fishermen for 50 years. If they don't have what you want, it doesn't exist. **Bailey's Charters** has been working the waters around Campbell River since Nixon was president. They also do wildlife tours for CAN $70. ☎ 250-286-3474, www.baileycharters.com. **Top Guides**, ☎ 800-287-3474, 250-287-4475, www.topguides.ca, runs a variety of boats and can set you up with specialized trips. Another good choice is **Calypso Charters**, ☎ 888-225-9776, www.calypsofishingcharters.com.

Kayaking: Campbell River is a great kayaking base. **Coastal Spirits**, ☎ 888-427-5557, www.kayakbritishcolumbia.com, leads trips along the shores of Quadra Island for CAN $89. A half-day paddle is only CAN $59. **Coast Mountain** has an enjoyable trip through the Surge Narrows for CAN $95. They also rent kayaks. ☎ 250-287-0635, www.coastmountain-expeditions.com.

Snorkeling: Paradise Found takes you snorkeling in a salmon river. When the fish are running, this is a chance of a lifetime to see things from their level. ☎ 250-923-0848.

Where to Eat

 There's nothing marvelously special in town, but you're not going to suffer, either. For quick fish & chips, try **Joey's Only**, at Discovery Harbour. Seven bucks gets you lunch. In the same place is the **Harbour Grill**, a little more upscale. **Bee Hive Café**, 921 Island Highway, is another good cheap seafood choice.

If you're tired of seafood and want some spice, head to **Baan Thai**, 1090B Shoppers Row, where you can burn off your tongue on real Thai cooking.

Where to Stay

 You won't have any trouble finding a place to stay in Campbell River. Island Highway is lined with hotels, including **Above Tide Motel**, 361 Island Hwy., ☎ 250-286-6231, with doubles from $65; **Bachmair Suite Hotel**, 492 S. Island Hwy., ☎ 250-923-2848, with suites, including fireplaces, for CAN $100; and the **Passageview Motel**, 517 Island Hwy., ☎ 250-286-1156, with doubles from CAN $70.

Downtown, try **Coast Hotel**, 975 Shoppers Row, ☎ 250-287-7155, with doubles from CAN $155, or the **Haida Harbourside Inn**, 1342 Shoppers Row, ☎ 250-287-7402, with doubles from CAN $60.

Campers can try the **Thunderbird RV Park**, 2660 Spit Rd., ☎ 250-286-3344, with full hookups and showers, or **Parkside Campground**, 6301 Gold River Hwy., ☎ 250-287-4278.

▪ Quadra Island

Captain Vancouver visited Quadra Island in 1792, braving Cape Mudge at the southern tip of the island, the narrowest spot in the Discovery Passage between Vancouver Island and the mainland, and home to fearsome riptides. Many travelers going south to Fort Victoria ended up shipwrecked in these wild waters, despite the lighthouse erected in 1898. Quadra attracted logging, mining and fishing industries in the late 19th century, far ahead of development on the surrounding islands. Today, Quadra is known for its natural beauty – it has many beaches, coves and inlets surrounded by some of the clearest water in the world, making it an ideal destination for kayaking and diving.

There are three communities on the island: Cape Mudge is home to the First Nations Kwakwaka'wakw people; Quathiaski Cove, the commercial center and the largest of the towns; and Heriot Bay, a longtime stop for steamships sailing the coast. BC Ferries has hourly trips between Campbell River and Quathiaski Cove – it's a 10-minute ride.

Attractions

 Stop by the **Tourist Information Booth** one block east of the ferry terminal on Harper Road. Take Cape Mudge road south of the ferry terminal to the **Kwagiulth Museum & Cultural Centre**, ☎ 604-285-3733, open July-August, 10 am-5:15 pm. The museum houses an impressive collection of potlatch regalia, artifacts, as well as masks, blankets and carvings. Check out the adjacent carving center and workshop. There are also special summer programs, including Kwakiutl puppet theater and petroglyph tours. Open 10 am to 4:30 pm daily in summer.

Adventures

 Visitors could spend days hiking, biking or paddling around the island. Try the walk between Cape Mudge and the 100-year-old lighthouse (via the road or beach); hikes in Rebecca Spit Provincial Park (near Heriot Bay, to the northeast of Quathiaski Cove); or the more ambitious hike up Chinese Mountain (mid-island) to get a 360-degree view of the area. Bikes are available for rent at **Island Cycle**, ☎ 250-285-3627. Island **Dreams Adventures**, ☎ 250-285-2751, and **Spirit of the West Adventures**, ☎ 800-307-3982, will both get you out on the water. For divers, there is wreck diving. In 1996, the former HMCS *Columbia*, a 366-foot 2,900-ton destroyer, was scuttled off Maud Island. The warship now lies in about 100 feet of extremely clear water. Also excellent is the small island of Steep, southwest of Quadra, with a variety of colorful sea life. **Abyssal Dive Charters**, ☎ 250-285-2420, and **Discovery Charters**, ☎ 250-285-3146, are two operators who know the waters well.

Where to Stay

 There are many excellent accommodations on the island. **Tsa-Kwa-Luten Lodge**, ☎ 800-665-7745, on Lighthouse Road beyond Cape Mudge, however, is a rarity. The lodge, built on the site of an old Salish village, from which it takes its name, was built using the design of a Kwagiulth "Big House." The rooms are luxurious; the food features traditional First Nations dishes such as salmon, mussels, fiddlehead ferns and dulse. Doubles are CAN $90-150, including either Jacuzzi or personal fireplace. From your room, you can walk down the beach to petroglyphs and shell bluffs. A nice splurge.

■ Cortes Island

Even though it's only a 45-minute ferry ride from Quadra Island's Heriot Bay, Cortes Island is home to a different group of First Nations people; the Coast Salish Klahoose. One of the old villages, Tl'itl'aamin, had an unusual ritual. Cheryl Coull wrote about it in her excellent *Traveller's Guide to Aboriginal BC*. Young women in the village would drive porpoises into a shallow lagoon, by frightening them with clam shell rattles; there, the young men would wrestle the animals to demonstrate their strength.

Attractions & Adventures

Most visitors today come to Cortes Island to walk or bike through the old-growth scenery, enjoy the white sandy beaches, or to paddle the quiet waters around the island. The ferry docks at Whaletown Bay are home to an old whaling station, which you can explore. An unusual sight is **Wolf Bluff Castle**, ☎ 250-935-6764. Built from scratch by a local resident, it's a real castle, five stories tall, complete with dungeons and three turrets. The castle is open for public viewing. You can even rent a room here in the summer. Camping is good at both Smelt Bay and Manson's Landing Provincial Parks. **Misty Isles Adventures**, ☎ 250-935-6756, will take you out on the water or land.

■ Strathcona Provincial Park

It's 55 miles/89 km west from Campbell River to Gold River. The road, Highway 28, passes through Strathcona Provincial Park.

There's not much in the way of attractions along the road, and once you're in Gold River, you end up turning around and heading back pretty quick. Still, it's a beautiful drive, with lots of scenery, some great places to camp, and plenty of chances to get out of the car and hike.

> **WARNING:** *This is pretty serious cougar country and there's no shortage of bears, either. Keep a clean camp and make some noise when you're hiking.*

Strathcona Provincial Park is the biggest park on Vancouver Island, at more than 450,000 acres. It stretches almost from coast to coast and includes the highest point on the island, **Mt. Golden Hinde**, at 7,237 feet/2,200 meters. The other big natural wonder in the park is **Della Falls**, 1,450 feet/440 meters high.

Victoria & Vancouver Island

Adventures on Foot

 Hiking: Take the **Karst Creek Trail**, a 1.2-mile/two-km loop through a pretty dramatic landscape of streams and sinkholes. The **Upper Myra Falls Trail** is one mile/1.6 km to a waterfall lookout.

For something longer, there's a six-mile/10-km hike along the **Elk River Valley**, which finally climbs up to Landslide Lake. A good half-day hike. If you're fit, **Price Creek Trail** takes four or five hours, and there are some scrambles over logs and some steep sections. The trailhead is at Ralph River Campground.

Rock Climbing: There's a great rock climbing area in the park, at Crest Creek. It has more than 300 routes on cliffs up to 130 feet high, with plenty of permanent bolts and anchors, and routes for every level up to 5. 10 or so. No camping is allowed at the site.

Where to Stay

 There are two **campgrounds** in the park. **Ralph River** is quite a ways off the main highway, on the shore of Buttle Lake. **Buttle Lake Campground** is also on the lake, but a whole lot closer to the main road. the telephone number for both sites is ☎ 250-337-2400.

Finally, there's **Strathcona Park Lodge and Outdoor Education Centre**, ☎ 250-286-3122, which runs wilderness skills classes, kind of like the NOLS (National Outdoor Leadership School) in the States. Check for current programs.

■ Gold River

You move into pure Great Bear Forest rainforest topography as you get closer to Gold River, with towering Sitka spruce, old-growth forest and trees bigger than you've ever seen.

Gold River is a little town of about 2,000 people. It sits right on the edge of the **Bligh Island Marine Park**, named after Captain Bligh, who was here with Cook in 1778; they refitted their ship the *Resolution* here.

BLIGH, THE OTHER STORY

Bligh is much maligned; he was probably the second greatest sailor history has ever seen (behind only Cook, and Cook was never tested the way Bligh was). But the movies of the *Mutiny on the Bounty* have permanently screwed Bligh's amazing record. Not only was he a brilliant sailor – nobody else could possibly have kept a crew alive in an open boat for more than 2,600 miles of emergency sailing – he was also the best writer of his generation. Cook was almost illiterate; Bligh was an artist. It's nice to see something beautiful dedicated to his memory.

The main reason people come to Gold River is because it offers the easiest access to Nootka Sound. Hop the MV *Uchuck III*, which has regular service to the Sound. Nootka Sound was once the single most important point on the west coast of North America: it was the main sealing grounds for generations.

Gold River Info Centre is at the junction of Highway 28 and Scout Lake Rd., ☎ 250-283-2418.

Adventures on Water

You are here to fish or to hang out on the water. **No Limit Adventure Tours**, ☎ 250-283-2388, has eight-hour wildlife tours – good chance to see bears – for CAN $200, and tours of the Upana Caves for CAN $5, followed by a beachcombing walk.

Where to Eat

Food choices are somewhat limited in Gold River. Head for the **Manila Grill** for pizza and other fare. The food is simple, but good.

Where to Stay

The best place to stay in town is the **Ridgeview Motel**, 395 Donner Court, ☎ 250-283-2277, with doubles around CAN $90. Campers can hit **Peppercorn Trail Motel & RV Park**, 100 Muchalat Dr., ☎ 250-283-2443. It has rooms from CAN $50 and camping sites from CAN $18.

■ Nootka Sound

From Gold River, you can jump the boat to Nootka Sound. The MV *Uchuck III* is 136 feet long and has both day and overnight sailings – don't do overnight unless you really have to, since you'll miss all the scenery that way. The ship started off as a mine sweeper during WWII, but now can take up to 100 passengers for the scenic run along the western edge of Vancouver Island.

It's not a cheap way to get around, but they have some packages that can save you a few bucks. Their Kyuquot Adventure takes you through Nootka Sound and Tahsis Inlet; you overnight at Kyuquot and return to Gold River the next evening. Adult fare is CAN $310, including accommodation.

There are also quick trips to Friendly Cove from Gold River for CAN $40; if you want to get out in the First Nations village, though, you have to shell out another fare to go ashore. Times and schedules change, so check with the office, ☎ 250-283-2515, for the latest offerings.

Nootka Sound has been inhabited for more than 4,000 years. When the Europeans showed up in the 1700s, they found a highly developed culture – as with most groups along the Pacific Northwest coast, food was never a big problem, so the people had time to develop their arts and lifestyles. The Nootka hunted seals, whales and other marine mammals, and they ate well from the rich salmon streams. They lived in communal houses and kept slaves (people captured during wars). As in most Northwest groups, being the chief was not easy, because you had almost no power (although you did get lots of slaves) and way too many responsibilities. If your people didn't like what you had to say, they'd just up and move away.

The one thing the Nootka didn't have much use for were the abundant sea otters. However, the Europeans saw them, yelled *Yipee!*, and moved in to stay.

In 1774, Captain Juan Perez first sailed into Nootka Sound; Cook showed up four years later: "We no sooner drew near the inlet when we found the coast to be inhabited and the people came off to the Ships in Canoes without showing the least mark of fear or distrust. We had at one time thirty two Canoes filled with people about us.... They seemed to be a mild inoffensive people, shewed great readiness to part with any thing they had and took whatever was offered them in exchange."

There was endless wangling over who had the rights to the Sound. Somehow, the locals never got taken into consideration. Finally, in 1793, the Nootka Convention was signed, which made the bay something of an open territory, but soon after, the decline of Spanish power left the place almost solely to the British.

And they went nuts. They had one philosophy – if it moves, kill it.

It didn't take long for the Brits to completely degrade the environment. Within a decade or two, there was nothing left to kill, so they packed up and moved out. Incredible riches had flowed from Nootka Sound. But once the otters ran out, there was no reason to come around. The place was soon forgotten.

Today, Nootka Sound is just a very, very pretty place in the middle of nowhere. Not many people bother to come, which is reason enough for making the effort.

There are three small towns in Nootka Sound – **Zeballos**, **Fair Harbour** and **Kyuquot**. Kyuquot is the largest of them, with about 300 people.

Package Deals

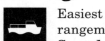 Easiest is to let the people who own MV *Uchuck* handle your arrangements with one of their packages. Contact **Nootka Sound Services** at ☎ 250-283-2325. If you're looking to spend more time in the Sound, pack your kayak and book a room at Zeballos River, in **Mason's Motor Lodge**, ☎ 250-761-4044. A little more swank is to get a fishing package or kayak tour from **Nootka Island Lodge**, ☎ 250-752-0455, with accommodation and activities running CAN $699 for kayaking, CAN $999 for fishing, both on a two-night/three-day arrangement.

Fishermen can also try **Nootka Sound Charters**, ☎ 250-283-7194, which has trips year-round.

■ Onward to Port Hardy

The final section of Highway 19 to Port Hardy alternates between old-growth forest and old logged areas. Not a whole lot of people head up this way, but Port Hardy, 144 miles/235 km from Campbell River, makes a good jumping-off point for BC Ferries trips to Prince Rupert or the Queen Charlotte Islands. From Rupert, you can link up with the Alaska Marine Highway and catch ships all the way out to the Aleutians.

There's a good hike at **Seymour Narrows**, seven miles/11 km north of Campbell River. It's a seven-mile/11-km route that leads you to an overlook point of the narrows. Up until 1958 – when it was blasted beyond recognition – this was a huge hazard to navigation, as the channel squeezed into nothing, causing tides that could move faster than 10 knots over hidden rocks.

Keep heading north. At the turnoff for Sayward, 39 miles/64 km north of Campbell River, you can head down the side-road to see the Salmon River, which offers the best steelhead fishing in BC. Steelhead are interesting fish. Biologists called them trout for a very, very long time, even though they lived in the ocean and spawned in rivers. A couple of years ago, they got switched to salmon in their official designation. The fate of the Dolly Varden, for those who are keeping track, is still up in the air, with continued trout status looking likely.

The **Salmon River Wildlife Reserve** takes in prime bird habitat; trumpeter swans stop here on their migration.

Go another 55 miles/90 km north and you'll hit the side-road to **Zeballos**, over in Nootka Sound. You need a good car for this road, which is un-paved, but if you missed getting to Nootka from Gold River, here's an-other chance. Just down the road is **Little Hustan Cave Regional Park**, which has easy-to-explore caves. Bring a flashlight, dress warmly and don't even think about going in alone.

From roughly Sayward to Sointula, the road moves inland, following the Nimpkish River. This is a pity, because the coast here overlooks John-stone Strait, which has a resident pod of orca and is on both the hump-back and gray whale migration route. You can get to Johnstone Strait by taking the road down to Telegraph Cove, a tiny village on Alert Bay.

■ Telegraph Cove

Adventures on Water

 Kayaking: If you have a kayak, look no further. Put in, head out. The paddling here is some of the best in the world, with sheltered waters and abundant wildlife. Really, it's the paddlers who are keeping the town alive.

Adventures in Nature

 Go whale-watching with **Stubbs Island**, ☎ 800-665-3066, to see the orca. **Tide Rip Tours**, ☎ 250-339-6294, does bear-watching and coast trips.

Telegraph Cove is a cool place to walk around. Take a stroll on the board-walk and check how the town booms in the summer. Come winter, this all shuts up tight.

Where to Stay

 You can stay at **Hidden Cove Lodge**, ☎ 250-956-3916, in Port McNeil (three miles/five km from Telegraph), and get a room with water views for CAN $100. Campers should hit **Alder Bay Resort**, also in McNeil, which has shaded spots. ☎ 250-956-4117.

Because Telegraph Cove is so small – although this is changing, as there are huge development plans in effect – Port McNeil has most of the ser-vices. Stop there for the **Info Centre**, on Broughton Blvd., ☎ 250-956-3131. If you're collecting big stuff in Canada, Port McNeil offers the "worlds largest burl." Hey, it's a logging town. And it makes more sense than putting up a girder and calling it the world's largest fly fishing pole.

■ Alert Bay

Across the channel from Telegraph is Alert Bay, by Cormorant Island. You can hop the ferry from Port McNeil for a chance to see the local Kwakwaka'wakw First Nations culture (you've probably seen it spelled Kwakiutl more often – and for ease of recognition, that's what we use in this book – but be aware that this spelling is fading fast).

Attractions

 The **U'Mista Cultural Centre**, on Front St. (turn left from the ferry), is the one thing you can't miss in town. There are daily programs in summer, and you can see what a traditional house looked like before the coming of the Europeans. Inside, there are some beautiful masks, finally returned to their rightful place after having been seized early this century in one of the government's potlach raids. ☎ 250-974-5403 for a current program.

> **BIGGEST:** Just outside is the tallest totem pole in the world, 173 feet/53 meters tall. It was actually surpassed by the pole overlooking Victoria Harbour, but that one turned out to be a hazard to the floatplanes using the harbor as a landing strip, and so it got whacked in half. Nobody's too worried about this one. Maybe it's not the peak of totem carving, but it is certainly big.

Walk over to the **'Namgis Burial Grounds** (turn right off the ferry). This is as close as you'll ever be to what life was like before Cook and his bunch showed up. Keep your distance and stay respectful, though, as this is still an active cemetery and the locals don't want you in it.

Adventures on Water

 Kayaking: If you don't have your own kayak, rent from **Little Rock Kayaks**. The company also leads guided trips. ☎ 250-974-2221.

Where to Stay

 If you're going to stay in Alert Bay, the **Orca Inn**, ☎ 250-974-5322, has doubles from CAN $50, or you can camp at the **Alert Bay Campground**, which has water views. ☎ 250-974-5213.

■ Malcolm Island

Sointula, the main community on the island, had its origins as a Finnish socialist community, established in 1901. The village still lives up to its name, a "place of harmony," as a modern fishing community with a very relaxed atmosphere. Most visitors come here to fish, walk the beaches or just relax. Try the **Beautiful Bay Trail** in Bere Point Regional Park – an easy six-mile/10-km round-trip beach hike. Orcas are often seen in this area. During the summer, stop by the **Finnish Museum**, housed in the Old School, ☎ 250-973-6353.

The ferry ride out here from Port McNeil takes 25 minutes.

The tri-island BC Ferries runs between Port McNeill on Vancouver Island, Sointula on Malcolm Island and Alert Bay several times per day, seven days a week. Current schedules are available at www.bcferries.bc/ca/schedules/northern or ☎ 250-386-3431, 888-223-3779.

■ Port Hardy

Port Hardy is the end of the line for road travelers. There are some logging roads you could head west on from here, getting you to Winter Harbour, Port Alice or Mahatta River, but honestly, except for the scenery, there's little reason to go. Port Hardy is where the pavement runs out.

About 5,000 people call the town home, and they've made it a very enjoyable place to spend a few days. Once you're done here, you can head to points south on the road, or catch BC Ferries north to Prince Rupert and the Queen Charlottes.

This is a working town. People are making their money here from the forest and the ocean, so fishermen and loggers rule.

The **Info Centre** is on Market St., ☎ 250-949-7622. It's open daily in summer, weekdays the rest of the year. **BC Ferries** is in Bear Cove, just a few minutes from town.

The **Port Hardy Museum** is at 7110 Market St., ☎ 250-949-8143. It has good Kwakiutl artifacts and local history.

Adventures on Foot

 The best things in Port Hardy are free. The place has beaches you have to see to believe.

Hiking: There are 14 miles/23 km of sand beach at Cape Scott and, closer to town, you can walk the shore in **Tsulquate Park**.

Adventures on Water

Kayaking: Hit the water with **North Island Kayak**, ☎ 250-949-7707, which rents kayaks and leads guided trips into Johnstone Strait.

Fishing: Fishing has taken a hit lately. This used to be the place to come for coho, but there's been a crash in the population of that species. There's still plenty of salmon fishing around, but at least for the moment, the glory days are over.

Where to Eat

 There aren't many choices here. Try **Oceanside**, downtown, for seafood. For quick and cheap, there's **Captain Hardy's**, with fish and chip lunches.

Where to Stay

 You won't have any trouble finding a place to stay. The only time it can get tight is when one of the big ferries comes in from the north late at night, and everybody on the ship is desperately looking for a place to crash.

Glen Lyon Inn, 6435 Hardy Bay Rd., ☎ 250-949-7115, has rooms with kitchenettes and balconies overlooking the water. Doubles from CAN $85. **The Northshore Inn**, 7370 Market St., ☎ 250-949-8500, also has good ocean views, and they'll pick you up from the ferry. Doubles start at CAN $75.

Pioneer Inn & RV Park, 4956 Byng Rd., ☎ 250-949-7271, overlooks the Quatse River. Doubles from CAN $90; RV sites CAN $17.

Getting Out

 Most people come to Port Hardy to leave. It's the terminus for the BC Ferries' *Queen of the North*, the pride of the fleet. This ship makes runs between Port Hardy and Prince Rupert, and it's a very popular trip just for the scenery – this is what cruise ship passengers do the Inside Passage for. Advance reservations, especially if you want to load a vehicle, are strongly suggested. ☎ 250-386-3431, 888-223-3779, www.bcferries.com.

The Gulf Islands

Scattered between the mainland and Vancouver Island are dozens of smaller islands, where there are resorts, wineries and a lot of vacation homes the size of shopping centers. BC Ferries runs regular ships to many of these islands, but with the exception of popular Salt Spring, not many people bother to visit. We offer up a few of the highlights here.

Northern Gulf Islands

■ Denman & Hornby Islands

These pretty, quiet islands, located 46 miles/75 km north of Nanaimo or 12 miles/20 km south of Courtenay, off the coast of Vancouver Island, are popular among local artists. Both are chock full of art galleries, markets and outdoor recreation at one of the islands' five provincial parks, including one of the warmest (sea) swimming spots at Tribune Bay Provincial Park on Hornby Island. **Fillongley Provincial Park** on Denman offers great beachcombing and walks through old-growth forests Ferries make the 10-minute trip from Buckley Bay on Vancouver Island for Denman Island every 40 minutes from 7 am to 11 pm; the ferries then travel from Denman to Hornby, also a 10-minute trip. Current schedules are available at www.bcferries.bc/ca/schedules, or you can call ☎ 250-386-3431 or 888-223-3779.

■ Gabriola Island

This pretty island that offers a mix of both residential and wilderness experiences is just a 20-minute ride from Nanaimo (ferries travel approximately every 40 minutes). There are three provincial parks, including **Gabriola Sands**, on the northwest end of the island, that has perhaps the best beaches. Near there are the **Malaspina Galleries**, where you can explore strange sandstone formations. At 20 square miles/50 square km, Gabriola is small enough to easily tackle on a bicycle – an 18-mile/30-km ride would allow you to stop at beaches, forests and petroglyphs.

Southern Gulf Islands

In the Strait of Georgia lie the southern Gulf Islands. These islands, part of the same archipelago as Washington State's San Juan Islands, number about 200, but most are tiny, uninhabited and without ferry service. Many of the islands were home to First Nations communities; later, homesteading started ranching and farming; logging and fishing followed.

The proximity of the largest islands to the mainland, combined with a mild Mediterranean-like climate, makes them a popular spot for both mainland and Vancouver Island commuters, weekenders and travelers.

The populated southern Gulf Islands are Gabriola, Galiano, Mayne, Pender, Salt Spring and Saturna. Outdoor activities are popular in all the islands: kayaking, canoeing, bicycling, hiking, beachcombing and diving, are just a few of the options.

There are many more islands than we cover here. These are just a few highlights to get you started.

■ Galiano Island

 Named after a Spanish explorer in the late 18th century, Galiano is the second largest of the southern Gulf Islands and is by far the driest. It's an excellent spot for birders – over 130 species live here. Start at **Visitor Info** on Sturdies Road, near the ferry terminal, to map out an itinerary. **Galiano Bluffs Park**, just a short jaunt from the ferry terminal, lies 400 feet/120 meters above Active Pass, and gives hikers excellent chances to see sea lions, seals and other marine and bird life. You can also watch some of the largest ships in the BC Ferries fleet pass directly below the bluffs. Most of the population lives on the southern end of the island – if you want to get away from (the relative) hustle and bustle, head north. **Dionisio Provincial Marine Park**, at the north end of the island, is accessible only via boat or on foot and is quite unspoiled, with beautiful mountain views and many rare flowers. **Montague Harbour Provincial Marine Park**, site of an ancient Coast Salish settlement, has three stunning white shell beaches.

Ferries run to Sturdies Bay from Tsawwassen twice a day (60-minute trip) and from Swartz Bay three or four times per day (90-minute trip). There are connections to Mayne, Pender, Salt Spring and Saturna.

■ Mayne Island

 During the Fraser River & Cariboo gold rush of 1858, Mayne Island was used as a stopping point for miners on their way to the mainland from Victoria. Thousands of men passed through Miner's Bay – many came back to Mayne Island and other southern Gulf Islands when the rush died. Japanese farmers moved here, to some of the best agricultural land in the islands, growing flowers, fruits and vegetables. Many of the historic buildings are preserved today. Get an island map at **Visitor Info**, just past the exit from the ferry terminal, on the right. Stop at the museum, housed in the old jail, open on weekends. Also of note is the **St. Mary Magdalene Church**, dating from 1898. The 353 lb/160 kg sandstone baptismal font was brought in 1900 on a rowboat by the determined (and strong) Canon William Paddon and Ralph Grey.

BC Ferries all dock at Village Bay; service is twice a day from Tsawwassen (90-minute trip); and from Swartz Bay three to four times a day (45-minute trip). Village Bay is a major transfer point for ferries all around the southern Gulf Islands.

■ Pender Islands

 The Penders, geologically one island, were made into two when a canal was dredged in 1903. The islands are now joined by a bridge. The **Info Centre** is located just a short distance from the ferry terminal.

Hiking on the islands is excellent: a favorite is the **Enchanted Forest Trail**, while **George Hill** and **Mount Norman Parks** (all on South Pender) have large trail systems with many options to suit the experience and timetable of the hiker. There are numerous beaches here; the most interesting is **Medicine Beach**, at the north end of Bedwell Harbour (near the bridge connecting the island). This area is the site of an early First Nations settlement. Extensive excavations have been done here – check at the library to see some of the artifacts recovered. There is also a wetland area just beyond the beach – a good area for birding.

All ferries land at Otter Bay, on North Pender; from Twawwassen twice daily (1½-2½ hrs) or Swartz Bay (35 minutes) at least five times per day.

■ Salt Spring Island

 Salt Spring is the largest and most heavily populated of the Gulf Islands. Salt Spring, population 10,000, is also the most geographically diverse, with the highest peaks in the Gulf Islands and several lakes. You can "do" the island in a quick two- or three-hour tour, but many travelers find they want to stay longer. There is a large community of artists here – stop at studios or galleries that catch your eye. **Visitor info** is available year-round in the village of Ganges, 121 Lower Ganges Rd., ☎ 250-537-5252 or 866-216-2936; www.saltspringtoday.com. Pick up a listing of the current cottages for rent and B&Bs here, as well as information if you're heading to Saturna Island.

Attractions

Most travelers land in Fulford Harbour – from here, stop at **St. Paul's**, a tiny church built about 1883, overlooking the harbor.

If you happen to arrive on a Sunday, stop by the market, next to Fulford Inn, just beyond the dock. On the road to Ganges, you'll pass **Ruckle Provincial Park**, which has lovely walk-in campsites at CAN $14 per night. **Mill Farm Regional Park**, down the road from Fulford Harbour, lies on the edge of Mt. Bruce, the tallest point in the Gulf Islands (2,300 feet/700 meters) and a popular starting spot for hang-gliders.

The village of **Ganges** is the focal point on Salt Spring – stop here to enjoy the outdoor Saturday market and explore art galleries and bookshops. The very quiet **Vesuvius** is a small community that was home to the island's first settlers, a group of freed American Blacks in 1857.

If you're planning to spend time on Salt Spring Island or to do an in-depth tour of the southern Gulf Islands, pick up the indispensable *Southern Gulf Islands*, by Spaulding, Montgomery and Pitt.

Where to Stay

This is a sampling of the wide variety of lodging available – check with the visitor center for a complete list.

Hastings House, 160 Upper Ganges Rd., ☎ 250-537-2362, is the posh place to stay. It was modeled after a British estate in 1940. The food is outstanding – if you don't want to blow your wad on a room, at least stop by for brunch. Doubles from CAN $450-700.

The Beachcomber Motel, 770 Vesuvius Bay Rd., ☎ 250-537-5415, offers more modest rooms, some with ocean views or kitchenettes, from CAN $79-99.

Green Acres Lakeside Cottage Resort, 241 Langs Rd., ☎ 250-537-2585, has fully-equipped housekeeping cottages on St. Mary Lake, the Gulf Islands' largest lake, from CAN $135-145.

Ferries dock at three different spots on the island: Tsawwassen ferries come in at Long Harbour; Swartz Bay ferries go to Fulford Harbour; and Crofton runs take you to Vesuvius Bay. There are connections to Pender, Mayne, Galiano and Saturna Islands. Current schedules are available at www.bcferries.bc/ca/schedules, or ☎ 250-386-3431 or 888-223-3779.

■ Saturna Island

This lightly populated island (300 residents) is an ideal spot for a quiet getaway. It is most popular with day-trippers. The island takes its name from an 18th-century Spanish ship, the *Saturnina*. While the island was long occupied by First Nations people, pioneers came late to the area in the 1870s. Saturna offers much natural beauty, but relatively few modern conveniences. The accommodations are excellent, but there aren't many of them; there are no public campgrounds, and few stores or commercial attractions.

Kayaking and canoeing here are excellent; **Lyall Harbour** is a good launching stop for paddlers bound for Boot Cove or Winter Cove Provincial Park. Make sure to hike **Mt. Warburton Pike** – the highest point on the island at 1,611 feet/490 meters – where there are excellent views. **East Point Park** has a protected beach area with wonderful sandstone formations and excellent wildlife viewing. Orca are frequently spotted here.

Most people who come to Saturna visit **Saturna Island Vineyards**, ☎ 250-539-5139, www.saturnavineyards.com. Tours and tasting are available May through September.

Ferries land at Lyall Harbour; from Tsawwassen generally twice a day (1½-two hours) and from Swartz Bay three or more times per day (1½-two hours). There are connections with Mayne, Galiano, Pender and Salt Spring Islands.

Vancouver & Environs

Vancouver

Check any poll of the best cities in North America and you'll see Vancouver near the top of the list. The only places that beat it are Victoria and, sometimes, San Francisco.

The biggest city in BC, Vancouver is famed for letting its residents go from working in a high-rise office buildings all day to paddling kayaks, skiing, mountain biking or pretty much any other outdoor activity before sunset.

The city is the art and culture capital of the province, as well. There's plenty of theater, good museums and, during the annual Film Festival,

Vancouver is a cultural hotspot.

Vancouver & Environs

N

VANCOUVER ISLAND

STRAIT OF GEORGIA

SEA TO SKY HWY

Clinton

97

Powell River   Pemberton   Lillooet   Cache Creek

Whistler   99

Lillooet
Lake   Ashcroft   Kamloops

Garibaldi
Park   Stein   Logan Lake

Nanaimo   Squamish   Valley   Lytton
Park

12   Merritt

Lions Bay

Harrison
Lake   5

Yale

VANCOUVER   Kent

Hope

Abbotsford

Victoria   Bellingham   100 KM

9   100 MILES

© 2004 HUNTER PUBLISHING, INC

you see people lined up around the block waiting to get into flicks you've never heard of. There's live music somewhere every night of the week, plus all the advantages of a university town.

Then there's the wild. Stanley Park is one of the biggest municipal parks anywhere. Get off a trail here and you'll forget that you're in the middle of a city of more than two million residents. Twenty minutes from downtown can put you in the deep forest.

Vancouver is also Canada's melting pot. When Hong Kong emptied out before the Communists took over, about half the people who fled ended up here. There are huge sections where almost nobody speaks English; a recent survey determined that 50% of people in lower mainland – Vancouver and environs – were born outside Canada. But it's not just the Chinese influence. Walk down Commercial Drive, and within a block you'll have a choice of restaurants serving ethnic cuisine from Ethiopia, Costa Rica, Thailand and Jamaica. And that's just the start.

There's a little something for everybody here.

■ History

Vancouver was kind of inevitable. You're at the mouth of the river here, looking at the ocean. Where else are you going to build a city?

Cook came through here, but didn't linger. Same with Vancouver himself. He charted the region, but didn't stay. Nootka Sound was more interesting, and there was still the problem of a Northwest Passage to work out.

The **Hudson's Bay Company** arrived in the 1820s and jumped for joy. Everything it wanted was here: ample hunting, a trade nexus, water access, a landscape that was easy to secure. The first HBC site was at Fort Langley, east of what's now Vancouver. It was not the best place. It took them 30 years and several major fires to realize that all they had to do was move downriver a bit to find a better spot. In the 1850s, **New Westminster** was founded, and by the 1860s, sawmills lined the river's edge.

> **DID YOU KNOW?** The official beginning of Vancouver was in 1867, when Hasting's Mill was founded in what was to be called Gastown, named for Gassy Jack Deighton – how's that for a way to go into history?

The railways came in 1886 and solidified the city's importance. It was the terminus, the place that, sooner or later, all West Coast shipping had to move through. There was a slow, steady growth, but it wasn't until the 1960s when Vancouver started to come into its own. With the growth of Whistler to the north, the town started to gain a reputation as an outdoor sports mecca. Add on a healthy job market in the financial center of BC, and the place boomed. A million people were in town by the early 1970s.

In addition to all its other attractions, Vancouver is now one of the biggest film production centers in the world, trailing only Hollywood, New York and Mumbai (Bollywood), India. Odds are a whole lot of the TV shows you watch – X-Files, Stargate – and a good half the movies you see were filmed around Vancouver. There's always filming going on somewhere in town. On one recent trip, we saw a guy in a long black coat standing at the edge of the roof on a 30-story building. People glanced, then walked on. Just another day of filming.

In July, 2003, Vancouver succeeded in its bid for the 2010 Olympics. We were in BC Place when the official announcement was made, which was really interesting and quintessential Canada: 15,000 people cheered for about five minutes, then they all nicely filed out and went on about their business. No overturned cars, no riots, nobody selling t-shirts.

Canada is such a wonderful place.

And Vancouver is its premier city.

Vancouver

■ Basics

Start any visit to Vancouver downtown, at the **Info Centre**, 200 Burrard St., in the Waterfront Centre, ☎ 800-435-5622, 604-683-2000. There's the usual wide assortment of brochures and pamphlets, and also a very helpful staff that really knows the city.

> **AUTHOR TIP:** While you're walking around, be sure to pick up a copy of *The Georgia Straight*, a local weekly free newspaper that's got listings of all the current films, gallery shows, plays and more.

■ Downtown Attractions

For the most part, we're going to keep you downtown at first, then move out in concentric circles, farther and farther from the city center. The only exception is in the museum section, where the one place you absolutely can't miss – and the one that you really shouldn't miss – are some distance from downtown.

Tours

Vancouver is a big place and it can be hard to get a handle on where everything is. A city tour is good to get your bearings and see town highlights – and there are plenty to choose from.

Walkabout, ☎ 604-720-0006, has CAN $18 walking tours. One shows you downtown, starting with the Hotel Vancouver, the prettiest old hotel in town, and then works its way over to Gastown, where the best shopping is. The other option takes you to Granville Island, through the markets and the art institute, and on to the float homes that line the channel.

The Vancouver Trolley Company, ☎ 604-861-6508, has several programs. Their West Coast heritage tour, offered in summer, takes you to the Museum of Anthropology, the very cool little fishing town of Steveston, the Gulf of Georgia Cannery, and more, all for CAN $48. For the same price, they'll take you out to Grouse Mountain.

Vancouver Harbour Tours, ☎ 604-688-7246, does 75-minute narrated tours of Burrard Inlet. There are three departures a day in summer.

Vancouver Champagne Cruises, ☎ 604-688-8072, runs sunset harbor cruises that include an all-you-can-eat buffet for CAN $60; if you just want the cruise, it's only CAN $25.

West Coast Sightseeing, ☎ 604-451-1600, ☎ 604-535-2317, takes you on a couple of whirlwind trips: one hits Canada Place, GM Place, Gastown, Stanley Park, Granville Island and a few other spots for

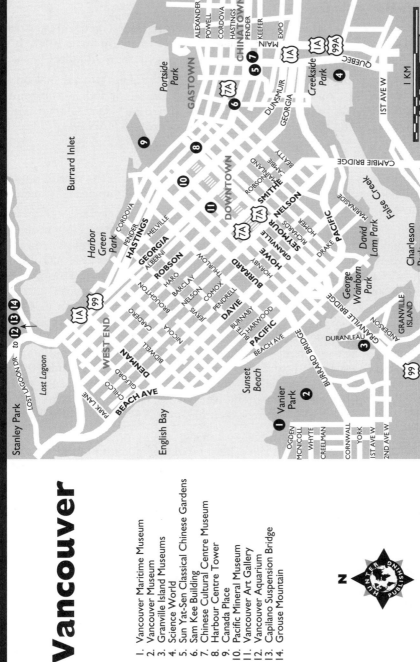

Vancouver

1. Vancouver Maritime Museum
2. Vancouver Museum
3. Granville Island Museums
4. Science World
5. Sun Yat-Sen Classical Chinese Gardens
6. Sam Kee Building
7. Chinese Cultural Centre Museum
8. Harbour Centre Tower
9. Canada Place
10. Pacific Mineral Museum
11. Vancouver Art Gallery
12. Vancouver Aquarium
13. Capilano Suspension Bridge
14. Grouse Mountain

© 2004 HUNTER PUBLISHING, INC.

CAN $47; the other takes you around the city and out to Capilano Suspension Bridge for CAN $55.

If you've ever wanted to try riding a hovercraft, you've got your chance with this company on their 30-minute trip through Burrard Inlet. It's CAN $30 for adults, CAN $15 for kids; trips leave near Canada Place.

There are a couple of flightseeing options. **Baxter Aviation**, ☎ 604-683-6525, and **West Coast Air**, ☎ 604-606-6888, do scenic flybys and regularly scheduled flights to points around the Sunshine Coast. Glacier trips run about CAN $170; quick town flybys start around CAN $85.

Museums

Vancouver has two of the best museums of their kind in the world, plus a few others that are world-class. Even if you don't like museums, you simply have to see these.

First on the list is the **Museum of Anthropology**, at the University of British Columbia. This is about a 20-minute drive from downtown, on the pretty university grounds at 6393 NW Marine Dr., ☎ 604-822-3825. Eight bucks gets you into the main gallery, which tends to stop people dead in their tracks as soon as they walk past the ticket booth. You go through a hallway, on either side of which are some simply stunning First Nations carvings. This all opens into a large main room with, flat out, the best classic totem pole collection in the world. There are memorial poles, house posts, doorways, bentwood boxes and more. Look up the hallway to the left and there's a Bill Reid sculpture of a bear fishing. Outside, there are more poles and a reconstructed clan house. It's reason enough to come. We have traveled all over the Northwest, been in pretty much every art gallery and museum there is, and there is nothing of this quality elsewhere.

But it's not just the poles. At the other end of the museum building is the Reference and Research collection, which has pieces from all over the world in glass cases. The selection of Kwakiutl masks alone stops us for an hour each and every time we come here, with variation upon variation upon variation of the raven theme. But there are also pieces from the Inuit, Salish, Tsimshian and other tribes, as well as art from around the world (surprisingly, the Japanese and Chinese collections aren't anything special). If you've ever wanted to compare canoe paddles from a dozen cultures, this is the place to come. One warning, though: this area is not well signed. Each piece has a little reference number on it, and if you want to find anything out about it, you're stuck with looking at the massive books that sit on tables around the collection. It makes browsing and quick comparisons a little difficult, and we've talked to some people who came out quite mad because they didn't know what they were looking at, and it was too hard to find out. Understandable. But the quality and variety of pieces here simply cannot be matched, and should not be

Above: Downtown Victoria, see from the harbor. (© Readicker-Henderson)

Below: Butchart Gardens, Victoria. (© Readicker-Henderson)

Totem poles, Victoria. (© Readicker-Henderson)

Above: Longhouse along the Campbell River. (© Vivien Lougheed)

Below: Chinese Gate along the Campbell River. (© Vivien Lougheed)

Driftwood on a Campbell River beach. (© Vivien Lougheed)

Above: Clan house detail. (© Readicker-Henderson)

Below: Traditional carving. (© Readicker-Henderson)

Boat launch on the Campbell River. (© Vivien Lougheed)

Above: Vancouver skyline. (© Vivien Lougheed)

Below: Vancouver Science Centre. (© Readicker-Henderson)

Above: Rafting on the Lillooet River. (© Vivien Lougheed)

Below: Bear cubs, Grouse Mountain. (© Readicker-Henderson)

missed. If we were in Vancouver for only a few hours, this is the only thing we'd do. It's that good.

The other museum of extraordinary quality in Vancouver is the **Maritime Museum**, in Vanier Park, 1905 Ogden Ave., ☎ 604-257-8300. Inside is the *St. Roch*, the first ship ever to navigate around North America – from the Northwest Passage to the Panama Canal. It's a small, tough boat, and you can go onboard and see how uncomfortable it must have been to work on. Also in the museum is a stellar collection of Cook artifacts: Joseph Baker's sea chest, a telescope used on Cook's ships and, most impressive, one of Cook's own sketchmaps. We're big Cook fans, so this piece stopped us dead in our tracks. There's a great pirate area for kids, plus special exhibits. It's a very good way to spend CAN $8 and an afternoon. You can get to the Maritime Museum by way of the False Creek Ferries, from Granville Island or the Science Centre (see below).

Vanier Park is where Vancouverites show up to fly kites on weekends, walk their dogs, sit in the sun. It's not only the home of the Maritime Museum, but also of the **Vancouver Museum**, 1100 Chestnut St., ☎ 604-736-4431, www.vanmuseum.bc.ca, admission $10 for adults. There's a good First Nations area, lots of stuff about when Vancouver was young, and special exhibits – a recent one explored the question of just who was the first to make it to North America: we all know it wasn't that lost Italian, but was it the Chinese, the Vikings, or someone else? There's a herbarium on the grounds, and also the **HR MacMillan Space Centre**, www.hrmacmillanspacecentre.com, which is a good place to park the kids while you look at the other stuff. In the Space Centre, there are multimedia shows, lots of rocket and science exhibits, a full-motion VR theater, with shaking chairs, 3D effects and more, and chances to find out if you have the skills an astronaut needs. It's a separate admission from the museum: CAN $12.75 for adults, CAN $8.75 for kids.

Hop the False Creek Ferry from Vanier Park to Granville Island. We'll get back to Granville later, but here in the museum section, there's one of those private nutcase museums that we have a serious soft spot for. The **Granville Island Museums**, at the corner of Duranleau and Anderson, ☎ 604-683-1939, CAN $6.50 for adults, has three separate museums that focus on: fishing, model boats and trains. The fishing museum has what might be the largest collection of fishing reels in the world, as well as ingeniously displayed fishing flies in more varieties than you'd think possible. The model boat museum displays, well, model boats. But these aren't like the kits you bought when you were a kid. These are lovingly detailed, scale models, and proof that if you don't watch TV, you have plenty of time to do other stuff. Finally, upstairs is the model train museum, which has literally thousands of different cars, and a really cool running layout. Check out the detail on the trees.

Vancouver

To continue your museum tour of Vancouver, hop back on the False Creek Ferry over to **Science World**, 1455 Quebec St., ☎ 604-443-7580. It's the building that looks like a big golf ball. Your CAN $12.75 admission gets you three floors of science experiments, from perspective and optical illusions, to gravity, to bugs and crawly stuff. There are regular shows and demos throughout the day, and your biggest problem once you get here will be hauling your kids back out. There's even a White Spot restaurant on the grounds, so you never have to leave once you're here.

Sun Yat-sen garden.

From Science World, you can hop on the Sky Train to go downtown, or walk a few blocks over to Chinatown for the **Sun Yat-sen Classical Chinese Garden**, 578 Carrall, ☎ 604-689-7133. This is an oasis of quiet (except when the tour buses roll in) in the middle of the otherwise bustling Chinatown district. Built in 1985, the gardens recreate a classic Chinese landscape courtyard garden. The idea is, from any angle of viewing, you should see an entirely different perspective and landscape. There are daily tours that can explain some of the features, but we think it's a little nicer to just show up and hang out solo for a while. CAN $7.50.

Hop on the Sky Train again to downtown for the last museums on the list. The **Vancouver Art Gallery**, 750 Hornby (at Robson), ☎ 604-662-4719, CAN $11, has frequently changing displays of world-class art. We were here for one that put paintings by Georgia O'Keefe, Emily Carr, and Frieda Kahlo side by side. There's a reasonable permanent collection, and some of the annoying, mediocre stuff that gets passed off as modern art – video terminals displaying static and dead cows, that sort of thing. It's a good idea to ask what's going on before you pay, as the frequently changing shows can mean not a whole lot will be on display sometimes.

A couple of blocks away, at 848 West Hastings, ☎ 604-689-8700, is the **Pacific Mineral Museum**, a small gallery of rocks and gems. There's a good shop on the ground level, and upstairs are some really pretty, shiny rocks. If you like this kind of thing, you'll really like this kind of thing. CAN $4.

Places & Parks

Most visitors are going to spend a fair chunk of their time downtown, and part of the joy of this is that as you walk around, you'll find surprising and unexpected beauty. That's the pleasure of a big town. There are the standard attractions that show up in most books, but quite frankly, we don't think you're going to bother to go see, say, GM Place, unless you go there for a hockey game. Same holds true for the Waterfront Station, which is a very pretty building, and if you need to catch the Sea Bus, the place to be, but otherwise, you could better spend your time elsewhere.

That said, within walking distance of the center of downtown, there are a few things you should check out.

Canada Place, right on the waterfront, is impossible to miss: it looks like a huge, docked cruise ship, and it is where all the cruise ships dock when they're in town. Inside there are some shops, a food court and the local IMAX theater. It's worth wandering around here for a bit.

Look up from almost any point in the city and you'll see the **Harbour Centre Tower**, 555 W. Hastings St., the best lookout point in the city. For CAN $9, you ride an elevator up one floor below the restaurant (the ride is free if you're eating up there). The large, circular area at top offers 360-degree views of Vancouver. It's especially impressive at sunset.

Keep walking past the tower and you'll end up in **Gastown**. We go into more detail on this in the shopping section, below. There are a couple of Vancouver's standard attractions here: the **steam clock**, which blows every 15 minutes, and the statue of **Gassy Jack**, where you can feel sorry for somebody named "Gassy." Jack was a sailor and politician who opened one of the first establishments here, the Globe Saloon, in 1867.

Head through Gastown to **Chinatown**. It's a big Chinatown, but quite frankly, the one in Victoria is a little more interesting. The big deal here is the narrowest office building in the world, the **Sam Kee Building**, at 8 W. Pender. Seeing its thinness is a little tricky, as until you hit the right angle, it looks like every other building on the block, but it's really not much more than 4½ feet wide. Nearby is the **Chinese Cultural Centre Museum**, 555 Columbia St., ☎ 604-687-0282. Especially now, the Chinese force in Vancouver is something to be reckoned with; in the suburbs, there are entire areas where you won't see a single shop sign in English.

Stanley Park

Just as New York has Central Park, so Vancouver has Stanley Park, a thousand acres of peace and quiet just minutes from downtown's business district.

It's prime real estate, jutting out into the water, with killer mountain views. There were First Nations villages here – some of their trails have been converted to hiking and biking trails. Today, ask around among Vancouverites, and you'll find most of them go to Stanley Park at least once or twice a month. Jog, bike, walk, picnic, check out the totem poles, ride a horse carriage, sit on the beach, fish, go to the aquarium.

You'll find something to do here.

> **AUTHOR NOTE:** Parking in the park can be a hassle; be prepared, especially on weekends, to spend some time looking for a space.

If you've got the time, simply take the perimeter walk along the seawall. It's 5½ miles/nine km that loops back to where you started. It's a paved path, and it's neatly divided, keeping bikes and pedestrians separate. Take this division seriously: you can actually get a ticket for being on the wrong side. For those with wheels, the path is one-way only, counterclockwise around the park.

At the town edge of Stanley Park is the **Lost Lagoon**. It used to be a tidal flat, but not anymore. Heading counterclockwise from there, you walk along the edge of Coal Harbour – yacht clubs, people with more money than most of us – and can see **Deadman's Island**, which is now a military outpost. The name comes from its history as a Salish burial ground.

Keep going along the seawall and, as you come around the point, you'll hit a patch of totem poles. They're not great ones, but they're okay, and if you can get past the bus tourists, stop for a minute to enjoy them.

The seawall follows a narrow point of land through here; if you want to skip this, there is a street that cuts across from Burrard Inlet to Coal Harbour. The reason to hit this road is, of course, the **Vancouver Aquarium**, one of the best in the world. Inside are more than 250 species of swimming things, plants and more. If you haven't seen the big stuff out in the water, come here to get a good look at dolphins, seals, beluga whales and, of course, otters. There's even an Amazon exhibit with sloths, and moths big enough to block out any light they fly up to.

If you've been wondering what's under all that ocean, this is a must-stop. Open 9:30-7 in summer, 10-5:30 the rest of the year. ☎ 604-659-3474. www.vanaqua.org. Admission CAN $14.95 for adults. Ask about the behind-the-scenes tour, where a naturalist shows you how they're keeping all these critters alive.

Because of the aquarium, the east side of the park tends to be the busiest. If you're looking for a little more peace and quiet, head into the thickly wooded west side, taking trails out to Second Beach or Third Beach.

If you don't want to walk or bike around the park, you still have a couple of options. There's a free shuttle bus that runs between points – this can be especially useful in getting you from the parking lot to the aquarium. There are also carriage rides that take you past the hot spots – the noon gun, the totem poles, etc. The ticket booth is at the rose garden on the southeast side of the park, and a ride will run you CAN $18.65. ☎ 604-681-5115. They can also sell you a combo ride/aquarium ticket that will save you a few bucks.

For visitors, the aquarium is the thing. Odds are, you're not going to be in Vancouver long enough to need the park for an escape valve. But knowing it's there changes the feeling of the entire city: these people were smart enough to know how important an empty space can be.

Granville Island

 It's a little world unto itself: Granville Island, on the south side of False Creek, is a hip place to walk around, get something to eat and watch the town go by. No visit to Vancouver is complete without stopping here. It's tiny – you can walk around the entire place in just a few minutes – but there's a lot crammed in.

Show up early in the morning at the **Granville Island Public Market**. Any food item you could imagine is on sale here. Stop in to one of the bakeries first thing in the morning for some of the best goodies in Vancouver; for your picnic later, there are endless fruit, vegetable and meat stands. Thanks to Vancouver's widely diverse ethnic makeup, you can find stuff from all over the world here. It's the best market in western Canada.

Coming out of the market, you'll walk along one of two roads; either is jammed with small art galleries, gift shops, chandlers – yes, this is still a working harbor area – and outdoor outfitters.

Among the more interesting attractions on Granville are the Granville Island Museums (see above, page 133).

There are four theaters on the island, so pretty much any time of year something is going on. There are also regular arts festivals, street performances, and more. To find out what's happening while you're in town, call the central information number, ☎ 604-666-6655, or visit www.granvilleisland.com.

▪ Out-of-Town Attractions

North of Town

Head across the bridge to the northern suburbs of town and follow the signs to the Capilano Suspension Bridge and Grouse Mountain, two big suburb attractions.

Vancouver

Folks enjoy the thrill of walking across this swinging bridge.

The **Capilano Suspension Bridge** is one of the most popular attractions in all of Vancouver. If you watch a TV show on the city, you will see the bridge.

It's a bridge.

It's a pretty bridge, spanning a 230-foot drop into the gorge below. When you walk on it, the bridge swings and sways and makes a lot of people scream and cling to the rails.

The first bridge was built here more than 100 years ago, for the entirely practical purpose of getting people across the gorge. Now, once you cross, there are some pleasant walks in old-growth rainforest – if you haven't had a chance to see any, this is a great spot in which to appreciate some really big trees. There's a very large gift shop here and some First Nations stuff, including canoes and five totem poles. There are also regular music and dance performances. There is a CAN $13.75 fee to enter the compound that includes the bridge.

Leaving the bridge, keep an eye on the north side of the road for the **Capilano Salmon Hatchery**, inside Capilano River Regional Park. It's free and you can walk around and see what stages salmon go through before they hit the dinner plate. The park itself is a quiet spot, and there are good walks along the river, with lots of rapids and rainforest. This is a really great picnic destination.

Grouse Mountain is just a little farther up the road. Park your car and hop on the tram for the ride to the top, at 3,600 feet/1,100 meters. This is one of the most popular recreation sites in all of Vancouver, as people come here in the summer for biking and hiking, and in the winter for skiing.

It's CAN $19.95 to ride the Skyride up and down, but if you hike up (which takes a normal person maybe two-three hours, but there are those who run it in under 40 minutes) and buy something in one of the shops at the top, you get a free descent.

While you're up there, there are very cool things to see, including some of the best chainsaw carvings in BC scattered around the trails (we particularly like the one of insects eating the tree trunk). There's also a bear habitat that has two grizzlies. They are not related; both were orphaned, and then put here. As of this writing, they're about three years old and are big, big bears already. Because they're so used to people watching them, they frequently come right up to the fence to watch you. They're playful, they're fascinating, and if they're not in the mood to be watched, they do have places to hide.

If you're looking for views from the absolute top of the mountain, take the **Peak Chairlift** up the last 400 feet//120 meters to the peak. This is included in your Skyride ticket, so why not? Once you're up there, you can look around the peak a little and, on a clear day, the views are spectacular.

There are guided walks around the forest on the mountain, and regular displays of falconry and hawking that offer a good chance to see raptor birds up close. In summer, there are lumberjack shows three times a day.

But mostly, people come to Grouse Mountain for a chance to throw themselves back down the hill. You can rent a mountain bike for CAN $20, and hurtle yourself down one of the groomed trails; guided trips, with a lesson and a rental, run about CAN $100, and it's worth it if you've never done this sort of thing before. Paragliding off the mountain starts at CAN $165.

In winter, CAN $42 gets you a lift ticket for the day, and the closest boarding and skiing terrain to just about any major metropolitan area in the country. There are lessons, rentals and more available.

For questions about any of the major activities, phone guest services, ☎ 604-980-9311.

There's one more reason to go to Grouse Mountain: it has one of the best restaurants in town, and flat out the best view of any eatery in BC. The **Observatory Restaurant** has local-ingredient specialties and a great cheese plate. There's also a bistro on the grounds. It has the same view, but simpler dishes at lower prices. When it's warm out, the bistro's patio is the place to be. See our review of these eateries on page 144.

South of Town

Head out past the airport and the town of Richmond – a must stop for anybody interested in Chinese culture – and there are a couple of things you'll want to check out.

There are two excellent botanical gardens. The **VanDusen Botanical Garden**, 5251 Oak St., ☎ 604-878-9274, is open year-round. Special attractions include the Chinese medicinal garden and the herb garden. There's a hedge maze and something flowering all year. CAN $7.

The **Bloedel Floral Conservatory**, in Queen Elizabeth Park, at Cambie and 33rd Ave., ☎ 604-257-8570, is open every day of the year except Christmas. It has a lovely greenhouse and 95 acres of native plants and exotic trees. CAN $4.

The **Gulf of Georgia Cannery** is a National Historic Site, located at 12138 4th Ave., in Richmond, ☎ 604-664-9009. The Pacific Northwest would have been nothing if it weren't for canneries – once the Russians had finished killing everything with fur, the fishing industry carried the day. Ever wondered how to make a can by hand? You'll find out. In the days before flash freezing, there were strict regulations on how long a fish could be in the hold before arriving in a cannery, hence all the cannery sites dotted up and down the coast. They were cultures in and of themselves, with worker houses and service industries all of their own. They created quintessential company towns. At Gulf of Georgia, there are live cannery demos, films, educational exhibits on the fishing industry and, of course, we know all roads lead to the gift shop. This is a good place to spend a few hours. CAN $6.50.

The **Buddhist Temple** of the International Buddhist Society rises up over the highway to Tsawassen like a vision from another land. It's huge, it's beautiful, it's classic Chinese pavilion-style architecture. There are weekly meditation classes, a pretty garden that you can wander around and several worship halls. If you've never been to the Orient to see the sacred architecture, come here. Admission is free (donations accepted) and anyone is welcome, as long as they're respectful.

Finally, quite a ways out of town – you're looking at close to an hour from the city center – is the **George C. Reifel Migratory Bird Sanctuary**. The refuge covers upwards of 800 acres. Several hundred bird species come through here – on one visit, there was the incredibly rare (at least around here) red-necked phalarope. There's nothing more fun than to hang out with birders who've just spotted a rarity. There are good trails all through the sanctuary, an observation tower and a small shop/office. It's CAN $5 to get in. A good time to come is Sunday mornings, when there's a regular group of birders who show up to out-do each other. These helpful people will show you what's what. Phone to find out about special programs that might be running and to ask for directions, as the sanctuary can be a little difficult to find – it does appear on most maps of the city, though. ☎ 604-946-6980. To get close, take Highway 99 south to River Road, just across the Fraser River. Follow this to River Rd. West, and turn right. This will get you to Westham Island Road, which, if you're watching the signs carefully, will get you to the sanctuary.

It's worth the effort.

■ Adventures

 Above, in Stanley Park, Grouse Mountain, and a few other sites, we've listed some chances to get out and get adventurous. A lot of what people live in Vancouver for – the wild – is actually a ways out of Vancouver, north near Whistler. We cover those destinations in the relevant section of this book, rather than here in the Vancouver chapter.

On Water

While you're in town, you need to paddle the inlet. There's no better way to get views of the city and to stretch your arm muscles.

Kayaking: Ocean West is our outfitter of choice. They have half- and full-day trips around Vancouver, including a Stanley Park and English Bay paddle suitable for any level (for beginners, if the wind is kicking up, there can be some small waves that make things a little exciting). Introductory paddles start at CAN $60/person for groups of four. For more advanced paddlers, they offer a good capsize and recovery class for CAN $70/person for a group of four. They also have longer excursions, including multi-day trips in the Gulf Islands and Johnstone Strait. If you've ever wanted to paddle with killer whales, that might be your big chance. ☎ 604-688-5770, www.ocean-west.com.

Eco Marine, ☎ 604-689-7575, has introductory paddles in False Creek for only CAN $49.

Takaya Tours, ☎ 604-904-7410, rents kayaks and leads trips but, more importantly, they have canoe cultural programs. For CAN $55, you paddle a traditional First Nations canoe while your guide tells you some of the history of the land. They also have nature walks that fill you in on how the First Nations people used the plants of the forest before there were drugstores on every corner. And for something really different, if you're in Vancouver at the right time, they have a full moon paddle for CAN $40. Night paddling is a thing unto itself.

Fishing: Fishermen can call **Bites-On Charters**, which serves as a central booking organization for trips around Vancouver. Chinook and coho are here in the summer, the really big chinook come in the fall. ☎ 877-688-BITE.

On Foot

Canada West Mountain School, ☎ 604-878-7007, www.themountain-school.com, shows you the freedom of the hills with a wide variety of classes. Basic mountain skills classes that get you expedition-ready run CAN $485 for four days. Rock climbers can take three-day courses for CAN $210 that take you from the flat land to climbing with the big boys.

Also for rock climbers are the guided trips on the Squamish Chief (see the Squamish section, page 155), maybe the most perfect granite slab in the world.

■ Shopping

 Back when we lived in Japan, we'd ask our students what their hobby was. The ones that didn't say "sleeping" inevitably said "shopping." Or, as a friend recently put it, "people like to buy things in astonishing, numbing, unbelievable excess."

Either way, Vancouver is the place to be. Anything – anything – you want, it's here. There's CAN $200/ounce coffee that is made of beans that have gone through the digestive system of small, wild cats. There's world-class art. There are enough souvenir stores to sink an aircraft carrier.

> **AUTHOR TIP:** Any time you spend more than CAN $50 in one location, save the receipt and get it stamped when you leave the country. Use it to claim some of the tax back.

Most guidebooks send you to downtown Robson Street for shopping, but it's kind of hard to figure out why. Mostly, what you'll see there is travelers from Asia heading to the Gap, Eddie Bauer and other stores of that ilk that sell the exact same stuff you can get back home. The Virgin Records at the corner of Robson and Burrard is very good, with some items you won't find back in the States, but **A&B Sound**, at 556 Seymour St., only a few minutes away, is a little cheaper.

There's a **Murchies** at 970 Robson St., a half-block from Virgin. It's the best place to buy tea in Vancouver. There's a well-stocked **Chapters Bookshop** at 788 Robson (Robson and Howe, catty-corner from the museum), which has a fantastic selection of BC books, and titles on anything else you might need.

But for the most part, go to Robson to eat – we'll get to that in the next section – because despite what everybody else says, with a few exceptions the shopping is generic.

You're better off heading to **Gastown** to spend your money. A few minutes' walk from the center of town, Gastown has better souvenir stores than Robson, and much, much better serious stores, as well.

We figure you can find the souvenirs yourself. As for art, Gastown is the place to be. Start with **Hill's Native Art**, 165 Water St., ☎ 604-685-4249. There's something good in here at every price range, from simple jewelry to very lovely masks, to – if you've got the room for it – decent-sized totem poles. We spend money here pretty much every time we visit.

The Inuit Gallery, 206 Cambie St., ☎ 604-688-7372, right across from the Steam Clock, has museum-quality First Nations art. It's a good place to come to see what the best of the best looks like.

Another quality gallery is **Spirit Wrestler**, 8 Water St., ☎ 604-669-8813, which has a good assortment of both traditional and modern art.

Images for a Canadian Heritage, 164 Water St., ☎ 604-685-7046, has modern paintings, lots of bone carvings, and some Inuit art.

For something completely different on Water St., try **Brendan Moss, Esq.**, 110-332 Water St., ☎ 604-662-8171, for antique maps and prints. We went in here with a very odd request: "We need frogs and turtles." It took a while, but we walked out with a pair of 200-year-old prints for a bargain price. Brendan Moss, Esq., has some great stuff.

For more art, back towards the center of town is the **Marion Scott Gallery**, 481 Howe St., ☎ 604-685-1934, which sells top-quality Inuit pieces.

And now for something at the other end of the scale. In summer, there's the **Vancouver Flea Market**, 703 Terminal Ave., ☎ 604-685-0666, which features upwards of 350 tables of *stuff*. Who knows what you might find.

For your specialist interests, when you're at the Info Centre, be sure to pick up a copy of the *Greater Vancouver Antique & Collectable Guide*, and *Guide to Secondhand & Antiquarian Bookstores of Greater Vancouver.* For truly specialist interests, take a walk down Granville Street, which has pawn shops and, to phrase it delicately, fetishist shops.

One more street we recommend for any serious shopper is **Commercial Drive**, which is kind of between downtown and Burnaby. This is the ethnic area of town, with endless restaurants serving food from around the world. Mixed in are fruit and vegetable stands – if you've ever wanted to try a durian (illegal in the US), here's your chance – new age shops, magazine emporiums, and more. It's like nowhere else, which is why it's so much fun. Spend an hour, spend a day. There's plenty to wander through.

■ Where to Eat

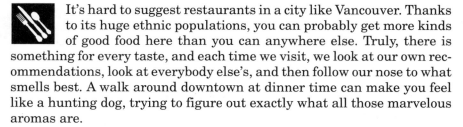

It's hard to suggest restaurants in a city like Vancouver. Thanks to its huge ethnic populations, you can probably get more kinds of good food here than you can anywhere else. Truly, there is something for every taste, and each time we visit, we look at our own recommendations, look at everybody else's, and then follow our nose to what smells best. A walk around downtown at dinner time can make you feel like a hunting dog, trying to figure out exactly what all those marvelous aromas are.

That said, if you walk around downtown Vancouver for any length of time, you'll come to the conclusion that at least half the meals consumed in the city have to be at buck-a-slice pizza places. There's one about every hundred yards.

But if that's not your thing, you won't have any trouble finding a place that offers what you want.

Cin Cin, 1154 Robson, ☎ 604-688-7338, is a local favorite that serves incredible Italian and seafood dishes. It's regularly rated as one of the best restaurants in town. Most entrées, made in the wood-fired oven, are around CAN $20, but with dessert and wine, you're probably looking at about CAN $80 per couple for a meal. The food is well worth it.

The Opus Hotel, 322 Davie St., ☎ 604-642-6787, is the home of the **Elixir** and the **Opus Bar**. The bar is where the swank come to see and be seen; it's also the place to come if you're after sashimi or maybe sheep's milk feta to go with your martini. The Elixir serves French cooking that will remind you that a big chunk of Canada started off as French. Get your credit card out and live it up.

You don't always expect the best food to be in hotels, but you're not going to be disappointed at either of the Fairmonts. At the Waterfront, try **Herons Restaurant**, ☎ 604-691-1818. It may be the only place in the world where they could get me to eat pave of grilled baby leeks and actually enjoy it. These people can cook. Most entrées start around CAN $30.

At the **Fairmont Hotel Vancouver**, in the center of town, at 900 West, there's wonderful halibut, free range chicken and, of course, fresh-caught salmon. Entrées run CAN $30-40. ☎ 604-669-9378.

There are three restaurants at Grouse Mountain, one of which is our other choice for a fancy night out: The **Observatory Restaurant** has specialties that use local ingredients, from tea-soaked pork to excellent seafood. The cheese plate here is a meal in and of itself and it has some of the best cheese we've ever eaten. Entrées start around CAN $30.

The bistro, also on the mountain, has the same great view and simpler dishes at lower prices. People gather on the patio when it's warm out. Finally, there's **Lupins Café**, the place to go for an après-ski cuppa. ☎ 604-980-9311.

Blue Water Café, 1095 Hamilton St., ☎ 604-688-8078, has won just about every award imaginable in town for their seafood. Fresh oysters are a specialty, as is sushi. Quite thoughtful for a seafood restaurant, they also have a tasty vegetarian menu. Entrées around CAN $20.

Sticking with that vegetarian idea, head to **Naam**, 2724 W. Fourth Ave., in Kitsilano, ☎ 604-738-7151. It has salads, chilli, Oriental dishes – all for under CAN $10.

Raincity Grill is a local favorite; they've been around forever, downtown at 1193 Denman St., ☎ 604-685-1193. It's what's called West Coast cuisine, without the attitude. Good food, reasonably priced – you can have lunch for under CAN $20.

A Kettle of Fish, 900 Pacific St., ☎ 604-682-6661, is another local seafood favorite. It's on the pricey side, but with a good wine list and only the freshest local ingredients.

Granville Island is a good place for cheap eats, as well as some fancy food. We tend to just hit the public market, picking and choosing from the stalls. But if you're wanting to sit for a while, go to **Bridges**, under the bridge, ☎ 604-687-4400. On cold nights, you can sit out on the balcony and wrap yourself in a blanket while you eat great seafood. Prices start around CAN $20.

If you're looking for cheap eats with an ethnic flair, there are two areas to hit. **Robson St.**, in and among the fine places like Cin Cin and the buck-a-slice pizza shops, is chock full of noodle, sushi and dim sum cafés. We firmly believe that you should let your nose lead you in situations like this, not us. If it smells good to you, that's the place to go.

By the same logic, when you start feeling peckish, head to **Commercial Drive**, for possibly the widest variety of ethnic fare available on any single street anywhere in the world. Mediterranean, African, Caribbean, South American, Central American: you name it, it's here, all right outside the Commercial Drive Skyride tram stop. There are also a bunch of open-air markets and grocery shops where you probably won't recognize half the things for sale.

For something completely different, hit the **Lilliget Feast House**, 1724 Davie, ☎ 604-681-7044. It's a replica of a traditional longhouse for the Coast Salish. Really, we think you owe it to yourself to try eating like a Native once. Try the Feast Platter, which gives you the biggest sampling. Come hungry. A couple should be able to get out for around CAN $60.

■ Where to Stay

 On average, Vancouver is the most expensive place to stay in BC; there are some good deals, though, and even at the higher priced places, what you're getting is a lot more than you'd get elsewhere.

We're going to break the city into two parts, downtown and the outskirts. Downtown is going to cost more, but it's also a whole lot more convenient. If you have a car and are planning to stay downtown, check about parking with the hotel: that can add another CAN $10-20 to your price for a night.

Downtown

Let's start on the luxe end of things. The **Fairmont Hotel Vancouver** is a city landmark at 900 Georgia St., ☎ 604-684-3131. It's an old railway hotel, with all the charm you'd expect of something predating cookie-cutter architecture. Doubles start around CAN $275.

For water views, try **Delta Vancouver Suite Hotel**, 550 Hastings St., ☎ 604-689-8188. It's within easy walking distance of everything and has very comfortable rooms starting at CAN $240 for a double.

The **Fairmont Waterfront** is right next to Canada Place and has all the swank you'd expect from the Fairmont chain, with doubles from CAN $270. 900 Canada Place, ☎ 604-691-1991.

The **Opus Hotel** is a new boutique hotel at 322 Davie St., ☎ 866-642-6787. The choice of movie stars and trendsetters, rooms start around CAN $250, but there are some decent package deals, like a spa package for CAN $449, and – a rarity for a fancy hotel – a dog package, where you can stay with Fido who gets his own treats, toys and a copy of *Modern Dog* magazine to read while he's doing his business.

You can stay downtown without cracking that CAN $200 point. The **Holiday Inn**, 1110 Howe St., ☎ 604-684-2151, has doubles from CAN $150. Nearby is the **Inn at False Creek**, 1335 Howe St., ☎ 800-663-8474, with doubles from CAN $120. The inn is within walking distance of Stanley Park.

The Canadian chain of **Sandman Hotels** has pleasant rooms at 180 Georgia St., ☎ 604-681-2211, with doubles starting around CAN $100. This is a good budget choice.

Century Plaza Hotel and Spa, 1015 Burrard St., ☎ 604-687-0575, has great views of town from the upper floors. It's still an easy walk to anywhere you might want to be downtown. The spa is a big draw. Doubles from CAN $150.

Comfort Inn Downtown, 654 Nelson St., ☎ 604-605-4333, is newly renovated. Doubles from CAN $120.

Howard Johnson Hotel Downtown, 1176 Granville St., ☎ 604-688-8701, was also recently renovated and is within easy walking distance of downtown. Doubles from CAN $130.

Granville Island keeps you in the downtown area, without keeping you in downtown. The **Granville Island Hotel**, 1253 Johnson St., ☎ 604-683-7373, is a little pricier than some of the downtown options, but it gives you an entirely different angle on the city. It has pleasant rooms, most with water views. Doubles from CAN $200.

There is a downtown hostel, **HI Vancouver**, at 1114 Burnaby St., ☎ 604-684-4565. Dorm beds from CAN $20.

Outside Downtown

Vancouver is a huge city, very spread out. Get away from downtown, and prices drop, but you might be making a trade-off for time spent getting from place to place.

Accent Inns, a high-quality, low-price local mini-chain, has two good locations, one by the airport and one in Burnaby by a Sky Train stop – about a 15-minute ride into downtown. The **Burnaby Hotel**, 3777 Henning Dr., ☎ 604-473-5000, has doubles from CAN $89. Across the street is the studio where they film *Stargate SG-1* and a few other TV shows. You never know who you might see. The **Accent Inn** by the airport is at 10551 St. Edwards Dr., ☎ 604-273-3311. Give them a call from the airport and they'll pick you up with a free shuttle.

Also out by the airport, try the **Radisson President**, 8181 Cambie Rd., ☎ 604-276-8181, 800-333-3333. It's far enough away from the airport to cut down on traffic and noise, but close enough to be convenient. It is about 20-30 minutes from downtown, depending on traffic. Doubles from CAN $175.

Atrium Inn, 2889 Hastings St., ☎ 604-254-1000, is a good choice on the outskirts. It's simple, but comfortable, with doubles from CAN $100.

Best Western Exhibition Park, 3475 Hastings St., ☎ 604-294-4751, is right off Highway 1, only three miles/five km from downtown. With doubles from CAN $89, this is one of the better deals around.

There are a couple of other good deals from the hotel chains outside the downtown area. The **Days Inn** at 2075 Kingway, ☎ 604-894-5531, has doubles from CAN $80; the **Holiday Inn Vancouver-Centre**, 711 Broadway, ☎ 604-879-0511, moves you upscale a bit, with doubles at CAN $159.

The hostel of choice if you can't get in the one downtown is at **Jericho Beach**, 1515 Discovery St., ☎ 604-224-3208. This is actually a lot nicer than the downtown property, with great views and a free shuttle service to downtown. It just eats up more of your time to get around. Dorm rooms from CAN $18.

Camping

There is nowhere to camp in town; anywhere you can park your RV or pitch a tent is going to be a ways out. RV parks and campgrounds are also frequently full, so call first, especially in summer.

Capilano RV Park, 295 Tomahawk Ave., ☎ 604-987-4722, is the closest you'll find to town – over the Lions Gate Bridge. It has a pretty nice campground, with a pool, laundromat and more. Full hookups start at CAN $35. It's a little bleaker for tents; you just have to try and find a spot on the grass.

Vancouver

Richmond RV Park, 6200 River Rd., ☎ 604-270-7878, is down near the airport. It has a good riverside location and better tent sites than at Capilano. Tent sites are CAN $17, RV sites start at CAN $23.

Parcanada, near the Tsawwassen ferry terminal, is about 30 minutes out of town on Highway 17, next to a water park. This is the place to be if you've got kids. Tent sites run CAN $18, RV sites start at CAN $22. ☎ 604-943-5811.

There are no provincial parks that offer good camping close to the city. **Golden Ears** is 25 miles/40 km north, out on Highway 7. It is huge, with more than 400 sites, but you're a long ways out.

■ Transportation

 Vancouver is the province hub. As such, it has plenty of ways to get in or out.

Getting Here

All major **airlines** fly into Vancouver. The airport is about 30 minutes from downtown, but it's an easy back and forth on regular buses. The one caveat about Vancouver's airport is that the international terminal may be one of the worst, most inconvenient designs of any airport, anywhere. Sometimes we've gotten in and out in under 30 minutes, but we've run into people who've been in the airport five hours and still haven't made it through security. Take all the "at least X hours early" warnings seriously.

There's a CAN $10 airport fee you have to pay before they'll let you to security. They say it's an airport improvement fee and, considering how nice it would be if they improved the place, let's hope they're telling the truth.

One bonus is that, if you're flying back to the United States, you go through US customs here.

> **AUTHOR NOTE:** If you've been saving your receipts for the tax refund, there is a station in the airport to get them stamped. It's in the international terminal, near the Fairmont Hotel.

If you have time, take a look at the fantastic artwork in the main terminal. It's some of the best First Nations stuff on display anywhere outside of the museum at the University of British Columbia. Make the effort to walk through, if your bags aren't too heavy.

Going into town from the airport, it's about a CAN $30 ride to downtown. There are also fixed-price limousine rides, which can save a few bucks for a large group. City buses leave from directly in front of the terminal. There's no way to miss them. There are no Sky Tram stops at the airport.

Amtrak (☎ 800-USA-RAIL), and **VIA** (☎ 800-561-8630) both serve Vancouver. There are daily trains from Seattle by Amtrak, and points east by VIA. If you come in on Amtrak, you go through customs at the train station, which is near the Science Center – about CAN $30 taxi ride to the airport, half that to most points downtown. Again, there's no convenient Sky Tram stop.

Greyhound (☎ 604-482-8747) branches out all through the province, and to pretty much anywhere else a bus can go. If you only want to get to Whistler, try the **Perimeter Coach**, ☎ 604-266-5386, which runs regular trips between Vancouver and the mountains, with stops in Squamish between.

To Victoria, **Pacific Coastlines** has daily service. They drive you to the ferry, load you on, drive you into downtown Vic. ☎ 604-662-8074.

BC Ferries has two terminals that serve Vancouver: to the south is Tsawwassen, which will get you the boat to Victoria; to the north, from Horseshoe Bay, you can catch ships to the Sunshine Coast and Nanaimo, on Vancouver Island. During rush hour, any ferry in and out of Vancouver is going to be jammed. You can make reservations for an additional charge – well worth it if you can't wait for the rush to die down. ☎ 888-223-3779, www.bcferries.com.

THE FUN WAY OUT

If you have the time and a few bucks to spare, the **Rocky Mountaineer train** is one of the glory rides of the rail world. It's a luxury way to get from Vancouver to Banff, with, on the shortest version, an overnight at a hotel in Kamloops. The train runs only during daylight hours, so you don't miss any scenery; packages range from four to seven days. This is a train lover's delight, with beautiful panoramic views of the incredible scenery. ☎ 800-665-7245, www.rockymountaineer.com.

Getting Around Town

In the city, you'll find Vancouver has a very good **bus** system. It gets crowded, but it's only CAN $1.50 a ride. There's also a pretty good **Sky Tram** system, which can get you from downtown to Burnaby and beyond. For visitors, the tram is good for staying in Burnaby hotels (which are cheaper than those downtown) or for getting from downtown to the Science Center and points past Chinatown. Price depends on how many zones you go through – a two-zone ticket is CAN $3.

Vancouver

On the buses or the Sky Tram, what you buy is the right to ride for a specific amount of time. If, say, you go from your hotel in Burnaby to downtown for a quick errand, the same ticket can get you back. Check the time printed on your ticket or on your bus transfer to see if you really need to buy another. The same ticket can get you on a bus, tram or on the Sea Bus, which is mostly useful for commuters heading to North Vancouver.

The Sky Tram runs on an honor system: there are no ticket takers. However, there are guards who work the trains at random, and it's not a cheap fine if they nail you for riding without a ticket.

You can buy day-passes at any Sky Tram station or from most tourist shops nearby. Look for the "Fare Dealer" sign.

Finally, to get around Granville Island, the Maritime Center and the Science Center, there's **False Creek Ferries**, which run tubby little boats back and forth between points. Hop on, hop off – a boat hits each stop every 15 minutes or so.

North from Vancouver

Roadside lupins.

When Vancouverites get enough money to get out of town, they head to the **Sunshine Coast**, a lovely piece of coast that stretches north from the big city into... well, what's becoming suburbs of the big city. There's a ways to go yet, but as more and more people look to escape, escape becomes harder and harder to find.

The routes that take you in and out of the Sunshine Coast can get jammed. Try to avoid the highway and the BC Ferries on Friday afternoons and Monday mornings, when the rush is on; otherwise, you won't have much trouble getting around. If you travel on any of the BC Ferries ships that link the small towns of the Sunshine Coast, you stand a reasonable chance of seeing orca from the boat.

For the purposes of this book, though, there's really only one important stop on the Sunshine Coast. Sure, you can go anywhere and probably have a good time, but a quick trip up to Powell River will show you a landscape that blew Jacques Cousteau away. And how often do you get a chance like that?

▪ Powell River

Powell River has about 17,000 people who call it home – actually, there are four towns kind of mushed together that make up Powell River, but that's not really important. Most of the people here are making their living off some aspect of the logging industry – there's a huge pulp and paper mill in town – or on taking people to the outdoors.

Visitor Info is at 4690 Marine Ave., ☎ 604-485-4701, www.discover-powellriver.com. Open 9-9, Monday-Saturday in summer.

Start your trip at the **Powell River Historical Museum**, on Marine Ave., ☎ 604-485-2222. There are good First Nations artifacts, and one of the biggest photo archives in the province. You can spend a lot of time here, seeing what the town was like way back when. Open daily in summer, 10-5. CAN $3.

That will about do it for you, as far as staying indoors in Powell River goes, unless you want to tour the pulp mill: there are daily tours in summer. ☎ 604-483-3722 for reservations. It's fun for people who like big machines.

Adventures in Water

Diving: What brought Jacques Cousteau here was the diving. If you're certified, you must come. It's that simple. Cousteau came and was awed by the giant wolf eels – they can grow to 10 feet long – and the giant Pacific octopus. Until you've seen one of these guys walking along the sea bed, striding on its six-foot arms, you simply haven't lived. There's also a 10-foot-long bronze mermaid statue – fits into that Canadian desire to make big *things* to set the towns apart – and the wreck of the HMCS *Chaudiere*, which was sunk in the early 90s to form an artificial reef.

The best diving is in winter, when the visibility can exceed 100 feet/ 30 meters, but if that sounds a little chilly for you, it's still a great spot any time of year. Check with **Good Diving and Kayaking**, at the Lund Hotel (☎ 604-483-3223) for gear and a guide to the more than 100 dive sites around town.

Kayaking: Good Diving and Kayaking can also show you how to stay above the water. The most popular paddle route is the Powell Forest Canoe Route, which takes four to eight days, depending on the side-trips you feel like tacking on. The basic route is about 37 miles/60 km, but you can extend that to more than 150, if you've got strong arms and a good sense of curiosity.

Put in at Lois Lake, 18 miles/30 km out of Powell River. From there, you'll paddle Horseshoe, Dodd, Windsor, Goat and Powell lakes (most people take out at Powell). There's about six miles/10 km of portaging along the way, with the single largest stretch at just over 1½ miles/2½ km.

Rent a canoe from **Wolfson Creek**, 9537 Nassichuk Rd., ☎ 604-487-1699; they also have guided trips and can get you good maps of the route. If you weren't able to get a reservation for Bowron Lakes, this is a really, really good alternate.

Adventures on Foot

 When it's time to dry off, take a hike. The **Sunshine Coast Trail** covers 110 miles/180 km from Saltery Bay to Sarah Point; Powell River comes in near the end. Pick a chunk, or try the whole thing. If you weren't able to get onto the West Coast Trail, this is not a bad alternative. For up-to-date trail descriptions, log on to www.sunshinecoast-trail.com.

Where to Eat

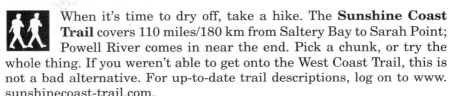 Food in Powell River is good and cheap. **Laura's Fish & Chips**, next to the ferry terminal, is a local favorite. It offers take-out only, but you're right by the docks, so it's not at all hard to find a nice spot overlooking the water. **Rocky Mountain Pizza & Bakery**, 4471 Marine Ave., another good choice, is the place in town for breakfast, with its own bakery. The rest of the time, you're looking at pizza pies, the best along the coast.

For something a little more upscale, try **Shinglemill**, at the Powell Lake Marina. It has steak, seafood and more, starting around CAN $15.

Where to Stay

 Powell River has a lot of hotels, but it's a good idea to call ahead, just to be sure you've got a bed. This town really can get a lot of traffic from the big city.

Marland Motel, 7156 Thunder Bay St., ☎ 604-485-4435, is a good budget choice, with rooms from CAN $60. **Seaside Villa Motel & RV Park**, 7274 Hwy. 101, ☎ 604-485-2911, is in the same price range; they also have full RV hookups.

Seabreeze Resort, 10975 Sunshine Coast Hwy., ☎ 604-487-9534, has cabins, and is also a good choice if you're looking to pitch a tent. Cabins from CAN $100.

Move 12 miles/20 km up the coast and you'll come to **Desolation Resort**, 2694 Dawson Rd., ☎ 604-483-3592. It has cabins and apartment-style rooms overlooking the water, with doubles from CAN $120.

Downtown is the **Coast Hotel**, part of a Canadian chain. Good quality. 4660 Joyce Ave., ☎ 604-485-3000. Doubles from CAN $100.

Camp at **Willingdon Beach**, ☎ 604-485-2242, with sheltered sites right on the beach. RV hookups are available.

Transportation

 If you don't drive in yourself, you have a couple of options. **Malaspina Coach Lines**, ☎ 604-485-5030, has service between Powell River and Vancouver. You can also get to Powell River by ferry. BC Ferries makes regular runs from Comox, on Vancouver Island.

THE SEA TO SKY HIGHWAY

If you're going to take only one scenic drive in British Columbia, this should be it. It's about an hour and a half between Vancouver and Whistler, via Lion's Bay and the lovely little town of Squamish. It's a road that is stuck on a narrow bit of land between mountain and sea, with amazing views of Howe Sound and the ranges beyond. Then, at Squamish, the road moves inland, opening views of thick forest and the jagged peaks of Black Tooth, Mt. Garibaldi and others. Along the way, if all that gets a little too much, you parallel the Cheakamus River, which runs in rills and rapids by the highway.

This road was both the backbone and the bane of the Vancouver 2010 Olympics bid. It's narrow, it's twisty and, even on good days, it can get crowded. Between now and 2010, they're going to widen, straighten and hope that they can steer more people onto boats, at least as far as Squamish.

Now's the time to go. See it before it's too late.

■ Squamish

Squamish is the only town of size between Vancouver and Whistler. Most people use it as little more than a place to get off the road and have a quick bite. That's a serious mistake. This little town has a lot of charm and, for the adventurous, more to do than just about anywhere else around. All you have to do is look at the great granite wall of The Chief – the second-largest granite massif in the world, behind the Rock of Gibraltar – to get an idea of the rock climbing possibilities. Squamish is also a prime destination for windsurfers and rafters.

We're treating Squamish and **Brackendale** as one spot because they are so close.

History

Squamish had long been the place to be for the local Coast Salish and Squohomish. First contact with Europeans happened in 1792, when Vancouver came this way. He loved the place – "it was no inconsiderable piece of good fortune to find a little cove in which we could take shelter, and a small spot of level land on which we could erect our tent," and he thought the people here were commercial geniuses. "We expected to find some difference in their general character. This conjecture was however premature, as they varied in no respect whatever, but in possessing a more ardent desire for commercial transactions; into the spirit of which they entered with infinitely more avidity than any of our former acquaintances, not only in bartering amongst themselves for different valuables they had obtained from us, but when that trade became slack, in exchanging those articles again with our people; in which traffic they always took care to gain some advantage.... Iron, in all its forms, they judiciously preferred to any other article we had to offer."

Not much happened after that for a while. During the 1850s, the valley was a common route to the interior for gold miners, but the town itself didn't start to appear until the turn of the century. It wasn't until there was a logging boom around 1900 that the place started to grow.

Still, it took the highway coming through in 1958 for things to really kick-start. Today, about 15,000 people call Squamish home, but it's growing fast – as prices in Whistler and Vancouver move out of sight, Squamish is still affordable, scenic and, so far, unspoiled. It's a good place to get off the road for a little while, to slow down and walk around. It's a place we make a point of coming to each time we're out this way.

Basics

The **Squamish Visitor Info Centre** is on the main street at 37950 Cleveland Ave., ☎ 604-892-9244, www.squamishchamber.bc.ca.

If you're coming from the north and planning to get on the ferry at Horseshoe Bay, stop at the Info Centre for directions. It will make your life a lot easier.

You can get to Squamish by **Greyhound Bus**, ☎ 604-482-8747. There's also **Alpine North Van**, in Brackendale, ☎ 604-898-3387, with service between Squamish and Whistler.

Attractions

The two big, standard Squamish attractions are the West Coast Railway Heritage Park and the BC Museum of Mining.

The **West Coast Railway Heritage Park**, near the BC Rail Station, ☎ 604-524-1011, has more than 60 vintage railway cars, including our favorite, a snowplow. Don't miss the 1890 business car to see what travel was like when it was still civilized. There's a station reconstruction, a miniature railroad for kids to ride on and a picnic area. CAN $6 admission. Open 10-4 daily.

BC Museum of Mining is pretty hard to miss: it's the gigantic building on the side of the highway south of town. Mining created British Columbia, in a very real sense, and this is one of the best mining museums you're going to come across. It's certainly one of the largest. Pan for gold, take the train through the underground tunnel to see where more than 1,200 million pounds of copper came from, and find out just how happy you are not to be a miner. ☎ 800-896-4044, www.bcmuseumofmining.org, CAN $9.50 for adults. Summer hours are 9 am-4:30 pm.

Adventures on Foot

Hiking: Squamish Estuary makes for great walking. Take some binoculars if you're looking to add a species or two to your life list of birds. There's a free handout at the Info Centre that shows the trails, but there are three main ones, all of which take about an hour. The Forest Loop starts at the end of the mall. Swan walk begins on Training Dyke Road and takes you along the central channel, where you stand a good chance of seeing trumpeter swans in season. Meadow Loop starts just off Vancouver St. – walk past the library and around the sewage plant. This trail gets you the best view of wild territory – in fact, it's a little hard to follow the trail in places – and takes you out to the edge of the central channel.

Rock Climbing: The Chief is the second-largest granite face in the world – only the Rock of Gibraltar is bigger. Check at **Vertical Reality**, 38154 2nd Ave., ☎ 604-892-8248, for the latest on the best routes – there are more than 1,600 in the area – which range from a walk-up that anybody reasonably fit can handle, to a multi-day climb. **Squamish Rock Guides**, ☎ 604-898-1750, can help you get up the face, as can **Slipstream Rock and Ice Guides**, in Brackendale, ☎ 800-616-1325 or 604-898-4891.

Adventures on Water

Whitewater Rafting: Elaho River Adventures, ☎ 800-713-7238 or 604-898-4633, has introductory whitewater trips for CAN $79, or a more gentle float for the same price. If you want bigger rapids, their wilderness whitewater trip, for CAN $109, takes in Class III and IV rapids.

Windsurfing: Squamish is the best place in BC to go windsurfing – in fact, it's generally rated at just below the Columbia River as the best place in the world. There's nobody in town who guides trips (due to insurance issues), but you can rent gear and get advice at Sea to Sky Ocean Sports, 37819 Second Ave., ☎ 604-892-3366, www.seatoskyoceansports. com.

Adventures on Wheels

 Mountain Biking: There are more than a hundred mountain bike trails in the Squamish area. There's a free guide to them available at the Info Centre, but among the most popular are **Alta Lake**, with single-track for beginning and intermediate riders, and **Smoke Bluffs**, if you can handle jumps.

Adventures in Nature

 Birding: For birders, the above-mentioned trails are a good place to start in town. But if you're a serious birder, come back in the winter, when the area between Squamish and Brackendale can have upwards of 3,000 bald eagles – a bigger concentration than anywhere in the world, except for Haines, Alaska.

> **WARNING:** *The eagles are here for the late-season salmon – which means at the beginning of the eagle season, you should be obeying all **bear** precautions, since they kind of like salmon, too.*

The birds start showing up in October, and there's good action through February, although December is the best time to come.

You can show up any time you want – it's not like they're hard to spot – or you can go on a guided bird walk. **Canadian Outback Adventure Co.**, ☎ 800-565-8735, has 90-minute narrated walking tours for CAN $59 if you're already in Brackendale, CAN $69 if they drive you in from Whistler, CAN $99 if they drive you from Vancouver.

Where to Eat

 This may be the only place where Squamish could stand to improve a little. There are all the usual fast food suspects out next to the highway. If you want something with a little more character, try the **Eagle's Nest**, 41340 Government St., which has a pleasant atmosphere, good seafood and steaks. For picnics, stop at the **Sea to Sky Deli**, 40380 Tantalus.

Where to Stay

AUTHOR TIP: If you're heading south to Vancouver, you can save a few bucks by staying the last night here, then getting into town first thing in the morning.

The budget choices downtown are the **August Jack Motor Inn**, 37947 Cleveland Ave., ☎ 604-892-3504, with doubles from CAN $75, and **The Garibaldi Budget Inn**, 38012 3rd Ave., ☎ 604-892-5204, with doubles from CAN $50.

A bit nicer is the **Howe Sound Inn & Brewing Company**, 37801 Cleveland Ave., ☎ 604-892-2603, with doubles from CAN $105.

Just off the highway is a **Best Western**, 40330 Tantalus, ☎ 604-898-4874, with doubles from CAN $80, and the **Super 8**, 38922 Progress Way, ☎ 604-815-0883, with doubles from CAN $95.

Camping

Alice Lake Provincial Park is eight miles/13 km north of Squamish. It's small, but very, very nice. However, it can quickly fill up with Whistler overflow, so check early in the day, or reserve at www.discovercamping.ca or ☎ 800-698-9025.

Elaho Adventure Lodge & Campground, at Mile 21, off the Alice Lake Junction, has sites for CAN $15; rooms in the lodge start at CAN $60 for a double. ☎ 800-713-7238.

Paradise Valley Campground, 3520 Paradise Valley Rd., ☎ 604-898-1486, has sites with full hookups for CAN $25.

South of Squamish is **Porteau Cove Provincial Park**. You get good ocean views here, but you're 12 miles/20 km out of town. Reserve at www.discovercamping.ca, ☎ 800-698-9025.

■ Whistler

BC, as this book should make perfectly clear, is one of the most enjoyable patches of real estate in the world. That said, if BC has a centerpiece, the place where it all comes together, it's Whistler. Famous for having the best skiing in North America, Whistler is actually a year-round destination – in fact, there's more to do in summer than in winter.

Set in a location that's dazzling even by BC standards, Whistler has rivers to paddle, rocks to climb, miles of bike paths. It's also got zip lines, downhill mountain biking for all levels and almost any other outdoor activity you could ever want. And when you're done, it has a couple of the finer restaurants in western Canada.

Okay, so the town itself looks like the world will after the McDonalds corporation finishes conquering the planet – a nasty, overdeveloped hellish architecture that will be painfully familiar to anybody who's hung out in a ski town over the past decade. If you're unfamiliar with the modern resorts that lack taste, you're in for a little shock: Swiss chalets from hell.

However, once you get past that, you're going to have serious fun here. This place is amazing. And it has plenty of festivals, including World Ski & Snowboarding events in April and December; a Classical Music Festival in August; a Street Festival in September; and the Food & Wine Festival, Cornucopia, in November.

History

 Whistler, as a quick look around will tell you, hasn't been here for very long. If it had, it would have a lot more individual character, instead of looking as if it came off a drawing board in a corporate office – which is exactly what happened.

The stunning natural scenery here has always brought people to the area, but the road in was awful and driving it just wasn't worth the effort. The town's modern history dates all the way back to 1965, when the road from Vancouver got paved. That started the influx.

The idea behind resort development at Whistler was to attract a winter Olympics. However, for the past 40 years, the Olympic committee, busy cashing in bigger bribes, has passed Whistler by. That all changes in 2010, when Vancouver and Whistler share the Olympics.

Between now and then, there are going to be some changes. The road in to Whistler is frequently two-lane, very curvy and very scenic – it's one of the prettier drives you're ever likely to take. In order to handle the influx of traffic the Olympics will bring, that's got to go. There are transportation plans in the works, including the deluded idea that most people will be willing to get on a boat in Vancouver, take a fast ferry to Squamish, and then load on a bus to Whistler. Yep. Sure. Right.

Whistler itself is not planning much development for the Olympics. They already have phenomenal ski runs, so only a few new ones need to be made, and only two new hotels are planned.

But with the road issues looming for the Olympics, the thing to watch is the highway. There are plans to shut it down eight hours a day for work – that's not likely to happen during the life of this edition, but it's coming.

Issues aside, why did the Olympic committee pick Whistler? Because it's world class, that's why. Plain and simple. It will showcase Canada's best as no other Olympics ever has. Meanwhile, already the median house price is over a million bucks – Whistler residents say that won't get you much more than a tear-down – and it is expected to go up. Whistler might just end up being loved to death.

DID YOU KNOW? The town was first named after the whistling sound marmots make when they're alarmed. They've got a fair amount to be alarmed about right now, but if past history is any indication, it should turn out okay. On our last visit, we watched bears watching mountain bikers. Whistler gets along, because the beauty overwhelms everything else.

Basics

 Whistler is not a budget location. Lodging is among the most expensive in BC – only downtown Vancouver compares. And most activities are, by BC standards at least, on the pricey side. They get away with it because it's worth it.

You can drive yourself to Whistler or you can take the **Perimeter Coach** up from Vancouver. Regular runs can get you to or from the Vancouver Airport or any hotel. ☎ 604-905-0041 in Whistler, or 604-266-5386 in Vancouver.

Greyhound, ☎ 604-932-5031, has daily service from Vancouver.

Once you're in Whistler, you don't need a car. In fact, most of the town is pedestrianized, and if you've got a car, you're going to find it's more trouble than it's worth. When booking your hotel, make sure you know exactly where to go to park, or you're not going to enjoy your entrance into the village.

Whistler's Visitor Centre is right off the highway at 2097 Lake Placid Rd., ☎ 604-932-5528. It's well marked; you can't miss it. **Whistler Central Reservations**, ☎ 664-5625 or 800-944-7853, can help find you a place to stay in town. It's run by Tourism Whistler, and they know what they're doing. For the scoop on the town via the Internet, try www.tourismwhistler.com.

To hook up to the web when in town, there are a lot of cybercafés in the village. Cheapest, though, are the coin machines in the lobby of the Crystal Hotel, where you get 10 minutes for a buck.

When you get to town, pick up a free copy of *Whistler This Week*, available all over town. It's got good ads, and it will give you an overview of what's going on.

Adventure Outfitters

 You can have more fun in a shorter amount of time in Whistler than anywhere else in western Canada. Get out of the overdeveloped town and head into the woods.

If you arrive in summer, the first thing to do is rent a mountain bike and get on the slopes. If you're here in winter, get your skis on and head the same direction.

There are a bunch of one-stop shops for tour booking. Go in and talk to a couple different ones before you decide. Pick people you trust and like.

Back Roads, ☎ 604-932-3111, just below the tramway on the Village Walkway, is a good one-stop shop for adventures. Floats on the River of Golden Dreams run CAN $50. For CAN $109, you can get on their nature walk to Cheakamus Lake or Nairn Falls. Peddle-paddle trips start at CAN $70. If you need to rent a bike, they've got good ones for CAN $50 a day.

Whistler Valley Adventure Center, ☎ 604-938-6392, can book pretty much any activity you'll want to try, from easy nature walks (CAN $48) to wakeboarding, horseback riding, jet boat tours and more.

Whistler Eco-Tours, ☎ 877-988-4900, www.whistlerecotours.com, also has a wide variety of programs. Float the River of Golden Dreams for CAN $90, do a bear awareness tour (no promise of bears) for CAN $79, or take a pedal-paddle trip for CAN $89. They also have fishing guides at CAN $150 a half-day.

Whistler Activity Central, ☎ 604-935-4528, can book it all.

Adventures on Foot

Climbing: Great Wall, ☎ 604-905-7625, www.greatwall-climbing.com, has Whistler's only indoor rock climbing gym. It's not big, but it's pretty, and it includes a 5.13 crack. A day pass is only CAN $15. They also have a really good variety of outdoor programs: four-hour trips with basic instruction run CAN $85. Kid's two-day rock classes are CAN $180. If you're looking for a taste of more, try their wilderness adventure trip. CAN $105 gets you a rock climb, zip line, rappel and a Burma bridge crossing. Finally, if you've been looking for a way to get away from the kids a while, try the kid's climb and dine. For CAN $59, your kids get pizza and time in the rock gym, while you get out for dinner with your spouse for three hours. This is one of their most popular deals.

Escape Route, in the Marketplace, ☎ 938-9242, www.whistlerguides. com, books glacier tours for CAN $129, and day hikes in the backcountry from CAN $129. They've also got one-on-one guides available, if you have a special route in mind.

This is the place to go for rock climbers and mountaineers. Introductory rock classes are CAN $195; lead climbing – if you don't know what that is, you're not ready to do it – goes for CAN $250; and a rescue class for CAN $125. Mountaineers can take a crevasse rescue class – a bargain at CAN $195. In winter, they'll guide ice climbing for CAN $195. If you need mountain gear, come here. It ain't cheap, but it's the real stuff.

Adventures on Wheels

Biking: In summer, Whistler is biker's paradise. There's no shortage of places to rent a bike in town. Basic bikes start around CAN $35/day. If you want a good bike – full suspension, etc. – expect to pay CAN $65-75/day. **Back Roads**, ☎ 604-932-3111, just below the tramway on the Village Walkway, has good bikes for CAN $50 a day. A bike suitable for the Mountain Bike Park runs CAN $70 for a half-day, CAN $95 a full day, including body armor.

> **AUTHOR NOTE:** The city has a helmet law that is very strictly enforced. There's a CAN $75 fine for riding around without a lid.

The Valley Loop is a clearly marked trail that takes you around Alta Lake, along the River of Golden Dreams, and gets you back to town. It's about six miles/10 km of easy pedaling that takes two hours or so. There are only a couple of hills to contend with. It's a good way to see the valley.

If that's a little tame for you, you'll need to hit the bike park.

What do you do with ski runs when there's no snow? Bomb down them on bikes, of course. A lift ticket to **Whistler Mountain Bike Park**, ☎ 604-932-3434 or 800-766-0449, is only CAN $35/day. For that, you get access to two lifts, 4,000 vertical feet of trails – more than 40 miles/60 km of trails – and even a couple of jump parks. Whatever your level of mountain bike experience, there's a trail for you. You're going to want a very good bike for this, with front and back suspension. Disk brakes won't hurt, either. You're officially insane if you go up without body armor – most good bike rental companies include it.

The bike park has private instruction available. Fees run CAN $165 for a half-day of lessons. **Alpine Bike Tours** also have good instructors and offer an excellent program. They charge CAN $135 for a half-day. Unless you're very happy and comfortable on your own bike, this is money well spent.

ATVing: Whistler ATV, ☎ 604-932-6681, has 90-minute trips for CAN $89, two hours for CAN $99. They run on some good bushwhacking trails.

Adventures on Snow

Skiing: We're not going to dedicate a lot of space to skiing – if you know how to ski, you already know Whistler is the place to be; if you're looking to learn how to ski, there's no reason to look elsewhere.

Skiing is why Whistler is famous. It's not the views, it's the mountains you can throw yourself down. It has some of the best skiing anywhere in the world – *Ski Magazine* has named it Number One in North America five years in a row. It's got the longest season in Canada – actually, the season never ends – and has an average annual snowfall of 30 feet, falling on more than 7,000 acres of skiable terrain, including 90 groomed runs. Best of all, the top of the peaks is only around 5,000 feet – they've got a huge vertical rise, the biggest on the continent for ski peaks – so you don't have to deal with altitude.

If you're coming in winter, check for ski/lodging packages, which are offered by most hotels.

If you're buying your lift tickets à la carte, three days out of four starts at CAN $201; you can get half-day beginner lessons for as little as CAN $85.

Escape Route, in the Marketplace, ☎ 604-938-9242, www.whistler-guides.com, has backcountry ski and snowboard tours starting at CAN $195. Instructional two-day courses on how to do the big stuff run CAN $295. Multiple-day ski tours are also available.

If you want to get way off the beaten track, you need to go heli-skiing. **Whistler Heli-Skiing**, ☎ 604-932-4105, www.whistlerheliskiing.com, offers a three-run day for CAN $625 and a four-run day for CAN $705. These are not beginner trips. Talk to the staff to make sure you're up for it before you plunk down your credit card.

Snowmobiling: In winter, try **Outback Rentals**, ☎ 604-932-2080, for snowmobile tours and sleds. A high-performance machine will set you back CAN $189 a half-day.

Adventures on Water

Captain Holidays, ☎ 604-905-2925, www.kayakwhistler.com, has half-day whitewater trips for CAN $175. Intro trips for kayaking start at CAN $80, including instruction on the Eskimo roll. You'll need to learn this if you're planning more intensive paddling on the coast.

Wedge Rafting, ☎ 604-932-7171, www.wedgerafting.com, is right next to the gondola. If you've never done whitewater rafting before, try their trip on Green River, for CAN $69. It has some good rapids, but nothing too scary. A little more ambitious is Birkenhead River, for CAN $87. Late in the year, try the Elaho-Squamish run, the prettiest of them all. It's a full-day trip, for CAN $99, and combines good rapids with some easy floats.

Whistler River Adventures, also right by the gondola, ☎ 604-932-3532, runs the same rivers for CAN $69 on the Green, CAN $87 on the Birkenhead, and CAN $149 for the Elaho-Squamish.

Whistler River Adventures also has jetboat tours. Blasting down rivers in a highly overpowered aluminum boat is great fun. Four-hour trips (about 2½ hours on the water) on the Lillooet run CAN $95; a trip through the Lillooet Narrows is CAN $139.

Adventures in the Air

 Ziptreck Ecotours, ☎ 604-935-0001, with an office right below the tram, takes you into the woods of Blackcomb, hooks you onto a steel cable with a pulley, and zips you across the river. It's very safe – they've had 80-year-olds do this. The longest line is 1,100 feet, and it's 180 feet above the river. This may be the only time you'll ever see old-growth forest from the top. It's a lot of fun, and a very, very well-run operation. The 2½-hour tour, which incorporates five ziplines, runs CAN $98. More thought went into designing this trip than pretty much any other we've been on in Canada.

If you're looking to hook onto a different kind of line, **Whistler Bungee**, ☎ 604-938-9333, throws you off a bridge down to a river for only CAN $90. Two jumps and a T-shirt to show off to your friends cost CAN $140.

Shopping

 If you can avoid shopping in Whistler, you'll do your wallet a favor. There aren't many bargains here. There are plenty of skate shops, even more ski shops, and lots of stuff you could buy somewhere else cheaper.

Of course, there are just a couple of exceptions that must be mentioned. **Black Tusk Gallery**, 101-4359 Main St., near the Marketplace, ☎ 604-905-5540, has absolutely first-rate Pacific Northwest art, some of the best you'll find anywhere.

R&G Gold & Silver, on the Village Stroll near the Crystal Lodge, has cave bear teeth and other fossils. How can you beat that? ☎ 604-938-3307.

Where to Eat

 Whistler is geared toward people who have been out all day and want to pig out or drink all night. There are some excellent restaurants here. When you get hungry, just take the Village Walkway; something will catch your eye. Everything listed below is on the walkway, unless otherwise noted. Five minutes of strolling will open up a couple of dozen restaurant choices.

Araxi, in Village Square, ☎ 604-932-4540, www.araxi.com, is one of the town's best eateries. It uses fresh, local ingredients and is the winner of every award in the book. It's not as expensive as you might suppose but, if it's too much, look across the walkway to the **Amsterdam Pub & Café**, a very popular local spot. Seafood and pasta dishes start at CAN $20.

The Mongolie Grill is a Mongolian stir-fry place, where your bill is done by weight – figure CAN $12 or so to fill up. Near Village Centre. ☎ 604-938-9416.

Zog's Dogs is just below the chairlift and offers the cheapest meal in town. A hot dog will run you four bucks or so, or you can get a Beaver Tail, a fried-bread meal with a wide choice of toppings, for CAN $4-6.

For Japanese food, try **Sushi Ya**, in the Marketplace, the far end of the walkway from the chairlift. It can get pretty crowded in the evening. Nearby is Le **Crêperie**, with French-Canadian-style dinner crêpes.

Off the walkway, but only half a block behind the Marketplace, is Whistler's most popular restaurant: **Splitz Grill**, 104-4369 Main St., ☎ 604-938-9300. It has zero atmosphere, horrible noise blasting at you from the stereo system and hamburgers good enough to get the place a Zagat rating. CAN $10 gets you a meal deal and will spoil you for ever eating a burger anywhere else. If there's one don't-miss spot in Whistler, this is it.

Where to Stay

This is going to hurt. There are no bargains in Whistler; it's one of the more expensive places to stay in BC. Also, if you're driving in, be sure you know in advance how to get to the hotel and where to park your car. Most of what you'll want to do in Whistler is in a pedestrian-only area.

Whistler can be fully booked, especially in winter or during one of the festivals. Check with **Tourism Whistler's** reservation office, ☎ 604-664-5625 or 800-944-7853, if you need help finding a place.

Whistler Lodging Company, ☎ 800-777-0185, books more than 700 hotel and condo rooms in town. Give them your budget, see what they can do for you.

Virtually all of the options below will have some kind of ski/lodging package if you need one.

Whistler's grand dame is the **Fairmont Chateau Whistler**, ☎ 604-938-8000, a great place to break the bank. Right up against the mountain, in the upper village, it's pure five-star luxury. The restaurant is said to have the second-best wine list in BC. Doubles from CAN $475.

If that's a bit much, in the lower village is **Delta Whistler Village Suites**, 4308 Main St., ☎ 604-905-3987, right next to the tram. It has good mountain views from rooms in the back. Doubles from CAN $269. The same company owns a slightly less swank property at 4050 Whistler Way, ☎ 604-932-1982, with doubles from CAN $179.

Coast Whistler Hotel, 4005 Whistler Way, ☎ 604-932-2522, is a good choice in the moderate range. Doubles from CAN $109.

Glacier Lodge and Suites, 4573 Chateau Blvd., ☎ 604-905-4144, has everything from basic rooms to huge suites. There's a deli, exercise room and more. Low-end doubles from CAN $140.

The Crystal Lodge is centrally located in the Village, at 4154 Village Green, ☎ 604-932-2221. Doubles start at CAN $125.

Blackcomb Lodge, 4220 Gateway, ☎ 604-932-4155, has a sauna and an indoor pool. Doubles start at CAN $139, but another CAN $20 gets you a room with a kitchen.

If all this is out of your budget, there's a **hostel** on Alta Lake, ☎ 604-932-5492, with dorm rooms for under CAN $25. It's a ways out of town, though, and it can be hard to find a spot. You could also try **Whistler Lodge**, 2124 Nordic, ☎ 604-932-6604, with dorm rooms around CAN $25.

Camping

There isn't much to choose from close to town. **Riverside RV Resort**, 8018 Mons Rd., ☎ 604-905-5533, is about a mile from the Village. Full hookups run about CAN $45; tent sites, CAN $25. They also have some cabins that start at $125.

Brandywine Provincial Park is seven miles/11 km down the road towards Vancouver; **Nairn Falls Provincial Park** is 17 miles/28 km north. That's as close as you're going to get with public campgrounds. Both are open only in summer and charge CAN $12/night. ☎ 604-888-3678 for reservations at either place.

■ Leaving Whistler, Heading North

 The Sea to Sky Highway isn't the only beautiful road in this part of the world. If your plans take you north from Whistler to Williams Lake or the Bowron Lakes canoe circuit – or even east, towards Kamloops and the Okanagan Valley – **Highway 99** north, through Pemberton and on to Lillooet, before meeting up with Highway 97 just north of Cache Creek, is the road to travel.

There's not a whole lot on this road – just amazing river, canyon and mountain scenery – but it's one of the most beautiful, uncrowded roads in BC.

> **AUTHOR NOTE:** This stretch of Highway 99 has a lot of twists and turns, and it's a narrow, narrow road in places. The passengers are going to have a great time; there are quite a few points, though, when the driver might be too occupied to enjoy the view.

Vancouver

About a half-hour outside Whistler, you hit **Nairn Falls Provincial Park**. A 15-minute easy hike takes you back to the falls, which are nearly 200 feet high. There are 88 campsites in the park; this is, from the north, as close as you're likely to find a campsite near Whistler during the high season.

The small town of **Pemberton** is just another four miles/seven km north of the falls. About 900 people live here – a lot of them work in Whistler, but can't afford the cost of living there. But here's how hard Pemberton is looking for a way to set itself apart: residents call their town the "disease-free capital of the world for seed potatoes." Okay.

The road branches just north of town. The left fork goes to D'Arcy and **Birkenhead Lake Provincial Park**, which is a nice spot to camp for a day or two. You can fish the lake for Dolly Varden, trout and whitefish. The tiny town of D'Arcy is the end of the road, unless you have a good 4WD vehicle – then you can head up over the Seton Portage and eventually get to Lillooet (tell somebody if you're doing this; a breakdown puts you deep in the middle of nowhere).

Those not driving Jeeps are better off sticking to the main Lillooet Road. You parallel the Fraser River – sometimes the road clings to cliffs over the riverbanks. Besides the mountains and water, there's the occasional tiny farm or homestead, making you wonder how these people got so lucky as to live in a spot like this.

Camp at **Marble Canyon**, 26 sites, ☎ 250-851-3000. It has hiking trails and views of the 1,000-foot-deep canyon.

Marble Canyon is about the only place to stop until you get to Lillooet. The road curves, it climbs, and then, after you've moved into a landscape that looks like high desert, you leave the river behind and begin a long, slow descent to Lillooet.

A LUMPY STORY

All of this area was thoroughly checked for gold during the Cariboo Rush. Of course, somebody had the bright idea of bringing camels back here – this got tried all over Canada and Alaska, and it failed each and every time. Here, in 1862, a guy brought in 23 camels, but the camels just couldn't take the terrain; they're not built for the sharp edges, or even for the wet of this part of the world. Some died, some were killed, some got loose. There were camel sightings for a decade or more.

Lillooet

Lillooet started off thanks to the Cariboo gold rush. It was a transhipment point where you ditched the boat that had taken you up the Harrison and Anderson lakes and got onto the Cariboo Road. In 1863, more than 15,000 people called Lillooet home, as it was a classic boomtown.

Now, long after the bust, it's a pretty little town of about 2,000 people.

Visitor Info is at 790 Main St., ☎ 250-256-4556. Open daily in summer, afternoon only in the shoulder months, closed in winter. Next door is the town's **museum**, which features artifacts from Ma Murray, who published a newspaper here in the 1930s. It also has some good First Nations stuff.

The attraction to Lillooet is the drive in or out; there's not a lot of reason to linger. Top off the gas tank here – any direction you go, the next station is a ways down the road. If you get here late at night and need a place to stay, there are some good choices. **Mile-0-Motel**, ☎ 250-256-7511, 616 Main St., has rooms with views of the river starting at CAN $48 for a double.

For campers, the full-service **Cayoosh Creek Campground**, ☎ 250-265-4180, is just outside of town, near the junction of Highway 12 and 99. It has sites from CAN $16. There's also **Fraser Cove Campground**, 1.2 miles/two km north of town, off Highway 99. ☎ 250-256-0142.

It's 46 miles/75 km from Lillooet to Highway 97, which puts you on the main road in central BC. Head east for Kamloops, or north for Williams Lake, the rodeo town of Quesnel, and on to Prince George. See *Central British Columbia* chapter for details.

Vancouver

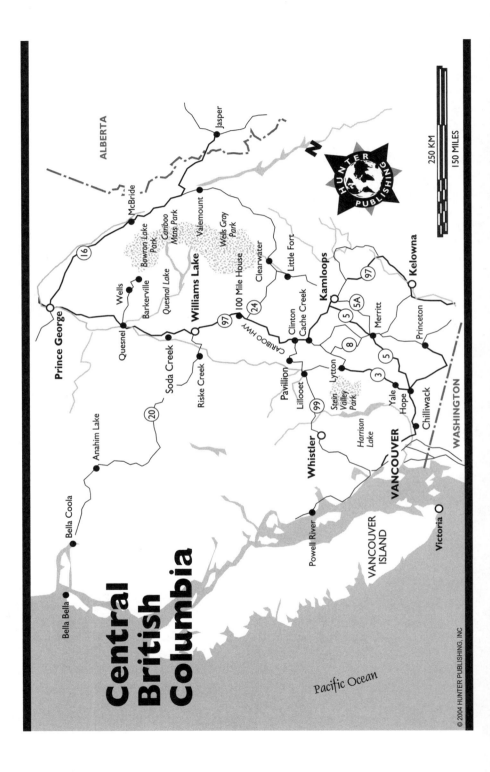

Central
British
Columbia

Pacific Ocean

© 2004 HUNTER PUBLISHING, INC

250 KM
150 MILES

ALBERTA

Jasper

McBride

Bowron Lake Park
Cariboo Mtns Park
Valemount
Wells Gray Park

16

Wells
Barkerville
Quesnal Lake

Quesnel

Williams Lake

100 Mile House

Clearwater

Little Fort

Kamloops

97

Kelowna

Prince George

Soda Creek

97

24

Clinton
Cache Creek

5A

5

Merritt

97

Princeton

Riske Creek

CARIBOO HWY

Pavillion
Lillooet

Lytton

Stein Valley Park

8

3

5

20

Anahim Lake

99

Whistler

Harrison Lake

Yale
Hope

Chilliwack

WASHINGTON

Bella Coola

Powell River

VANCOUVER ISLAND

VANCOUVER

Victoria

Bella Bella

N

HUNTER PUBLISHING

Central British Columbia

Cariboo Country & the Fraser River

Leaving Vancouver for the eastern parts of the province, you have two options that get you to the exact same place. Highway 7 follows the north side of the Fraser River; Highway 1, the south. Both are going to get you to the lovely little town of Hope. From Hope you can head due north through Lytton toward Cache Creek, or east toward Kelowna and Kamloops. The third option, Routes 97 and 22A, which more or less parallels the US-Canada border, isn't really going to get you anywhere you want to go.

Along Highways 1 & 7

Vancouver and its suburbs stretch on for quite a while, taking in the towns of Surrey, Langley, Cloverdale and more. You can never run a highway through too many towns, or change the speed limit too many times, according to Canadian road designers. So you're likely to see more towns than you want to, particularly if you're coming from Victoria by ferry and trying to get out into the province. Just go with it. They're pretty little suburbs and, eventually, they end and you're in the countryside.

Along Highway 1, stop at **Fort Langley**, the site of the first European settlement in the Fraser Valley. This is the best place to jump from the north to the south side of the river, or vice-versa, via the **Albion Ferry**, ☎ 604-467-7298. It's free, it runs every 15 minutes, and it's worth getting on just to say you crossed the mighty Fraser.

Visitor Info in Fort Langley is at 23245 Glover Rd., ☎ 604-513-8787.

But the main reason to stop in town is to see **Fort Langley National Historic Park**, one of the refurbished HBC posts. The first post was built here in 1827; that didn't work out too well, so in 1838, they built a new fort, farther upstream. That didn't go so well, either: it burned to the ground only two years later. They tried one more time, a bit farther upstream, and that location is where the park is now.

At its peak, this was one of the busiest posts in Canada, and it served as a central depot for other HBC posts, sending out nearly 40,000 pounds of Fraser River salmon to more distant forts each year.

This spot was important enough that when BC officially became a crown colony in 1858, the announcement was made here, in the Big House; Fort Langley was actually the first capital of the new province, but that lasted only a year.

By 1866, there was no need for the post at all. It was shut down and left to rot until 1923, when preservationists got hold of it.

Today, you can wander around the reconstructed post (only the storehouse remains from the original fort) and ask questions of the very knowledgeable staff, who hang out in period costume (this is a great summer job for university history majors). The park is open daily from March through early November. Admission is CAN $5, and it's money well-spent to see how the HBC managed to become the second-largest empire the world has ever known – only Kublai Khan ruled over more territory. ☎ 604-513-4777.

Just a bit farther up the road, in the town of Langley, is the **Canadian Museum of Flight**, at the Langley Airport, Hangar 3. ☎ 604-532-0035. For aeronautical fans, the big draw here is a Handley Page Hampden bomber, one of two surviving in the world. This one was dredged up from the Straits of Georgia in 1986, restored and put on display here.

Keeping on Highway 1, the first town of size you hit is **Abbotsford**. The city is one of Canada's largest berry-producing areas, growing strawberries, raspberries and blueberries. It's also the first Canadian city you'll hit if you're coming north from Seattle. There is no shortage of banks in the city center ready to change your US dollars for the more interesting-looking Canadian dollars.

The road winds northeast, getting closer and closer to the mountains. Snow-covered much of the year, these are the Coast Mountains, which extend for nearly 1,000 miles inland.

There's a helpful tourist information stop outside **Chilliwack** and, for people who've just driven up from Washington State, this should be one of your first stops in Canada, if only to take a look around the first of the wonderful **BC Tourist Infocentres**, ☎ 604-858-8121. It's at 44150 Luckakuck Way (how can you go wrong with a street name like that?). Load up on brochures of the nearby parks and activities.

The city itself has the **Minter Gardens**, 52892 Bunker Rd., ☎ 800-661-3919, a world-class botanical array. In summer, when the flowers are in bloom, it's a great place to laze away a few hours while you rest from driving. You'll see the entrance from the highway, off exit 135.

Also in Chilliwack is the **Canadian Military Engineers Museum**, the first of many transportation/engineering museums along the BC highways. This one focuses on how the CME has helped develop this part of Canada. The museum is on the Canadian Forces Base, 45820 Spadina Ave., ☎ 604-795-5210. There's also a city museum and archives, both on Yale Road. Take the same exit as for the CME Museum, but turn west.

There are plenty of places to sleep and eat around Chilliwack, but if you've got the energy for another 45 minutes or so of driving, continue on towards the mountains, to Hope. Along the way, there is the very popular **Cultus Lake Provincial Park** (fishing, boating, almost 300 campsites; ☎ 800-689-9025). The word Cultus comes from the First Nation's Sto:lo language: it means "bad, worthless." Cultus is one of the most popular parks in this part of the province, even though there's supposed to be a Slellucum – a giant spirit bear – that lives around here. On summer weekends, this park is an escape valve for Vancouverites, and can be very full.

The road also passes **Bridal Falls Provincial Park** – which has the sixth-highest waterfall in Canada, at 403 feet – and Harrison Hot Springs, where you can soak away the pains of driving. The hot springs are at the southern edge of Harrison Lake, and they've been in constant use for as long as anybody can remember – the Salish used them, and when gold miners came into the area, they found out this was the place to soak the sore muscles they got from failing to strike it rich.

If you want to get out for a soak yourself, you have two options. You can stay at **Harrison Hot Springs Resort** and shell out CAN $165 or so for a double in the superb lodge with access to the pools, a spa and restaurants. The resort is at 100 Esplanade, ☎ 604-796-2244. Alternately, go to the public pool, downtown, on Harrison Hot Springs Rd. CAN $7.50 gets you in, and you can camp at **Bigfoot Campgrounds**, 670 Hot Springs Rd., ☎ 604-796-9767, which has full-service sites.

Near the springs is the **Agassiz-Harrison Museum**, 6947 Lougheed Highway, ☎ 604-796-3545, housed in an original 1893 railway station. It now sits on the property of Agriculture Canada's Agassiz Research Station. Check for the current schedule of summer tours, which are usually offered in the early afternoon. Open 10-4 daily, May to September.

Every road has a direction it should be driven. We're describing Highway 1 one according to the direction you're most likely to go: west to east. And it's beautiful that way, as the mountains draw ever-closer before the road heads right between peaks. But if you find yourself coming back out this way, east to west, you'll discover that it's even more dramatic as you come out of the mountains. It's like coming out from under a very beautiful thunderstorm, into broad daylight.

The road follows the path of the Fraser River. The mountains generate a lot of clouds, and it can get cold here very fast. The Fraser River is one of BC's most important rivers – and the canyon the river has cut is one of the province's most dramatic spots. There are several provincial parks along the river, with great camping in each and every one.

> ## ON THE TRAIL
>
> Along the river used to be the Cariboo Wagon Road, which from 1862 to 1870 took more than 10,000 miners north to the Cariboo goldfields. One miner imported 23 camels to haul packs on the trail and, until his camels died, he probably got a lot closer to rich than most of the would-be miners.

The Fraser is great for whitewater rafting, especially around Lytton, which is at the north end of the canyon, at the junction of the Fraser and Thompson rivers.

■ Hope

Hope was just a quiet little spot in the middle of nowhere until it burst into the world's view in 1982, when it was chosen as the site for filming *Rambo: First Blood*. Many of the shops have autographed pictures of Stallone and, for the movie buff, there is a self-guided Rambo Tour, which points out all the famous backdrops for the movie.

Of course, once everybody forgot the movie, the town went back to being a quiet little spot in the middle of nowhere. However, it's a beautiful little spot, with quite a venerable history.

The first settlement was built in 1848, when the HBC put up a trading fort. Only 10 years later, it became a boomtown, when gold was struck in the nearby Cariboo region. Hope was a jumping off point, serving steamboats on the Fraser River; shops and sawmills soon followed.

Unlike most boomtowns, Hope outlasted the gold rush, thanks to a silver rush: right as everybody was about to pack up and go home, there was the fortuitous discovery of silver on Silver Peak in 1873. The early 1900s brought the railway, which ensured continued slow growth. The town was officially incorporated in 1928.

Hope is a scenic little town with plenty of attractions to justify getting off the highway for a little while.

A good place to start your tour is at the **Tourist Infocentre** and museum, 919 Water Ave., ☎ 604-869-2021. In front of the building is a funny-looking contraption that is a restored gold mill. Inside you'll find interesting farm and mining tools, as well as many objects from everyday life, such as a gentleman's mustache teacup with a special ceramic plate covering part of the cup so that a mustache wouldn't get wet. There is no admission fee; the staff in both the museum and Infocentre are informative and helpful.

ON LOCATION

Rambo isn't the only movie to have been made here. A couple of dog movies – *White Fang II*, and *Far From Home* were both filmed in Hope, and much of the excellent mountaineering movie *K2* was filmed in the Fraser Canyon. Jack Nicholson and Sean Penn hung out in town to film *The Pledge*, and Sidney Poitier was here for *Shoot to Kill*.

Attractions

 Hope claims to be the "Chainsaw Carving Capital." This is partly an indication that people go a little stir-crazy here in winter, but also recognition of a genuine Canadian art form. If you really are interested, there's a pamphlet on the carvings tour at the Info Centre, but it's more fun to just stumble on these and be surprised.

HOPE CARVERS

The tradition of carving here started off in 1991, when a tree in Memorial Park had to go, because of root rot. A local artist argued for making this into something worthwhile, so he hacked away with his saw until there was a carving of a bald eagle with a salmon in its talons. Now there are a couple of dozen giant carvings scattered around town. There are several bears, a mountain goat and more.

On the corner of Park and Fraser is **Christ Church** that claims to be the oldest in mainland Canada still on its original foundations. It was consecrated 1861 and services have been held ever since.

Just outside the town are the **Othello/Quintette Tunnels**, a set of railroad tunnels built in 1910 as part of a project to link this area with the BC coast. The cost of building in this area was tremendous; the average cost per mile was CAN $136,000, and one mile held the record for being the most expensive in the world, at CAN $300,000. Of course, modern roads often cost that much per foot now. Today you can visit the tunnels at any time, except during the winter months; there are no hours or fees. A walk in the beautiful Coquilla Canyon is peaceful and relaxing, and there are picnic tables along the way. The tunnels are fairly dark, so a flashlight might be handy. Continue through the tunnels and you'll pass over a gorge cut by the roaring Fraser River. Getting the trains through here gave the engineers nightmares for years.

Hope is a good place from which to launch side-trips into the wilderness. There is excellent fishing and river-running in the area, as well as hiking, winter sports and gold panning. Hang-gliders from around the world come here to jump off the mountains. Ask at the Tourist Infocentre for additional information.

Where to Stay

 You won't have any trouble finding a place to stay in Hope: there are plenty of choices, most under CAN $75.

Best Continental Motel, 860 Fraser Ave., ☎ 604-869-9726, is right off Highway 1 and has good views. All the rooms have fridges. Doubles start at CAN $55. **Inn Towne Motel,** 510 Trans Canada Hwy., ☎ 604-869-7276, has Jacuzzi suites. Doubles from CAN $54.

Maple Leaf Motor Inn, 377 Old Hope-Princeton Way, ☎ 604-869-7107, has newly renovated doubles from CAN $55.

For campers, **Othello Tunnels Campground & RV Park**, 67851 Othello Rd., ☎ 877-869-0543, is just 10 minutes away from the tunnels. It has tent sites, full hookups and showers.

Coquihalla Campground is overlooking the Coquihalla River. It has nice treed sites, showers and a laundromat. ☎ 888-869-7118.

Transportation

If you're not in your own car, Hope is a regular stop for **VIA Rail** (☎ 800-561-8630) and **Greyhound** (☎ 800-661-8747) bus services.

The road continues along the Fraser River, through Hell's Canyon. It's scenic and amazing, and it's very dangerous driving, so use caution.

North from Hope

Leaving Hope, you've got to decide which way you want to go. If you're headed north, there are two choices. Both are scenic, but one's more dramatic and slow, whereas the other is a good, fast road that makes for a pretty drive.

The Coquihalla, Rte 5, leads straight from Hope up to Kamloops. Except for the small town of Merritt (there's no reason to stop unless you need to buy gas), there's nothing on this road but a toll booth (CAN $10 for a car) and a few rest stops. The road cuts through scenery that's particularly beautiful in the fall when the leaves are changing colors – and it's the fastest way north. Once you're in Kamloops, you can head towards Jasper, to Kelowna, or east to Cache Creek.

We've got to suggest you take the Coquihalla only if you're in a hurry, though – you easily cut an hour and a half off your northern travel time – because Route 1, which parallels the Fraser, is so much more beautiful.

Truly, there's nothing on the Coquihalla. That's how we can write up nearly a hundred miles of road in a couple paragraphs. It's pretty, it's a very good road, it's the middle of nowhere.

Three warnings on the Coquihalla: there are a lot of steep grades, so in summer, your car can have trouble with overheating if it's not in great shape; in winter, these steep grades and the high altitude of the road means there can be serious snow conditions. Do not get on this road in winter without first checking conditions and being prepared: snow tires, chains, emergency kit. Also, remember that Merritt is the only place along the entire length of the road to buy gas. When you're leaving Hope or Kamloops for the Coquihalla, check your fuel.

Route 1 follows the Fraser River, from Hope north. This is a beautiful road, lots of twists and turns and dramatic canyon views. There are also a few really cool places to stop along the way, and if you're a river rafter, this is the place to be.

It's about 60 miles/100 km from Hope to Lytton, the first town of size you'll hit, but don't plan on hurrying through this region. There are plenty of things to see, places to stop, and it's well worth the time simply to plan on an hour or so watching the river flow.

The Fraser has always been BC's most important river. It cuts through the heart of the province, emptying out just south of Vancouver. Really, it's the river that made the province, as it was used for a highway by early explorers, by First Nations traders, and by military expeditions. The HBC never could have dealt with BC without the Fraser opening the landscape for them.

Alexander MacKenzie and his men used the river to explore BC in 1793. They started their work in 1789, looking for a freshwater route to Cook Inlet – where Anchorage, Alaska, is today. That didn't quite happen. First, they went north along the Peace River, ended up in the Great Slave Lake, and found what's now the Mackenzie River, in the Yukon and Northwest Territories. It empties out in the Arctic Ocean, a long, long way from Cook Inlet.

In 1793, they gave it another shot, heading down the Fraser. The Fraser is kind of a tricky river: it's huge, wide, and flat in some places, but in others, it gets a little nasty. The town of Yale marks the southern boundary of the nastiest section. It was here that the river was blocked by Lady Franklin's Rock, a huge black boulder in the middle of the river, which kept steamers from going any farther north.

LADY FRANKLIN

Lady Franklin is a story in and of herself. Her husband was the great lost cause of the mid-1800s, a man who was once governor of Tasmania, and then got in way over his head as an Arctic explorer. In 1845, Franklin, at the command of two ships, went north looking for the Northwest Passage. By 1847, it was clear that he was deeply lost, and for the next 20 years – yes, 20 years – search parties went out looking for him from every conceivable angle. In doing so, they mapped out half the geography of the northeast Arctic, and the career of one of the greatest polar explorers ever, John Ross, was nearly destroyed when he gathered evidence from the Inuit that, in their last days, the remnants of the Franklin Expedition had resorted to cannibalism.

Lady Franklin herself never gave up. She was sure her husband – by this time in his 60s – was still out there, alive and well. She came to the Fraser thinking that Franklin and his men may have made it as far as the mouth of the Mackenzie, and then worked their way down. That didn't happen, but there's the rock here that bears her name, a monument to a lady who absolutely would not quit.

If the story intrigues you, one of the best books on the search for the Northwest Passage is Canadian Pierre Berton's *Arctic Grail*, a classic.

■ Yale

Yale is a pretty, small town today, but it was once a boomtown: because river traffic had to stop here, it was a transshipment point, the origin of the Cariboo Wagon Road, which led north and serviced the 1858 Cariboo gold rush.

Attractions

At one point, more than 30,000 people lived in Yale. Not anymore. Now there are fewer than 200. But it's worthwhile to pull off and take a look at the **Yale Museum**, 31179 Douglas St.,

☎ 604-863-2324, which has good displays of the gold rush history. In summer, the museum offers walking tours of the town.

Yale also has the oldest church in British Columbia that's still on its original foundation, **St. John the Divine Church**, on Highway 1. It dates back to about 1859, and it's worth a quick stop to see.

Adventures on Water

Rafting: The Fraser and the nearby Thompson rivers are the place to raft in British Columbia, and Yale is home to one of the best outfitters, **Fraser River Raft Expeditions**, ☎ 800-363-RAFT, www.fraserraft.com. You'll see their headquarters off the highway. (There's also a fantastic little B&B on the grounds, a restored 1864 house, with Fraser views and simple rooms from CAN $60; it's a very quiet and peaceful place to stay.)

They run single and multiple-day trips on both float rafts and power rafts – the power rafts are more stable, you're a lot less likely to go in the water, and you get to see more scenery because they can move more quickly through the slow spots. On the other hand, your wilderness experience will include the sound of a motor.

Their trip on the Thompson, which runs CAN $105, takes you from Spence's Bridge down to Lytton, and includes Class IV rapids – the full-day version of this trip takes in 25 separate sets.

If you're looking for an experience more like what the earliest travelers had, take their power raft trip on the Fraser, which includes shooting Hell's Gate (see below). It's also CAN $105. For longer trips, there are three days on the Ashcroft, ending at Yale, for CAN $390, or six days, from Soda Creek to Lillooet – amazing scenery all the way, rapids that will leave you screaming – for CAN $1,288. This is a good operation, run by good people. You'll be glad you went out with them.

Yale to Lytton

Leaving Yale, the road hugs the river and the mountains; there are seven tunnels along the way, as well as the tiny town of **Spuzzum** (population about 30) and **Alexandra Bridge Provincial Park**, 14 miles/22 km past Yale. The first bridge across the Fraser was built near here in 1863, as part of the Cariboo Wagon Road. That was replaced in the 1920s; the bridge that you drive across now is the third. From the park, there are lovely views and, if you're looking for a picnic spot by the river, look no more.

Another five miles/eight km up the road is **Hell's Gate Airtram**. The tram is open in summer from 9-6. ☎ 604-867-9277. Hell's Gate stopped more than its share of explorers over the years. Mackenzie's crew got through the first batch of rapids leading up to the gate, but then quit when they saw what was up ahead.

How did the Fraser River get its name? Because Simon Fraser wasn't going to let something like a suicidal stretch of river stop him. He got past the stretch that stopped Mackenzie and kept going, noting along the way that there were paths carved along the cliff faces, and that the First Nations men had developed techniques to stand in the river and spear fish, even in currents that should have knocked them down. And, as George Bowering writes in his marvelous *Bowering's B.C.*, Fraser noticed "many graves covered with small stones all over the place."

The group did not shoot Hell's Gate in their canoes. They weren't quite that dumb or determined. Leaving all their gear behind (except their guns, of course), they set out on the same paths the locals used, paths that, according to Fraser, "no human being should venture." Fraser bought new boats near what's now Yale, and finished his first descent of the river. It took modern rafting technology to make shooting Hell's Gate possible, and it's actually kind of sad that anybody with a hundred bucks or so can rip right through a passageway that stopped people for centuries.

Today, Hell's Gate is a tourist attraction. Ride the airtram across the canyon (CAN $10.50) and you get great views of the canyon (which is actually even less passable now than when Fraser was here, after a 1914 rockslide). Once you're across, the **Salmon House Restaurant** is a good place for lunch.

The small town of **Boston Bar**, north of the gate, is the put-in site for rafting trips through the canyon. This was one of the more important mining spots during the Cariboo rush, but not many people have stuck around since.

REO Rafting runs the **Nahatlatch River Resort**, ☎ 800-736-7238, www.reorafting.com, right outside Boston Bar Run. They run the Thompson for CAN $99, or do Class V on the Nahatlatch for CAN $150. They've also got multiple-day packages. Two nights of camping, plus rafting and rock climbing runs CAN $210; rafting and kayaking are CAN $270. Stay at the resort for CAN $60 in a tent cabin, CAN $45 in a teepee, or CAN $150 in a log cabin with a private bath. Rates are cheaper in the middle of the week.

There's not much else but scenery between Boston Bar and the town of Lytton, the biggest town between Hope and Cache Creek with nearly 400 residents. It's a pretty town, right at the junction of the Fraser and Thompson rivers, and has quite a few things to see around town.

■ Lytton

Attractions

 Start at the **Info Centre**, 400 Fraser St., ☎ 250-455-2523. It's open daily in summer, weekdays October through May. The main thing you'll need here is a map to the Stein Valley Nlaka'pamux Heritage Park (see below) and a map to the nearby Pit House. It's also well worthwhile to stop in the museum next door, where there are good displays of Cariboo history and some great historical photos of the region.

The **Pit House** is up the road to Lillooet; you'll pass a few horse ranches, then see what's really nothing more than a turnoff and a gate. Hike down the road (or drive, if the gate happens to be open), and you'll eventually come to a traditional pit house of the sort the First Nations people in this region used for thousands of years. More than half of the circular house was underground, with a log roof covering it. It was warm in winter, cool in summer and easy to defend – the perfect dwelling. Check at the Info Centre, as there are rules and regulations regarding access to the area.

To get to the **Stein Valley Nlaka'pamux Heritage Park** (call for open times, ☎ 250-455-2304), cross the Fraser via the reaction ferry (open daily, runs on demand from 6:30 am to 10:30 pm). From there, drive three miles/five km to the parking lot at the edge of the park. The main attractions here are some good hikes and views of the Stein River. If you like what you see, you can string together a multi-day hike from the parking lot all the way back to Tundra Lake, nearly 60 miles/100 km away. There are regular campsites along the way, and a couple of suspension bridges and cable car crossings – not for the person afraid of heights. This takes you through Lytton First Nations Reserve land, so show respect, and camp only in the designated sites.

Headed the other way, northeast from Lytton, you hit **Skihist Provincial Park** right outside of town. There's a campground and a day-use area. A hiking trail leaves from the campground and takes two or three hours for the whole thing. You get some great views, as well as an education on the health of the forest – this is the unlogged area that's closest to Vancouver, so there's a mix of new and old forest. Like so much other forest in BC, this is under attack by pine beetles, spruce beetles, Douglas-fir beetles, and an assortment of worms. None of this does happy things to the trees, but nobody's figured out a cure yet.

Adventures on Water

 Rafting: If you haven't booked your rafting trip from one of the outfitters mentioned earlier, try the **Kumsheen Rafting Resort**, ☎ 800-663-6667, www.kumsheen.com, in Lytton. Day-trips on the Thompson start at CAN $119; two days on the Thompson and Fraser runs CAN $319. They've got quite a few combo packages available, with multi-sport trips and stays at the lodge.

Another outfitter is **Hyak**, which has day-trips on the Thompson for CAN $109, or two-day trips for only CAN $249. They've been running the rivers here for more than 20 years. ☎ 800-663-RAFT, www.hyak.com.

Adventures on Foot

 If you're looking for something a little more sedate to do around Lytton, try **gold panning**. There's a three-mile/five-km section of the Fraser that's set off for public hand-panning. You probably won't get rich, but it was gold that brought people here in the first place, and you owe it to yourself to take a shot. For kids, stop by Caboose Park, which looks more like a model train than the real thing.

One of the beauties of Lytton is that it's where the Fraser meets the Thompson. It's worth some time simply to sit and watch these two mighty rivers blend – and we've seen bears right at the confluence, as well, so you never know what might walk in to your photos.

Where to Stay & Eat

 Lytton is a tiny town and a good choice for an overnight, especially if you're planning a raft trip. Food at the town's **Acacia Leaf Café** is actually quite good, and the **Totem Motel & Lodge**, 320 Fraser St., ☎ 250-455-2321, is a cottage-style place, nicely kept up, and off the highway. Doubles from CAN $55. A good place to call it a day.

Lytton to Cache Creek

It's an easy and scenic 50 miles/85 km from Lytton to Cache Creek. You'll go through the small town of **Spence's Bridge** – not too far from here was where they drove the final spike on Canada's Northern Pacific line.

Ashcroft, another 25 miles/40 km north and off a small side-road, is worth a look. In 1862, a couple of lawyers came here from England to start a ranch. They held races, and when they couldn't find any foxes for traditional fox hunts, started out after coyotes. Their house, Ashcroft Manor, is now a museum, with a teahouse and gift shop. It's a testament to what people can do when they have vision. Nearby is the **Ashcroft Museum** proper, 404 Brink Street, ☎ 250-453-9232, which has First Nations displays, as well as a good explanation of the importance of the Chinese to the region. This seems particularly appropriate now, since a

Above: O'Keefe Farm, Vernon. (© Vivien Lougheed)

Below: Waterwheel outside of Hope. (© Readicker-Henderson)

Above: Snowmobiling offers great challenges. (© Vivien Lougheed)

Below: Vermillion Pass in the Kootenays. (© Vivien Lougheed)

Fort Steele Historic Park. (© Vivien Lougheed)

Beautiful dogs provide the steam in dog-sled races. (© Vivien Lougheed)

Above: Along Highway 93 to Kootenay National Park. (© Vivien Lougheed)

Below: Fort Steele Historic Park. (© Vivien Lougheed)

Shopping at Radium Hot Springs. (© Vivien Lougheed)

Above: Pinnacles Provincial Park just outside of Quesnel. (© Vivien Lougheed)

Below: Hoodoos near Radium Hot Springs. (© Vivien Lougheed)

St. Andrew's Church, Barkerville. (© Vivien Lougheed)

newspaper headline in late 2003 stated that nearly half the people living in lower BC were born outside of Canada. Any walk around Vancouver leaves you wondering just how many people stayed in Hong Kong for the turnover. Maybe a half-dozen, at most. Summer hours are 10-6 every day.

From Ashcroft, take the road north out of town, and that will lead you out of the forest and the canyon to the town of Cache Creek.

■ Cache Creek

Cache Creek, despite the dry-looking land around (it's almost like the Badlands), is actually on a floodplain; most of the town nearly washed away during the floods of 1990. Overall, it's an unusual landscape, plopped right in the middle of all these mountains and lakes. The land hasn't quite recovered from the last time a volcano went off here, and the cactus and sagebrush make it look as if Clint Eastwood would be perfectly comfortable riding his horse around here.

That said, there's not a whole lot here, and since the faster Coquihalla opened, traffic through the town has dropped considerably.

Where to Stay

Because the town was once a major crossroads, it has a good assortment of places to stay; many people make it their first stop on the way to the Alaska Highway, as Cache Creek is a comfortable day's drive north of Seattle. The **Sandman** (☎ 250-457-6284) has doubles from CAN $75; the **Best Value Inn Desert Motel** (☎ 250-457-6226) has doubles at CAN $50, and the **Sage Hills Motel** (☎ 250-457-6451) has doubles from CAN $50.

There's camping at the **Brookside Campsite** (☎ 250-457-6633), a mile east of town. It offers full hookups for around CAN $15. Another good camping option, if you don't mind a few more minutes in the car, is **Hat Creek Ranch**, seven miles/11 km north of town.

HAIRY HISTORY AT HAT CREEK RANCH

Hat Creek Ranch was first opened as a roadhouse around the 1860s by a man named Donald McLean, a deeply unpopular man, who was later killed. Three of his sons took after dear old dad, and ended up hanged in 1881 for murder. You do have to give the family credit for recognizing a beautiful place to live, though.

Hat Creek Ranch today is a BC Heritage Trust Site, and the buildings you can tour (free, although they ask for donations) include the roadhouse, barns and a blacksmith shop. You can also book trail rides here. They have a very small campground, with sites for only CAN $10. ☎ 250-457-9722. Pitch your tent in the Old West for a night.

Cache Creek to Williams Lake

From Hat Creek Ranch, the road west is Highway 99, to Lillooet. If you're headed south towards Whistler, go this way. It's gorgeous, one of the prettiest roads in the province.

Northbound, you're on 97 headed towards a long series of what were once stops on the Cariboo Wagon Road. The road parallels the Bonaparte River and, especially now that most people take other roads, there's a remote feeling to this stretch. The tiny town of **Clinton** was the junction of a pair of roads to the goldfields, and today it's well known in BC as being the kind of town for people who just don't quite fit in elsewhere.

Just north of Clinton is the turnoff for **Big Bar Lake Provincial Park**, ☎ 250-398-4414. Come back here for the camping, or a chance to hike glacial eskers. There's also a pretty good chance of seeing marmots in the area.

Chasm Provincial Park is on the main highway, 14 miles/22 km north of Clinton. It's worth the stop here to see **Painted Chasm**, a slice in the volcanic landscape that has some pretty dramatic color to it. The volcanoes erupted as long as 25 million years ago; the chasm was carved out by glacial meltwaters at the end of the last Ice Age, 10-12,000 years ago.

The towns on this stretch of road have numbers as frequently as they have names. **70 Mile House** was 70 miles from the start of the wagon road in Lillooet. There's a roadhouse here you can tour, but not much else.

Still, this is ranching country, and that means they do things big here. **Gang Ranch** is west of the highway on Meadow Lake Road. It's about a 31-mile/50-km trip back to the ranch, which was once the largest cattle ranch on the continent; even today, when it is considerably smaller, it still covers more than a million acres. In addition to running cattle, the ranch also operates a small **B&B**, ☎ 250-459-7923. This is a good chance to spend the night and see what real cowboys with more land than some eastern states have to do to get through the day.

100 Mile House, the biggest stop between Cache Creek and Williams Lake, has about 7,000 residents. It's a center for all the ranches that surround the town, as well as for logging concerns. **Visitor info** is on the highway at the Chamber of Commerce building, ☎ 250-395-5353. It's easy to spot, since there's a pair of giant skis outside, in yet another one of those BC shots at having the world's biggest something: gold pan, skis, fishing pole, whatever. You really have to wonder who in the city councils thinks of these things. Still, they make for interesting stops and a good peek into the psyche of lesser-traveled regions in Canada.

Right behind the center is a small wetlands; the helpful people inside Visitor Info can tell you which birds you're likely to see – there's a display board as well – and direct you to a larger wetlands, about five miles/eight km away. Birders might come here for a picnic and perhaps some waterfowl to their life list.

There are great fishing lakes all around 100 Mile House: try your luck at Mahood Lake, Hathaway Lake, Horse Lake, Ruth Lake or Canim Lake. These are all excellent moose sites, as well.

The 100 Mile District Historical Society has been hard at work at the **108 Heritage Site**, where they've gathered buildings from around the district and put them up here, in one spot. If you missed Hat Creek, here's another chance to see what ranch life was like at the turn of the century. There's a ranch house, telegraph house and a barn that they say is one of the biggest log barns in all of Canada. The site is open from late May into September. ☎ 250-791-5288.

Lac la Hache bills itself as "the longest town in the Cariboo" – maybe they couldn't think of a giant *something* to put outside the town, so they hit on this instead. Or maybe they were just too busy looking at the beautiful lake to care. Fish the lake for trout, camp at **Lac la Hache Provincial Park** (☎ 250-389-4414), eight miles/13 km north of town. Just past the campground is **Cariboo Provincial Nature Park**, ☎ 250-398-4414, a walk-in-only park that has some easy trails that lead to beaver ponds and birding areas.

You can get a look at the lake with the **Shoreline Resort**, ☎ 250-396-7441, which has parasailing and Jet Ski rentals. Ten minutes in the air attached to a sail will run you CAN $40.

■ Williams Lake

Williams Lake started off as a big stopping point for miners headed to the goldfields. However, when a local refused to loan money to the builders of the Cariboo Road, they bypassed the town and it pretty much died. Today it's home to one of Canada's largest rodeos (July 1 – book well in advance or plan on staying far outside of town). For birders, there's excellent watching in the marshes around town. If you're planning to go to Barkerville or the Bowron Lakes, this is actually a much nicer, more scenic place to stay than Quesnel, where most people end up.

Attractions

The **Info Centre**, ☎ 250-392-5025, is at the south end of town, on the highway. They'll tell you the place to go in town is the **Museum of the Cariboo Chilcotin**, which includes the **BC Cowboy Hall of Fame**. It's at 113 4th Ave., ☎ 250-392-7404, open Monday-Saturday in summer, 10-4, CAN $2 admission. Inside, you will find out more about ranching and cowboys than you ever need to know. It's a lot of fun.

Adventures on Foot

Stop by **Red Shred's** on 1st Ave. This is information central for rock climbers, mountain bikers and other adrenaline junkies. It has all the gear you need, and ideas on where to use it. **Esler Lake** has good climbing routes already established if you're traveling with your own gear.

Adventures on Water

Boating: If you have a rodeo boat and know what to do with it, try the **Quesnel River**, between Likely and Quesnel forks. Pick up a map at Red Shred's and be prepared for Class IV rapids.

Fishing: Fishermen just need a copy of *Cariboo-Chilcotin Fishing Guide*, available at the info center. No matter what lake species you're after, this will point you to the right place.

The Rodeo

Of course, the big deal in town is the annual rodeo, and if you can get reservations – or don't mind driving in from a ways out of town – it's worth attending. There are more than CAN $100,000 worth of prizes, and rodeos daily, as well as tractor pulls, raft races and barn dances. Pretty much anything you can think of that might go with a rodeo is happening here. All you have to do is grab your hat, pick up a corn dog from one of the food vendors and dive into the action. Phone well in advance for tickets, ☎ 800-717-6336; find out more at www.williamslakestampede.com.

Where to Eat

Williams Lake has all the usual road food choices, but for something different, try **Laughing Loon Neighborhood Pub**, 1730 S. Broadway, which has a pleasant atmosphere and a very large menu. But when they say one of the dishes is hot, believe them. It took five Cokes to get through the very delicious medium-heat stirfry we tried.

Where to Stay

Z^z Our first choice for a place to stay is the **Drummond Lodge Motel**, overlooking the lake (☎ 250-392-5334). It has good rooms, friendly people and fantastic lake views. Get a room with a balcony and you're set for the night. There's also an RV park on the grounds. Rooms in the hotel start at CAN $75; RV sites run CAN $27.

Other good choices include the **Sandman**, 664 Oliver St., ☎ 250-392-6557, with doubles from CAN $85, and the **Overlander Hotel**, 1118 Lakeview Crescent, ☎ 250-392-3321, with doubles from CAN $77.

Campers can go to the **Williams Lake Stampede Campground**, 850 S. Mackenzie St., ☎ 250-398-6718, with full-service sites priced around CAN $18. If you're in a tent, go north of town to the **Wildwood Campsite**, ☎ 250-989-4711, eight miles/13 km outside of town, which has shaded tent sites for CAN $15.

The Road to Bella Coola

Feel like striking out for the middle of nowhere? The road to Bella Coola might be just what you're after. It's a two-day round trip – Bella Coola is 280 miles/456 km from Williams Lake – but there's been a lot of roadwork recently, and it won't be as rough as it was just a few years ago. The rewards are a chance to go through the Tweedsmuir Provincial Park, which is probably bigger than the county you live in back home, and some wild and remote territory that you'll be the only kid on your block to ever see. Not a whole lot of people head down this road; only about half of it is paved, and if the weather's been bad, you can end up very sorry that you gave it a shot. Before heading out, be sure to check with people at Williams Lake for the latest conditions.

> **WARNING:** *There are a lot of logging roads and dirt roads that lead off the main highway. Don't even think about going on them unless you've got 4WD and somebody knows where you're going. If you get stuck out here, you're a long, long way from help.*

At **Riske Creek**, just west of Williams Lake, you can do jet boat tours of the Chilcotin River with **Cariboo/Chilcotin Jetboat Adventures**, ☎ 877-RIV-TOUR, 250-659-5800. An hour through the canyon runs CAN $63 and, in summer, this includes a stop to watch the Chilcotin and Shushwap First Nations people dip-netting for salmon along the river, a technology that hasn't changed much for a couple of thousand years. A full-day trip runs CAN $135. They also have cultural tours for CAN $135 that include a boat ride, the salmon dipping and a visit to a traditional village. For a few bucks more, you can arrange overnight stays in a teepee, which wasn't quite what the people around here ever lived in, but it's fun anyway.

You can't be in a hurry on this road. Stop at the **Chilcotin Lakes** to fish, or camp overnight at **Ts'yl-os Provincial Park** (☎ 250-398-4414), which has two campgrounds on the shores of Chilko Lake. These are the traditional ranges of the first Nations Xeni Get'in. The mountain that gives the park its name is the guardian of the people (on your map it's probably shown as Mt Tatlow, almost 1,000 feet/ 3,000 meters high).

About 60 miles/100 km west of Williams Lake, you'll pass the small First Nations village of Anaham and, just past that, the almost as small community of Alexis Creek. You stand a good chance of getting gas here.

Leading off Alexis Creek is a road aimed north to the **Bull Canyon Provincial Recreation Area** and **Nazko Lakes Provincial Park**. It's only six miles/10 km or so to Bull Canyon, about the same to Nazko, a popular canoeing area. To get to the put-in, take Alexis Lakes Forest Road 28 miles/45 km to the Nazko Lake Canoe Route; from there, it's three miles/five km to the staging area at Deerpelt Lake. You can easily put together a multi-day canoe trip back here and not see another soul, but check road conditions at Alexis Creek before you leave.

The road to Bella Coola stretches through both the Chilcotin/Cariboo country (the Fraser River area) and the coastal area. In the upper reaches, the river opens out into lake after lake, giving you enough fishing choices to make your head explode: Puntzi Lake, Tatla Lake, Eagle Lake, One Eye Lake, Nimpo Lake.

Tatla Lake has a ranger station and marks the landscape change from interior to coast, as you leave ranching country and move into forest. Problem is, a lot of this forest has been attacked by the various beetles that have been hard at work in BC, and so the view ain't what it once was. Still, as you climb into the Coast Mountains, you'll get lovely views, both backwards and forwards. The Coasts are some of the most dramatic mountains in a province full of dramatic mountains. Just squint a little to see past the tree blight.

About 50 miles/80 km west of Tatla Lake is a historic marker commemorates how little interested the locals were in the coming of Europeans. In 1861, someone came up with the bright idea of building a road from Bute Inlet to Quesnel. He didn't check this with the local Tsilhquot'in first, though, and since they'd already had a few less-than-savory encounters – smallpox, rape, pillage, the usual – they wanted to bring all this incursion to an end. In 1864, the Tsilhquot'in started making raids on the road builders, killing 18 in all. But then they were lured into peace talks, where they were promptly arrested and executed. Really, they should have seen that coming.

The biggest town between Williams Lake and Bella Coola is **Anahim Lake**, with about 500 people, 195 miles/316 km west of Williams Lake. If you're looking for a hotel to break the drive, this is probably your best bet. Try **Anahim Lake Resort**, ☎ 250-742-3242, with doubles from CAN $65, or **Dew Duck Inn**, ☎ 250-742-3782, with doubles from CAN $85.

Anahim Lake is also the place to stock up if you're going to head into Tweedsmuir (see below).

Just past Anahim Lake, you start climbing into the Coast Mountains. After the peak, there's nothing but a long, downhill slide to the ocean, through really spectacular scenery. Once you're over the range, you're in the coastal rainforest, with plenty of views of glaciers – when the clouds lift. Look closely, you'll see a completely different ecosystem, with the poor coastal soil – only six inches deep or so most of the time – taking over from the richer inland landscape. On the coast you're in the Great Bear Rainforest, part of the same midlatitudes rainforest that stretches, more or less, from Seattle to Skagway. Plants here have to eat each other, and the only way to get nutrients is to wait for something else to die. A fallen log will provide a nursery for other plants, and it's not at all uncommon to see an older tree with literally hundreds of other plants growing on it.

The big attraction over the mountains is **Tweedsmuir Provincial Park**, nearly 1.8 million acres of protected land in the middle of nowhere.

Tweedsmuir Provincial Park is the second-largest provincial park in British Columbia; see page 242 for information on access to its northern reaches.

Here in the south section, you have the only road that goes into the park. The road is open year-round, of course, since it's the only way to Bella Coola, but all the park facilities close with the first snowfall. There is a gravel road that leads north from where Young Creek meets the Atnarko River. There's a campsite at the junction or, if you head north, you reach the Rainbow Range Trail and the tent-only sites along the Octopus Lake Trail. It's a five-mile/eight-km walk from the trailhead up to Rainbow, another 40 miles/16 km of fairly easy hiking out to Octopus Lake. Another easy – and shorter – hike option is the hour or so hike to the kettle ponds, from the Big Rock/Kettle Pond picnic area. Kettle ponds are created when glaciers drag really, really big rocks around. It's very interesting.

> **WARNING:** *In the park, obey all proper bear precautions. If you're carrying food, make sure it's in a bear-proof container.*

Overall, we've got to agree with the BC Parks brochure on Tweedsmuir that states: "Outdoor recreation opportunities are almost unlimited, but persons not prepared to be completely self-sufficient or who do not wish to employ a professional guide should not contemplate a visit."

In other words, know what you're doing, or don't get off the road. You'll get killer views from the highway, whether you lace up your hiking boots or not.

Not far past the Rainbow Range trailhead, westbound travelers start their final climb, up to 5,300 feet/1,600 meters; there's a 2,000-foot/600-meter dip, another 1,000-foot/300-meter climb, and then it's all downhill. But remember that when you're headed back. This stretch of road takes a little extra time.

The Young Creek Picnic Site offers a long (17-mile/28-km) hike back to the Hunlen Falls. But once you're there, you get to hang out at a single-drop waterfall that plunges 850 feet/260 meters.

Camp at Atnarko River, and be sure to stop in at the Tweedsmuir headquarters, just west of the campground. It's open only in summer, but if you're thinking about going into the park at all, don't do it until you talk to these people and find out the latest conditions. ☎ 250-398-4414.

There's more camping 16 km west of the headquarters at Fisheries Pool.

Westbound traffic exits the park 16 miles/26 km west of headquarters. Enjoy the killer views here of the Coast Mountains. If you've gotten this far, the hard part is over, with only about 30 miles/50 km more to Bella Coola.

At Burnt Ridge, you cross the Nuxalk-Carrier Grease Trail, which follows the original route Alexander Mackenzie used when he crossed BC in 1793. It takes 18 days or so to hike the entire 260-mile/420-km trail.

 If you're interested in this hike, get a copy of *In the Steps of Alexander Mackenzie*, by John Woodworth, and touch base with the Alexander Mackenzie Trail Association, Box 425, Stn A, Kelowna, BC, V1Y 7P1.

■ Bella Coola

Remember, you didn't come here for the town, you came here for the experience of getting to the town. Bella Coola has its attractions, but the real fun is just knowing that you got here, and you'll get to see all that really cool stuff again on the way out.

When Mackenzie got here, he was, to say the least, tired. He was also the first guy to cross North America, a little fact he doesn't get nearly enough credit for, just because Lewis and Clark had better PR.

He got here – you can't really get to where he stopped – and wrote, "Alexander Mackenzie, from Canada by land, the twenty-second of July, one thousand seven hundred and ninety-three." So the guy was no poet. His art was all in his ability to travel through anything.

Attractions

Visitor Info is in the **Bella Coola Valley Museum**, in the middle of town. ☎ 888-863-1181, 250-799-5767. It's open from June-September. The museum has stuff from the town's early Norwegian heritage, some HBC stuff, and First Nations history. CAN $2 admission.

Ask at the Info Centre for directions to the **Thorsen Creek Petroglyphs**, about six miles/10 km outside of town. There are more than a hundred petroglyphs here.

Adventure Outfitters

Everything you'll want to do in Bella Coola is outside Bella Coola, and you'll need to shell out for a charter. Try **White Surf Ocean Adventures**, ☎ 250-982-2520, for day trips to Mackenzie Rock, Larson Bay – where they've got some of the biggest cedar trees in the world – or fishing trips. **Avid Adventures**, ☎ 250-982-2642, guides fishing trips in the area.

Where to Eat

Most of the restaurants are in the hotels. **Bella Coola Valley Inn**, on Mackenzie St., ☎ 250-799-5361, has a good restaurant and rooms, some with kitchenettes. Doubles from CAN $75. If they're full, try the **Bella Coola Motel**, on Clayton St., ☎ 250-799-5323, with doubles from CAN $65.

Where to Stay

There are actually more places to stay back down the road at Hagensborg, 14 miles/23 km down the highway. **Bay Motor Hotel**, ☎ 250-982-2212, has a lounge, coffee shop and pub. Doubles from CAN $69. **Brockton Place**, ☎ 250-982-2298, on the highway about 10 miles/16 km east of Bella Coola, is another good choice. Doubles from CAN $79.

Campers can try **Camping Select**, in Hagensborg. It has good shaded spots. Sites start at CAN $15. ☎ 250-982-2448.

Transportation

If you don't want to drive out of town, you do have options. BC Ferries runs its Discovery Coast Passage from June to September. You'll need to plan ahead for this, especially if you want to load a car onto the ship. There are some scenic stops along the route, where you can get out and take a quick look around – Shearwater is an old cannery village, Ocean Falls an old pulp and paper mill boomtown. But the real goal of the trip is to get to Port Hardy, at the tip of Vancouver Island. From there, you can link with other BC Ferries that will get you to Prince Rupert and the Queen Charlottes on BC Ferries, or to Rupert and points north on the Alaska Marine Highway. Again, book early. BC Ferries: ☎ 250-386-3431, www.bcferries.com.

Williams Lake to Quesnel

Heading north on Hwy. 97 again, between Williams Lake and Quesnel (pronounced Kwe-nel), you pick up the Fraser River one more time. At the tiny Soda Creek Xats'ull First Nations site, 10 miles/33 km north of Williams Lake, a traditional pit house village offers salmon bakes and cultural programs in summer. Check with Xats'ull Information, ☎ 250-297-6323, to see what's going on. The Xats'ull have been here for a couple of thousand years, making use of the rich resources of the Fraser. Soda Creek was once a lot busier than it is now, as it's the southernmost point of navigability on the Upper Fraser River: from here, you can head north 400 miles or more on the river without hitting anything horrible, like Hell's Gate. The gold rushers came this far, then switched to the paddlewheelers that once roamed the river.

There is a one-car reaction ferry at **Marguerite Ferry**, 38 miles/62 km north of Williams Lake. There's not much reason for you to use it, but it's kind of nice to see. In winter, when the river freezes, there's a hand tram.

■ Quesnel

Quesnel – get ready for it – bills itself as "home of the world's largest gold pan." It's the last major city between southern BC and the Cariboo – the area you've been traveling through – and the nearly empty but incredibly scenic northern reaches of the territory, which begin at Prince George.

The fact that the best the town can come up with is a huge gold pan should tell you that the interest lies outside the town itself. There's nothing at all wrong with Quesnel: it's a pleasant little town with all the services you'll need, and it's a perfectly reasonable place to stop for a day. But except for the third week of July, when it hosts Billy Barker Days (see Barkerville, below), there's not a whole lot going on in the town itself.

Attractions

Quesnel Info Centre is a little tricky to find, but it's at 705 Carson Ave., ☎ 250-992-8716. Follow the signs off the main road, and be prepared for at least one U-turn. The staff at the center can fill you in on everything going on in the scenic town, including a one-hour walking tour of the downtown area that's an enjoyable way to get out of the car and stretch your legs. They also have a checklist of local birds: everything from the green-backed heron to the Calliope humming-bird. They even get white pelicans through here, just one of the 259 species on the checklist.

One reason Quesnel gets a lot of BC tourists is that it has a casino, the **Billy Barker Casino Hotel**, 308 McLean St., ☎ 250-992-5533, 888-992-4255. The hotel is actually quite pleasant, and if you're in a gambling mood, this casino is one of your only choices in the entire province.

Try striking it rich the old-fashioned way, **panning for gold** at the city-owned area at the confluence of the Quesnel and Fraser rivers. Outside of this spot, most of the land is somebody's gold claim, and it's best to steer clear.

Heritage Corner at Carson and Front streets has the remains of an old riverboat and the best bet for food in town, the **Heritage House Restaurant**, 102 Carson Ave., ☎ 250-992-2700, which is in an old HBC trading post. If road food is getting to you, **Karin's Deli & Health Foods**, 436 Reid, downtown, has salads, sandwiches and organic choices. Another good choice for fresh food is the Saturday **farmers' market**, held from May to October, at 97 and Kinchant, downtown. It's a must-see if you're going through town on the weekend.

Once a year, the entire town turns out for **Billy Barker Days**, which include one of the biggest rodeos in BC. It can be hard to find a place to stay during this frantic time. Downtown is closed off for an open-air crafts fair and the parade, and everybody in town turns out in period costume. For details and a schedule, ☎ 250-992-1234.

Where to Stay

The rest of the year, you won't have any trouble finding a place to stay. Quesnel's main drag is one hotel after another. As we mention above, Williams Lake is a bit more scenic, but if you need to stop in Quesnel, you'll still enjoy your evening.

There are the usual chains in town: **Sandman**, ☎ 250-747-3511, with doubles from CAN $85, is at 940 Chew Ave.; the **Travelodge**, ☎ 250-992-7071, has doubles from CAN $60. They're downtown at 524 Front St.

You can also get a room at the **Billy Barker Casino Hotel**, 308 McLean St., ☎ 250-992-5533. Doubles start at CAN $70, but there are some much nicer rooms, with Jacuzzis, for more.

Fraser Bridge Inn & RV Park, ☎ 250-992-5860, 100 Ewing Ave., is a good budget choice, with doubles from CAN $50.

■ Barkerville & the Bowron Lakes

Billy Barker was an old Cornish gold miner who struck it rich in 1862, triggering the Cariboo rush. Billy pulled out CAN $1,000 in gold during the first two days. Remember, for comparison, that the Klondike rush was started on about CAN $40 worth of gold and a lot of speculation.

Outside Quesnel is Barkerville, a fun old mining camp/tourist trap sort of place. It's a half-hour outside of town, but it's a pleasant drive, and there's a good chance of seeing moose on the way. Barkerville is a restored gold mining town with over 100 structures and people around to interpret the various exhibits. The town of Barkerville originally sprang up right after Billy hit it rich. For a while it was the largest city west of Chicago and north of San Francisco, with more than 10,000 people running around, but it was pretty much a ghost town by 1900. Today, it's a very, very popular destination, especially for people from BC. Take the kids out for a stagecoach ride, or just pretend there's a chance you're going to strike gold in the river – they'll let you take a shot at panning in the Cottonwood River. Some people find the town hokey, but most folks really enjoy it. Adult admission is CAN $8, and the park is open daily, 8-8. However, if you're heading out in winter, call first, ☎ 250-994-3332, to see what's going to be open once you get out there.

There are three **campgrounds** at Barkerville, plus a couple of hotels. **Kelly House**, ☎ 250-994-3328, offers rooms in a heritage house at CAN $95 for a double. **The St. George Saloon**, ☎ 250-994-0008, 888-246-7690, done up like it was still the gold rush and tattered miners are about to walk in

Adventures on Water

Canoeing: Near Barkerville is **Bowron Lake Provincial Park**. Head east on Highway 26; then turn onto the gravel road right by Barkerville. If you've got a canoe, this is the spot you've looked for all your life. The chain of lakes, rivers and streams here adds up to about 70 miles of the best paddling you'll ever find. You can pick up a map of the circuit in Quesnel. To be sure that everyone gets a primo experience on the lakes, reservations and registration are required, and no more than 50 people are allowed on the circuit in a day. For reservations, ☎ 250-992-3111. The circuit is open from May to October, and you have zero hope of just rolling in and getting on the lake. You'll have to plan this one ahead.

At the main parking lot, there's a visitor center where all travelers must register, and, before they go out on the lake, watch a video. If you're going to do the full circuit, there's a CAN $50 fee; just the west side runs CAN $25.

There's a campsite by the center, but out around the lake are cooking areas and cleared spaces for three to seven tents. There are a couple of cabins along the way, but they're for emergency use only.

You can fish for your dinner along the route, but you will need a fishing license. Remember that this is bear country, and take all appropriate cautions. All the camping areas have bear-proof food caches.

The beginning of the route is almost enough to make most people turn back: a 1½-mile/2½-km portage from the center to Kibbee Lake. After a very short paddle there, you get to portage again, this time 1.2 miles/two km to Isaac Lake. Once you're that far, though, you're made. Isaac Lake is 23 miles/38 km long. It is prone to high winds, but if you stick reasonably close to the shoreline, you should be okay.

At the south end of the lake is an entrance to the Isaac River. The current is pretty fast here, so be careful. You're on the river for another 1,300 feet/400 meters before you'll see the portage sign – don't miss it, because if you go any farther, you'll be in whitewater. It's a short portage to McLearly Lake, Indian Lake and Kibbee Lake. Part of this takes the Cariboo River, where there are a lot of sweepers and a strong current. On Lanezi Lake, stick to the north shore.

Get off the Cariboo at Unna Lake, unless you think you can successfully navigate your canoe over an 80-foot/24-meter waterfall. Take Unna Lake to Babcock Creek, and be sure to use the portage through the rapids. From there, it's pretty straightforward, as the lakes link up. The entire route is 71 miles/116.4 km, with about seven miles/11 km of portages.

Obviously, the quick description here is not going to be enough for those heading out by canoe. Get good maps, as well as current advice from the registration center. And be sure to plan early.

If you like the sound of this but you're not an experienced paddler, contact **Bowron Lake Canoe Kayak School**, ☎ 250-747-0228, www.bowron-school.com. For the newest paddlers, an intro course is only CAN $30; the most advanced runs CAN $150, and almost takes you to the level where you can teach classes yourself.

Adventures on Foot

Hiking: If you want to see some of the scenery without paddling, keep driving past the registration center to Kruger Lake Forest Service Road; turn west and keep going until the road dead-ends at Littlefield Creek. From here, you can pick up the Goat River Trail, part of Canada's National Hiking Trail. The other end of the trail is at Crescent Spur, maybe eight or nine days walk away, off the Yellowhead Highway.

Although the hike does run along a few forest service roads, it's mostly deep wilderness, and you've got to be ready to be alone out here. Take all bear precautions, and let the Forest Service know where you're going and when you expect to get out.

You can pick up a basic brochure on the hike, but it has nothing more than a paragraph or two on the 33-mile/54-km middle section of the trail. Get good topo maps in Quesnel, or check with the Fraser Headwaters Alliance, ☎ 250-968-4490, www.fraserheadwaters.org, for the latest on the trail.

Barkerville to Prince George

North of Quesnel, you're faced with pasture land, farms, tree-covered hills in the distance, and lots and lots of wildflowers in season. There's gas, food and lodging available at regular intervals, and some provincial parks good for camping, including Cottonwood River and Ten Mile Lake, before you roll north to Prince George, where southern BC meets its great North.

Prince George (page 235) offers a choice of directions. You can continue north to the Alaska Highway (page 285), or take the shortcut and head west along the Yellowhead Highway (page 233), connecting with the Cassiar Highway (page 268).

The Okanagan, Kootenays & Eastern BC

This section of the province may have some of the most diverse landscape anywhere in Canada: from the high mountains at the western edge of the Rockies, to the desert climates of the Okanagan, to the thick forests outside Kamloops. It's an area that sees few visitors – when they do come, they hurry on past, with other destinations in mind – but they're missing out.

The Okanagan Valley

The Okanagan extends, roughly, from Vernon, in the north, to Oliver, in the south. It's one of the most popular vacation destinations in the province for people who already live in the province: there are endless stretches of vacation homes and RV resorts, waterslides and stuff to take you away from home for a week or so.

But that's not why most everybody else goes to the Okanagan. The valley has two big attractions: fruit and wine. It's the perfect mobile picnic.

The Okanagan Valley is some of the best farmland in Canada. It's also as far north as anybody has ever been able to grow wine grapes. There are about 50 wineries in the valley and, although they're all pretty small – there are single properties in Napa that cover more land than everybody in the Okanagan combined – they produce roughly 18% of total wine sales in BC. And in what's truly unusual for a wine-growing region, roughly a quarter of the grapes are grown by First Nations people.

Because the Okanagan has so many microclimates – one estimate puts it at 28 quite distinct regions – the wines from the north end of the valley are entirely different from the ones at the south end, only 50 or 60 miles away.

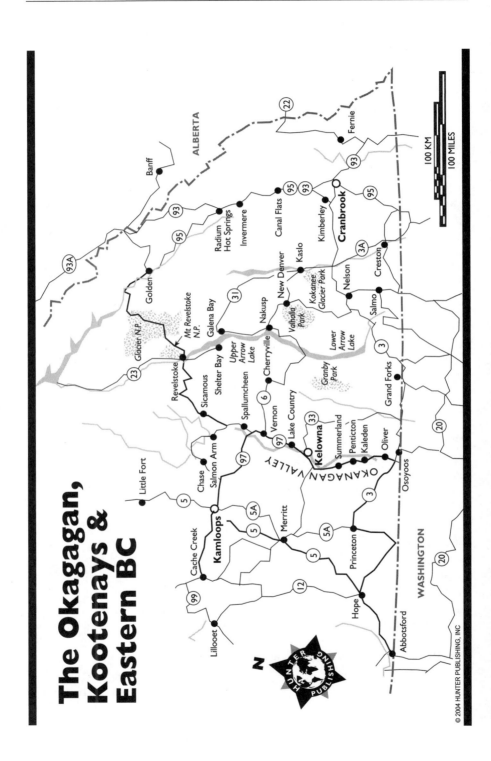

The Okagagan, Kootenays & Eastern BC

ICE WINE

The Okanagan also produces ice wine – well, not recently, but we'll get back to that. Ice wine was first developed in Germany, and it involves harvesting the grapes after a hard freeze. The wine that results (mostly whites, a few rare reds) is nothing like any other wine you've ever tasted. As one woman told us, sipping her glass of ice red, it was "like drinking liquid strawberries." It's good stuff. Expensive, but highly enjoyable.

The problem of late has been that the Okanagan Valley has been hit hard by global warming. It's always been one of the warmest spots in BC during the summer months, but now that's stretching into winter. There hasn't been a good, hard freeze for four or five years, so the ice wines are getting harder to find and, of course, more expensive. A few people are still making them, but we may be seeing the last of this marvelous local product.

Eastern BC

Growing wine in the Okanagan offers up a few other hazards that most vintners never have to face: marmots and bears like to get into the grapes, for instance. One winery has bobcats threatening the rabbits on the property. And another has a sea monster. Okay, lake monster.

Most of the wineries are turning out more or less the same varieties: a Pinot Noir, a Cabernet Franc, a Merlot, and maybe a Pinot Gris. But, thanks to the widely varied landscape, the tastes from one end of the valley the other change dramatically.

The Okanagan isn't like any other place in BC. Spend a day or two here.

■ Valley Basics

 The road through the Okanagan travels the shores of **Lake Okanagan**, first on one side, then on the other. The entire stretch of road, except where the mountains move in too close, is lined with town, a thin strip of settlement that extends the length of the valley.

This has caused a few problems. The Kelowna fires of 2003 – started, ironically, by a fireman who tossed his cigarette away while he was installing a satellite dish – caused massive evacuations and burned out the mountains behind town. You won't see the damage as you travel through the valley, but it was utterly devastating to the people who lived in the region. For more than a month, the sky was black, and when we were in Kelowna at the peak of the fires, the sky glowed red at night. Lots of houses were destroyed, and lots more were threatened.

Despite the heavy settlement, the Okanagan lives on agriculture. Every October, there's a wine festival – if you want to come, make your reservations well in advance, because every hotel room is jammed full. There is also an ice wine festival in January, and music festivals all summer.

You're not going to run out of things to do here.

We're going to describe the Okanagan from south to north, starting with Osoyoos, right on the edge of the valley. We're not going to give you every fruit stand along the way (they're everywhere in the valley). Stop when you see one that looks good and you won't be disappointed.

The Okanagan is organized; there are plenty of roadside signs leading you to the major sites, and every winery that offers tastings is easy to find, well signed and pretty much always open. In winter, check at the VQA shop in Penticton to see who's open but, come summer, just get to the valley and start looking.

Kelowna Airport serves the Okanagan Valley with **Air BC,** ☎ 250-542-3302, and **West Jet,** ☎ 800-538-5696. Flights to Vancouver and Edmonton are the most useful.

■ Osoyoos

Osoyoos is a junction town, where Highway 3, the main east-west road in the southern province, meets Highway 97. Highway 97 runs the length of the Okanagan and on to Sicamous, eventually meeting up with Highway 1, from Golden and Jasper in the east to Kamloops and Cache Creek to the west.

Osoyoos is a small town on the edge of **Osoyoos Lake**, one of the warmest lakes in Canada. Why? Because Osoyoos itself is the very northern tip of the Sonoran Desert – which goes all the way down to Mexico – and is itself one of the hottest spots in Canada. The thermometer has hit 42°C (109°F) a couple of times here.

Osoyoos Information is at the highway junction. ☎ 800-676-9667, 250-495-7142.

You should stop and take a look at Osoyoos simply to see the desert, which is kind of unusual up here. There are cactus, rattlesnakes and everything else you'd expect from a good desert, including encroaching development that's wiping the whole thing out. **The Desert Center**, just off Highway 97, ☎ 250-495-2470, has an interpretive display showing what the desert is all about. CAN $4.

Osoyoos has the only First Nations winery. Although First Nations peoples own a lot of the land in the valley, this is the only place where they're turning the stuff out themselves. **Nk'mip Cellars**, 1400 Rancher Creek Rd., ☎ 250-495-2985, shows how you can get wine from the desert.

For more on First Nations culture, hit the **Nk'mip Desert Heritage Center**, right by the winery. Admission is CAN $7, and they have good displays and programs to show you what life was like here for the last few thousand years.

The Osoyoos desert was once the habitat for burrowing owls – they're little things and, like the name says, they live underground. (Up the road a bit in Oliver, we'll get to Burrowing Owl Wineries.) Just north of Osoyoos there's a wildlife reserve, where there are some efforts to reintroduce the owl. Meanwhile, there's good birding along the riverbanks. Turn off the main highway at Road 22.

■ Oliver

The small town of Oliver bills itself as the wine capital of Canada. Maybe so. Maybe their old accolade as the cantaloupe capital of Canada didn't get them very far with tourists. Anyway, some of the best wineries are down on this end of the valley, and the valley itself is a lot more rustic and less frenetic than points farther north.

Oliver **Info Centre** is on 93rd St., just off 362 Ave., ☎ 250-498-6321.

Wineries

 There are several wineries in Oliver that make the visit to town worthwhile. At the north end of Osoyoos Lake, take Road 22 east. This brings you around twists and curves, a small area overlooking the river that has great birding, and to two of the best wineries in the Okanagan: Burrowing Owl and Black Hills.

Burrowing Owl is one of the very few wineries in the valley that charges for tastings. However, the two bucks you drop in their pot supports efforts to reintroduce the burrowing owl into its natural habitat, here at the south end of the Okanagan. The winery has only been around since 1993, but already it's one of the primo properties in BC. Try the Pinot noir or the Cabernet Sauvignon – these wines are rare in the valley. Bottle prices start at around CAN $30.

Time your visit to Burrowing Owl carefully, because they also have one of the best restaurants in the valley. The lunch menu includes such delicacies as Atlantic baby shrimp in a curry, for CAN $12.50; for dinner, try the sockeye salmon.

The winery is the impressive building to the east off Black Sage Road. You can't miss it. ☎ 877-498-0620.

HELP THE OWLS

If you just want to help the good work with the owls, get in touch with **The Burrowing Owl Conservation Society of BC**, 2165 Palmerston Ave., West Vancouver, BC V7V 2V7.

Our introduction to BC wine came about at the British Columbia Wine shop in Victoria. We asked an obviously knowledgeable customer what his favorite wine was and, without hesitation, he said, "Black Hills, Nota Bene." The clerk smiled, nodded and immediately refused to sell us a bottle. "It's the king of reds," she said. "I have to ration it, and even so, we run out almost right away."

Black Hills Winery, ☎ 250-498-0666, is just up the street from Burrowing Owl. It's not as fancy – Burrowing Owl, like most of the wineries in the valley, has a tasting area and a place to sit down; Black Hills has a warehouse. But if you want to try what's largely considered the prime wine in BC, head here. It's about a mile past Burrowing Owl, on the opposite side of the road. Buy a bottle and stash it for a few years.

You can get back onto the main highway by going straight along Black Sage Rd. to Orchard Grower's Lane (322 Ave.). Stay on this and, immediately after crossing the highway, head up the hill on Road 8 (326 Ave.) for Gehringer Brothers and Hester Creek. **Gehringer Brothers** (☎ 250-498-3537) is one of the few wineries still trying to make ice wine, although it hasn't worked out too well of late. They've got a back stock, though, and it's worth the stop. The friendly staff is very knowledgeable. How often do you get a chance to go to a winery that has "Watch for Marmot" signs on the road in?

Right across the road is **Hester Creek**, ☎ 250-498-4435. It's fascinating to see how two properties, next door to each other, make such different – and good – wines.

Go back down to the highway and turn south (right), to Road 11, where you'll hit **Iniskillin Winery**, ☎ 250-498-6663, another good property, with very reasonable prices. And, unlike so many of the other wines produced around here, you can drink it today, instead of having to cellar it.

THE GOLDEN MILE

This whole stretch of road is called the Golden Mile; it goes on for quite a bit more than a mile, though, and we're just hitting the highlights here. Keep an eye out by the roadside and you'll see signs taking you to dozens of small wineries.

Tinhorn Creek Winery is up Road 7. This is a must-stop, simply because not only do they have good wine, they have the best demonstration garden in the valley, showing how Okanagan vintners do their stuff. They face unusual hazards, including bears that come down from the hills to eat the grapes but, thanks to the sunshine days here, which are unusually high, it all works out. Tinhorn Creek consistently wins top awards for its Cabernet Franc.

In addition to the usual tasting room and the great demo garden, Tinhorn Creek has some good package deals. You can book a four-day/three-night package that includes lots of winery activities and a stay in one of their suites. It costs CAN $965 for two people – swankier suites are available. One night runs CAN $190, if available. The three-hour tour of the winery is well worth the time. ☎ 888-484-6467, www.tinhorn.com.

If you need to get back to Vancouver, from the small town of Kaleden, between Oliver and Penticton, you can jump on Route 3A, which leads to Highway 3. From the junction to Vancouver takes about four hours, depending on traffic. The road is very beautiful, as it follows the banks of the Similkameen River and goes through Manning Provincial Park before taking you to Hope and Highway 1. There are a lot of twists and turns, and plenty to gawk at.

■ Penticton

This is next town up the road, one of the bigger settlements in the valley. Most of the town's 30,000 residents make their living off some form of agriculture, be it growing, shipping or processing. Penticton is set right at the southern shore of the lake, and it makes a good base for exploring the rest of the valley.

The **Info Centre** is at 888 Westminster Ave., ☎ 250-493-4055. In the same building is the VQA shop, the best wine shop in the valley. They have bottles from more than 40 vintners, and these people know their stuff. Anybody considering a few days of winery touring should stop here.

Penticton is a highly cultured town, proud of its place in the valley and of its recreational opportunities. Their **Jazz Festival**, held in early September, draws people from around Canada, and acts from around the world. If jazz isn't your thing, show up in June for their official **Elvis Festival**. Who knows, maybe The King himself, thinner and gray, is lurking in the crowds.

Penticton Museum & Archives is at 785 Main St., ☎ 250-490-2451. It's one of the better ones you'll find in Eastern BC, with lots of displays on the lake as a trade center, the coming of the railway, and more.

The lake used to be a lot more convenient than the road, and there's a remnant of this with the **S.S. *Sicamous***, a sternwheeler moored near downtown. First launched in 1914, the ship ran until 1935. Now they're working at restoring it, bringing it back to its former glory. The work is

Eastern BC

ongoing, but you can tour the ship from April 1 through December 15. The ship was huge, more than 200 feet long, with three towering decks. When it was running, you could get a private stateroom for just $2.50; breakfast onboard was a buck. The sternwheeler is 24 feet wide, with 20 paddles that are each 20 feet long. Moored next to the *Sicamous* is the ***Naramata***, also built in 1914. We love this kind of attraction. Located at 1099 Lakeshore Dr. West, ☎ 250-492-0403. CAN $4.

You can access the **Kettle Valley Railway** from Penticton. This railway route that was several hundred miles long has mostly been turned over to walkways and bike paths. One of the historic bridges was heavily damaged in the 2003 fires, but there's still plenty of it out there. For guided trips on the trail, **Kettle Valley Trail Tours**, ☎ 250-496-5220, has a 12-mile/20-km bike tour for CAN $39. They run daily bike shuttles between Penticton and Chute Lake for CAN $23.

There is still a railway working part of the line. The **Kettle Valley Railway**, ☎ 877-494-8242, runs twice-daily trips in summer. You ride a train pulled by a 1924 Shay steam engine, and there's good hokey fun, like a staged hold-up. The basic run is 90 minutes and costs only CAN $16 for adults. A hold-up run, which also includes a BBQ, runs CAN $35. Those are held every other week or so in summer.

If you're in Penticton in winter, the place is still hopping. **Apex Mountain Resort**, ☎ 250-494-6400, southwest of town on Green Mountain Rd, has 2,000 vertical feet of runs just a half-hour outside town. Considering that a lot of the view from the mountain is desert, it's a little surprising that they have an annual average snowfall of 20 feet, but there it is. Lift prices are CAN $48/day for adults.

If the snow hasn't hit yet, go to the south edge of town, at Skaha Lake, where there's the Skaha Climbing Bluffs. Off South Main, turn on Crescent Hill; follow the dirt road to the parking lot. It has a granite face and plenty of overhang, providing a good workout. The **Crux Climbing Centre** in Kelowna can get you a site map (☎ 250-860-7325).

Where to Eat

 You won't go hungry in Penticton, but, with a few exceptions, you probably won't be dazzled, either. We suggest **Burrowing Owl Winery** (☎ 877-498-0620) in Oliver for lunch or dinner (see above). It has great views and great food.

BC's "restaurant of the year" in 2003 was **Theo's Restaurant**, 687 Main St., ☎ 250-492-4019. Greek specialties, perhaps best summed up in their Web address: www.eatsquid.com.

Okanagan Surf & Turf, 21 Lakeshore Dr., ☎ 250-493-8221, has lake views and is a good place for an evening out.

Where to Stay

 There's no shortage of choice in town. If you're rolling into town late at night, just head to **Lakeshore Drive**, which is lined with hotels.

The **Sandman** is right across the street from the Visitor Centre and VQA shop. It has very big rooms, with doubles from CAN $85. ☎ 250-493-7151.

If you want water views, try the **Waterfront Inn**, 3688 Parkview St., ☎ 250-492-8228, overlooking Skaha Lake. Doubles from CAN $65.

Closer to Okanagan Lake is **Rochester Resort**, 970 Lakeshore Dr., ☎ 250-493-1128; doubles with kitchenettes start at CAN $60. Nearby is the **Spanish Villa Resort**, 890 Lakeshore Dr., ☎ 250-492-2922. It has lake-view suites, with doubles starting at CAN $85. In the same neighborhood is the **Crown Motel**, 950 Lakeshore Dr., ☎ 250-492-4092. Doubles from CAN $70.

Transport

If you're not driving yourself, **Greyhound** comes in daily from points north and south. ☎ 250-493-4101.

If you want to fly into the Okanagan, you'll need to start in Kelowna, the next major town up the road. See above for details on service.

Leaving Penticton, Highway 97 goes along the east shore of Okanagan Lake. There's an alternate route, up the east side, on Naramata Rd., where there are a few more wineries around the small town of Naramata.

If you stay on 97, you run between small vacation towns, lots and lots of fruit stands, and more wineries. Sumac Ridge overlooks the lake just north of Summerland. Greata Ranch has maybe the best views of any winery in the Okanagan, overlooking the lake just south of Peachland. This is one of the newer estate wineries in the valley, and it's doing things right.

Just north of Peachland is the junction to Highway 97C, which will take you east to Merrit and the Coquihalla Highway. This is the quickest route back to Vancouver from the Okanagan Valley. The road between Peachland and Merrit is kind of interesting. It cuts across the absolute middle of nowhere, crossing high mountain passes through deep forest. There's a fence that goes the length of the road, though, because what the road really cuts through is animal migration territory. There are lots of underpasses under the road to try and steer the moose, deer and elk from harm. You get good scenery up to the Coquihalla.

AUTHOR NOTE: Check your gas tank before you get on the road, because there's nothing between the Okanagan and Merrit.

■ Kelowna

Kelowna is the biggest town in the valley, with nearly 150,000 people in the area. When you drive in on the highway, it looks huge and busy: you're stuck in traffic with shopping malls and hotels on either side of the road. But Kelowna is also cooler than Penticton, and vacation ground zero for much of the population of British Columbia. Water slides, miniature golf – all that fun kind of stuff that died out from the United States back in the early '70s.

The first permanent non-native settlement in BC was built here, in 1859, when Father Charles Pandosy set up his Immaculate Conception Mission. Up until then, the local First Nations people had been getting only traders and HBC forts; now it was time for the one-two punch of Christianity to come in and tell them that they'd had everything desperately wrong for thousands of years. And the HBC soldiers had been setting such a good example for so long....

With all that good clean living going on, it wasn't long at all before a town sprung up. Within a couple of decades of Father Pandosy's arrival, the region was bustling with sawmills, farms and fisheries. A lot of the valley's agriculture originally centered on tobacco, but that pretty much petered out in the early part of the 20th century.

Today, Kelowna makes it as one of the most popular vacation home areas in all of western Canada, as an agriculture and transshipment point, and serving the residents of the valley with everything they need from the big city without actually having to go to the big city. Get off the main highway in Kelowna and the place slows down considerably.

The **Kelowna Info Centre** is at 544 Harvey Ave. – don't worry, that's just another name for Highway 97. ☎ 800-663-4345, 250-862-3515.

Attractions

 See where it all began at the **Father Pandosy Mission**, on the corner of Benvoulin and Casorso roads. It's open daily in summer from 8 am; admission is CAN $2. There's a restored mission, chapel and schoolhouse.

There's a worthwhile self-guided walk through the town's **cultural district**. Park at Cawtson Ave., by the Lake City Casino. On Cawston is the **Art Ark**, three connected art and crafts galleries, as well as Turtle Island Gallery, which features First Nations art.

Keep heading away from the lake to the corner of Cawston and Ellis and look left for the **Old Cannery**, which actually started off as a cigar factory. When the tobacco industry collapsed, it didn't take long to figure out where the future was: fruit. And so the cannery was born.

On the same corner is the **Laurel Packinghouse**, first built in 1917, as part of the same bright idea that started the cannery. Inside now is the **BC Orchard Industry Museum**, which traces the agricultural history of the valley. It's open Tuesday through Saturday, all year, ☎ 250-763-0433. When you're done there, stop in at the VQA wine shop in the same building.

Follow Ellis to Queensway, and turn right for the **Kelowna Museum**, 479 Queensway, ☎ 250-763-2417. Not a bad local museum, it's got early transport, fossils and all the usual frontier days stuff. It's open Monday-Saturday, 10-5 in summer, Tuesday-Saturday, 10-5 the rest of the year.

Right behind the museum is the **Kasugai Gardens**, a sister-city deal between Kelowna and Kasugai, Japan. It's free, it's a good place to sit and relax for a few minutes. How Japanese it is, we'll leave up to you to decide.

Kelowna really is kind of like stepping back in time, with all those fun activities that disappeared when the United States got too jaded for its own good. We miss that stuff.

Drive a go-kart at **Westside Family Go-Kart**, 2101 Okd Okanagan Hwy., ☎ 250-768-6877; or play on the water slide at **Mariner's Reef**, just south of town on Highway 97, ☎ 250-768-7644; and, best of all, play a round of miniature golf at **Scandia Golf & Games**, 2898 Hwy. 97, ☎ 250-765-2355.

Finally, if you're feeling a little more modern and aggressive, hit **Safari Ridge Paintball**, ☎ 250-769-0239, and shoot the person who's been driving you nuts in the car for the past week. It's at the junction of Hwy. 97 and Horizon Drive.

The **Okanagan Valley Wine Trail** goes from Kelowna north to Vernon every Saturday evening from mid-July to mid-October. For CAN $79, you get the train ride, dinner and a theme car. For CAN $30, you get just the train ride. ☎ 250-712-9888.

Adventures on Water

Boating: Sparky's, at the Grand Okanagan Lakefront Resort, rents out small boats to get out onto the lake. ☎ 250-861-8001. If you want somebody else to do the work for you, take a ride on the **MV** *Fintry Queen*, at Bernard Ave., ☎ 250-763-2780, which does two-hour lake cruises for CAN $10.

OGOPOGO

Why do you want to get onto the water? Simple: to spot Ogopogo. You get two million bucks if you can prove it. Ogopogo is the Okanagan's answer to the Loch Ness Monster. It's the same kind of monster, a long loopy thing, living in the bottomless depths of the lake. Reports of this lake dweller vary. Supposedly, it's between 15 and 50 feet long, has a head like either a goat, horse or sheep, and it wriggles through the water like a worm. It has the same humps that Nessie does, with some reports of the humps hitting five feet above the surface of the water. Ogopogo ain't new: the First Nations people knew he was there, and they used to offer sacrifices to him to keep him away from their boats. Ogopogo sightings make the news from time to time – he's one of the usual megafauna that gets trotted out along with Nessie and Bigfoot – but definitive proof is still lacking. Snap the shot, claim the money. Or just put the camera back down and be glad that the world always will hold some mystery.

Wineries

 You can hit the wineries yourself. The one we think you can't miss here is **Gray Monk**. Turn west on Berry Road off the highway and follow the signs. The winery is right on the lakeshore, and it serves as an official Ogopogo watch station. If anybody is going to see the thing, they will probably do so from here.

This winery got started when a psychic decided it was a good place to grow grapes. He was right. Gray Monk is one of the premier wines in the Okanagan. There are daily tours and, of course, a very good wine shop.

If searching out the wineries is too much – or if you're worried about your driving after a full day of tasting – there are plenty of options with wine tours.

Accent Inns, right in downtown Kelowna, ☎ 800-663-0298, has accommodation/tour packages. You overnight in the splendid hotel – these people do budget hotels right – and then take a four-hour winery tour. Prices start at CAN $185 per room. Two-night packages start at CAN $392, and they include a CAN $100 voucher at the **Birch Grill**, one of the better local eateries. Good people, good operation.

Okanagan Wine Tours, ☎ 250-868-9463, has four-hour winery tours for CAN $47, or full-day tours for CAN $105.

Tasteful Tours, ☎ 250-769-1929, has a three-winery tour for CAN $30 and a four-winery tour for CAN $35.

Wildflower Trails and Wine Tours, ☎ 250-979-1211, has a combo tour for CAN $95. The morning is spent hiking to check out the valley, and the afternoon is a winery tour. The easy hike is a good way to see things you're otherwise going to miss in the valley.

 The serious wine-lover should pick up a copy of *British Columbia Wine Country*, by John Schreiner, the definitive book on vintners in the province. It's available at VQA shops and all bookstores around town. A lot of the wineries also sell copies.

Where to Eat

 Like most towns in the valley, Kelowna doesn't have anything fancy. **Bagel St. Café**, 526 Bernard St., is a good place for a quick bite. Nearby is the **Lunch Box**, 509 Bernard St., where you can get in and out of pretty much any meal for under CAN $10.

If you're looking to move upscale, **Yamas Taverna**, 1630 Ellis St., is regularly voted one of the best Greek restaurants in the Okanagan Valley. Entrees top out around CAN $15.

Christopher's Steak & Seafood Restaurant, 242 Lawrence Ave., serves top-quality food in a pleasant setting. Figure CAN $20 for entrées.

Where to Stay

 Drive into town from any direction and you'll see countless hotels. As you read these listings, remember that Harvey Avenue is Highway 97. You won't have any trouble finding a place to stay, except during the Wine Festival in early September, when you won't get a room without advance reservations.

We like the **Accent Inn**, 1140 Harvey Ave., ☎ 250-862-8888. This is one of five hotels in a family-run chain, and the family does it right. Doubles from CAN $99. See *Wineries*, above, for special packages.

There's a **Coast Resort**, 1171 Harvey Ave., ☎ 250-860-6060, and a **Sandman**, 2130 Harvey Ave., ☎ 250-860-6409, in town as well. Doubles run around CAN $100.

Alpine Lodge Motor Inn, 1652 Gordon Dr., right off the highway, ☎ 250-762-5444, has some suites with Jacuzzis, as well as some loft rooms. Doubles from CAN $95.

Chinook Motel, 1864 Gordon Dr., ☎ 250-763-3657, is a good, clean budget choice. Some rooms have kitchens. Doubles from CAN $60.

The Oasis Motor Inn, 1884 Gordon Dr., ☎ 250-763-5396, charges about 10 bucks more than the Chinook for its good rooms. They'll pick you up from the airport.

Camping

There aren't a lot of options for campers. **Bear Creek Provincial Park**, ☎ 604-689-9025, six miles/10 km from downtown off Hwy. 97, is beautiful, way back in the trees, and pretty much always full. If you miss out, head another 14 miles/23 km back on the same road to **Fintry Provincial Park**, ☎ 604-689-9025, which gets a little less traffic just because it's farther out.

In town, there are some private campgrounds, but they're pricey and kind of sterile. You'll see their signs from the road, but they're more for long-term RV stops than for travelers passing through.

Transportation

Kelowna Airport serves the Okanagan Valley with **Air BC**, ☎ 250-542-3302, and **West Jet**, ☎ 800-538-5696. Flights to Vancouver and Edmonton are the most useful.

Greyhound serves all the Okanagan Valley. In Kelowna, the station is at 2366 Leckie Rd., ☎ 250-860-3835.

South of Kelowna, at Peachland, you can pick up Highway 97C, which will lead you to the Coquihalla and on to Vancouver. If you're looking to go the other direction, Highway 33 leads from Kelowna west and south until it hits Highway 3, just above the Canada/US border. From here, it's 30 miles/50 km to Osoyoos, or you can head west to Creston and on to Cranbrook to get into the Kootenays and the southern end of the Rocky Mountain parks.

■ Vernon

It's about a half-hour drive along the shores of the lake from Kelowna to Vernon, at the northern end of the valley. From here, you can continue up Highway 97A to Enderby and Salmon Arm or Sicamous, which gets you to Revelstoke and Jasper, or you can head west on Highway 97B to Kamloops, the biggest crossroads in central British Columbia.

Vernon was a cattle ranching area that got taken over by orchards. It's cooler and wetter than points south, although it has been hit hard by the recent warm winters.

Attractions

Vernon Info Centre is on the highway at the north edge of town, ☎ 250-542-1415.

There are some good attractions in this town that most people overlook. The **O'Keefe Ranch** is eight miles/13 km north of town, on the road to Kamloops. Stop in to see how good the life of a cattle baron was by touring the O'Keefe Mansion. You can also check out the church, and see what the other end of the economic scale was like by going in the Chinese bunkhouse. The Chinese were a major force in the early settlement of British Columbia. The ranch is open in summer from 9-5, as late as 7 pm in July and August. CAN $6.50.

Closer to town, there are two places that we think you should visit: Planet Bee and Bella Vista Vineyard.

Planet Bee, 5011 Bella Vista Rd., ☎ 250-542-8088, www.planetbee.com, is an apiary with "western Canada's largest outdoor honeybee observatory." Killer bees, which have taken over most of the southern United States, have not yet made it to Canada – probably the cold will keep them out. There are two species of mites, though, that are devastating the honeybee population. Considering bees are about all that keep us alive on this planet – no bees, no pollination, no food – anybody trying to save them is aces in our book. In summer, you can take apiary tours – this is a really, really popular school field trip. The shop is open year-round, and you can taste from their sample bar. We bought a bunch of their leatherwood honey. It didn't last long. They also have other bee products, including royal jelly healing items and beeswax candles. We never go to the Okanagan without stopping here for a honey fix.

If you look up the hill and to the right from Planet Bee, you'll see **Bella Vista Vineyards**, 3111 Agnew Rd., ☎ 250-558-0770, the northernmost vineyard in the Okanagan. Don't miss it. Most of the vineyards are selling sizzle as much as wine: they have that European flavor, trying to draw you in. Bella Vista is something a little different and much more laid back. It has only two varieties – they say, "all you need is a red and a white" – and is the only organic winery in the region. A fish pond provides water and fertilizer to the fields, while sheep keep the weeds down and fertilize things a bit more. Random rabbits that make the winery home provide dinner for local bobcats. A bottle of the very nice Lady in Red will run you less than CAN $20. A good place.

Highway 97 to Kamloops

Two roads lead north out of Vernon: 97A takes you to Revelstoke, Kicking Horse, Glacier National Park and on to the Rockies. Highway 97 takes you to Kamloops, Cache Creek and points in northwest BC. There's also 97B, but it's nothing more than a feeder line between 97 and 97A. Take 97 and you hit Highway 1 at the tiny town of Monte Carlo; take 97B and you hit 1 at Sicamous.

Highway 97B is a good road through forested areas, small farms, streams and such. It's heavily traveled by logging trucks, so don't think about hurrying. There's no real reason to stop along the way, except just east of

O'Keefe Ranch (see *Vernon* section) where there's a bird sanctuary at Swan Lake. It has good waterbird habitat.

The junction with Highway 1 comes at the tiny town of Monte Creek, which is a pretty little place, famous for a stupid moment in history when the "gentleman bandit" Bill Miner held up a Canadian Pacific Railway train near here, in 1906. Problem was, he and his gang grabbed the wrong car. He made CAN $15 on the heist (according to one Kamloops brochure, "a few dollars and a packet of kidney pills" – love that kind of detail), probably not enough to stable his horse. They did make a movie about him, though, *The Grey Fox*, which made only slightly more at the box office than the original robbery netted.

The final stretch of road to Kamloops follows the Thompson River through a wide, pretty valley that has seen a lot of industrial action.

■ Kamloops

Spend enough time in the province, and sooner or later you're going to end up in Kamloops, the most important crossroads in this part of BC. It's a nice town, an easy place to pass a day or two. There's some good hiking, some birding, a couple of historical attractions. Also, if you've been in smaller towns for a while, Kamloops has all the conveniences of the big city, including fast food and bookstores.

Kamloops started early in the 1800s as a fur trading center. It was an important stopping point during the gold rushes of the 1860s, and when the railway came through in 1886, the town's future was solid. There was even a movement to have the town made the capital of BC.

Today, Kamloops lives as a shipping and service center for everything around it. There are some huge mines near town, and a lot of logging goes on in places you're not likely to see – you will see the trucks full of logs moving through, though. This is also prime ranching country.

Kamloops Info Centre is off exit 398. Open daily in July and August, weekdays the rest of the year. ☎ 800-662-1994.

Attractions

There are three main attractions in the town itself: the train, the boat and the First Nations center.

The boat is the **MV *Wanda Sue***, an 85-foot/26-meter sternwheeler. She makes two-hour trips on the Thompson River and, along the way, a narrator fills you in on local history. CAN $13.50. 1140 River St., ☎ 250-374-7447.

The train is the ***Spirit of Kamloops***, at the Kamloops Heritage Railway, 510 Lorne St., ☎ 250-374-2141. The steam locomotive was built in 1912 and it now pulls two cars: an old coach and a hayrack car that's been converted for passengers. Trains run on Friday, Saturday and Sunday at 10 and 11:45 am. The fare is CAN $13.50. You can buy a CAN $25 combo ticket that gets you the train, the paddlewheeler and a stagecoach ride. Purchase it at any of the three attractions.

Secwepemc Heritage Park and Museum is at 355 Yellowhead Highway, on the banks of the Thompson River, only a few minutes from downtown. This is the headquarters of the Secwepemc Band. In addition to a school and an arena on the grounds, there's a museum and what they call a "living laboratory" that features the traditional Secwepemc lifestyle.

You can tour the very good museum and then take a look at the archeological site, a winter village that was used 1,200-4,000 years ago. There's another, reconstructed winter village that shows changes in how the people lived, and what they did. This is one of the better attractions of this type. Open Monday-Friday, 8:30-4, CAN $6. ☎ 250-828-9801.

If you're just looking for a place to kick back in town, head down to the banks of the Thompson, where there is good birding. There are lots of parks, as well as places to hang out along the riverbanks.

Just outside of town is the **Lac du Bois Grasslands**: take Highway 5 to Halston, turn left, then follow the signs. This is one of the largest grasslands in BC, and it's completely protected, although there are a lot of people using it for hiking, fishing and more. It's worth coming out here to see what this area – in fact, pretty much everything from here to Texas – looked like, once upon a time.

Adventures on Foot

 Hiking: Mt. Dufferin, just outside town, has a lot of hikes and also good mountain bike trails. If you're looking for a hike with no risk of getting run over by logging trucks, try the Lac le Jeune Circuit Trail, which runs from Lac le Jeune Provincial Park up to Ross Moore Lake. The whole trail is about 15 miles/25 km long, but part of it can be done as a half-day out-and-back excursion.

Rockhounding: Kamloops has some good geology around, perfect for rockhounding. At **Deadman River**, just up Deadman Road off Highway 1, there's a good chance to find agate and petrified wood; at **Little Fort**, up Highway 5 by the Thompson Ferry crossing, there are fossils; **Hat Creek** has amber deposits. **John Ratcliffe**, ☎ 250-554-2401, leads geology and fossil tours, with lots of regional history thrown in.

Adventures on Snow

 Skiing: Kamloops is a convenient base to the local ski resorts. Sun Peaks is less than an hour away, Harper Mountain even closer. **Logan Lake** has 22 miles/36 km of cross-country routes.

At **Sun Peaks**, ☎ 250-578-7222, there's a vertical rise of almost 3,000 feet/900 meters. In summer, the mountain is turned over to bikers. An all-day lift pass for you and your bike is only CAN $26; there are rental places on site, too, if you don't have the right kind of gear. In winter, lift tickets run about CAN $50/day.

Harper Mountain is a lot smaller, the kind of place you take your kids to learn to ski. Lift tickets are only CAN $28. ☎ 250-372-2119.

Where to Eat

Don't expect a whole lot. There's pretty much every fast food company known in Kamloops, but not a lot else.

Try **The Old Steak & Fish House**, 172 Battle St., for surf and turf, with organic salads. **The Amsterdam**, 369 Victoria St., ☎ 250-377-8885, offers up original-style Dutch pancakes. **D'Agostino**, 258 Victoria St., ☎ 250-372-1111, has good, cheap lunches, with tasty pasta dishes that get you out for under CAN $10.

Where to Stay

Because it's a crossroads, you won't have any trouble finding a place to stay in Kamloops. The **Accent Inn**, 1325 Columbia St., ☎ 250-374-8877, is the place of choice. It has good, clean rooms that show attention to detail, with doubles from CAN $89. Best of all, it's next door to a miniature golf course. The world needs more of these well-placed inns.

Other Canadian chains in town are **Coast**, 339 St. Paul St. downtown, ☎ 250-372-5201, with doubles from CAN $175; and the **Sandman**, 550 Columbia St., ☎ 250-374-1218, with doubles from CAN $75.

The Alpine Motel, 1393 Hugh Allan Dr., ☎ 250-374-0034, has nice views and some rooms with fireplaces and kitchens. From CAN $70.

The Grandview Motel, 463 Grandview Terrace, ☎ 250-372-1312, has a heated pool and some rooms with kitchenettes. Doubles from CAN $75.

Camping

The best place is **Paul Lake Provincial Park**, ☎ 250-831-3000, about 12 miles/20 km out of town off Hwy. 5. It offers beautiful sites and very basic facilities.

Transportation

If you don't want to drive to Kamloops, there are plenty of other options. **VIA Rail** stops here three times a week on its run between Vancouver and Jasper; ☎ 800-561-8630.

Greyhound can get you here from almost anywhere in the province; ☎ 800-661-8747.

At the airport, book flights with **Air BC**, ☎ 888-247-2262, which connects to Vancouver, the Okanagan and beyond.

If you're driving, from Kamloops you can head south on the Coquihalla past Merrit and down to Hope and the quick route to Vancouver. Or you can go east on Highway 1 to Cache Creek – a pretty drive, following the Thompson River.

If you want to move north, Highway 5 takes you through pretty much the middle of nowhere, past the tiny towns of Little Fort, Blackpool and Vavenby before skirting **Wells Gray Provincial Park**. This park covers nearly a million acres, and it's almost roadless. The Park Info office is in Clearwater, on Highway 5, ☎ 250-587-6150. From here, you can also get to a couple of campsites, including Clearwater Falls Creek and Clearwater Lake. But that's about it for roads into the park. If you want to get in deeper, get your topo map at the park office. Practice all bear precautions on the park's trails. **Wells Gray Chalets Wilderness Adventures**, ☎ 250-587-6444, leads hut-to-hut hikes in the park in summer, and skiing trips in winter. They also have instructional trips and avalanche courses.

From the park, Highway 5 crosses the Cariboo Mountains and meets up with the Yellowhead Highway at Valemount, right outside Jasper National Park. Highway 5A avoids the first part of the Coquihalla (although not the toll booth). There's not much reason for going on this, unless you're looking for backcountry scenery.

The other reason to go on Highway 5A is to get on the top end of what might be the longest canoe route in North America. From Valemont, you can paddle Kinbasket Lake all the way down to the dam at Mica Creek – about 60 miles/100 km. Once you've portaged the dam, there's another 60 miles/100 km of gentle paddling on the very long, very narrow Lake Revelstoke, which ends at Revelstoke Dam, just above town. If you still want to be in the water from there, put in again on the south side of Highway 1 and paddle all the way down almost to the city limits of Castlegar. There are a few towns – Revelstoke, Nakusp, Burton – along the way to replenish supplies, but mostly you'll have the place to yourself. It's not rough water – although you need to know how to handle weather – so as long as you've got the muscles and the fortitude, anybody can take it on.

A few more things in Valemount: **Wildfoot Tours**, ☎ 250-566-4007, leads quick birdwatching tours for only CAN $15. These give a preview of what you're going to see while on the water.

If you don't feel comfortable hitting the water by yourself, **Wildways Safaris**, ☎ 250-566-0098, has daily raft trips on the Fraser. **Scenic Moun-**

tain Tours, ☎ 250-566-4650, has guided canoe trips on the Fraser for $52, or they'll rent you a canoe for $30/day.

The other way out of Kamloops is east on Highway 1. There's a junction at Monte Creek, which offers Hwy. 97 south to the Okanagan (see above), or you can stay on Hwy. 1 through the Salmon Arm and Sicamous until you hit Revelstoke, Glacier National Park and Golden, before moving into Yoho National Park and Banff.

■ Revelstoke

Envy the ski bum, the guy who figures out a way to make a place like Revelstoke home. Maybe he lives in a lousy apartment, but everything outside the door is simply amazing.

Revelstoke is a small town of fewer than 10,000 people, right on Highway 1. The town is smack dab between Revelstoke and Glacier national parks. What are you in the mood for? It's here.

In that great Canadian tradition of making something large and useless to bring attention to yourself, Revelstoke claims it has the world's biggest sculptured grizzly bears. Okay. There aren't many grizzlies in the area, although blacks are common. On our last trip through, we saw a young black thinking about crossing the road and found ourselves yelling out the window, "No, Bear!" just to try and discourage him from getting smashed by traffic.

Revelstoke Visitor Info in summer is at the junction of Highways 1 and 23. In winter, it's downtown at 204 Campbell Ave. Learn from our experience here: if you're in an RV, you ain't gonna get anywhere near the downtown office. ☎ 250-837-5345.

Attractions

 There's only one real attraction in town, the **Revelstoke Railway Museum**, 719 Track Ave., ☎ 250-837-6060. Open daily in summer, call before you come in winter. Revelstoke has always been a town that lived on the railway, and this is one of the better railway museums in BC. It has a steam engine, and offers a chance to see how the upper crust traveled in a luxury car. CAN $5 admission.

If you're really curious, there's also a **piano museum** in Revelstoke, at 117 Campbell Ave., ☎ 250-837-6554. Call ahead for hours.

Adventures on Foot

 Hiking: You didn't come to Revelstoke to be inside. You came here because it's got hotels and campgrounds, both of which are in very short supply in Glacier Park (see below), or you came here to get into **Mt. Revelstoke National Park**.

Drive east of town to the Meadows in the Sky Parkway. This is a short road – only 15 miles/25 km – but what it lacks in length, it more than makes up for in scenery. Climb through the switchbacks up through a subalpine forest to the high mountain meadows beyond. Park at Balsam Lake, where you can pick up a free shuttle to Heather Lake (shuttle hours are 10-4 daily in summer). From there, you can climb the final stretch – it takes a half-hour or so – to the peak for the best views. There are other trails at the top, including the **Giant Cedars Trail**, a short boardwalk trip that goes by 800-year-old trees, and the **Skunk Cabbage Trail**, which is short and offers plenty of signs to fill you in on the flora around you.

There aren't a lot of trails in Revelstoke: this is real wilderness. The five-mile/eight km **Lindmark Trail** leaves you gasping as you climb nearly 3,200 feet/1,000 meters from near the park gate up to Balsam Lake. It's going to take you a while.

Much of the park is closed due to lingering snow – the road may not open until well into June. Check with the park office in Revelstoke, 313 3rd, ☎ 250-837-7500, for latest conditions and trail updates.

Selkirk Mountain Experience, ☎ 250-837-2381, www.selkirkexperience.com, leads guided hikes into the **Selkirk Mountains**, including hikes to the Durrand Glacier. Week-long trips, including the helicopter ride to the glacier, are CAN $1,340. Three-night trips are only CAN $695. They also have easier, shorter hikes and can get you out for some glacier skiing.

Adventures on Wheels

Biking: You can let your wheels do the work for you, biking down the Parkway. **Summit Cycle Tours**, ☎ 250-837-3734, drives you up, shows you around, then points you downhill. CAN $69. Understand what overgripping the front brake can do to you.

Adventures on Water

Canoeing: As mentioned above, Revelstoke is a midpoint on the huge **Revelstoke Lake/Arrow Lake canoe route** – more than 122 miles/200 km of gentle paddling. The only thing that limits you is your ambition and your rotator cuffs. It's a 31-mile/50-km paddle from Revelstoke south to Shelter Bay, where you can have somebody pick you up, if you don't want to try the entire route.

Adventures on Snow

Skiing: Revelstoke is a ski bum kind of town. Kicking Horse, near Golden, is more famous, but you're not going to suffer here. Powder Springs, over on Mt. McKenzie, has a small vertical rise and trails for all levels, and the play area is expanding. It has 2,000 feet/

610 meters of vertical powder and, if you know what you're doing, you can arrange heli-skiing trips here. Reach the resort at ☎ 250-837-5151. They'll do snow-cat trips as well, so the total skiiable area extends to upwards of 13,200 feet/4,000 vertical meters. Check for lodging/ski packages.

> **AUTHOR TIP:** When you're done climbing, hiking or biking, head to **Albert Canyon**, 22 miles/35 km east of Revelstoke on Highway 1, where there's a natural mineral pool and a restored ghost town. This is the kind of hokey tourist trap that is absolutely irresistible.

Where to Eat

 Just hit **MacKenzie Ave.**, walk along and see what catches your eye. It's where everybody goes to eat.

Woolsey Creek Café, 212 Mackenzie Ave., has breakfasts and lunches for under CAN $10. One of the better spots in town, usually jammed with locals.

For pizza, try **Claudios**, 204 MacKenzie Ave., where you and a friend can get out for under CAN $20.

If you want to combine food with toy shopping, try **Bertz Outdoor Equipment and Café**, 217 MacKenzie Ave.

Where to Stay

You should be able to turn up any time of year and find a place to stay. **Canyon Motor Inn**, 1911 Fraser Ave., ☎ 250-837-5221, has decent rooms, some with balconies. Doubles from CAN $79. **Columbia Motel**, 301 Wright St., ☎ 250-837-2191, is another good, basic choice. Doubles from CAN $45.

Move a little upscale with the **Glacier House Resort**, 679 Westsyde Rd., ☎ 250-837-9594. They have a spa, killer mountain views and rooms with fireplaces. There's also an indoor pool. Doubles are a bargain, starting at CAN $75.

Regent Inn, 108 Victoria Rd., ☎ 250-837-2107, is not a bad place to pamper yourself. It offers Jacuzzi suites, a sauna and more. Doubles from CAN $109.

If you went out to the hot springs and liked what you found, **Canyon Hot Springs Resort**, ☎ 250-837-2420, 22 miles/35 km from town, has tent sites, log cabins and that great 1950s feel. Oh, and the hot springs. Doubles from CAN $95.

Camping

You thought Smokey Bear was only in the US? Wrong, wrong. **Smokey Bear Campground** is three miles/five km west of Revelstoke. It has full-service sites, fire pits and a good location in the woods. Smokey would approve. ☎ 250-837-9573.

There's a **Good Sampark** on Nixon Rd, just off Highway 23. It has all the services and everything you expect from Good Sam. ☎ 250-837-3385.

Williamson Lake Campground is just out of town on Airport Way. It has good lake views and nice sites. ☎ 888-676-2267.

If you're looking to get a little more remote, there are several campgrounds along the road to **Shelter Bay**, including some nice provincial park sites, up to BC's usual standards.

Transport

VIA Rail stops here on its run between Vancouver and Jasper; ☎ 800-561-8630.

Greyhound can get you here from almost anywhere in the province; ☎ 800-661-8747.

At the airport, book flights with **Air BC**, ☎ 888-247-2262, which connects to Vancouver, the Okanagan and beyond.

South from Revelstoke: The Arrow Lakes

Before we take you east to Glacier National Park, we need to go south for a couple of pages. Drive south from Revelstoke to Shelter Bay; there, you can catch a free ferry over to Galena Bay.

From Galena Bay south, past the pretty town of Kaksup, you're in the Arrow Lakes, a kind of hidden treasure in the middle of BC. They call this the valley of hot springs, but if soaking isn't quite your thing, and you want to go for a paddle or a hike, come here. Not many people make the effort to visit, which is a good thing.

There's not much in Galena Bay except for the ferry. The crossing takes about 30 minutes, and the ship, which is free, leaves every hour.

Head south along the lakeshore to the main city in the Arrow Lakes region, Nakusp. "Main city" isn't saying much here: it's a town with fewer than 2,000 people. But look one way, you've got the lake; look the other, and there are the Selkirk Mountains.

The main stop here is the **Nakusp Hot Springs**, just outside of town on Highway 23. Admission of CAN $6 gets you into a large, circular pool – the two halves are different temperatures. There are camping sites and a few short hiking trails, but mostly you should treat it as a place to soak road-weary muscles.

Also in the area is the **Halcyon Hot Springs**, 18 miles/30 km north of town on Highway 3. This one is new, and it has a bistro complete with natural foods, camp sites and hiking trails. It's not as well known as Nakusp, so is perhaps a little less crowded.

From Nakusp, you have two road choices. South takes you farther along the lake – take this for remote paddles, where you can put in and not see anybody else on the water. The road ends at the very small town of **Fauquier**, where you can catch a free ferry across the lake and get onto Highway 6, which will lead you to Vernon and the Okanagan Valley.

Alternatively, from Nakusp, head east on 31A, to **New Denver**. There's not much going on there. Its 500 residents just found a beautiful spot in the middle of nowhere. The area had a lot of rich mines – zinc, lead and silver – but that's pretty much petered out now. Still, if the mining history interests you, stop at **Silvery Slocan Museum**, at the corner of 6th and Marine, ☎ 250-358-2201, which has lots of stuff on logging and mining in the valley. Open daily in July and August, 10 am-4, plus weekends in off-season, pmsgw@netidea.com.

Right outside town is **Valhalla Park** and **Slocan Lake**. This is largely pure wilderness, so most people see only the edge of the park that you can get to from the lake. Get to the west side and take the five-mile/eight-km lakeshore trail, or head inland on Beatrice Lake, which takes you up to a couple of small lakes, and then into the Beatrice Lake cirque. The area has stunning views, and you'll probably have them all to yourself.

For more, get in touch with the **Valhalla Wilderness Society** in New Denver, 307 6th St., ☎ 250-358-2333, people fighting the good fight in this area. They were instrumental in getting the park declared, and they're now working on saving the Kermodie bear (there's a small pocket of them in Goat Range Provincial Park).

From New Denver, you have two choices. Head south to Castlegar and the road to Vancouver or, more interestingly, go east to Kaslo.

Head east and south on 31A. The first place you need to stop is **Sandon Ghost Town** which, considering the scenery around it, makes you wonder how stupid the people were who left this town. At its peak, the place had nearly 30 hotels and saloons, feeding off miners coming in for the silver rush. Lesser known is that, during World War II, this was remote enough that they put up a detention camp for Canadian-Japanese. The US involvement in these concentration-camp-like facilities (take a look at Yuma, Arizona, or Heart Mountain, Wyoming) is pretty well known; the Canadian side of it hasn't been recognized quite as much.

Sandon is a ghost town. There's a shop and a museum, open daily from June into September. Makes for a pleasant side-trip.

The small town of **Kaslo** offers the only access to the **Purcell Wilderness Conservancy**. Head north out of town, following the lake shore, then turn inland at Cooper Creek. This doesn't get you into the Conservancy, but it gets you as close as you can get. From the wide-spot-in-the-road town of Argenta, pick up the trailhead to **Earl Grey Pass**. It's only 37 miles/61 km through utter wilderness. Along the way, you've got to get yourself across creeks on a couple of cable cars but, other than that, it's not too bad for any serious hiker.

> **WARNING:** *This is bear country, and it's really remote bear country. Know what you're doing, tell people you're going, or expect to die in an uncomfortable fashion.*

On the other side of the lake is **Goat Range Provincial Park**, 160,000 acres of protected landscape. There's one campground, at Trout Lake. If you want to get into the park, you're in for serious wilderness hiking. Quite frankly, BC Parks kind of hopes you don't make it into the park as they are trying to reestablish the goat and bear – grizzly and Kermodie – populations.

From Kaslo, follow the shore south to the ferry at Balfour (see below) or west into Nelson and Castlegar, before catching feeder roads to Vancouver or the Okanagan.

■ Glacier National Park

Meanwhile, back on the main Highway 1, if you want to see Glacier, you'll have to get out of the car. The view from the road isn't all that glacial anyway. It has mountain scenery and affords you a good chance of spotting bears, but not a lot in the way of glacier. About the only glacier you're likely to see is **Great Glacier**, and that can be shut down by weather.

Glacier National Park covers about 245,000 acres, with the highway cutting right through the middle. Inside the park, there are upwards of 400 glaciers and, around them, a widely varied landscape, with everything from rainforest to scree just uncovered by the retreating ice. The Selkirk Mountains tower above, dominating every view.

If you want to get good looks at ice, you're going to need to lace up your boots. Luckily, there are some easy hikes into the park, as well as a couple of slightly more challenging ones.

Right off the road, try **Loop Brook** (just under a mile) or **Abandoned Rails Trail**, which is even shorter. Both show remnants of a train line that once passed through here (the train from Jasper to Rupert does still cut through the park on an active line).

Eleven miles/18 km in from the park's west entrance is a pullout and campground for the **Illecillewaet Glacier** – with that name, no wonder everybody just calls it the great glacier. The glacier is retreating pretty quickly. You can get closer to it on the **Illecillewaet Trail** from the campground. The trail is just under three miles/five km each way, with an elevation gain of about 1,000 feet/300 meters. At the end, there's a scree field you can work your way up to get even closer to the ice.

Also from the campground, there's the **Asulkan Valley hike**. It's a little easier than the Illecillewaet Trail, though a mile or so longer. The Asulkan Valley hike will take you along the stream bank back into a beautifully forested valley. Once you're at the end of the trail, you're looking straight at an icefield. And there's nothing like that glacier blue.

More determined and experienced hikers can try the **Avalanche Crest Trail**. It's just over 2.5 miles/four km each way, with a climb of more than 2,000 feet (800 meters). You start at the campground, climb through the forest, and then hit a ridge line with great glacial views.

The **Rogers Pass Information Centre**, ☎ 250-837-7500, is just north of the actual pass, the high point on this stretch of highway. It's housed in old railway buildings, and inside you can get the latest on trail conditions, bear sightings and the park's history. Particularly interesting is the model train, which shows some of the nightmares involved with trying to run a railway through here. A single avalanche in 1910 killed 63 workers.

If you're going to hike in the park, you need to buy a park pass here – your car will be checked. A one-day pass runs CAN $5 per person, or CAN $10 for a vehicle. The center is open 8-7 in summer, 9-5 the rest of the year.

The park has two campgrounds. **Illecillewaet**, two miles/3.2 km south of Rogers Pass, is open in summer, and it's the best base if you want to hike in the park. It's not a great campground, but it'll do. **Loop Brook Campground**, 2.5 miles/four km south of Illecillewaet, is a lot smaller and more scenic. No reservations are taken for any of these sites, so you just need to show up early and hope.

When you're driving through the park, you will change time zones. Why they couldn't run the boundary along provincial borders is anybody's guess. If you're going east, by the time you get out of the park the world is an hour behind you. Going west, it's an hour ahead. This is particularly important to remember if you're heading into the Rocky Mountain parks, which have set opening hours.

■ Golden

The lovely town of Golden has a close-to-perfect location: the road junction can take you south to Radium Hot Springs, east into Yoho, or west into Glacier National Park. From Golden, you're only a few minutes away from Kicking Horse, one of Canada's premier ski slopes. And the Kicking Horse River meets the Columbia here, so there's outstanding paddling and rafting.

You've got to wonder how the town stays small.

Attractions

The **Info Center** is at 500 10th Ave., ☎ 800-622-4053, 250-344-7125.

There aren't a lot of attractions in town. You come here to be outside, but if you're curious, the **Golden Museum**, is at 1302 11th Ave., ☎ 250-344-5169. There's a blacksmith shop and an old log school. It's not a bad place to kill an hour between trips out.

The Northern Lights Wildlife Center, 1745 Short Rd., ☎ 250-344-3798, is a wolf breeding area, set up by a private company. You're not likely to see wolves in the wild – we could count the number of times we have on our fingers – so this isn't a bad option. They also lead trips into the wilderness, to try and get that elusive wild wolf photograph. Admission to the center is CAN $10, and you can hang out and see what wolves do when they're not up to normal wolf business. Open 9-9 in summer, 10-6 in winter.

Adventures on Foot

Hiking: How ambitious are you feeling? There's a little something for everybody here. The **Moonraker trails** offer more than 27 miles/45 km of hiking and biking, including loops from Cedar Lake to Canyon Creek. Start at the end of Canyon Creek Road, bring a lunch and watch for bears.

Adventures on Snow

Skiing: The main reason to come to Golden is that it's the town closest to **Kicking Horse Mountain Resort**, ☎ 866-SKI-KICK, www.kickinghorseresort.com. The resort has got the longest gondola ride in the Rockies, full skiing facilities – you can hang out here for an entire season without running out of options – and more. The resort has all the facilities you'd expect: restaurants, school, lodge and plenty of places to rent gear. Lift tickets start around CAN $50.

In summer, you can still ride the gondola, which drops you at 7,700 feet above sea level. On a clear day, you get views that there's no point in us describing. Like mountains? This is the place to be. From roughly the last week in June through the last week in September, gondola rides are CAN $16; if you want to ride the gondola and have lunch at the top, from noon to four, it's a deal for CAN $25.

Once you've reached the top, there are a number of hiking trails to take you around the summit area. You can also hike or bike all the way down to the bottom, which is not at all a bad way to spend a day.

Golden Guides, ☎ 866-SKI-KICK, at the resort can book you on pretty much any kind of trip you're after, from whitewater rafting to fishing and hiking.

Adventures on Water

 Boating: Because of the river confluence here – the wild Kicking Horse with the calmer Columbia – there's a water trip for every taste. **Wet & Wild,** ☎ 250-344-6546, has easy trips on the Columbia. If that's too sedate for you, try **Alpine Rafting,** ☎ 250-344-6778, which will take you on the Class IV Kicking Horse, or **Rocky Mountain Rafting Company,** ☎ 250-344-6979. At the Kicking Horse Resort, **Golden Guides,** ☎ 866-SKI-KICK, can book you on river rafting, canoeing, kayaking or float trips.

Another one-stop booking service is **Golden Mountain Adventures,** ☎ 250-344-4650, www.adventurerockies.com.

One float option is along the **Columbia Valley.** The floodplain is a perfect wetland habitat for more birds than you can shake a spotting scope at. The region extends from just north of Golden all the way south to Invermere; right outside Golden, try Reflection Lake for prime birding.

Adventures in the Air

 Parasailing: After you've traveled enough in BC, you get a little overloaded on beautiful mountain scenery. There's so much of it, so very, very much of it. If you're looking for a slightly different perspective, throw yourself off the mountain. **Golden Guides,** ☎ 866-SKI-KICK, books you on a tandem parasail off Mount 7, where the gondola drops you off. It's not something to try on your own.

Adventures on Wheels

 Mountain Biking: One day, somebody woke up and thought, what can we do with all these ski trails when there isn't any snow? Simple answer: give them over to the pedalheads.

You can rent bikes at the Kicking Horse Mountain Resort. Just take the gondola up and you have nearly a mile of vertical drop to work your way back down. The trails are well marked and there's something for every level here – 18 trails, 11 of which are good for beginners and intermediates. Day passes for the lift run CAN $30.

If you've never thrown yourself down a mountain on a bike before, it's a good idea to have somebody tell you how to do it. Check with the **Golden Cycling Club**, goldencyclingclub@canada.com.

BEARS

The Kicking Horse resort has the largest enclosed grizzly bear sanctuary in the world. Twenty-two acres are set aside for a pair of bears, Boo and Cari. Similar to the one at Grouse Mountain, near Vancouver, the idea at the sanctuary is to take these once-orphaned bears, give them some room to run, draw people in, and slip some education in on them. Grizzlies are one of the most endangered animals on the planet for a couple of reasons, the biggest of which is that there are too many people in grizzly bear habitat. It takes a massive amount of space to be a grizzly bear, and the available room is forever being shrunk by suburbs and weekend homes. The other reason is that most people don't know squat about bears, so grizzly/human encounters almost always end up badly. Stop in and get to know your bears.

Where to Eat

 If you're going to ride the gondola up at Kicking Horse Resort, you might as well stop and have some food. The **Eagle' Eye Restaurant** is nicely done, and you'll spend more time looking out the windows than at your food. You can have lunch for under CAN $20; dinner is going to run rather more. ☎ 250-344-2330.

Golden

Ledgendz Diner, on the highway, ☎ 250-344-5059, has your standard roadside food and a 50s theme. For breakfast, try the **Dogtooth River Café**, next to the bridge, ☎ 250-344-4547, which has a bakery.

Kicking Horse Grill, 1105 9th St., is a good choice for late lunch or dinner. This spot serves local foods using local ingredients. Most dishes run under CAN $20. ☎ 250-344-2330.

Eastern BC

Places to Stay

The area is geared up here for a huge influx of visitors in winter. In summer, you won't have much trouble finding a place to stay.

A very budget choice is the **Goldenwood Lodge**, 2493 Holmes Deakin Rd., ☎ 250-344-7685, which has little cottages and lodge rooms starting at only CAN $50 for a double.

Golden Rim Motor Inn, 1416 Golden View Rd., ☎ 250-344-2216, is another good budget choice. It has a sauna and an indoor pool, as well as some Jacuzzi suites. Doubles start at only CAN $59.

Moving upscale a little, **Hillside Lodge & Chalets**, 1740 Seward Frontage, ☎ 250-344-7281, is a bit out of town, with great views of the Blackberry River. The rooms have balconies, and there's a spa and outdoor hot tub. Doubles from CAN $100.

Closer to town, **Alpen Rose Cabins**, 448 Althoff Rd., ☎ 250-344-5549, has private cabins, some with a fireplace. It's a pity this sort of thing has disappeared from the landscape; we remember driving across the US and Canada in the 1960s, staying in nothing but cabin-style hotels. Doubles from CAN $75.

Camping

Golden Municipal Campground is on 9th St. It's quiet, has full facilities and, although it's not exciting, it is convenient. ☎ 250-344-5412.

McLaren Lodge, at the east edge of town, 1509 Lafontaine Rd., ☎ 250-344-6133, has views, some cabins and a pleasant campground.

Outside of town is the **Donald Station Campground**, ☎ 250-340-8422, 2603 Big Bend Hwy., 14 miles/22 km west of Golden. It has full hookups, showers and a laundromat.

Transport

You can fly into Golden via **Montair**, ☎ 604-946-6688; that will get you to and from Vancouver. If you're heading anywhere else, **Greyhound** is your only choice. ☎ 800-661-8747.

From Golden, it's only an hour into the massive Rocky Mountains park complex. Your other choice is to drop south into the Kootenays – heading to Cranbook, Creston and Kootenay Lake.

The Kootenays

The BC/Alberta Rockies get most of the world's attention, but this part of the province has a couple of other mountain ranges that are worth spending some time in: the Selkirks and the Purcells. Just to get you on board geographically here, go to Glacier National Park, climb any mountain, and look south. To your left will be the Purcells; to your right, the Selkirks. Inside the mountain ranges are long, beautiful valleys, lakes upwards of 100 miles/150 km long that make for perfect paddling, and a ton of parks and wilderness areas.

The towns tend to be small, mostly ways to get somewhere else, but there are a few attractions: the hot springs just outside Banff; the great train museum in Cranbrook.

We're going to describe the valleys of the Kootenays by taking you up the two roads, both beginning in Creston, at the southern edge of the province. From Creston, you can take the east fork, which leads you right between the two ranges, or the west fork, which puts you east of the Purcells and leads to Banff, Jasper and the BC/Alberta Rockies.

▪ Creston

Creston is your quintessential crossroads town, with road options to the north and east – described above – as well as south to the US border and west through a lot of tiny farming towns, eventually getting you to Vancouver. If you are looking to go west, we really suggest you go north a bit first. The landscape gets better, the road a little less frustrating. From Creston to Osoyoos is just one long string of tiny towns with traffic lights, punctuated by farm fields and forest.

Creston itself is the agricultural center where residents of all these tiny towns come to do their shopping. Not many people live in Creston – about 5,000 – but it's the biggest thing in the area and, sooner or later, all southern BC roads will get you here.

Attractions

Creston **Info Centre** is at 1711 Canyon St, on Highway 3. Open daily in July and August, weekends only the rest of the year. ☎ 250-428-4342.

The main reason to come to Creston is the **Creston Valley Wildlife Management Area**, about six miles/10 km northwest of town. This wide, long valley is a floodplain, taking the waters of the Kootenay River every spring. There's nearly 13,000 acres of protected wetlands in the valley, so it's a birder's paradise. More than 250 species come through, including swans – there's nothing quite like seeing wild swans and realizing they really are birds, not just big stupid decorative things that live on park lakes – Canada geese, snow geese and more. In all, there's one of the highest counts of nesting species anywhere right in this valley. If you get tired of birds, there are also Western painted turtles and spotted frogs.

The **park center, ☎** 250-428-3259, is open daily in summer. From it, hiking trails – more than 21 miles/35 km in all – lead out to the wetlands and to a birdwatching tower. It's CAN $3 to get into the center, which offers guided trips out onto the water that are well worth your time. Stop in and make a few ticks on your life list.

Where to Eat

 Creston is a crossroads, so there are plenty of fast food choices and no shortage of hotels. For food, try the **Creston Valley Bakery**, 113 10th Ave., for breakfast or pick up a sandwich for a picnic later. **Munro's**, 1403 Canyon St., has steak and seafood and is one of the more popular places in town.

Where to Stay

 All the hotels are easy on the budget. **Bavarian Orchard Motel**, 3205 Hwy 3., ☎ 250-428-9935, is, as the name suggests, set in an orchard. It has suites, some with decks, and doubles from CAN $55. **City Centre Motel**, 220 15th Ave., ☎ 250-428-2257, is only a block off the highway. Despite the name, it's a quiet location, and you can walk to most of the town attractions. Doubles from CAN $55.

Sunset Motel, on Highway 3, ☎ 250-428-2229, is another good choice in the same price range.

Highway 3A

Take 3A north through the small towns of **Wynndel**, **Sirdar**, **Sanca**, **Boswell** and more. All of these little towns are on the banks of the huge **Kootenay Lake**, which is more than 60 miles/100 km long. If you have a boat or want to go for a paddle, this is the place to be. The lake is also the site of some serious fishing – the world's biggest rainbow trout (up to seven pounds/16 kg) come out of this lake. Try flipping that on the grill with a little spatula.

There are two parks on the lake accessible only by boat: **Midge Creek** has six campsites on the west side of the lake; **Pilot Bay** has just two sites on the east side, near the ferry landing.

Which brings up the next fun thing you can do on Kootenay Lake: take the free ferry. From Balfour on the west bank, over to Kootenay Bay on the east bank, this is the longest free ferry in North America, with two ships running, almost every hour in the summer. In winter, it's about every 90 minutes. It's 5.5 miles/nine km across the lake, and the crossing takes about 40 minutes. From the west side, you can catch Highway 3A down to Nelson, or 31 up to Kakusp and the Arrow Lakes, then catch the ferry at Galena Bay over to Shelter Bay, where you pick up Highway 23 to Revelstoke. For more options, see the *Arrow Lakes* section, above.

Going east from Creston, you cross the Purcell Mountains into a wide valley region between here and the Rockies. There are a few things worth stopping at along the way, as you head east and north into Banff.

■ Cranbrook

The biggest town in southeast BC, Cranbrook has little to offer. Driving through, it's large, ugly and industrial. Two things make it worth a stop, the Canadian Museum of Rail Travel and Fort Steele Heritage Town.

Attractions

Tourism Info is at the junction of Highways 3 and 95. It's open year-round, ☎ 250-426-5914.

The Canadian Museum of Rail Travel, 1 van Horne St. North, ☎ 250-489-3918, is, plain and simple, the best train museum in BC. Any train fan is going to simply love it here.

There are beautifully restored cars – luxury sleepers, a dining car, a solarium and more. Tours take you through each car, including a caboose, where you see that maybe it wasn't really the best place on the train. These are all in like-new condition; nowhere will you get a better idea of what travel was like during the classic age of rail. There's also a good movie shown, and a model train set up. Get here around lunch time and you can have tea in the restored Argyle dining car. The museum is open 10-6 daily in summer, with regular tours – the short tour is enough for most people, the CAN $10 long tour is a better choice for serious train nuts.

Fort Steele Heritage Town, 15 minutes out of town on Highways 93/95, is open year-round, although not as much happens in the winter. It's set up to look like a town in the 1890s, when this was a booming mining town. Killed when the railroad passed it by, the town's now restored with a theater, a bakery, a general store and horse-drawn wagon rides, among other things. It's a good place to take the kids for a day. ☎ 250-417-6000. Admission to the park is CAN $6 (free in winter), with extra charged for theater shows.

Where to Stay & Eat

$Z^{Z^{Z^z}}$ If you end up spending a night in Cranbrook, you're going to be mostly stuck with road food as there aren't that many fine dining options. There are, however, lots of places to stay, befitting the largest town in the region. Go to Cranbrook Street and take a look around. You're not going to have any trouble finding a place.

The Heritage Inn, 803 Cranbrook St., ☎ 250-489-4301, has decent rooms and some suites, with doubles from around CAN $100. Cheaper are the **Kootenay Country Comfort Inn**, 1111 Cranbrook St., ☎ 250-426-2296, and **Lazy Bear Lodge**, 621 Cranbrook St., ☎ 250-426-6086, both of which have doubles for around CAN $60. Clean, good choices.

The Nomad Motel, 910 Cranbrook St., ☎ 250-426-6266, has a heated pool and every room has a fridge and a microwave. Doubles from CAN $50.

If, for some reason, you want to skip the Rocky Mountains and the incredible scenery therein, there is a quick way through to Alberta, taking Highways 3/93 out of Cranbrook, east to Fernie and into Alberta at Crowsnest Pass. If you're in a hurry to get to Calgary, this would be the route to take.

There's not much reason to stop in **Fernie** in the summer, but in winter, the **Fernie Alpine Resort**, ☎ 250-423-3555, comes alive, and it has some of the best – and least discovered – skiing in BC. The vertical rise is over 2,800 feet/850 meters, and the weather patterns bring plenty of snow – as much as 30 feet/nine meters a year, with great bowl skiing. Lift tickets are CAN $56 for a day of skiing. If you come in summer, put your bike on the lift for CAN $26/day. If you're coming in winter, be sure to ask your hotel about lift/lodging packages. It's how they make their business.

The **Best Western**, 1622 7th Ave., ☎ 250-423-5500, is quite convenient. Some rooms have fireplaces and Jacuzzis. Doubles start at CAN $110. **Cedar Lodge** has suites, kitchenettes, an indoor pool and a sauna. It's at 1101 7th Ave., ☎ 250-423-4622. Doubles start from CAN $70. If you want to stay right next to the slopes, try **Lizard Creek**, 5346 Highline Dr., ☎ 250-423-2057. It has some kitchenettes and rooms with fireplaces. Doubles start at CAN $80. Also nearby is the **Riverside Mountain Lodge**, 100 Riverside Way, ☎ 250-426-5000. It offers hot tubs, a sauna and even a water slide that's open year-round. Doubles are CAN $59 at the low end, but nearly CAN $900 at the high end.

Heading to the Parks

From Cranbrook, you're looking at a few hours yet to get into Banff. It's a pleasant drive, though, with mountains on either side and good river scenery. Stop for the night to camp at **Whiteswan Lake Park**, a popular provincial park near Canal Flats. It has a big lake that offers good walks along its shoreline. ☎ 250-422-4200.

From Whiteswan, you can take the logging road back to **Top of the World Provincial Park**, which has some hiking and good backcountry camping in the shadow of Mt. Morro, which is more than 9,500 feet/3,000 meters tall.

Stay on the main highway – which parallels the Columbia Wetlands Wildlife Management Area, so it's a good place to have your spotting scope at the ready – up to the **Dutch Creek Hoodoos**, 12 miles/20 km past Canal Flats, at the north end of Lake Invermere. Hoodoos are pillars left by erosion. What usually happens is that a capstone prevents the pillar itself from eroding, while everything around it melts. It's a classic and fascinating geological trick.

Just beyond the hoodoos, you'll get good views of the Columbia River. This river was somewhat problematic in the early days, as both Canada and the United States wanted it. Canada put forts as far south as Oregon (that's why there's a Vancouver in Washington State) and the US nearly started a world war over what it saw as its divine right to own most of British Columbia. The river still is a point of tension, as fishing rights and water rights – the battle for the new century – are ongoing issues.

Fairmont Hot Springs Resort, ☎ 250-345-6311, is near where the river hits the lake. It has golf, a ski area restricted to hotel guests and the less-exclusive hot springs pools, which you can get into for CAN $7. Lovely rooms in the lodge start around CAN $150. If you're the lodge sort, you'll have a good time here. Otherwise, you might be a little happier up the road at Radium.

The small towns of Windermere and Invermere are set along the river banks. Finally, you come to Radium Hot Springs, the gateway to Banff.

■ Radium Hot Springs

Radium Hot Springs is the most important town between Cranbrook and the parks, and it's really nothing more than a crossroads lined with hotels. Still, it's a good place to stock up on picnic supplies before you head into the parks – everything is cheaper here than it is in Banff – and if you're coming out of the parks, soak your hiking-weary muscles in the springs.

Attractions

 Visitor Info is right on the highway, 7585 Main St., ☎ 800-347-9704, 250-347-9331. It's next door to a grocery store, so it's a convenient one-stop spot.

The **hot springs** themselves have been a destination since the 1890s, when the first pools were built. Today, there are several pools, the hottest of which has water just under 100°F. There is indeed radioactive material in the water, which people figure is bound to cure something. Don't worry; you won't come out glowing. A day pass is CAN $10. Between soaks, you can walk some of the hikes right by the pools. ☎ 250-347-9485 to reach the people who run the springs.

Where to Stay

 The town of Radium Hot Springs isn't really much more than a line of hotels. If you want an early start in the park, you'll save a lot of money staying here, instead of in Banff.

Apple Tree Inn, 4999 Highway 93, ☎ 250-347-0011, has some suites and kitchenettes. You can walk to the hot springs from here. Doubles from CAN $45.

Big Horn Motel gets you off the main road, 4881 St. Marys, ☎ 250-347-9522. Doubles from CAN $65.

Park Inn, 4873 Stanley St., ☎ 250-347-9582, has some rooms with full kitchens, as well as some with Jacuzzis. There's also an indoor pool. Doubles from CAN $75. **Chalet Europe**, 5063 Madsen Rd., ☎ 888-428-9998, is a bit higher up the scale, with some suites, and rooms with balconies and fireplaces. Doubles from CAN $100.

Radium Hot Springs Lodge, 5425 Highway 93, ☎ 250-347-9341, has saunas, whirlpools, suites and more. Good ski packages. Doubles from CAN $120.

Camping

You can go on into Kootenay to camp – we'll cover that in the Parks chapter – but here, there aren't many choices. **Canyon RV Resort**, on Sinclair Creek Loop Rd., ☎ 250-347-9564, has sites along the creek and full services.

Northern British Columbia

British Columbia has two great highways headed north, the Cassiar Highway and the Alaska Highway. They both start farther north than most people bother to go. That makes it good for you: you get more scenery, more fun and fewer people.

The Alaska Highway gets all the publicity, but there's also the incredibly beautiful, remote Stewart-Cassiar (usually just called the Cassiar), which picks up from the Yellowhead Highway just south of Kitwanga and comes out 21 miles/ 34 km west of Watson Lake, in the Yukon. The Cassiar is faster, more consistently scenic (although there is nothing to match the grandeur of Stone Mountain or the Kluane Range), and considerably shorter. It's also a lot rougher, with almost no services along the way, and it's frequently full of trucks going too fast for conditions, taking a shortcut to Alaska. There are even a few places where the road doubles as an air-strip.

The other significant route in Northern BC, the Yellowhead Highway, takes you west to Prince Rupert and the coast, where you can catch a ferry over to the Queen Charlotte Islands.

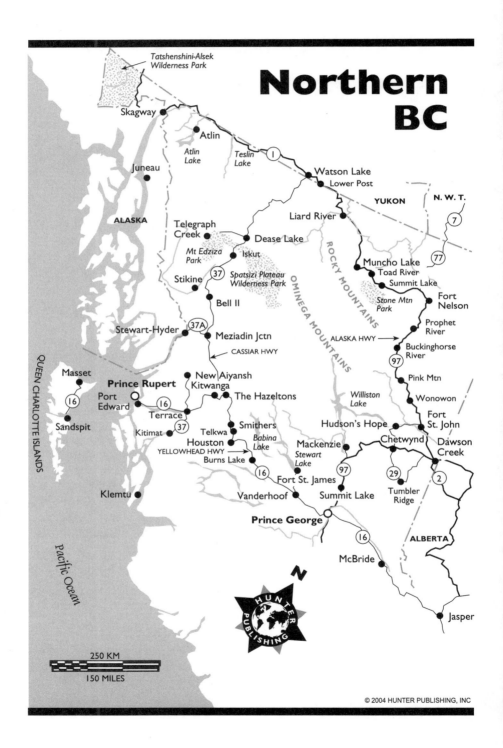

Northern
BC

Tatshenshini-Alsek
Wilderness Park

Skagway

Atlin

Atlin
Lake

Teslin
Lake

Teslin
①

Watson Lake
Lower Post

YUKON

N. W. T.

⑦

Juneau

ALASKA

Telegraph
Creek

Liard River

Dease Lake

ROCKY MOUNTAINS

Mt Edziza
Park

Iskut

Muncho Lake
Toad River
Summit Lake

⑦⑦

Stikine

③⑦

Spatsizi Plateau
Wilderness Park

Stone Mtn
Park

Fort
Nelson

Bell II

OMINEGA MOUNTAINS

Prophet
River

Stewart-Hyder

③⑦A

Meziadin Jctn

CASSIAR HWY

ALASKA HWY

Buckinghorse
River

⑨⑦

QUEEN CHARLOTTE ISLANDS

Masset

Prince Rupert

New Aiyansh
Kitwanga

The Hazeltons

Williston
Lake

Pink Mtn

Wonowon

⑯

Port
Edward

⑯

Terrace

Smithers

Hudson's Hope

Fort
St. John

Sandspit

Kitimat

③⑦

Telkwa

Babina
Lake

Mackenzie

Chetwynd

Dawson
Creek

Houston

YELLOWHEAD HWY

Stewart
Lake

②

Burns Lake

⑯

Fort St. James

⑨⑦

②⑨

Klemtu

Vanderhoof

Summit Lake

Tumbler
Ridge

Prince George

⑯

ALBERTA

Pacific Ocean

McBride

N

Jasper

250 KM

150 MILES

HUNTER PUBLISHING

The Yellowhead Highway

Jasper to Prince George

There's no delicate way to say it: if you're coming out of the parks system, through those fantastic vistas in Banff and Jasper, the Yellowhead is going to be more than a little let-down. On the other hand, if you're using the Yellowhead to get into the parks, at least you're saving the good stuff for last.

As it goes, the road from the parks to Prince George is good, but fairly uninteresting, mostly following the course of the Fraser River. Farms and ranches dot the landscape, and the forests are a mixture of evergreen and deciduous trees. There really isn't anywhere to stop and camp along this road. There are a couple of motels near the northern park entrances, but once you've left them behind, you're pretty much stuck on the road until you get to Prince George.

You hit Highway 16 just a couple of miles out of Mt Robson park. To your left, as you're heading west, is Mt. Terry Fox Provincial Park, named after one of Canada's great heroes.

TERRY FOX, A MAN TO ADMIRE

Although he was born in Winnipeg, Terry Fox grew up in Port Coquitlam, near Vancouver. When he was 18, he was diagnosed with osteogenic sarcoma – bone cancer. His right leg was amputated six inches above the knee in 1977.

Kind of like Lance Armstrong going on to win at the Tour de France after his cancer battle, Terry, while he was still in the hospital, decided to run across Canada to raise money for cancer research. This became what he called the **Marathon of Hope**.

As soon as he could, he started training. Eighteen months later, he felt warmed up, so he began his run across Canada in St. John's, Newfoundland on April 12, 1980. Not many people cared at first, but it didn't take all that long for this man – who really did run, with a kind of hop in his step – to start getting attention. Lots of it.

But Terry didn't make it all the way across the country. On September 1st, after 143 days and 3,339 miles/5,373 km, Terry had to stop running, just outside of Thunder Bay, Ontario because cancer had appeared in his lungs. He died on June 28, 1981 at age 22.

But the work went on. To date, the annual Terry Fox Run, held in cities all over Canada, and even overseas, has raised more than CAN $300 million for cancer research.

It's quite fitting that one of the most beautiful mountains in Canada is named after Terry. He towered above most of us.

The junction with Highway 5 (which takes you south toward the Okanagan) is at Tete Jaune Cache. About 150 people live here, stretched out along the banks of the Fraser River. You can get gas here, and maybe something to eat, but don't count on it. It's better to make the run to **McBride**, 37 miles/60 km farther east. About 2,500 people live there; if you want to linger, **Visitor Info** is in the caboose at Robson Square Shopping Centre, ☎ 250-569-3366.

The trailhead for the **Goat River Trail** is off Loos Road, about nine miles/15 km west of McBride. This is an eight- or nine-day hike that takes you to Route 97 and the Bowron Lakes Canoe circuit (see page 192 for more). Know what you're doing before attempting this trail, and let people know you're headed into the middle of nowhere. The Fraser Headwaters Alliance, ☎ 250-968-4490, www.fraserheadwaters.org, can give you the latest on trail conditions.

For the next 122 miles/200 km, until you get to Prince George, you're paralleling the Fraser. There are a few attractions along the way, including **Kakwa Recreation Area**, located up a branch road just outside Kidd. You're going to need a 4WD car to get the 53 miles/87 km to Kakwa, but once you're there, you'll probably have the place to yourself. This is fantastic wildlife country, with moose, black and brown bear, and more.

Purden Ski Village, ☎ 250-565-7777, www.purden.com, is 37 miles/60 km east of Prince George. It's a T-bar hill, and there's a double chair. It's nothing compared to what you can get around Banff, or farther west in Whistler, but you could kill a winter day here.

Bowron River Rest Area, three miles/five km farther up the road, is day-use only. Come here to see the state of the forest. There was a ferocious spruce beetle infestation here, so it was opened for logging to try and get the beetles under control before they spread. Now it's the largest silviculture plantation in the world, covering upwards of 95,000 acres.

Willow River Forest Interpretation Trail, 21 miles/34 km out of Prince George, is a 1.2-mile/two-km trail that takes you through a variety of ecosystems and gives you a good idea of what's what in the local forests. It is a good place to see animals, and is a recommended spot to get off the road and stretch your legs.

Watch for moose 18 miles/30 km before you get to Prince George. There's a raised platform off the north side of the highway over a good moose marsh. Remember, injuries by moose are far more common than injuries by bears.

Tabor Mountain Ski Resort, ☎ 250-963-7542 – another small one – is just 12 miles/20 km outside of town. Popular with locals, it's got a triple chair, but a vertical drop of only about 800 feet.

Prince George comes up in a tangle of railway lines and industrial buildings. It's not the prettiest spot in the province, but it is the most important town in the northern reaches.

■ Prince George

Prince George itself is the largest city in northern Canada; if you're heading north on the Alaska Highway, it offers the last chance before Whitehorse to stock up on necessities at something that resembles a reasonable price and to get your fill of junk food.

Prince George is a transport city: the railway runs through here, the river traffic runs through here. That makes it important, but not exactly the most exciting spot for visitors. There are some good, cheap restaurants and a couple of attractions that are well worth the time.

Because it's a hub, Prince George is an easy place to get to, whether you've got your own transport or not. **VIA Rail** stops at PG on its Rupert-Jasper run. ☎ 800-561-8630. **Greyhound** connects PG to Rupert and Vancouver, via Kamloops; ☎ 800-661-8747. **Air BC** has daily flights to connect PG and Vancouver; ☎ 888-247-2262.

Attractions

 Start at the **Visitor Info Centre**, on the corner of Victoria St. and Patricia Blvd. It's open year-round. This is a must-stop, as it has stuff on the entire northern region, as well as many points south. Whichever way you're thinking of going from George, you'll find some info on it here. ☎ 250-562-3700, www.tourismpg.bc.ca.

The main attraction in town is the **Prince George Railway and Forestry Museum**, 850 River Rd., ☎ 250-563-7351. It's open May-October; admission is CAN $3.50. This is the best railway museum in BC. There's also a good display of early fire trucks and heavy equipment. It's all laid out in a huge field, so you can just wander and see what interests you. Many of the cars are open, so you can get in and take a look around – don't skip the caboose, to see how early trainmen lived. The highlight of the collection is the 1903 Russell snowplow, which is made out of wood and is truly a thing of beauty.

The **Fraser-Fort George Regional Museum** is at the end of 20th Ave. It has lots of displays on the area's history – both natural, with lots of stuffed animals, and cultural, with displays of Carrier arts. There's also a theater, lots of stuff for kids and an Internet café – not too many of those north of here, so you may want to stop just for that. Admission is CAN $8. ☎ 250-562-1612.

Across the street is the **Fort George Railway Station**, which has a half-mile mini steam train that runs on summer weekends. This whole area is the original site of Fort George, an HBC fort established by Simon Fraser. Fraser, as we point out elsewhere, was just a fun guy. More than anyone else, his drive and precision and control-freak nature opened BC to exploration. He was of a generation of explorers that simply doesn't exist anymore, able to cross frozen streams, eat nothing but rotted biscuit and still have time to break treaties with the locals. Okay, that sounds snide, but Fraser was, really, a marvel.

SIMON FRASER

In May 1808, Fraser left Fort St. James with four canoes, 19 *voyageurs*, a pair of First Nations guides, and some flunkies. They got to Prince George (then Fort George), did a bit of trading and, despite all sanity, headed south along what's now the Fraser River. Fifteen years earlier, Alexander Mackenzie had been turned back by the rapids at Hell's Gate. Fraser went through, passing, as he wrote, "where no human being should venture." He and his crew – after a few days of hanging on cliff sides, wishing they were mountain goats, navigating their canoes through impossible rapids, and trying to cling to the cliffsides with rickety ladders – were the first people to shoot the length of the Fraser River. When he got there, he turned around and went back. People were different in those days.

If you're in town on a Friday night from August-October (not December, though), take a look at the **Prince George Astronomical Society's telescope**. There are open houses at the observatory, during which the public can visit. Admission is by donation, but do call first – ☎ 250-564-4787 – to make sure they're on for that week.

From May to September, stop at Prince George's **Saturday Farmer's Market**, in Courthouse Plaza, first thing in the morning. This is the center of BC's farming districts, and the only other place in the province where you can get produce like this in the Okanagan.

Prince George has long depended on the huge stretches of surrounding forest for its robust economy. The single largest Canadian forestry company is based in Prince George, and in summer, you can take a tour that shows you the whole process, from seedlings to pulp. It's a four-hour tour, and it's free. Check at the Visitor Centre at the intersection of Highways 16 and 97. ☎ 250-563-5493.

There's also a demonstration forest, east of town on Highway 16. See above for details.

Adventures on Foot

Hiking: For serious hikers, the **Alexander Mackenzie Trail** is accessible from Prince George. The trail stretches from here to Quesnel, then along the Dean Channel (near Bella Coola on the Pacific Coast). It takes about three weeks to hike the entire trail, which began as an Indian trading route, with furs and obsidian as the main goods. Alexander Mackenzie, the first to cross the Americas from coast to coast, reached the Pacific in 1793 (well before Lewis and Clark) and used this route for the last part of his trip. Mackenzie was one of the great ones, a mad explorer who was not happy unless he was in the middle of nowhere (although he did retire fat and rich in England). The Mackenzie River, which runs from Great Slave Lake in the Northwest Territories to the Beaufort Sea, was one of Mackenzie's better-known canoe trips.

> **AUTHOR NOTE:** Get topos, get the latest from locals, know what you're doing before you even think about getting on this trail.

Where to Eat

PG is not a luxury dining kind of place. All the usual fast food suspects are here.

Our first choice is **Moose McGillicuddy's**, 1778 Highway 97, ☎ 250-563-8667, is a local landmark in Hawaii; here, the food is every bit as good. Best hamburgers we've had in this part of the country, and great service too. You can be in and out for under CAN $20.

Foodteller, 508 George St., ☎ 250-563-2946, makes for a good night out. It offers steaks, pasta, seafood, and more, starting around CAN $20.

Ric's Grill, 547 George St., ☎ 250-614-9096, is part of a mini-chain, with a couple of other locations in BC and Alberta. It offers steaks and seafood at reasonable prices.

Where to Stay

PG is used by people coming through town and stopping for a night, so there are many quite reasonable hotels in town. Try the **Connaught Motor Inn**, ☎ 250-562-4441, with doubles

Northern BC

from CAN $70, or the **97 Motor Inn**, 2713 Spruce St., ☎ 250-562-6010, a little cheaper, for comfortable budget accommodation.

Another reasonable choice is the **Carmel Motor Inn**, 1502 Hwy. 97, ☎ 250-564-6339.

To move up a little on the luxury and price scale, there's a **Sandman** in town, 1650 Central St., ☎ 250-563-8131, with doubles from CAN $85, and a **Coast Inn**, ☎ 250-563-0121, with a pool, sauna, gym and three restaurants. It has doubles from CAN $125.

Prince George has a good **B&B association**, ☎ 888-266-5555, www.bbcanada.com (click on Northern BC, then Prince George), which offers a free booking service. They have some splendid properties on file, so just tell them what you like in a B&B, and they'll set you up.

Camping

Campers can head out to the **Prince George Municipal Campground** (no phone) at 4188 4th Ave. Sites are priced from CAN $12. Other choices include the **Blue Spruce RV Park,** on Kimball Rd, just west of Highway 16, ☎ 250-964-7272, which has pull-through sites and full hookups for around CAN $20.

West from Prince George

The western territory opens up via the Yellowhead Highway west from Prince George. The Yellowhead is in excellent shape: smooth, wide, not heavily traveled. It stretches through alternating patches of forest and farmland, with a few glaciers in the mountains and hints of things to come along the way. If you take the Yellowhead all the way to its end, you get to Prince Rupert, a lovely town that feels more like Alaska than Canada – and, in fact, Alaska is only a few miles up the coast.

You leave Prince George on the same kind of low, rolling scenery that you come in on. Cross the bridge over the Fraser River, the city's earliest lifeline, and you're out of there. This is farming country, and you can plan on getting through the first stretch of the road pretty quickly.

About 28 miles/45 km from Prince George, you'll see **Bednesti Lake** on the south side of the road; this was an important village site for the Dakelh First Nations people who lived here before the coming of the HBC. A plaque here gives a little history, if you need to get out and stretch.

Another 18 miles/30 km up the road brings you to the geographical center of British Columbia – it's on the other side of the trailer park.

■ Vanderhoof

The first town you hit moving west from PG is Vanderhoof, with a population of a bit under 5,000. It's a logging town and a ranching center for the outlying areas.

Attractions

 There's not a lot to do in Vanderhoof, but it's a nice little town. Stop in at the **Visitor Info Centre**, just north of the highway on Burrard St., ☎ 250-567-2291.

HERBERT VANDERHOOF

Here's an odd bit of history. The town's name comes from Herbert Vanderhoof, a man who was a PR flack for the Canadian railways in the early 1900s. He thought this spot would make a perfect writer's retreat, and so he started to plan one, along with a luxury hotel. Neither ever came off, but the loggers loved the spot, and the town, named after a failed dream, started to grow.

Heritage Village is on the western edge of town. It has reconstructed buildings from the 1920s and a small museum that displays stuffed birds and all the things you would have needed to survive here 80 years ago – lots of tools. It's worth a quick look and the CAN $2 admission. Open daily 10-5, ☎ 250-567-2991.

Adventures in Nature

 The other big attraction in the area is the **Vanderhoof Bird Sanctuary**, at the northern edge of town, along the banks of the Nechako River. Upwards of 50,000 migrating birds come through here in spring and fall. Out of migration season, it's a good spot for a picnic.

Adventures in Culture & History

 Take Stoney Creek Road seven miles/11 km south of town to the village of **Sai-K'uz**, a Dakelh village. Take a look at the potlach house, which has some arts and crafts for sale.

There's a wonderful side-trip to **Fort St. James**, up Highway 27. It's about 50 miles/80 km, and well worth the effort.

Fort St. James was a Hudson's Bay Company headquarters site. Today it's a living history park, where visitors can wander around restored sites and talk to people costumed as 1800s trading post folk. The fort is in a

Northern BC

beautiful location, on the edge of a huge lake, and the people inside really know their stuff.

The HBC was the single most important force in settling western Canada, and it was all on the basis of a single, very simple idea: fur sells. The Fort St. James warehouse has a good display on the different furs that were traded, from the luxurious otter pelt to weasel skins and scent glands from minks. You'll see the presses where skins were flattened for easy shipment, and get a good idea of the kind of insular world these people created for themselves. To quote from Peter Newman's outstanding book *The Company of Adventurers,* "The Company's wilderness settlements were eventually modelled on contemporary defensive architecture.... They were situated inside a quadrangle of wooden bastions mounting various gauges of cannon, joined by palisades of upright logs, sometimes with iron points. The main buildings were meant to be unassailable redoubts with parapets pierced by embrasures for fixed eight-pounders."

Fort St. James was actually taken over by First Nations forces at one point in its history. Really, despite their fortifications, the HBC posts were here because they were allowed to be here; the men inside were desperately outnumbered and entirely dependent upon the goodwill of the Natives for everything they needed.

James Douglas was the man who turned the HBC into what it was in the western reaches of Canada – Douglas was driven, organized, and utterly fearless; he was also married to a First Nations woman who could help him get around in the local languages. In 1828, Douglas heard that a man named Tzil-na-o-lay, who had been accused of murder five years before, was living near Fort St. James. The fugitive was hanging out in the house of a man named Kwah, who had been a good friend to the HBC – he'd once saved Simon Fraser and his crew from dying of starvation, and he was the driving force behind much of the fur trade in the area.

Douglas, though, in an unusual mood for a trader, put Western justice above practicality, and went out after Tzil-na-o-lay, who was beaten to death.

Kwah didn't much care for this abuse of his hospitality, so he and a bunch of his men went out and captured Ft. St. James. It didn't take much doing. As the story comes down, Kwah had Douglas pinned to a table, a knife at his heart, when Douglas's wife came in to save the day. She went straight for the pile of trade goods, and started throwing presents at the warriors, telling them that if they left her husband, they could have it all.

Kwah was insulted by the attack on his house, but he was a practical man, too. Reparations struck him as being a good idea, so he and his men loaded up on goodies and headed out. He was banned from the fort for six months.

Douglas got it a bit worse. He'd been diminished in the eyes of the locals, and there began to be regular threats against him, small skirmishes, just enough to keep him on his toes. It wasn't long after the confrontation with Kwah that Douglas got transferred to Fort Vancouver – nowhere near what's now Vancouver, but much farther south, in the disputed region around the Columbia River – to be the accountant.

Take the side-trip. There's nowhere else in BC where you can see how the western expansion of Canada came about. Where else are you going to find out that an HBC clerk made the princely wages of 50 pounds a year, more than double what an interpreter would make for explaining to the clerk exactly what was going on?

Fort St. James is open May-September, 9-5. There's a small museum and reception center on the grounds, which is open year-round but, in winter, you're not going to see much else. Admission is CAN $4 and absolutely worth it.

Adventure on Water & Foot

 If you've come out this far, you can go just a bit farther north to Germanson Landing North Road, which opens up the **Takla-Nation Lakes**. There's a multi-lake canoe route through here, as well as a wide variety of hiking trails.

Where to Stay

 Hotels are nice and cheap here: get a good basic double room for about CAN $70 at the **Grand Trunk Inn**, 2351 Church Ave., ☎ 250-567-3188; the **North Country Inn**, 2645 Burrard, ☎ 250-567-3047; or the **Siesta Inn**, on Highway 16, ☎ 250-567-2365.

There's a campground at Sai-K'uz, at the **Riverside Park Campground**, 3100 Burrard Ave., ☎ 250-567-4710, and **Dave's RV Park**, 1048 Derkson Rd., ☎ 250-567-3161.

■ Onward from Vanderhoof

Once you get back on the Yellowhead, you'll pass Fort Fraser, a tiny community on the site of one of the first trading posts in BC, and **Beaumont Provincial Park**, which has campsites (☎ 800-689-9025 for reservations). There are, though, better campgrounds farther up ahead.

The scenery starts to get a little wild as you enter the foothills of the coastal mountains. By Burns Lake, you're in the pretty stuff. There's not a lot to see in Burns Lake, but there is the **Heritage Center**, ☎ 250-692-3773, if you need to get off the road and stretch a bit. Burns Lake is a popular recreation area, with lots of fishing and boating; it's also the access point for **Tweedsmuir Provincial Park**, the biggest in BC, 1.8 million acres.

Tweedsmuir has no road access or facilities from this side of things – the road to Bella Coola, farther south, cuts through the park and there are a couple of ways into it from there – but you can get at it by crossing Ootsa Lake (if you've got your own kayak, you could easily spend a few days on the lake), which forms the northern park border. Once you're inside, you're on your own. This is bear country.

For the serious paddler, you can link up a chain of lakes: from Ootsa through Whitesail, Eutsuk, Tetachuck, and Natalkuz, which will take you back to Ootsa. You'll need to do some portaging, and if you don't know how to boat in the wilderness, this is really just a cold, wet way to commit suicide.

Highway 16 starts to head north here, past the small towns of Houston (home of the "world's largest flyrod" – 60 feet long and 800 pounds) and Telkwa (which made *Ripley's Believe It or Not* for having three bridges over two rivers, all anchored on the same rock). Ripley was maybe having a slow week. The bridges are long gone, but the town is a pretty little spot, and there's a heritage walk with about 30 stops; pick up the free pamphlet at the museum, on Highway 16, ☎ 250-846-9656.

There's good camping at **Tyhee Lake Provincial Park**, just north of Telkwa. It's wheelchair-accessible and has good bird watching.

■ Smithers

Smithers has about 6,000 people, almost every fast food restaurant known, and not much else. It's a good halfway point between Prince George and Rupert on the coast but, unless you're really tired, there's no need to stop.

Smithers is another of those BC spots with a weird history. In the early days, it was a way-point for people headed to the Klondike but, because the government had decided the region was fertile and would make for good farming, they hatched a plan to move 8,000 Boer War veterans here. Problem was, they couldn't find 8,000 who wanted to come. Only a hundred applied, and about half of those sold off their allotment of 160 acres to speculators.

Smithers was also going to be passed by on the rail line: the plan was to send the train through Aldermere. Much like the Boers and their unwanted land, though, Aldermere didn't want the railroad; they were afraid it would turn their lovely little town into nothing but a huge collection of squatter shacks, and so they pushed to get the train through Smithers – which ended up, for a time, being called Squatterville.

Adventures on Foot

 Hiking: If you're looking to get into the bush, take the road out to **Babine Mountains Recreation Area**. Along the way, you'll go through **Driftwood Canyon Provincial Park**, which has some fossil beds. Most of them are plant fossils, but there are also a few fish and insects. Don't go up on the canyon walls looking for fossils – the walls are fragile, and you'll end up bleeding. It's okay to check the slope below, though.

Out by Babine Lake, you've got a no-roads park that covers 61,000 acres. Try the five-mile/eight-km **McCabe Trail** for good views of alpine meadows.

The Adventure Smithers Group, ☎ 250-847-3499, 877-610-8075, www.adventuresmithers.com, is a co-op of outfitters who can get you into the extraordinary bush around town. Excursions range from flightseeing and easy hikes to trips deep into the Spatsizi wilderness. Check them out.

Climbing: Bear Mountaineering, ☎ 250-847-2854, www.bearmountaineering.bc.ca, guides rock climbing, ice climbing and ski mountaineering. They've also got an avalanche survival course, 2½ days that could save your life. For serious mountain hounds, these are the people to call. They have trips ranging from short pitches to multi-day expeditions, including climbs of Mt. Logan, Canada's tallest mountain.

Adventures on Water

Rafting: You can take a whitewater raft trip on the Buckley River with **Suskwa Adventure Outfitters**, ☎ 888-5-GO-RAFT, www.suskwa.com. The run takes in a stretch of about 30 rapids, but nothing too hairy.

▪ The Hazeltons

Back on 16, Another 60 km down the road, you hit the complex of **Hazelton**, **South Hazelton** and **New Hazelton**. That's a lot of names for about a thousand people. The towns are overlooked by Mt. Rocher Deboule, rolling stone mountain – so named by miners who kept getting nailed by landslides. It was a bit more important to the First Nations Gitxsan, for whom it was the center point of their civilization.

Over in New Hazelton, there's a historic oddity: Russian anarchists robbed the railway's payroll. The plot worked once, so they thought they'd try it again. You know that scene in *Butch Cassidy and the Sundance Kid* where they're surrounded by the Bolivian Army? The Russian anarchists – were these guys lost, or what? – ended up playing out that same scene.

Attractions

 All three Hazeltons share the same **Info Centre**, at the junction of 16 and 62 north. ☎ 250-842-6571. The big guy out front is Jean Jacques Caux, a packer, a *voyageur*, legendary for the size of loads he carried on the trails. As the stories come down to us, the guy was also famous for changing his clothes only once a year – whereas, let's be realistic here, most other guys out working in the bush probably changed clothes two or three times a year.

The Hazeltons do open up two of the more interesting First Nations villages in the area. **'Ksan**, just outside of town, is a reconstruction of a traditional Gitxsan village, very beautifully done. Set on a quiet meadow overlooking a river, it has classically constructed tribal houses, complete with totem poles, and other carvings and paintings. It gives a very good feel for what these villages must have been like. Tours (CAN $8) leave every hour and take you into the different buildings to see the quite wonderful regalia room and carving room, while the guide tells you stories about the village and the culture. The tour is very well done. If you don't want the tour, but just want to walk around the village, that's CAN $2, but it's worth paying extra to get inside. There's also a quite large gift shop and a good museum. The village also runs the Kitanmax School of Northwest Coast Indian Art, which offers a four-year program that teaches traditional styles and techniques. There aren't many groups who are this organized passing on their heritage. Tours are May-October, and the village is open from 9-6. ☎ 250-842-5544. There's also a decent campground.

The other nearby village is **Kispiox**, also a Gitxsan village. It's 10 miles/16 km north of Hazelton. Come out here for the totem poles if you didn't see enough in 'Ksan.

From the Hazeltons, Highway 16 starts to dip south, running along the Skeena River and heading for the coast. The mountains dominating every view on a clear day are the **Seven Sisters**, some of the prettiest mountains in BC.

Along here, you enter Kermodie bear territory. Kermodies are a white subspecies of black bear. They are very, very rare, and you stand a better chance of being struck by lightning than seeing one. The only other place in BC where there's a population of these (also called spirit bears) is on Princess Royal Island.

COOPERATIVE KERMODIES

When Michio Hoshino, the best bear photographer ever, wanted to see a kermodie, it took weeks. When Jack Hannah decided to bring in his camera crew, he said he had a couple of hours. They had to get in, get the bear, and get out. Impossible.

Wasn't going to happen. The BC guide tried to talk them out of this, but Jack insisted.

The group landed on Princess Royal, and within two hours had all the bear footage they needed.

Lightning is more cooperative for some than others.

■ Terrace

To get an idea of what a Kermodie looks like, stop by the **Terrace Visitor Centre**, right on Highway 16, ☎ 250-635-2573. You could also give **Silvertip Eco Tours** a call, ☎ 250-635-9326. They guide bear trips – as well as jet boat tours and kayak trips – and might be able to make your Kermodie dream come true.

Terrace has always made its living off the river, the downhill slide to the ocean. It's a good town for fishing, and in August, there's a local festival, the Sternwheeler Days, harking back to the time when giant paddle-wheel ships worked the Skeena.

While you're in town, stop by the **Heritage Park**, 4113 Sparks St., ☎ 250-615-3000. Guided tours take you through buildings dating from the town's early days to give you that Wild West feeling. Displays cover mining, trapping and more. CAN $3.50.

If you're really looking for a trip, there's a 49-mile/80-km one-way side-trip to the **Nisga'a Lava Beds**, a lava flow about 11 miles/18 km long. It was left from an eruption around 1775 that might have killed as many as 2,000 people and rerouted the Nass River. According to the Nisga'a, the eruption was nature's retaliation: their children had begun to torment salmon. A few short trails go into the lava, and in summer you can join a guided four-hour hike. ☎ 250-638-9589 for reservations.

Where to Stay

Terrace has more hotels than any town between Prince George and Prince Rupert. **Northern Motor Inn**, 3086 Hwy. 16, ☎ 250-635-6375, is basic but comfortable, with doubles from CAN $70. A little cheaper is the **Rainbow Inn**, 5510 Hwy. 16, ☎ 250-635-6415, with doubles from CAN $55. There are also a couple of the standard Canadian chains: **Sandman**, 4828 Hwy. 16, ☎ 250-635-9151, with doubles from CAN $75; and **Coast Resorts**, 4620 Lakelse Ave., ☎ 250-638-2258, with doubles from CAN $85.

Camping

If you've got a tent, go back east on the road to Kleanza Creek Provincial Park. There are sites right along the river. One of the most perfect campsites we've ever stayed in was here.

Your other nearby camping option is at **Lakelse Lake**, on the road down to Kitmat.

■ Kitmat

If you have time, you can make a pleasant side-trip from Terrace down to Kitmat. It's 35 miles/57 km from Hwy. 16 to the end of the road in Kitmat.

Locals all go out to play on **Lakelse** Lake, which has more than 150 campsites, and can be very, very crowded in summer with families. For reservations, ☎ 800-689-9025. The lake has a winter population of trumpeter swans and is very popular for fishing. There's also a hot springs nearby, at Mount Layton, but we recommend you skip the natural pools, which are too hot, and try the pool at the Mount Layton Hot Springs Resort, ☎ 800-663-3862.

Kitmat is a port town and a smelter town; most of the population makes its living off one or the other. There's not a lot to see in town, but the road in is quite pretty and, if you drive to the far end of town and Radley Memorial Campground, you'll see BC's oldest Sitka spruce tree. It's more than 30 feet in circumference, 150 feet tall and 500 years old.

If you want to see how the industrial side of British Columbia works, you can set up tours at Alcan Kitimat, Eurocan Pulp and Paper, or Methanex – ask at the **Visitor Info Centre**, which is on the east side of the road as you come into town, ☎ 250-632-6294.

Once you're back on Highway 16, the scenery starts to look more Alaskan than Canadian. You're entering the great rainforest of the coast, which covers most of the area from Seattle all the way up to Haines and Skagway, Alaska. The mountains are rolling, the trees thick, the clouds low. The road runs right along the banks of the Skeena – there are some pullouts for views, but keep any eye out for the heavy truck traffic when you're getting back on the highway.

The river opens to the ocean, the road bends north, and you enter Prince Rupert, a town that, since its beginning, has been designed to be the end of the line.

■ Prince Rupert

History

 Founded in 1900, Prince Rupert is now home to about 18,000 people. The original idea for the town was that it was to be the terminus of the Grand Trunk Pacific Railway. The Grand Trunk was one of those great plans that didn't turn out quite like anybody thought it would. In preparation, more than 12,000 miles of territory were surveyed for the best route, nearly 900 miles of right of way was blasted through solid rock, and costs rose to more than CAN $10,000 per mile before the line was completed.

Plans for Prince Rupert were equally grandiose, and publicity started early. First, there was a contest to name the town. The rules were that the name had to have 10 letters or fewer, and represent the Northwest coast. Prince Rupert – yeah, it's got too many letters, they allowed the cheat – was second cousin to Charles II and son of Fredrick of Prussia. His Northwest connection came because he was the first governor of the HBC. For this marvelous bit of sucking up, three CAN $250 prizes were awarded to contest entrants.

The original plan was for the town to have as many as 50,000 people. This would have made it one of the biggest cities west of the Rockies at the time, but everything changed when Charles Hays, the man who was spearheading the building effort, went down on the *Titanic*. With him went the grandiose plans for the port – situated in the third-largest and deepest ice-free harbor in Canada. When he died, there were about 200 people in the town.

That wasn't necessarily a bad thing. While Hays envisioned something to compete with Vancouver, what happened instead was slow, controlled growth, resulting in a pleasant little city that maintains a very busy port, especially for pulp and coal.

Basics

 In addition to access from the Yellowhead Highway, the Alaska Marine Highway ferry system uses Prince Rupert as its secondary southern terminus. Southbound ferries that terminate here – ships that go on to Bellingham usually do not stop in Rupert – leave you with a very enjoyable drive farther south, through the Yellowhead Highway and southern BC, or you can hop on a BC Ferry and go a bit farther south, to the northern tip of Vancouver Island, before you start driving. Either option is more than scenic.

The local **AMH** number is ☎ 250-627-1744. For full information on Alaska's ferry system, check out our *Adventure Guide to the Inside Passage and Coastal Alaska*, the most complete look at the AMH.

Northern BC

In summer, there's a BC Ferries run every other day from Rupert to Port Hardy on the tip of Vancouver Island. The trip takes 15 hours and it is always run in daylight to provide maximum scenic enjoyment. Ferries also go from Rupert to Skidegate in the lovely Queen Charlotte Islands. Local phone number in Prince Rupert for **BC Ferries** is ☎ 250-624-9627; toll-free in BC, ☎ 800-663-7600.

For local charter flights, call **Harbor Air,** ☎ 250-627-1341, or **Island Air,** ☎ 250-624-2577.

Greyhound Bus connects Rupert to Prince George and Edmonton, with daily departures. ☎ 800-661-1145.

Rent a car at **Tilden Rental,** ☎ 250-624-5318.

Skeena Taxi, ☎ 250-624-2185, serves the Prince Rupert area.

There's an excellent **Visitor Information Centre** next to the small boat harbor in Cow Bay. It's open from 9 am in summer. ☎ 250-624-5637, 800-667-1994, or write Box 22063, Prince Rupert, BC, V8J 4P8.

Internet access at **Java Dot Cup,** 516 3rd Ave. West, ☎ 250-627-4112.

Attractions

 Rupert is a walking town. Just take a stroll from the archeological museum down to the train museum, and around the point towards the ferry terminal. Look one way, there's a beautiful town; look the other, and there's nothing but ocean, islands and fishing boats coming and going.

Still, there isn't a whole lot to do in Rupert except soak in the exceptional scenery – the town is most useful as a way to get somewhere else, as it's a port for both the Alaska Marine Highway and the BC Ferry system – but you're not going to regret a couple of days wandering the pleasant streets, either. It's one of the prettiest small towns in British Columbia.

Start touring the town at the **Museum of Northern British Columbia**. Check for guided heritage walking tours of the downtown area. The museum has a good assortment of Native artifacts, including a reproduction of a petroglyph known as "Man who fell from the heaven." It's a full-sized outline of a human body. There are elaborate displays of Native basketry and utensils. It's pretty easy to lose track of time in here, the quality of artifacts is so good. There are also regular guided programs to the carving shed behind the museum, which offers a look at a totem pole in the making, and where films are shown on the history of totem poles. Admission is $5.

In the summer, the museum runs archeological tours; tickets are sold at Tourist Info Centre. The tour, which is really more historical than archeological, takes you out on a boat to the old village of Metlakatla, stopping along the way at other points of interest. A knowledgeable guide fills you in on how to spot old native villages (watch for green swaths of land or parallel rows of rocks leading into the water), and offers a history of settlement in the area. It's a good introduction to local native culture. The price can't be beat, at CAN $24 for a 3½-hour trip. For more information, contact the museum at PO Box 669, 100 1st Ave. East, Prince Rupert, BC V8J 3S1. ☎ 250-624-3207.

The **Firehall Museum** details Rupert's historical fire stations, with the highlight of the exhibition being a 1925 Reo Speedwagon fire engine. It's just up the street from the Infocentre. Admission is by donation. ☎ 250-627-4475. Summer hours: Tuesday-Sunday, 9 am-noon and 1-5 pm. CAN $2.

Walk west along the waterfront to reach the **Kwinitsa Station Museum**. Along with an interpretive exhibit – a detailed history of how the railway has influenced Prince Rupert – the museum also features videos and has a good gift shop. It looks small on the outside, but this is a must-see. After all, the railway was what started the town and, of all the railway museums in British Columbia, this one gives you the best idea of what life was like at the stations (most museums concentrate on the trains). It has good photographs of railway workers and their tools, and is a great place to get an idea of what working on the railroad really was like. Admission is by donation, suggested at CAN $1. ☎ 250-627-8009.

The Station Museum has a great location right on the waterfront, with a little park nearby. It's the perfect spot for a picnic.

The other standard attraction of Prince Rupert is actually a few miles out of town. Head out on the Yellowhead Highway and take Route 599 – there's only one way to go and you can't get lost. Follow 599 for six miles and you'll reach the **North Pacific Cannery Historic Fishing Village**. Like coal mining communities in the Eastern US, cannery communities were towns unto themselves, with housing, stores, entertainment and more. The North Pacific Cannery opened in 1899 and ran continuously until 1981. It's now been reopened as a museum, showing the details of the canning process and how the canneries stayed alive. The museum offers excellent displays (ever wonder how they made cans before the machinery took over?) and good interpretive signs. Tours are run every hour, or you can walk the grounds yourself. Admission is CAN $10 for adults, and well worth it. ☎ 250-628-3538. Open seven days a week, 9 am-6 pm, May 15 to September 30.

Adventures in Nature

Khutzemateen/K'tzim-a-Deen Grizzly Bear Sanctuary. A lot of the operators listed below say they run trips into the Khutzeymateen wilderness, and that's sort of true. But they're really running on the very edges of it, in the Khutzeymateen Inlet, just outside the actual sanctuary. That doesn't mean you won't see bears –

there are a lot of bears out there to see (roughly 50 make the area home, which is quite a high density for grizzlies), and your chances are extremely good of getting a close-up view. But be sure to find out whether you're going into the very restricted reserve, or simply into the area.

The Khutzeymateen was Canada's first wilderness area set up specifically to protect grizzlies and their habitat. It covers a bit over 79,000 acres, ranging from the coast to mountains over 6,000 feet high. The official provincial park handout on the sanctuary says it all: the land is there for the bears, and "any human activity in the area is secondary.... While visitor use of this sanctuary is not encouraged, controlled viewing is permitted." And they keep a tight control on the viewing. This isn't a place where you can just turn up and take a look around.

All visitors to the sanctuary must register in the ranger station at the head of the inlet. And the rangers keep a close eyes on you. Each day, only one group of 10 people, maximum, is allowed into the estuary, the prime bear-watching spot. Officials would prefer it if you never even get out of your boat and just watched from the water, at least 100 yards from any bear. If you've got your own boat, you can turn up and anchor in the inlet, but you can't get off the boat unless you're accompanied by a park official. They are trying hard to make this a very inconvenient place to go. It's better for the bears that way, and we've got to encourage that. Bears have enough trouble. Let's give them some room and applaud Canada's efforts to tightly control the area. Ten people a day is enough.

For more information, contact BC Parks Khutzeymateen office, ☎ 250-798-2277.

If running on the edges of the sanctuary isn't enough for you, contact **Ocean Light II Adventures**, ☎ 604-328-5339, an official guide into the sanctuary itself. Four-day trips run about CAN $1,500 on the company's quite swank boat. These people know what they're doing, and they're serious about protecting bears inside the sanctuary. For true bear fans, this is the chance of a lifetime.

If you're looking for guided trips onto the water, **Prince Rupert Adventure Tours**, ☎ 800-201-8377, 627-9166, has a good variety at bargain prices. Their four-hour whale-watching trips are a deal for CAN $72, and they guarantee you'll see whales, or they'll take you out again for free. Trips to Khutzeymateen run CAN $140 for six hours. They also do a four-hour photography safari for CAN $80. Give them a call or stop by their office, in the same building as the Tourist Info Centre.

Adventures on Water

 Fishing: Prince Rupert is **salmon** country. Mid-May to mid-July, the place is a fisherman's dream come true. Even if you're here as late as September, you can pick up on the coho run.

There are a ton of local operators. Check with the Info Centre first, since they know the operators and can set you up with the people who will best match your needs. Remember, before booking a charter, always see what you're getting yourself in for, what's provided and what isn't, and what kind of boat you're going to be on. There are plenty of choices out there, including something that's just right for you.

Seashore Charters, ☎ 250-624-5645, in the trailer across from the museum, has wildlife watching, fishing and town tours. Fishing charters start at CAN $200/person for all day, with a minimum of four people. Whale-watching trips run CAN $75 and offer a good chance to see humpbacks, and possibly minkes or grey whales. Trips out to see bears cost CAN $175. If you're after a quick look at the town from the water, try their CAN $25 harbor excursion, which gives you a good view of the Rupert coastline.

Once you've caught the fish, **Dolly's Seafood**, #7 Cow Bay Road, ☎ 250-624-6090, can freeze or vacuum-pack your catch.

Kayaking: If you're looking to kayak, contact **Eco-Treks**, ☎ 250-624-8311, next door to the Info Centre. They've got quick paddles for novices from CAN $40. If you're after something more, there's a six-hour paddle at Lucy Island, where you've got a good chance of spotting seals and more among the blue lagoons and white sand beaches. The CAN $150 includes a Zodiac ride out. For birders, there's the Kayaking Quest tour, for CAN $60, which takes in a rhinoceros auklet sanctuary. Rhinoceros auklets are even more clumsy than most of the auk family. If you watch one, you'll wonder what kind of bad day Mother Nature was having when she came up with the design.

Eco-Treks also runs longer trips, including excursions to Khutzeymateen to see grizzlies, for CAN $595, in June and July, or overnight paddles to watch humpback whales, for the same price.

They rent kayaks, but you've got to know what you're doing before they'll send you out alone with one.

Adventures in the Air

 Flightseeing: Harbour Air, ☎ 250-627-1341, runs flightseeing trips, including flyovers of the Khutzeymateen wilderness – Canada's only grizzly sanctuary – for about CAN $250. **Inland Air**, ☎ 250-888-624-2577, also runs charters to Khutzeymateen, as well as quick flightseeing trips closer to town.

Palmerville Adventures, ☎ 888-580-2234, runs trips to Khutzeymateen, starting with a flight to the inlet, and then two hours of boating to watch for bears. Prices start at CAN $250.

Where to Eat

The place of choice is **Smiles**, at 113 George Hills Way, in Cow Bay. The menu includes seafood, wonderful carrot cake and other desserts. In business since 1922, it offers the best food in town and is the most popular eatery. You may have to wait for a table. Prices start around CAN $6. Nearby is the reservations-required **Cow Bay Café**, ☎ 250-627-1212, at 205 Cow Bay Rd. The menu changes according to what's fresh, but the food is always outstanding. Prices from CAN $12.

For a seafood night, head to **Boulet's Seafood** (☎ 250-624-9309), in the Pacific Inn. They serve crab, salmon and other dishes in a deluxe atmosphere (with deluxe prices). Reservations are required.

At the other end of the scale is the **Green Apple**, at 310 McBride. Stop in for a quick fill up of fish and chips. This is Prince Rupert's place of choice for a quick meal.

Where to Stay

Most of Prince Rupert's hotels are located along 1st, 2nd, and 3rd Avenues, between the ferry terminal and downtown.

Crest Motor Hotel, ☎ 624-6771 or 800-663-8150, 222 1st. Ave. West, is the nicest place to stay in town. Doubles start at CAN $140. **The Moby Dick Inn**, ☎ 624-6961, 935 2nd Ave. West., is conveniently located, features room/car packages, and has a pretty good restaurant on the premises. Doubles go from CAN $80. **The Inn on the Harbor**, ☎ 250-624-9157; 800-663-8155, 720 1st Ave., has good views and rooms starting from CAN $80.

The Aleeda Motel, ☎ 250-627-1367, at 900 3rd Ave West, near the ferry terminals, has doubles from CAN $70. In the same neighborhood is the **Totem Lodge**, 1335 Park Ave., ☎ 250-624-6761 or 800-550-9161, with doubles from CAN $75.

As with most towns, turnover in **B&Bs** is huge. It's easiest just to ask at the Info Centre, where there will be plenty of brochures on local spots.

Camping

There are two places to camp in Prince Rupert. The **Park Avenue Campground** is just a mile from the ferry terminal. There's not much atmosphere here, but it's a very convenient spot. Tents can get in anytime; RVs need reservations. The place is a big grassy patch by the roadside. ☎ 250-624-5861.

Just 14 miles/23 km outside of town on the Yellowhead Highway is **Prudhomme Lake Provincial Park Campground**, ☎ 250-847-7320, which features 18 spots, no facilities, but lots of trees and scenery.

Queen Charlotte Islands

❝ There is a pole that hold the centre of this world – it's a cedar tree in the middle of Haida Gwaii," says Cheryl Coull, quoting Michael Nicoll Yahgulanaas in her indispensable *Traveller's Guide to Aboriginal B.C.*

Haida Gwaii, more commonly known to the outside world as the Queen Charlotte Islands, is a triangular archipelago of hundreds of islands (just how many depends on what size rock you call an island). The islands are the ancestral home of the Haida, the coastal First Nations people who've inhabited this area for thousands of years. The heart of the Queen Charlottes is made up of two large islands – Graham to the north, and Moresby to the south, and four other main islands: Langara, Louise, Lyell, and Kunghit. The larger islands are bordered by two mountain ranges to the west and are separated from the mainland by the stormy Hecate Strait. Smack dab in the middle of the most active earthquake area in Canada, the Queen Charlottes are an otherworldly mix of snow-top mountains and fiords that plunge into the sea, mist-enshrouded forests and windswept sandy beaches.

Robert Bringhurst, in his amazing *Story as Sharp as a Knife*, describes the Charlottes: "Southern Haida Gwaii is an indissoluble tangle of land and sky and sea; in Swanton's words [a visiting 19th-century linguist] 'a ragged chain of mountains half submerged in the ocean.' Northern Haida Gwaii is broad, full of muskeg, low hills and tall Sitka spruce.... Well-hidden trails pierce the mountains of southern Haida Gwaii, surreptitiously linking the villages on the relatively sheltered east coast with those a world away... on the open Pacific. The links are there, and they were used. Yet every southern Haida village had its own light and weather. Each one was – and though the houses have long vanished, each still is – a world of its own."

According to Haida legend, these islands are the place where time began. The even older name for this area, Xhaaidlagha Gwaayaai, means "Islands at the Boundary of the World." Archeologists date the first human habitation to over 7,000 years ago, while Haida legends all start with the Raven, 10,000 years ago, creating the world here and filling it with the first Haida (he found them hiding in a clam shell).

The cedar trees that covered the islands were perfect for carving. The Haida had no written language, but they expressed themselves beautifully through their art and villages were filled with intricately decorated canoes, longhouses and totem poles.

The land was good to the Haida; they grew and prospered here until it just got too crowded. There may have been as many as 30,000 people living on the island chain, so the people in northern villages left in a series of canoe migrations to what are now the southern islands of Alaska.

First Haida contact with Europeans came in the late 1700s and sparked the same disasters as were repeated many times across the world: waves of smallpox epidemics decimated the population. Entire lineages were wiped out, villages emptied. Settlers from the mainland, social and governmental changes all took additional tolls on the Haida: by 1915, the estimated population of 7,000 people in the 1700s had been reduced to less than a tenth that.

Today, there are no cities on the islands and only a few small settlements, but fully half the population is Haida, and traditions are strong. The reason to go to the Charlottes is to get away, to escape the busy outside world and sink back into a land that's almost primordial. The islands have a spiritual and almost mystical air.

The Charlottes offer a landscape of snowy mountains, dramatic fiords, misty forests and windswept beaches punctuated by ancient First Nations villages dissolving back into the earth. Appealingly isolated, the islands, sometimes called the Galapagos of the North, are covered with rare subspecies of plants and animals, including the world's largest black bear, rare mosses and river otters and saw-whet owls found only in the Charlottes. The west coastlines are rocky and studded with coves; on the east, sandy desolate beaches lure even the most hardened beachcombers. Seventeen species of whales and dolphins pass through the waters surrounding Haida Gwaii; almost half of British Columbia's population of sea lions feed and breed here as well. The middle of the islands are covered by rainforests filled with giant cedars peppered with bald eagles.

■ Transport

Haida Gwaii is accessible by **BC Ferries**, ☎ 888-223-3779, and via air from Prince Rupert and Vancouver. There is a small cluster of towns near the port of entry. Visitors arriving via ferry sail into Skidegate, the main gateway of the Charlottes, at the southeast tip of Graham Island. There are six sailings per week to and from Prince Rupert in the summer months (June to mid-October) and three days per week the rest of the year. Reservations are strongly suggested for the six-hour trip, especially if you're bringing a vehicle.

The ferry terminal is 1.2 miles/two km south of Skidegate, and three miles/five km east of Queen Charlotte City. Ferries to Prince Rupert make a once-a-week stop in Port Hardy, at the northern tip of Vancouver Island, so it's possible to do a two-part sailing from Vancouver Island to the Queen Charlottes.

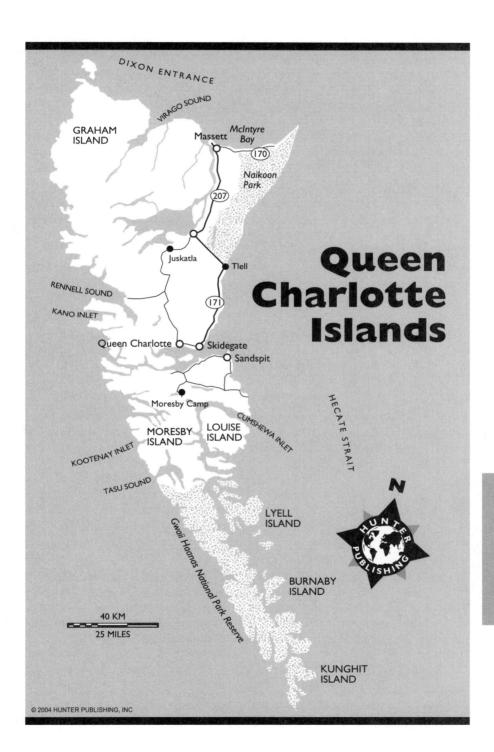

© 2004 HUNTER PUBLISHING, INC

There is also a local ferry connecting Skidegate to Allisford Bay (nine miles/15 km south of Sandspit) on Moresby Island. The ferry makes frequent trips between 7 am and 10:30 pm daily. The 20-minute trip gives visitors spectacular views of the busy Skidegate Inlet. It's cheaper if you purchase books of passenger and vehicle tickets at the booth at Skidegate.

The main airport at Sandspit has daily flights arriving from both Vancouver (with **Air BC**, ☎ 800-665-1177, or **Canadian West Airlines**, ☎ 866-835-9292) and Prince Rupert (with **Harbour Air**, ☎ 250-559-0052). **Hawkair**, ☎ 866-429-5247 or 800-487-1216, also offers service from Prince Rupert to a smaller airport at Masset. Other commercial air services, such as float plane and helicopter, are available at Sandspit, Queen Charlotte City and Masset. Contact **South Moresby Air Charters**, ☎ 250-559-4222, or **Vancouver Island Helicopters**, ☎ 250-637-5344.

A local airport bus meets and transports all passengers at Sandspit to Queen Charlotte City (three miles/five km west of the airport, CAN $14 per person). Taxis are also available: **Bruce's Taxi**, ☎ 250-637-5655; **Eagle Cab**, ☎ 250-559-4461; **Pete's Taxi**, ☎ 250-559-8622.

To best explore the islands, you'll need a car. If you're planning to rent, both **Budget**, ☎ 800-577-3228, and **Thrifty**, ☎ 250-637-2299, have offices at the Skidegate airport. **Rustic**, ☎ 250-559-4641, and **Twin**, ☎ 250-559-8700, are in Queen Charlotte City. Prices start at CAN $60 per day plus mileage – in high season, make reservations well in advance.

Because the airport is in the middle of the islands, we're describing the Charlottes from the north to the south, starting at Masset, the largest town in Haida Gwaii, on the northern end of Graham Island, near the Dixon Entrance.

■ Masset

Masset, accessible by air or via Highway 16, 67 miles/110 km from Skidegate, is the oldest municipality in Haida Gwaii, dating to 1909. It was originally named Graham City, for the Graham Steamship, Coal and Lumber Company that founded the town, but the name changed later to New Masset, then just Masset. Most of the town's residents work in either the fishing or lumber industries, though tourism is becoming increasingly important. Masset is a good base from which to explore the northern shores of Graham Island and even Langara Island.

Attractions

 Start out at the **Tourism Info Centre**, on the main road as you drive into town, ☎ 888-352-9292 or 250-626-3982. Open May 1 to September 30, daily, 9 am to 4 pm. Come here for details on the local hiking, beachcombing and clam-digging areas, as well as to arrange fishing trips for crab, halibut and salmon.

Most of the sights in Masset are just outside of town. Be sure to take the 16-mile/26-km drive past the airport along the north coast from town out to **Tow Hill**, in Naikoon Provincial Park. The park covers most of the northeast corner of Graham Island, over 130,000 acres, and the road out there takes you past mossy old growth spruce trees through the Tow Hill Ecological Reserve to the Rose Spit Ecological Reserve.

Adventures in Nature

 Take a walk around town to get oriented and see some of the early 20th century architecture (the church and schoolhouse date to 1912, the hospital to 1914) on your way to the **Delkatla Wildlife Sanctuary**, at the head of Delkatla Inlet. You can see upwards of 113 species of birds here, including sandhill cranes, trumpeter and tundra swans, and Canada, snow, Ross's and white-fronted geese. It's just over 1.2 miles/two km to the north of the village of Old Masset; walk or take a five-minute drive.

Adventures on Foot

 Hiking: Superbly situated campsites are available at **Agate Beach**, just west of Tow Hill, a 360-foot/110-meter cliff of columnar basalt, at the north end of the park. The sites (for vehicles and tents) are at the back of the beach, but have an unbeatable view of the Dixon Entrance and Tow Hill. Sites are CAN $14 during the summer and free the rest of the year. A short distance east are picnic grounds and a trail that leads to the top of Tow Hill. This 15-minute hike takes you to the second-highest point in the park and a good spot for photographs. On a clear day, you can see across the Dixon Entrance to Prince of Wales Island and the mainland in southern Alaska; to the west is Langara Island. Check out the nearby blowhole and the lovely tidal pools.

Just beyond the base of Tow Hill is a favorite walk (or bike trip) for locals along golden North Beach to Rose Spit, about six miles/10 km along the beach, depending on your route and the tideline. If you've got a mountain bike, you can ride halfway out to the spit and then leave the bikes and walk the rest of the way. Plan a full day for this trip if you're on foot, to hike out to the end of the spit and back. Clam digging and beachcombing are popular all along these northern shores. Note that these dunes are a fragile ecosystem. Stay on the trails. If you want to do a little clamming, razor clams are the safest to eat, but check with the visitor's center for current conditions before eating any other shellfish.

Continue to the tip of Graham Island, to Rose Spit and **Naikoon**, or "point town." Jutting seven miles/12 km out from the rest of Graham Island, this spot, sacred to the Haida, is the place named by legend where ancestors of the Raven clan were lured out of their hiding spot in a giant clam shell to take their place in the newly created world. Certainly, the landscape here, where the Hecate Strait meets the Dixon Entrance, full of boiling tides and ocean spumes, covered with muskeg, wind-stunted trees and agate-spotted beaches, has a sense of the otherworldly. Wildlife-viewing opportunities abound in the park: watch for whales, orca, dolphins and seals offshore – there may even be sea blubber, a kind of jellyfish that can have tentacles 10 feet/three meters long; on shore, there are black bear, deer, marten, beaver, wild cattle and even the shy river otter.

Ambitious hikers can travel south, the spectacular 58-mile/94-km length of Naikoon Park, from Tow Hill to Tlell, along East Beach. Allow four to six days for this hike. While there is some shelter and limited fresh water, carry adequate food and water, as well as a tide table.

Where to Eat

Your choices are pretty simple, but also pretty cheap. After a long beach walk, grab a coffee and a bit of local color at **Haidabucks**, on Main Street, ☎ 250-626-5548. Another place to catch up on the local news is **Marj's Café**, also on Main Street. ☎ 250-626-9344. **Pearl's**, on Main & Collision, ☎ 250-626-3223, offers Chinese food as well as seafood, while the **Mile Zero Grill**, on Collision Ave., is the place to have a burger.

Where to Stay

Masset has a selection of B&Bs, as well as a motel and a campground. Check in with visitor info for a complete list as B&Bs can come and go quickly. **Alaska View Lodge**, 12291 Tow Hill Rd., ☎ 250-626-3333, is right on South Beach, halfway between Masset and Tow Hill, and offers pleasant rooms, breakfast and private baths. Doubles start from CAN $90. **Singing Surf Inn**, 1504 Old Beach Rd., ☎ 250-626-3318, is the only motel in town and offers large airy rooms just off the main drag near downtown from CAN $90. **Harbourview Lodging**, 1608/1618 Delkatla St., ☎ 250 626-5109, offers comfortable rooms with shared baths, a communal kitchen and sauna at CAN $60-90.

For a splurge, try **Chinook Lodge**, 2062-2064 Maple Crescent, ☎ 800-492-4554. For CAN $115-135, you get your own two-bedroom guesthouse, completely furnished with all the comforts of home, including bicycles and canoes. Also swank is **Naden Lodge**, 1496 Delkatla St., ☎ 250-626-3322, offering waterfront rooms with many amenities. Rooms run upward from CAN $129.

Camping

Camp at **Daisy's RV Park and Campground**, 1440 Tow Hill Rd., ☎ 250-626-5280, near the Delkatla Wildlife Sanctuary. Large full-service sites run CAN $12-20, depending on services.

■ Old Masset

Legend has it that the west coast's first totem pole was carved in Old Masset (sometimes you'll see this spelled Massett; we're keeping it simple here). The town took its name as a gift from a European ship, possibly Spanish, that was damaged in a storm. Three villages in the area gave timber and provisions to the ship, allowing it to safely continue its journey. The captain tossed the name out like a party favor.

The present town, which covers the sites of the three older villages (Atewaas, Kayang and Jaaguhl), is the administrative seat of the Council of the Haida nation, and is a must-see for anyone interested in Haida history.

The village is a focal point for Haida artists, historians and archeologists. As you walk around the village, notice that some of the new houses have been made in traditional longhouse style. You may also see intricate spruce root weavings and carved totem fences. Be respectful during your visit to the community and artists' workplaces – this may look like a museum, but it's home to many people.

Make sure to stop at the privately owned **Ed Jones Haida Museum**, in the old blue schoolhouse, at the end of the coastal road. You'll get an idea of what the area looked like from the lovely historical photographs. Also on exhibit is Haida art, pre- and post-contact artifacts, and original Queen Charlotte totem poles. Generally open in summer on the weekends, from 9-5. Also check out **Haida Arts and Jewelery**, in the longhouse community building. You can see artists working at several local galleries and workshops. They include Jim Hart (daily, in summer, from 1-4) and Morris White, ☎ 250-626-3985. Check with the Village Office (in the large hall on Eagle Rd.) for details on local artists and attractions. You can also inquire here about permits for **Duu Guusd Tribal Park**. Over a century ago, villages dotted the coast from Old Masset to the western edges of Graham Island. Duu Guusd Tribal Park, created to protect the abandoned villages in this part of the island, covers much of the northwest coast of Graham Island, from Naden Harbour to Kiusta. There is currently only limited access to the park – check at the village office for information on special visitor's permits. North of the park is the spectacular and remote Langara Island, a birder's and fisherman's paradise.

■ Port Clemens

Heading south of Masset, along Masset Inlet, it's an easy 25-mile/40-km drive to Port Clemens. About halfway to Port Clemens is the lily-rimmed Pure Lake Provincial Park, a good place to stop for a picnic, a warm water swim or a paddle in a canoe.

Attractions

 Port Clemens is a small fishing village with a few amenities. It's mostly home to area loggers. It lies at the waterway crossroads of Masset Inlet and the Yakoun River, the longest river on Haida Gwaii and a major salmon run. Make sure to check out the pleasant **Port Clemens Museum**, on Bayview Dr., ☎ 205-557-4443, for a window into the community's WW I origins. Open afternoons in the summer; weekends only the rest of the year.

The village is best known for its proximity to the **golden spruce**, a 300-year-old, 164-foot/50-meter genetic oddity with golden needles (the chlorophyl in its needles broke down in the sun). Unfortunately, you can't see this tree today, as an off-island lunatic cut it down – scientists are trying to grow a new one from cuttings. Other golden spruces have since been spotted in the Charlottes, but none as notable as this.

Adventures on Foot

 Hiking: About three miles/five km south of Port Clemens, on Juskatla Rd., the **Golden Spruce Trail** winds along the Yokoun River. It is still worth doing, even though the landmark tree is gone. In summer, watch for salmon swimming up to their spawning grounds. Five miles/eight km down Juskatla Rd. from the Golden Spruce Trail is another hike to an unfinished Haida canoe. Carvers shaped canoes on site – start by burning out the center of the tree, then work endlessly with a series of hand adzes – before finally towing it back to the villages for the detail work. The largest canoes could carry 40 people and were 76 feet/23 meters long.

Where to Stay

 The **Golden Spruce Motel**, 2 Grouse St., ☎ 205-557-4325, has rooms for CAN $55-65, some with kitchenettes.

Onward from Port Clemens

 From Port Clemens you have a choice: you can continue south along Highway 16 to Tlell and Skidegate, or head southwest on inland logging roads 39 miles/64 km to Queen Charlotte City. If you decide to take the inland route, make sure you've got a full tank of gas and a useable spare tire. Logging trucks always have the right of way, regardless of circumstance. Juskatla is the local headquarters of the local logging company, Macmillan Boldel, 12 miles/19 km outside Port Clemens. You can get local logging maps and road conditions here, or check with any of the information centers. If the roads are clear, this is a scenic route, passing numerous streams and lakes.

■ Tlell

Continuing south, it's 14 miles/21 km to Tlell, a tiny community first homesteaded in 1904 and home of the oldest working ranch on Haida Gwaii (1911). The village, a traditional Haida fishing camp, offers access to the southern entrance of Naikoon Provincial Park (get a map at the park headquarters beside the highway, just south of the Tlell River bridge).

Attractions

 Tlell is a growing artist's community. If you're planning to be in the area in early July, plan to attend the **Edge of the World Music Festival**. Held the second weekend in July, it draws musicians from all over Canada for a long weekend of fun.

Stop by **Sitka Studio**, on Richardson Rd., ☎ 250-557-4241, to get a feel for some of the local art.

Adventures on Foot

Hiking: Northwest of the bridge in town is a picnic area and the trailhead for a 10-mile/16-km round-trip hike to the wreck of the *Pesuta*, a log barge blown ashore during a 1928 gale. This could also be used as a starting point for the hike up to the northeast corner of the park (see Masset, above, for details). The advantage of starting from the south is that you will often have the prevailing southeast wind at your back. The hike is 55 miles/89 km on the slightly inland Cape Fife route, or 58 miles/94 km to go round Rose Spit. Winds in this area average 15 mph/24 kmh and are stronger during storms. Plan accordingly.

Where to Stay

There are several new B&Bs. Find out who's in business when you're there at the Queen Charlotte City Info Centre. You can camp at **Misty Meadows**, just north of Naikoon park headquarters, for CAN $14 per site during the summer (free camping off-season).

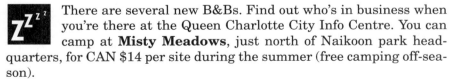

■ Skidegate

It's a short 22-mile/36-km drive south to Skidegate, but it's a beautiful one. The winding road along **Hectate Strait** offers spectacular whale-watching in summer months. **Halibut Bight**, 16 miles/26 km north of Skidegate, was a seasonal fishing site – today it's a rest stop providing a spot to pull off and walk the beach, watching for rainbows and whale spouts. A mile or so north of Skidegate you'll see **St. Mary's Spring**, marked by a wood carving. Legend says that if you drink from the spring, you'll return to Haida Gwaii. Just a bit outside of town, watch for a sign for **Balance Rock**. A short trail here takes you down to the beach to see the seven-foot/two-meter boulder left here by an ancient glacier. The boulder, which looks precariously perched, is best viewed at low tide.

Most people pass through Skidegate only because it's closest to where the ferry stops, but the town is more important than that. It was one of the few villages that survived the post-contact smallpox epidemics, so it has a longer continuous history than most spots on the island. Named for the son of the leader who met the first European otter hunters here in 1787, Skidegate today is still a focal point for Southern Haida culture.

Attractions

 The **Queen Charlotte Islands Museum**, at 2nd Beach Rd., a half-mile/.8 km from the ferry terminal, is a masterpiece combination of glass and cedar overlooking Hecate Strait and one thing you absolutely cannot miss during a visit to the Charlottes. It has an outstanding collection that includes ancient totem poles from abandoned villages, antique and contemporary carvings argillite (a soft black slate found only on Haida Gwaii), fur and bark clothing, and many personal, household and farm items. Combined with the excellent historic photos and prints by Haida artists, the museum gives visitors a window into the Charlottes of old. The natural history exhibits include a humpback skull and a good collection of stuffed birds. Admission is CAN $4. ☎ 250-559-4643.

After you've finished at the museum, stop out back at the wooden viewing platform and scan the horizon for whales. You can see whales anywhere along the beach in town – the grays are especially easy to spot as they rest and feed along the shallow gravel waters of the inlet.

Next door to the museum are the offices of the **Haida Gwaii Watchmen**, ☎ 250-559-8225. The Watchmen program was created in the late 1970s by a group of Haida volunteers to protect the old villages from vandalism, theft and overzealous tourists. Today, Watchmen live in several of the old villages in the summer, to check permits and act as guardians. You can get permits for visiting Gwaii Haanas here.

Just down the road you'll see a group of buildings, including a carving shed workshop. One longhouse-style building covers the Loo Taas, or "Wave Eater," the first canoe carved since 1909, that was commissioned for Expo '86 in Vancouver. The canoe was then paddled from Vancouver, carrying a group of passengers (including one of its designers, the acclaimed Bill Reid, the greatest Haida-style artist of the past century) on a three-week journey back to Haida Gwaii.

Most visitors to Skidegate eat and stay in Queen Charlotte City, three miles/five km west of the BC Ferries terminal in Skidegate.

▪ Queen Charlotte City

Queen Charlotte City is a business center for Haida Gwaii. The town, the second-largest on the islands, was the first registered township in the Charlottes. The headquarters for the **Gwaii Haanas National Park** are here, ☎ 250-559-8818. See below for details about the park.

The **Visitor Info Centre**, at 3220 Wharf St., ☎ 250-559-8316, is open 10 am to 7 pm daily from mid-May through early September. Call for hours during the rest of the year, or check online at www.qcinfo.com.

Shopping

Queen Charlotte City is an excellent place to shop for Haida crafts. Walk around town and see what catches your eye – Haida Gwaii has one of highest concentrations of artists in North America. If you need some reference material before you get started, stop by **Bill Ellis/Northwest Coast Books**, 720 Highway 33, ☎ 250-559-4681. **Joy's Island Jewelers**, ☎ 250-559-8890, has a good collection of contemporary artwork.

Where to Eat

Take a walk down 3rd Ave. and see what suits your mood. **Oceana**, 3119 3rd Ave., ☎ 250-559-8633, has Chinese cuisine, while **Claudette's**, at 3rd Ave. and 2nd St., ☎ 250-559-8861, is more gussied up, and priced accordingly. The **Hummingbird Café**, in the Sea Raven Motel, ☎ 250-559-8583, offers dinners using local seafood. For great views and local flavor, check out **Margaret's**, 3223 Wharf St., ☎ 250-559-4204, for breakfast and lunch. **Howler's Pub & Bistro**, ☎ 250-559-8600, overlooks the harbor and is a good place to eat, play or drink.

Where to Stay

Premier Creek Lodging has comfortable rooms with kitchenettes in the historic Premier Hotel building (dating from 1910), 3101 3rd Ave., ☎ 250-5559-8415, from CAN $55-75. **Sea Raven**

is the only motel in town. It's at 3301 3rd Ave., ☎ 250-559-4423, just down the street from the Visitor Centre. It has rooms with kitchenettes and private baths at CAN $75-95. **Spruce Point Lodge**, ☎ 250-559-8234, is a hybrid B&B, offering a private rooms from CAN $70, with breakfast brought to your room (or out on a deck overlooking the water).

■ Sandspit

Sandspit, on Moresby Island, is where most travelers coming via plane enter Haida Gwaii. A local ferry connecting Graham and Moresby Island runs several times a day (see *Transport*, above, for details). Due to its stormy winter weather patterns, Sandspit wasn't settled until the beginning of the 20th century, during the Charlottes' homesteading period. The settlement remained tiny until the end of WW II, when logging business moved here and the Royal Canadian Air Force opened an airstrip and a seaplane base at Alliford Bay.

Use Sandspit as a base, get your bearings and supplies, and then head out to the good stuff. Most of Moresby Island is inaccessible by road; the southern half of the island, along with smaller southern islands, is protected. You can drive south about 31 miles/50 km on the logging roads in north Moresby Island to the abandoned Moresby Camp, but it's best to check with the tourist information office before you set out, as these are protected sites and visitors are not always welcome.

The **Tourism Centre**, www.sandspitqci.com, is at the airport, ☎ 250-637-5362. Get details on rental vehicles, charters, tours and accommodation here; if you're arriving in high season, it's recommended to make reservations for the aforementioned well in advance.

Where to Eat

You can get a cup of joe and light snacks at **Java on the Spit**, at the airport, ☎ 250-637-2455. For something more substantial, stop by the **Eagle's View**, ☎ 250-637-2217, on Shingle Bay, downtown, or head to the **Sandspit Inn**. **Dick's Wok Inn**, ☎ 250-637-2275, is the place for Chinese cuisine and will even bag it for you to take out.

If you're getting ready to go to Gwaii Haanas, stop by the **SuperValu** grocery store on Alliford Road, next to the airport, to stock up on all your essentials. The fresh baked goods are a bonus.

Where to Stay

There is one motel and several B&Bs. As usual, check with tourist info in the airport terminal to get the most up-to-date info on the B&Bs.

The **Sandspit Inn**, ☎ 250-637-5334 or 800-666-1107, next to the airport, offers doubles (some with kitchenettes) from CAN $95. **Moresby Island Guesthouse**, just down the road at 385 Alliford Bay Rd., ☎ 250-637-5300, offers rooms with shared baths from CAN $65.

■ Gwaii Haanas National Park

Accessible only by plane or boat, this protected area includes a rare group of old Haida village sites that are a must-see. This area gives a sense of the ancient world one can rarely experience today. Legend has it that the site where the great ancestress, Foam Woman, gave birth to all women is hidden somewhere in south Moresby Island. Robert Bringhurst, in his beautiful *A Story As Sharp As A Knife*, tells a tale from this part of Haida Gwaii about a group of hunters trying to capture a harpooned orca with apparently supernatural powers:

> Big killer whales were spyhopping right there in the cove.
> They offered them tobacco.
> When they put another offering
> Of calcined shell with the tobacco,
> A bat scooped up the shell and the tobacco in its jaws.
> Then the biggest killer whales moved out to deeper water.
> Then the gods went back to the sea.

Get a permit from the park operators or the Watchmen's office in Skidegate before you go if you're not traveling with a licensed tour operator.

Watchmen preside over five main village sites: K'una (Skedan); T'anuu; Gandla K'in (Hot Water Island); Hlk'waah (Windy Bay); and Sgan Gwaii (Ninstints). Sgan Gwaii, listed as a UNESCO World Heritage Site in 1981, is one of the most popular villages to visit. Headquarters of the Kunghit Haida, "people to the south," it was an important fur trading site. As people here had heavier contact with the Europeans, it was one of the first to fall to the smallpox plague. There are no traceable descendants of the Kunghits, but they live on through the slowly sinking remains of 20 houses and magnificently carved poles.

This area is a destination for birders as well, as more than 370,000 pairs of seabirds – including tufted puffins, rhinoceros auklets and ancient and marbled murrelets – nest in Gwaii Haanas. Other types of wildlife abound, including orcas, and humpback and gray whales. There's a large sea lion rookery at Cape St. James.

There is a proposal to make a marine conservation reserve to protect the waters surrounding Gwaii Haanas. The reserve would still allow Haida traditional marine harvests as well as limited commercial fishing.

When to Visit

 Haida Gwaii is warmer and windier than the mainland. Prolonged rain is unlikely, but possible, while gusty winds, especially on the beaches, are common. Annual temperature averages vary little. Summer months have 18-20 hours of sunlight.

Attractions

 Masset has big **Victoria Day** festivals, complete with fireworks. **Skidegate Days**, the second weekend in June, include Haida war canoe races. Sandspit's **Logger Sports Day** in July (check dates with tourist info) – features competitions in traditional logging events, such as axe throwing and pole climbing.

Getting Out

 There are tour operators all over Haida Gwaii, offering a variety of services ranging from rental of vehicles to float plane drops to fully guided tours. Many motels and B&Bs also offer or can arrange these services. Check with the tourism centers and do some research, as offerings can change quickly. Talk to anyone you're considering *before* you book. Keep in mind that the weather in the Charlottes can turn on a dime (if you don't like the weather now, locals say, wait 20 minutes and it'll change). Allow a little extra time in your itinerary – this is not a place to rush or be rushed.

Adventures on Water

 Sailing: The area around the Queen Charlottes is a sailor's paradise. Cruising along the Inside Passage and the Alaska coastline is one of the great experiences of a lifetime. The waters here are for experienced sailors and boaters – if you don't fall into this category, you can hire someone else to do the work for you and just sit back and enjoy the view. Hypothermia is kind of peaceful, but it can be hard on your loved ones.

Fishing: Fishing here is, not surprisingly, excellent; Haida Gwaii has one of the world's most productive salmon fishing grounds. Chinook, coho and silver salmon are popular with anglers. Deep-sea fishing is also available; some of the largest halibut in the world are caught off the northern end of Graham Island.

Kayaking, Canoeing: Sea kayaking and canoeing are popular here. Operators offer guided trips through the archipelago, or you can go out on your own.

Adventures in Nature

 Whale-watching: Pacific grays visit the area in spring and summer (late April to June); you have a good chance of seeing one either on the ferry trip to the islands or while walking along the shoreline. Orca and the occasional blue or fin whales are also seen. Humpbacks feed during herring spawning season, February. Good spots to whale-watch from the shore include: anywhere along the beach in Skidegate; on the local ferry, Kwuna; on Rose Spit, northeast of Masset.

Guided tours will take you out in Zodiac boats suited up in warm survival jumpsuits, or you can go out in a heated boat. Most tour operators offer both half- and full-day whale-watching cruises, and the majority of them have hydrophones so you can listen to the whales. If you prefer, you can just watch for whales yourself, from any kind of fishing boat or sea kayak. For more info on whale-watching, check with the Whale Watch Operators Association Northwest at www.nwwhalewatchers.org.

Birding: The Charlottes are on the migration route for plenty of birds, so pack your spotting scope. Thanks to the remote location, which protects the birds, the abundance of food and water, and the fact that it's on the bird highway, makes the Charlottes a birders' paradise.

Keep an eye out for bald eagles and peregrine falcons. In the forests, there are hairy woodpeckers, saw-whet owls and, if you're lucky, a brown creeper or two. But sea birds are the real show: puffins, auklets, murres and murrelets, sandhill cranes, black-footed albatrosses, all four species of loon.... We could go on, but you've got the idea.

Good birding spots include the **Yakoun River**, near Port Clemens – the estuary brings in just about everybody, sooner or later – and **Kagan Bay**. The **Delkatla Wildlife Sanctuary**, near Masset, has perhaps the greatest variety of birds, as the terrain takes in the ocean, the shore and the forest. See *Masset* section for details.

You can charter boats out to some of the shorebird colonies in the outlying areas, but really, unless you're a hardcore, fanatic birder, this isn't such a great idea. The birds nest out here because they need space and privacy. We prefer to give it to them.

Haida Gwaii is an amazing destination, worthy of a trip by itself. We've tried to give you a just a taste of what it's like. If you're planning more than a few days here, we recommend a guidebook that focuses just on the Charlottes.

 Neil Carey, a longtime resident of the islands, wrote the *Guide to the Queen Charlottes*, an excellent book on the history of the islands. Also excellent is Cheryl Coull's *A Traveller's Guide to Aboriginal BC*.

The Cassiar Highway

If you've gone all the way west to Rupert – and it's well worth the trip – and then plan on doing the Cassiar, you'll need to do a bit of backtracking. Luckily, it's only a few hours, and it's very, very scenic.

Mile markers are almost nonexistent on the Cassiar; what's given here is mean distance from the junction of the Cassiar and Yellowhead highways, so keep an eye on your odometer. We're giving distances in miles rather than kilometers, because of the Cassiar's longstanding place as an alternate to the Alcan – there was actually quite a controversy over using the metric system on the Cassiar.

The junction for the Cassiar is in the middle of nowhere, but it's well signed, 365 miles/588 km to the west of Prince George. Be sure to gas up in Hazelton, which is spread out along the highway about 25 miles/40 km before the junction. Hazelton was a wintering spot for miners and prospectors working the interior; pack trains traveled the Telegraph Trail and ended up here.

Around you at the junction are the Seven Sisters Mountains. In this area there is some possibility of seeing a Kermodie bear, a rare subspecies of black bear. Kermodies are cream-colored – it's a form of albinism – and found only here and on some coastal islands. The other mainland spot where you might see them is in Terrace, farther along the Yellowhead Highway toward Prince Rupert.

If you're going to go this way, you've got to remember that there are very few services along the road. What services there are may be out of town, or out of business – there's a heavy turnover. Gas runs as much as 30¢ a liter more than on the main roads. Although the Cassiar is now almost all fully paved – at least what passes for pavement – construction sections become mud washes during rains. If the road is dry, the dust can be literally choking and blinding until the water trucks come by. There are still a couple of slippery single-lane bridges, lots and lots of potholes, frost heaves, and steep grades. Also, you should know that much of the road has been approved for small airplanes to land on. ☎ 900-451-4977 for a recording of Cassiar road conditions – the call is 75¢ a minute, and well worth it.

The Cassiar is a road you should consider only if you're camping and don't mind a bit of incredibly scenic hardship. Those looking for hotels often find themselves driving well past midnight. On the plus side, the drive is lovely and there's very little other traffic (except the long-haul trucks, which take this route). You certainly won't see any crowds of tourists. And maybe because of that, most people who have driven both the

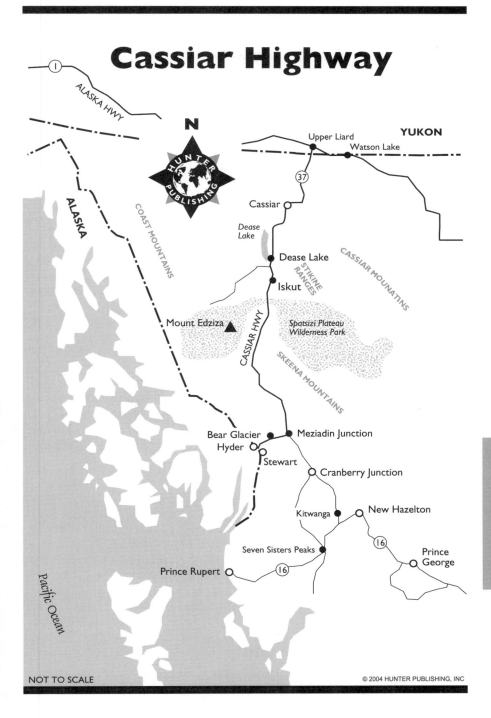

Cassiar Highway

N

ALASKA HWY

YUKON

Upper Liard
Watson Lake

ALASKA

COAST MOUNTAINS

37

Cassiar

Dease
Lake

Dease Lake

CASSIAR MOUNTAINS

Iskut

STIKINE
RANGES

Mount Edziza ▲

CASSIAR HWY

Spatsizi Plateau
Wilderness Park

SKEENA MOUNTAINS

Bear Glacier
Hyder

Meziadin Junction

Stewart

Cranberry Junction

Kitwanga

New Hazelton

16

Seven Sisters Peaks

Prince
George

Pacific Ocean

Prince Rupert

16

NOT TO SCALE

© 2004 HUNTER PUBLISHING, INC

Alcan and the Cassiar highways go back to the Cassiar. If you're looking for Northern solitude and beauty, this is the road to take.

The other advantage of moving inland to go north along the Cassiar is that it takes you to areas of British Columbia's coast that most people never see. From the lovely Victorian town of Prince Rupert to the more wild Iskut and the huge, connected park complex of Mt. Edziza and Spatsizi Plateau, to the rough and remote road back to Telegraph Creek and the Stikine River, the Cassiar opens more of British Columbia than any other single road in the province.

The beginning of the Cassiar Highway.

It's easy to make a loop trip: a few days on the Cassiar headed north puts you only a couple of miles from Watson Lake, Yukon, on the Alaska Highway. Then simply head south along the Alcan to take in the eastern part of the province, dog-legging off to the park system of Banff/Jasper/Kootenay, etc. If you like driving, you'll have the absolute time of your life, and it will give you a feeling for the variety of terrain in British Columbia in a way you'll never get otherwise. It's like a scenic highlights reel.

■ Kitwanga & Gitanyow

The first village you hit on the Cassiar is Kitwanga (turn east on the side road a quarter-mile after the junction). It has a National Historic Site commemorating the fight at Battle Hill; the first such site honoring the activities of the Natives in Western Canada. It's not exciting – it's a 40-foot/12-meter man-made hill – but it's worth a quick drive by. This was the site of a Gitxsan fortress, which included hidden chambers, trap doors and booby traps. The leader of the forces was a man named Nekt, who went into battle dressed like a grizzly bear. Luckily for him, he was killed in battle before the Europeans showed up and destroyed his world.

There are some **totem poles** in the village and **St. Paul's Anglican Church**, a prime example of Canadian wooden church architecture, which dates back to 1893. The bell tower is especially lovely. Kitwanga – or Gitwangak, as it was traditionally called – was on the trading route for candlefish oil (it was called the Skeena Grease Trail), which braided and branched as far as the Bering Sea.

Kitwanga is part of what's billed as the **Northwest Kultural Tour** that includes Kitwanga, Kitwancool (properly Gitanyow), New Hazelton, K'san, and Kispiox – a day-trip of about 125 miles/200 km that takes in some of the First Nations villages in southern BC. K'san boasts a reconstruction of a Gitksan village; Kispiox has great totem poles. These are all simple villages, not really tourist attractions, except for K'san, which is quite developed. You're perfectly welcome, but be polite.

Gitanyow is a recent change in name to the village of Kitwancool, at Mile 5, where you take the short spur to the west. Your map may show either one but, outside the village, more people are still calling it Kitwancool – it'll take a while for everybody to get used to the change. Gitanyow is home to an impressive collection of totem poles, including what is believed to be the world's oldest that is still standing in its original location; the pole is titled "Hole-in-the-Ice." More than 140 years old, it tells how a man saved his village from starvation by his skills in ice fishing. The art of totem carving is still very much alive in Kitwancool; half-carved poles lie on the ground among the poles that have been erected. Common figures on the poles include ravens, frogs and killer whales. For more on totem poles, see the *Introduction*, page 38.

Check at Gitanyow's **Information Centre**, next to the carving shed, to see if anybody feels like talking to you about the poles. This is one of the best places in BC to see poles.

■ Onward from Kitwanga & Gitanyow

Heading north, the road travels alongside **Kitwanga Lake**, with the Kispiox Mountains to the east. To the west are the massive Coast Mountains, which form a barrier between the shore and the interior of BC.

The first **camping** facilities are at **Cranberry Junction**, at Mile 53 (about Km 74). You'll find good **fishing** on the nearby **Cranberry River**, especially during salmon season. No services are available here; there's just the campground.

The Nass Road heads west at Cranberry Junction, leading back down to Terrace. The road is paved and improved gravel, leading past logging operations and a few First Nations villages. For scenery, there are dried lava flows in places.

Northern BC

> **AUTHOR NOTE:** At any campground in this area, watch for black bears. There's quite a population around.

Continuing north, the road follows the **Nass River**, one of BC's best salmon runs, and crosses the Meziadin River on a one-lane bridge nearly 200 feet/60 meters long at Mile 87.9. In autumn, you can stop and watch the salmon run in Hana Creek, at Mile 94.4.

RUN SALMON RUN

A salmon run is an amazing thing – on a large one, the water will be completely full of fish, packed gill to gill. The fish are struggling upstream, a little closer to death each minute, as they can hardly breathe in the fresh water. It is illegal to fish in a running stream, and it is illegal to harass the fish in any way. They've got enough problems without you. And, as you might recall from the incident of Canadian fishermen blockading an Alaska Marine Highway ship during the summer of 1997, fish are taken very seriously around here.

The highway reaches the banks of **Meziadin Lake** at Mile 99. Here is the junction with the road to Stewart and Hyder, two interesting old towns. At the junction, at Mile 96.2, **Meziadin Lake Provincial Park**, ☎ 250-847-7320, has 46 campsites and great views of the Coast Mountains. Some of the sites have great water views, too. You're in bear area here, so keep your camp accordingly. Sites are CAN $12. There's a boat launch and good canoeing and fishing on the lake. Gas and repairs may be available at Meziadin Junction Services, which also operates a small RV camp and restaurant on the shores of the lake. ☎ 250-636-9240.

■ Stewart-Hyder

The side-trip to Stewart and Hyder is an interesting one. It's a 40-mile/65-km access road, smooth and delightful, traveling between tight mountain ranges. You'll see several glaciers along the way; Bear Glacier, at Mile 15, is the best. Come here in early morning light for top-notch photos. There's a pullout where you can look across the river to the glacier. Look up at the old highway, several hundred feet up. The glacier used to reach all the way across the valley. A few miles farther is a huge accumulation of snow, which looks like a glacier, but is in reality the remnants of avalanches.

The scenery on the road in is nothing short of stunning. Beside the glacier are mist-covered streams and steep mountains that give the feeling that you're entering a different world as you head downhill from the interior's

Downtown Hyder.

plateau to the coast. If you've never seen the coast of Southeast Alaska, this is what it looks like – trees, water, mist, like a Chinese landscape painting run riot.

Stewart, despite being the northernmost ice-free port in Canada, has the most snow of anywhere in the North. Its record is 1,104 inches during one 12-month period.

These weather conditions have made Stewart the town of choice for filming Hollywood movies. *The Thing* (the John Carpenter version), *The Iceman* and *Bear Island* were all filmed here. More recently, the Robin Williams-Al Pacino film *Insomnia* came to town. Most of the crew stayed on yachts brought in by the producers, but locals will tell you quite elaborate stories of Robin Williams getting crazy in the woods.

The town of Stewart (population 1,200), which is in Canada, is primarily interesting for its juxtaposition to Hyder (population 100), which is in Alaska. Hyder residents tend to use Canadian money, attend Canadian schools and use the Canadian time zone. Hyder, in a very real sense, tries as hard as it can to be invisible. As soon as you cross the border into the Alaska town, the road goes to hell, for example, in an effort to keep people away. However, because of Canada's tax structures, the grocery store in Hyder, for instance, is much more popular than the one in Stewart.

Northern BC

Hyder also has more bars per capita than pretty much anywhere else in the world. You will have to stop at Canadian customs on the way back in, so be aware if this presents visa issues for you.

The two towns create an odd but very interesting juxtaposition, so it's well worth the couple of hours it takes to come down here.

Attractions

 The **Stewart Infocentre** is in the Chamber of Commerce Building on 5th Ave.; it's open in summer, and has a good variety of brochures on the area.

The towns lie at the head of the **Portland Canal**, a 90-mile/145-km saltwater fjord. George Vancouver came up this canal on July 29, 1793, looking for the Northwest Passage. Obviously, this dead end wasn't it, but he wrote: "Salmon in great plenty were leaping in all directions. Seals and sea otters were also seen in great numbers." Actually, had communications been better at the time, Vancouver might have skipped the canal entirely (his diary entry when he left said he was "mortified with having devoted so much time to so little purpose"). In August 1791, the *Columbia-Rediviva*, a US ship, was in the canal when "one canoe came alongside in which was six men extraordinarily well armed with spears daggers bows and arrows covered with mats in the bottom of their canoe." There was a bit of talk, a bit of trade, and a landing party was put ashore. It didn't come back, so the ship tacked in closer, and there "I saw my worthy friend Mr. Caswell laying dead in the bottom of the boat... stabbed upwards of twenty places." The ambush was apparently retaliation for the actions of an earlier ship (Vancouver was really behind here), the *Hancock*, which had opened fire on the locals.

The US Army Corps of Engineers came here in 1896. With the big gold rush in the Klondike two years later, the area was swamped with would-be prospectors. A few got lucky here, and both towns boomed for a brief period. Just before World War I, there were 10,000 people in town. When the boom went bust, about a dozen remained.

This area was originally going to be the terminus of the transcontinental railway, but the terrain leading in was simply too rough to cut a train line. The terminus got moved south to Vancouver, and Stewart/Hyder languished until the 1960s, when mining concerns moved in. The biggest of them, a copper mine, shut down in 1984. Today both towns are quiet, but pleasant.

There's not a lot to do or see. People come here for the glaciers, the bars and the bears. Or simply because the drive down from the Cassiar is so beautiful. That's about it, but it's really more than enough to justify the drive.

Hyder is worth a visit for a look at the bars, where the walls are covered in money, a tradition from the days of the miners. A miner would tack a bit of cash to the wall, scribbling his name across it. It was insurance against coming back broke from prospecting. The big deal, of course, is to get "Hyderized" at the Glacier Inn. Knock back a shot of 190-proof in one swallow, and you get a genuine Hyderized card to show your friends (they may wonder just what's wrong with you). The cards are numbered. Among Alaska and BC residents, there are bragging rights involved in having a lower-numbered card.

The towns get a little wild at the beginning of July for a combination **Canada Day/Independence Day** celebration, with parades, fireworks, pig races and more.

Adventures in Nature

 Wildlife-watching: Once you're across the border in Hyder, head right to Fish Creek. The **Fish Creek Wildlife Observatory** is three miles/five km outside Hyder; it's the easiest access of any of the bear observatories in Southeast. From July into September – as long as the fish run holds out – both black and brown bears show up to gorge on the salmon return here. There are very few rivers that the two types of bear share – Anan in Southeast Alaska is the only other accessible one – but you're not likely to see both kinds on any given day.

A viewing platform stretches out parallel to the creek. Forest Service personnel are on duty from 6 am to 10 pm. Bring lots of film, but remember: bears don't like flash bulbs. Never surprise anything with a mouth bigger than your head. Read our bear section, page 14, for how to behave at the platform.

That's the good side of the platform. In season, you will likely see a bear, and, because it's a small creek, you'll probably see the bear closer than you've ever seen a bear before. The downside is, because the platform is so accessible, it can get jammed. On a recent visit here, we came up with one bear and easily 150 people pushing to get the best angle with their telephoto lenses. The bears have got to be really, really puzzled by all this.

Glaciers: Once you're done with the bears, if you're in a decent car, keep heading out the road to **Salmon Glacier**. The best views are about 22 miles/35 km from the Hyder border, but if your appetite was whetted by Bear Glacier, it's worth the drive.

Adventures on Foot

 Hiking: If you're looking for a place to hike or boat, head to **Clements Lake**, seven miles/11 km northeast of Stewart. Other options are the **Sluice Box Trail** (the trailhead is near the dump), which is a nice short overview trail; or the **Titan Trail**, with the trailhead off Salmon River Road. The hike is 4.7 miles/7.5 km up to the Titan Mine.

Where to Eat

The **Bitter Creek Café** has pizza and Mexican dishes. For the trip ahead, stop in at **Brother's Bakery** for rolls, fresh sandwiches and a good selection of meats and cheeses.

Where to Stay

There are some good places to stay in town. All hotels, whether in Alaska or Canada, use the 250 area code, and prices are quoted here in Canadian dollars. Canadian hotels tack on a 15% bed tax to their rates.

The King Edward Hotel (☎ 250-636-2244) is the town's standard. It's downtown. Some rooms have kitchenettes, and there's a dining room that serves passable dinners. Rates start as low as CAN $70 for a double.

Ripley Creek Inn (☎ 250-636-2344), off the main road, is a bit smaller and a bit more swank, with a sauna and a few other perks. Some rooms have kitchens. Doubles start at CAN $90.

Camping

Campers can head to the **Rainy Creek Campground**, ☎ 250-636-2537. It has 98 spots under trees and short hiking trail behind the tennis courts (watch for bears). Prices start at CAN $16. Across the border in Hyder is **Camp-run-a-muck**, ☎ 250-636-9006 or 888-393-1199. Again, it's pretty basic, but you're a little closer to the bears. CAN $16.

■ Onward from Stewart-Hyder

The Cassiar used to be a nightmare of packed gravel and broken pavement. Not so much anymore. The road is smooth, for the most part, and the pavement is in good shape. There's not as much maintenance along here as there is on the Alcan, and there are more long-haul trucks taking advantage of the shortcut to Alaska, but as long as you're paying attention – there are still places with no center lines and a lot of curves – everything will be fine. This is a remote road; once you're on it, there are only a few places with services, so time your days out accordingly.

The Cassiar is so very much prettier than the Alaska Highway. The Alcan has stretches of more dramatic scenery but, for mile after mile of stunning scenery, there aren't many roads that can match the Cassiar.

It's quite scenic through here, with mountains all around and some lovely forests. It's prime bear area, so keep a close watch by streams for the

Robson Pass, Mt. Robson. (© Vivien Lougheed)

Not all trail bridges are easy to cross. (© Vivien Lougheed)

Above: Balance Rock, Queen Charlotte Islands. (© Vivien Lougheed)

Below: Tow Hill area of Haida Gwaii National Park. (© Vivien Lougheed)

Mt. Fitzwilliam near the Alberta border. (© Vivien Lougheed)

Raven Lake, east of Prince George. (© Vivien Lougheed)

Eagle wood carving, Queen Charlotte Islands. (© Vivien Lougheed)

Above: Trail signs like this one are used throughout BC. (© Vivien Lougheed)

Below: Bennington Dam on the Columbia River, Nelson. (© Vivien Lougheed)

Berg Glacier leads to Berg Lake. (© Vivien Lougheed)

bears who might be fishing. Those who want to try their luck at fishing should keep an especially close eye out before dropping their lines. There are also extensive patches of berry bushes, a bear favorite. And, with all the water around, there are also numerous moose, beavers and smaller mammals.

Your first chance for a break comes at Mile 153.6, **Bell II Lodge**. It has gas, food and lodging available year-round. ☎ 888-655-5566.

> **WARNING:** *You're in serious avalanche territory from about Mile 160 to 175. Use extreme caution in winter and spring.*

Mile 178 passes the **Dominican Telegraph Line**, which linked Dawson City and Vancouver. Built at the turn of the century, the line was also used as a trail to Atlin. You can still see a few telegraph cabins submerged in Echo Lake and a few stretches of the old trails that haven't been completely swallowed by forest.

Kinaskan Lake Provincial Park Campground is at Mile 225. It has 50 sites for CAN $12 each. You can fish the lake for rainbow trout. This is good moose country.

Mile 248 has the **Red Goat Lodge**, on Eddontenejon Lake, which rents canoes. Park your RV or stay in the lodge for CAN $85 a night. Campsites start at CAN $10. ☎ 250-234-3261.

At Mile 250 is the **Mountain Shadow Campground and RV Park**, a nice place tucked down in a valley away from the road. Unserviced sites (both wooded and gravel) are CAN $15 and come with clean facilities.

■ Iskut

The tiny town of Iskut, Mile 250, has several hotels. **Tatogga Lake Resort**, Mile 240.7 (☎ 250-234-3526), has a restaurant, gas station and campground. **Trappers Souvenirs** has a gift shop and a few cabins at Mile 256. Plan to stop early in the day, if possible.

Iskut, spread out and nearly empty, is a Taltan Indian town. The site forms the boundary between the Mt. Edziza and Spatsizi parks. **Spatsizi Provincial Park** is a wilderness area with no road access. You can enter on trails or fly in. On the river, there's a great week-long paddle trip. If you've got a mountain bike, the old railroad beds are just there waiting. **Mt. Edziza Provincial Park** is also a wilderness area, with no vehicle access. Again, you have to get in by plane or trail; easiest access is from Telegraph Creek (see below).

You cross the **Stikine River** at Mile 275. The Stikine is one of the last great rivers, yet to be tamed. Boating is excellent along its length (see below). West of the bridge is the Grand Canyon of the Stikine (with rock walls nearly a thousand feet high), the river runs Class V+. Below the canyon, the river is mostly Class II, with good shore camping. Watch for bears, and expect masses of mosquitoes in season.

■ Dease Lake

Dease Lake, at Mile 307, is the only town of any size along the Cassiar. The natives called it "Tatl'ah" (head of the lake), and its modern history goes back to 1838, when Robert Campbell was first opening the area for the Hudson's Bay Company. The lake was used as a boat-building site during the Cassiar gold rush (1872-1880), and the boomtowns that sprang up during this period – Laketon and Porter's Landing – are now ghost towns that make for an interesting side-trip. Gas, groceries and lodging are available year-round. Try the **Northway Motor Inn**, ☎ 250-771-5341, right on the highway, with doubles from CAN $75, or the **Arctic Divide Inn**, ☎ 250-771-3119, which runs about the same price.

There's an interesting side-trip from Dease Lake, down the Telegraph Creek Road.

■ Telegraph Creek & the Stikine River

Telegraph Creek Road was cut in 1874 by William Moore. Later, this route was used to haul supplies to Alcan construction camps – from Dease Lake, the supplies got ferried on the Dease River. The road is gorgeous, but should be attempted only by those in sturdy vehicles. An RV isn't going to make it. Check at Dease Lake for road conditions and a weather forecast before heading down.

The road is about 70 miles long and takes you to the town of Telegraph Creek, population about 400. Traders came in and tried to kick out the Taltan Indians during the early 1800s. The Taltans had the interesting habit of hunting bears with dogs. They bred a special type of dog, now believed extinct, that was insane enough to leap at a bear. Well, actually, almost any dog is insane enough to leap at a bear – we've seen weiner dogs go amok – but the Taltans had dogs that could win the fight, instead of becoming bear appetizers.

As with every other wide spot in the North, gold was eventually found near Telegraph Creek (in 1861) and a boomtown followed. During the Klondike rush, Telegraph Creek boomed again when it was on the "all Canada" route to the goldfields, with miners heading up the Stikine to Teslin Lake, then on the Teslin and the Yukon rivers to Dawson City.

This was not a happy route. It took would-be miners from the coast to the interior faster than any other means, and it didn't have any of the nasty mountains or glacier crossings that other routes did. The big problem was getting from Telegraph Creek up to Teslin Lake, where you could load gear onto a boat and head north. The *Klondike News*, on April 1, 1898, wrote, "The portage of 150 miles from Telegraph Creek to Teslin Lake is one that the traveler will never forget, even though made over a wagon road, and we would advise our friends to wait until the long-talked-of railroad is completed and go over this route by Pullman Car." Of course, if you had waited, you'd still be waiting.

And so, although hundreds of miners tried this route in the first years of the rush, not many made it. The miners traveled in winter, and the first thing that got them was the fairly constant 60-mph headwind that howls down off the glaciers all winter long.

Actually, not much that was supposed to happen at Telegraph Creek ever really did. The town was founded to support the telegraph line – it was easily accessible by river, a nightmare to reach by land. Rosemary Neering describes some of the hassle in her book *Continental Dash*: "The trip was the most miserable of all Morison's experiences in the region. For ten days, he was constantly wet, wading in cold water under teeming rain or soggy snow. He arrived at his destination, the miners' settlement known as Buck's Bar, now renamed Telegraph Creek in honor of the planned telegraph line, to find just two or three shacks and a dozen miners washing gold. These were the last holdouts of the hundreds who had flocked here in 1862. Most had returned down the coast on the HMS *Devastation*, sent to rescue them from hunger, cold and despair."

So, more than once, Telegraph Creek was going to be the next big boomtown. Never happened.

There's not much in Telegraph now. There's an airport, where it looks like the terminal is an abandoned truck camper (but no – there really is no terminal), and a few dozen houses, about half of which seem to be falling down. There's one store and there is the small church, which is really quite lovely but impossible to get a decent picture of because of the way the phone lines frame it.

You go to Telegraph Creek for the river.

If you want to be alone in the most beautiful countryside you can imagine, the Stikine River is for you. John Muir called it "a Yosemite 100 miles long," and we're convinced the only reason he didn't rave more was that he didn't have time to go upriver any farther.

The Stikine River – the name comes from the Tlingit for "Great River" – is about 400 miles/644 km long, starting deep in British Columbia. Fed by literally dozens of glaciers, the water in the river is a murky silver, laden with silt, and yet somehow enormous runs of salmon return to it each year.

The watershed of the Stikine is one of the largest on the continent, and it is the largest (over 20,000 square miles/50,000 square km) that is undammed. At its widest, the river is a bit less than a mile across, but most places are considerably more narrow, perhaps averaging a hundred yards or so from bank to bank.

TRAVELING SAFELY ON THE STIKINE

The main complication of traveling the river is that the channel is never the same twice. Huge amounts of silt are coming down the river, and the soft banks are cut away as the river digs new courses for itself. The lower reaches of the river, in particular, are heavily braided, with as many as 10 or 15 small channels reaching out. No chart can keep up with the river. In winter, storms howl through the Stikine valley, combining with deep freezes; you can pass acres of trees where the tops have been simply sheered off through a combination of freeze and breeze. This means that, at any time of year, there is a lot of debris in the water, snags and entire tree trunks waiting to reach out and grab your boat. There are log jams and sweepers (trees that extend into the water but are still attached to the bank) that need to be watched for. The lower reaches of the river are tidal, which can cause other problems. Plus, the water is really, really cold. Should you fall in, not only are you going to be dealing with the possibility of hypothermia, you've also got to worry about so much silt getting between the fibers of your clothes that it can drag you down before you have time to get hypothermia. The river requires attention, respect; it's not a simple float.

 Before hitting the river on your own, pick up a copy of ***Stikine River: A Guide to Paddling the Great River***, by Jennifer Voss.

Because of the remoteness of the river and the very few people traveling on it above Shakes, you have to assume you're on your own when you head out. Be prepared for emergencies. There is enough jet boat traffic running between Wrangell and Telegraph that you can't go for more than a day or two without seeing a boat – unless you're in one braid and they're in another. However, even if a passing boat sees you, they're not going to stop unless you're signaling – they don't want to interrupt your wilderness experience. To the usual first aid kit and emergency equipment, add a good signaling device.

Adventures on Water

 Outfitter Tours: The best way on the river, unless you're a crack camper and kayaker, is to let somebody else do the work. The fine people of **Alaska Vistas** are the only outfitters to run raft trips down the Stikine. For a paltry US $2,200 – only a bit more than hiring a jet boat just to get you back to Telegraph – you get first and last night at a hotel in Wrangell and five days traveling and camping on the river. Each evening is capped off with the best food you have ever eaten. You travel in an 18-foot self-bailing river raft, with plenty of time to get out and hike around, enjoy the scenery and sit back and relax in camp. This is one of the best deals in the state, and the trip's river time will be five of the best days of your life. Contact Alaska Vistas at ☎ 250-874-3006, www.alaskavistas.com. We have been lucky enough to experience a lot over the decade we've been writing these books. This is, quite simply, the best thing we've done in the North, and there's no way to recommend it highly enough.

You can't kayak the river above Telegraph Creek. Right past the town is the Grand Canyon of the Stikine, an area with Class IV and V whitewater. Below the town, there's nothing more than Class II, and the very fast current (about five knots) that makes running the river a gentle, easy blast – all 150 miles/242 km down to the river's mouth by the Wrangell airport.

Of course, anybody can go on the river at any time, although there are a lot of times you wouldn't want to be out there. No permit is required. The prime season for running the Stikine is May-August. There are heavy spring floods before that, and in late summer the wind begins to howl up the river, making paddling downriver a bit of a nightmare. In winter, the entire thing freezes up.

Independent Kayaking: If you are going to run the river on your own, the put-in point is Telegraph Creek. As mentioned above, you can get there by driving in from the Cassiar Highway, or you can hire a jet boat in Wrangell to take you up. You can also fly, but regulations make it impossible to fly your boat into Telegraph, unless you can collapse it and fit it inside the plane. Canada no longer allows boats strapped to the outsides of airplanes.

Alone, the trip will cost you US $1,000-1,500 to get a jet boat ride from Wrangell to Telegraph. The ride takes about eight hours. Keep this in mind if you're leaving your car in Telegraph while you hit the river.

> **AUTHOR TIP:** Telegraph is your last chance to stock up on anything and, as there is only one store, don't plan on finding much. Get what you need before you get to the river.

It takes three to four days (six hours a day) in a canoe or a kayak to get downriver from Telegraph to the mouth of the Stikine. Obviously, the more you want to get out and explore, the longer it's going to take. For however long you plan to stay on the river, remember that you are on your own. You need to be entirely self-sufficient.

Most people plan on their pick up around the Great Glacier. There is a developed picnic site here, and it's an easy place to tell your ride home where you'll be. There's an easy half-hour hike back to the glacier's pond, with great views of the glacial face and floating icebergs. If you fly over the area, you can see that the glacier once reached much farther ahead; there are two concentric rings, moraines, that show how far up the glacier once moved.

A popular side-trip on the river is to **Chief Shakes Hot Springs**, which is on a slough by the Ketili River. It's about two miles/2.5 km off the main channel and, at high water levels, paddling up to the spring is quite doable; if the water is running fast, particularly at the mouth of the slough, you can pretty easily line your boat up past the rapids. Once you hit the springs, you'll find the water is a toasty 122°F. There is another hot spring on the river, **Warm Springs**, across from the Great Glacier and just above the Choquette River. It's marked on many maps, but it has leeches.

Adventures in Nature

 Glaciers: Above the river is the **Stikine Icefield**, whose 2,900 square miles include **LeConte Glacier**. Most trips to the Stikine will stop by the glacier, a favored pupping ground for harbor seals, who have their pups on the ice floes that calve off the glacier. There are also moose aplenty, bear and even a few packs of wolves. In migration season, the Stikine sees as many as a quarter of a billion birds. Snow geese, teal ducks, sandpipers, eagles and more flock to the rich shoreline.

NATIVE GLACIAL MYTHS

Native mythology has quite a story about Great Glacier on the Stikine. It seems that, when they were first moving into the area, they found the river entirely blocked off by the glacier. There was, though, an opening in the glacial face through which water moved. They sent a couple of people up over the ice to see if the water came out anywhere, then sent a log through to see if it made the trip okay. Then they sent the most expendable member of the society, someone's grandmother. When she got through alive, everyone else decided it was okay for them to follow, and the journey continued.

Where to Stay

 There are two **B&Bs** on the river, one just below the Great Glacier, one on Farm Island. There's no real way to contact them in advance; if you're interested, just show up, and the odds are there will be room available. There are also six **Forest Service cabins** on the river, plus another six on the delta, which are not quite as scenic, but still great places to stay.

Camping

Camping on the Stikine is one of the great pleasures of life. There are plenty of wide beaches sheltered by alder, pine and spruce. Camp well above the water level – floods are generally seasonal, but anything is possible – and practice all bear safety precautions. We've seen only a very few beaches without indications that a bear has visited. You can get your water out of the river, but you'll need to boil it and wait for the sediment to settle, or filter it. If you're going to use filters, keep in mind what all the sediment is doing to your equipment.

Stikine Conservation

 The mere fact that the Stikine River is huge, remote and fairly pristine means that there are a lot of people who want to do something to it. The additional fact that many of its tributary rivers are rich in coal, gold and other goodies, means that the Stikine is facing serious threats. It's the last great undammed river on the continent, but that may not be true much longer.

The Iskut, perhaps the Stikine's main tributary, has been the site of mining activities for years. When you're on the lower reaches of the river, you may see a large plane flying low overhead; it's taking ore out of the mines on the Iskut at a rate of two or three loads a day. Before the plane, a hydroplane was used, a behemoth that literally killed the river. The turbulence it caused changed the river's habitat entirely, rendering the area largely sterile. Additional silt flowing into the Stikine, where the boat also went, made the river shallower and wider, greatly increasing bank erosion.

The mines on the Iskut are one problem; the huge coal deposit on the Spatsizi is another. There is simply no way to extract coal without damaging the Stikine's downriver flow.

There have been plans for years to dam the Stikine at the Grand Canyon (above Telegraph Creek). The river depends on regular flood cycles to maintain its equilibrium; without them, the river will die, the fish in the river will die, and the world will have lost another beautiful natural feature just so people can run their hairdryers.

FRIENDS OF THE STIKINE

The Friends of the Stikine have been around for a long time, trying to keep the river alive. They lobby actively for preservation of the river and its headwaters and, while a few of their positions may verge on over-conservation – in Wrangell and Telegraph Creek, there are fears that the FOS is trying to outlaw jet boats, which would cut off Telegraph and send Wrangell's economy into a tailspin – they are the only ones fighting for the river. Friends of the Stikine, 1405 Doran Rd., North Vancouver, BC V7N 1K1. ☎ 604-985-4659; maggie_paquet@- bc.sympatico.ca.

■ The Stikine River Corridor

If you look east or west of the bridge over the Stikine, as you cross the river on the Cassiar, you're looking at the Stikine River Corridor, a protected area that leads west to Mt. Edziza Park and east to Spatsizi Plateau Wilderness Park. This is a huge area of protected wilderness; except for the road town to Telegraph Creek, the only way in is by boat or float plane.

Mount Edziza Provincial Park covers over 410,000 acres of the Tahltan Highlands. It's a park of nature run wild: there's a volcanic landscape of perfect cones, lava flows, cinder fields, and more. Mt. Edziza itself (9,168 ft/2,787 meters) is, according to the Canadian Park Service, "a composite volcano consisting of thin basalt flows and a central dome of andesite, dacite and rhyolite with a glaciated crater nearly 8,300 feet/2,500 meters in diameter. The eruption that built the mountain and its central cone began four million years ago. Successive lava flows raised the dome above the encircling plateau and spread lava over an area 39 miles/65 km by 15 miles/25 km. The last basalt flow occurred only 10,000 years ago, at which time it solidified in place and plugged the central vent."

What all this boils down to is a landscape that looks like pictures of Mars – but with animals. On one fly-by of the mountain, we watched a wolf trot right out to the ridge line to watch us. Caribou are everywhere, and the biggest bears we've ever seen have all been along the Stikine River.

To the east side of the river, at the upper reaches of the Stikine, is the **Spatsizi Plateau Wilderness Park**. There is no road access to this 1.2 million acres in the middle of nowhere, so only go in if you know what you're doing. But, as Parks Canada says, its "True wilderness atmosphere, outstanding scenery and varied terrain make this park an excellent place for quality hiking, photography, and nature study. Lands within the park have an excellent capability for supporting large populations of wildlife."

This area is remote, and there aren't a lot of operators who can take you into the parks. Book a plane from Telegraph Creek or Smithers, down on Highway 16. If you're looking at the river, a hike east, into Spatsizi, is doable. Just don't even think of going west towards the canyon.

Back on the Cassiar Highway

 Back on the Cassiar, the road follows Dease Lake for a considerable distance; and, once you've passed Dease Lake, there is a daisy chain of other lakes, all with excellent fishing.

This area has produced some of the richest gold finds in Canada, including a 72-ounce nugget pulled out of McDame Creek in 1877, near the gold rush town of Centreville (Mile 381). Most of the gold is long gone, but there are still extensive jade mines – check out Jade City at Mile 370 – and, until 1992, there was a huge asbestos mine in the city of Cassiar, 10 miles/16 km off the highway. You can't get back there anymore, but it was amazing to drive into the town and see the oddly glowing green hill that dominated the buildings around it. The hill was made up of tailings from the mine, grown over by mosses. In the proper light, you could swear it was alive. Creepy.

Boya Lake Provincial Park, at Mile 394, has nice campsites on the lake, good boating and fishing on cloudy days. On clear days, the clarity of the water allows the fish to get a good look at you and know what's coming. The campground, ☎ 250-847-7320, has 45 sites at CAN $12 each. It's a good place to spend the night, with surprisingly few bugs.

The last 35 miles of the road to its junction with the Alaska Highway are paved, but the condition of the pavement may not be the best. The road is narrow and twisting, and there are many one-lane bridges as the road crosses the French River, the Blue River, Cormier Creek, and dozens of other waterways. At Mile 444 you leave British Columbia and enter the Yukon. If you've been driving with your headlights off, turn them on now, according to Yukon law. No more services are available until you hit the junction with the Alaska Highway at Upper Liard, 23 miles/37 km west of Watson Lake.

Northern BC

The Alaska Highway

It's called the Alaska Highway, but the longest chunk of it is in BC – as is most of the best scenery along the route. If it weren't for the Alcan, built in a frenzied period of war fears, much of the best of British Columbia would still be inaccessible.

■ The History of the Highway

 Although the highway is mostly in Canada, it was a US project – in fact, the US had already started building it in Canadian territory before they bothered to get Canada's permission.

On February 2, 1942, the US War Department called **Brigadier General Clarence L. Sturdevant** to a meeting. Sturdevant was the Assistant Chief of Engineers, and the War Department, shaken by developments in the Orient, decreed a new project: the construction of a highway to Alaska. If this project were proposed today, you would expect 10 years of study, at least a 100% budget overrun and engineers trembling at the thought of cutting a road through nearly 2,000 miles of bush and mud. But in the 1940s, the country was preparing for war. Only two days after the meeting with Sturdevant, a comprehensive plan was presented by the Chief of Engineers. The Alaska Highway was about to become a reality, and the North was about to explode in a frenzy of activity.

The Alaska Highway was designed to provide a military supply route to the threatened fringes of America; it was also to provide a supply line to a series of air bases – the **Northwest Staging Route** – which stretched in a chain from Edmonton, in Alberta, Canada, to Fairbanks, Alaska. The Northwest Staging Route had been established the year before, and the tiny airports – not much more than Quonset huts and dirt landing strips – were already overloaded with the influx of war materials as planes were ferried along the route from the US to the beleaguered forces of the Soviet Union, which had nearly collapsed under the Nazi advance.

By February 16, orders had been given and military engineers were heading North. Dawson Creek, in British Columbia, was chosen for the southern end of the highway; The city was served by a small dirt road, and it was the northern terminus of the Northern Alberta Railways, so it was a relatively easy place to bring supplies.

In order to get the road built as quickly as possible, a three-pronged attack was planned. Construction crews were to begin not only from Dawson Creek, but also from Fort Nelson, BC, Whitehorse, in Yukon Territory (where supplies could be brought in via the White Pass & Yukon Route Railway), and Big Delta, Alaska (today, Delta Junction), where the existing road from Fairbanks turned south.

The original plan was to build a simple, fast and serviceable pioneer road to open access to interior Alaska as quickly as possible. Standards were established. The clearing had to be at least 32 feet wide, the grades no more than 10%, the curves no less than a 50-foot radius, with a minimum of 12 feet of surfacing. The specs called for exactly enough road to get a military truck up, nothing more. The official orders said, "Further refinements will be undertaken only if additional time is available." However, once construction started and they found out exactly what was involved, refinements came about with amazing speed, almost on the heels of the pioneer road.

A Tough Road to Build

On March 9, 1942, nine days before the Canadian government officially agreed to allow the US to build a road through Canadian territory, troops began arriving in Dawson Creek. They were met by deceptively warm weather – about 50°F. But within days, they discovered the real character of the North. The temperature plummeted to 30° below zero, and snow and ice covered the ground and the tents where the soldiers lived. Less than a week after the first troops arrived, there were more than 1,100 soldiers in Dawson Creek. This was but a fraction of the more than 10,000 soldiers who would soon be involved in the construction, and they were all to learn the same lesson: Living conditions were not going to be easy. The end of February isn't exactly the best time to start a construction project in the North. Even today, all construction is done during the summer season, and only a few maintenance crews venture out in the dead of winter.

The highway was to cut through completely uninhabited country for most of its length; the few towns that did exist were tiny and unprepared for huge influxes of soldiers. Dawson Creek had a population of less than 500; Whitehorse had 1,000. The soldiers were forced to live on what they could carry.

Road construction moved along so quickly there was no chance to build permanent settlements or even refined living quarters. The soldiers lived in tents, although a few constructed small shacks mounted on skids that could be dragged forward as the construction progressed. They fashioned their own beds from boughs and government-issued sleeping bags.

The food they ate was equally basic: dehydrated potatoes, powdered milk, canned chili and corned beef. As sections of the road opened up and transportation problems eased, the menu changed slightly. Fresh meat and vegetables were brought in at the first opportunity. But, in general, the meals were monotonous, enlivened only when a soldier happened to kill some fresh game.

If the only problems had been food and shelter, the soldiers could have easily taken it; after all, life in the Army has never been luxurious. But working in the North brought a new array of problems. The soldiers were attacked by clouds of mosquitoes and biting flies. The mud was so deep in places that entire tractors sank. And then there was the weather: freezing cold, day after day, with temperatures reaching 40 and 50 below, and no place at all to get warm. (The miserable weather made the section of road around Muncho Lake one of the most popular for the workers; Liard Hot Springs was nearby.) When it wasn't freezing cold, other elements tormented the exhausted workers. On June 7, 1942, 4.47 inches of rain fell on Fort St. John. The workers were living in tents; the road became an impossible morass that could not be approached for two weeks. In December of 1942, just after the pioneer road had opened, but long before the work was finished, the temperature in Whitehorse did not rise higher than 20 below for two weeks, bottoming out at 67 below – cold enough to freeze exposed skin and to explode tires when the air inside them froze.

These problems, coupled with the difficulty in getting mail through and the lack of news from the Lower 48, led to serious morale problems among the workers. One entertainment they devised was to elect a "Sweetheart of the Al-Can." The sweetheart they chose was Rita Hayworth. The soldiers pooled their money and sent Lt. Jim Blackwelder to Hollywood, where he met Ms. Hayworth and took her picture. The story made the front page of *The Los Angeles Times* on June 11, 1943.

Despite all the difficulties, the road got built at a lightning pace. Workers cut trees down by the thousands; bulldozers followed closely behind, leveling a roadway. Construction moved forward at such speed that surveyors did their work from atop the bulldozers – barely able to keep ahead of the machinery. By the first of August, 858 miles of road had been laid out, 611 miles had been completed, and there were an additional 183 miles under construction.

But this incredible pace wasn't fast enough. The road had to be finished before hard winter set in. To support the Army, the Public Road Administration (PRA) joined in during the late summer. Its workers followed behind the troops who were creating the pioneer route, and began to improve and maintain the road, getting it ready for all-season operation. At the peak of operations there were 17,000 civilians working on the road, using 7,000 trucks, bulldozers and cars.

The work, for troops and civilians alike, was arduous. Workers faced terrain conditions that they had never encountered before. **Muskeg** was one of their first threats. A swampy area covered by low plants, muskeg looks solid, and sometimes is, but other places give way to the deep waters beneath. The muskeg areas were feared to be impassable, but the engineers developed skills at spotting them and were able to loop the road around many of the boggy areas. There were times when it couldn't be gotten around, however. On one three-mile stretch, the muskeg, three to four feet thick, had to be cleared by a dragline. Then the road bed had to be backfilled with dry clay transported from a considerable distance away.

Permafrost was a more serious threat. Delicate, frozen ground, the permafrost melted and sank the first attempts at roadbuilding, when the workers stripped the topsoil and tried to grade the ground beneath. The longer the permafrost was exposed and the underlying ground allowed to melt, the worse the conditions became. Finally, the engineers developed the technique of leaving the topsoil and increasing its insulating qualities by laying a bed of logs and brush. On top of that went the road surfacing. More than one vehicle was swallowed by the gaping, melting earth before engineers struck upon this idea.

The North is a land of water. More than 200 bridges were built, plus countless culverts and drainage areas. The road building crews worked miles ahead of the bridge builders, so equipment had to be forded across streams and rivers. There are accounts of tractors being taken through water so deep that only their air intake and exhaust pipes were visible above the water surface.

Bridges and culverts were built with whatever material came to hand, often the very logs that had been cleared from the water's edge. Just 10 days before the opening of the highway, the bridge over the Smith River was carried away by water and ice. Three days after that, 200 feet of the bridge on the Peace River was swept away.

When the PRA came along to erect permanent bridges, they faced the difficulty of attempting to work with steel in weather of 40 or more below zero. A touch of steel on bare skin was torture, and even the thick gloves worn by the workers didn't provide full protection.

Under the demands of the thousands of men and machines working on the highway, local transportation systems, such as they were, became overloaded. When the Army took over the White Pass and Yukon Route Railway, the railway's engines and rolling stock were decrepit and out of date. Yet they were the only means of getting equipment from the harbor in Skagway, up the 2,900-foot White Pass, and on to Whitehorse. Meanwhile, near Dawson Creek, more than 1,000 freight cars jammed the yards, but there was no equipment to unload them and take the cargo farther north.

And still the work went on at a furious pace, taking its toll in both machines and men. Near the Kluane River stands a monument to Lt. Roland Small, one of the soldiers who died during the construction.

What did the workers earn for their efforts? A laborer working for a contractor under the PRA made as little as 96 cents an hour. Tractor drivers made CAN $1.60 for an hour of freezing cold. Crane operators earned CAN $2 an hour. Room and board cost the workers about CAN $2 per day. The workweek was 70 to 77 hours long (of course, there wasn't much to do but work), and almost no overtime was paid. An ad for workers in the *New York Times* included this enticement, "Temperatures will range from 90 degrees above zero to 70 degrees below zero. Men will have to fight swamps, rivers, ice, and cold. Mosquitoes, flies, and gnats will not only be annoying but will cause bodily harm."

A Road in Use

By September 1, 1942, the entire road had been laid out; 837 miles were completed. On September 4, as part of the final push, the War Department created the **Northwest Service Command**, bringing all the disparate construction and transportation units under one command. And on September 28, the route from Dawson Creek to Whitehorse was given its baptism by fire. The first truck to take the road traveled the 1,030 miles in only 71 hours – at an average speed of 15 miles per hour. More trucks quickly followed, and by the beginning of October, there were regular cargo runs from Dawson Creek to Whitehorse.

The cold weather was coming. Lakes and rivers began to freeze, and there was widespread flooding. Against all odds, on November 20, 1942, the road was officially opened where the 18th Engineers and the 97th Engineers linked up the northern and southern sections at **Soldier's Summit**, on the shores of Kluane Lake. The road was completed, but not finished. The day before the road opened, the first convoy left Whitehorse for Fairbanks. It arrived only three days later. The first convoy to travel the entire route, Dawson Creek to Fairbanks, did so in 210 hours.

The pioneer road was in business, but it was rough, crooked (partly because the surveyors had worked from the tops of bulldozers, and partly to protect convoys from enemy aircraft), and so tiring that convoy drivers were changed every 45 to 90 miles.

The goal was to have more than a seasonal tote road. Furious construction continued, to provide an all-weather road by the end of 1943. But thaws in the spring had shown weaknesses. Transportation was interrupted, and men were stranded as the road turned into a long ribbon of mud. Brigadier General Ludson D. Warsham, who was in charge of the Northwest Division, ordered an all-out effort to get the road into shape, and over the next few months, it was straightened, ballasted, surfaced and widened. Permanent bridges were erected and, by October 15, 1943, the Alaska Highway was open for year-round use by military traffic.

The Alaska Highway opened to civilian traffic in 1949, but only a few intrepid and self-reliant motorists tried it. The trip was still months long, freezing cold and terribly muddy. It wasn't until the automobile boom of the late 1950s and early 1960s that traffic began to increase. Services along the road multiplied as the number of cars grew.

Improvements have continued over the years: paving, smoothing, construction of new bridges. A road that could once be traveled at only 15 miles per hour is now easily and comfortably traveled at 65 (unless you're behind an RV, which all too often seem to top out at 40). Towns along the highway have grown and thrived, and the road has opened endless possibilities for recreation and commerce, as it has opened the northwest section of the continent.

Alaska Highway
British Columbia

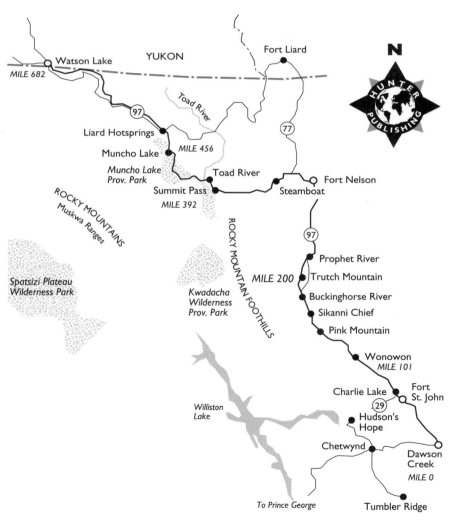

YUKON

Fort Liard

N

Watson Lake
MILE 682

97

Toad River

Liard Hotsprings

77

Muncho Lake
MILE 456

Muncho Lake
Prov. Park

Toad River

Fort Nelson

ROCKY MOUNTAINS
Muskwa Ranges

Summit Pass
MILE 392

Steamboat

97

Prophet River

ROCKY MOUNTAIN FOOTHILLS

MILE 200

Trutch Mountain

Spatsizi Plateau
Wilderness Park

Kwadacha
Wilderness
Prov. Park

Buckinghorse River

Sikanni Chief

Pink Mountain

Wonowon
MILE 101

Charlie Lake

Fort
St. John

Williston
Lake

29

Hudson's
Hope

Chetwynd

Dawson
Creek
MILE 0

To Prince George

Tumbler Ridge

Northern BC

NOT TO SCALE

▪ Dawson Creek

History

 Dawson Creek is Mile Zero on the Alaska Highway, the place where construction started. Now it's the place where Alaska Highway travelers stop to buy their first souvenirs of the road.

Dawson Creek and the surrounding area were first explored by a governmental boundary commission in 1879. Named for George **Mercer Dawson**, the area was first settled about 1912. Dawson was the kind of explorer who just doesn't exist anymore. He started off as a geologist, and in 1873-74 he set off to explore the 49th parallel from the Lake of the Woods to the Pacific. He suffered from bone tuberculosis but, instead of staying home and feeling sorry for himself, Dawson set out to see and study everything. If all that weren't enough, he's also credited with being "the father of Canadian Anthropology."

The town site of Dawson Creek was originally two miles west of its current location, but it was moved in 1930, to become the railhead for the **Northern Alberta Railway**. The railway became the life's blood of Dawson Creek. As the northernmost and westernmost railhead in Canada – called "the end of steel" – it was the only possible choice as the base for construction of the Alaska Highway. In 1941, the area's population was under 500; in 1942, it was 20,000, as soldiers and engineers moved in to begin the highway. Things have slacked off since then, and today about 11,000 people call the beginning of the Alaska Highway home.

Most people drive into Dawson Creek, but if you need to fly, **Air BC** has regular flights (☎ 888-247-2262). There's also **Greyhound Bus** service (☎ 250-782-3131).

Attractions

 We asked a local resident what there was to do in Dawson Creek. He replied, "Leave." It's not quite that bad, but there's no reason to plan a long stop here, either.

The main attraction in town is the cairn that says you are entering the Alaska Highway, the **Mile Zero Cairn**. To reach it, turn left when you enter the town from the south. The Mile Zero marker you see today is not the original; that one, which was in a slightly different location, was hit by a car. The new post is 10 feet tall and located at 102nd Ave. and 10th. It does not sit at the geographical start of the highway – the city fathers decided it was better for business to plunk it smack dab in the center of downtown. Let's face it, there aren't a whole lot of other reasons to go downtown.

One Halloween, the sign was stolen and replaced by a wooden privy.

The other attraction in Dawson City is the **Infocentre** itself at 900 Alaska Ave. (☎ 250-782-9595). It's all housed in a converted railway station. It has the standard array of brochures, making it a good place to stock up to see what lies ahead. But more interesting is the lovely **Dawson Creek Station Museum**, housing railroad artifacts on one side, and re-creating the look of a working station in the time before the highway, with a ticket office, baggage room and station master's quarters. On the other side is an excellent display of pioneer items and a geological and wildlife display – including serious mammoth bits, bigger than you're likely to see anywhere else in the world. There's also a good photo history of the building of the highway, with a video shown at regular intervals. Both sides are well worth a look. Open May to September, 8 am to 7 pm; entrance fee, CAN $3.

Outside the Infocentre, take a look at the **train engine** built in 1933. Next door is an old wooden grain elevator, now the **Grain Elevator Museum**, one of the last survivors of the many that once lined the tracks. Housed inside is an art gallery that features the works of locals, as well as traveling collections. It's open June to August, 10 am to 5 pm.

Dawson Creek is either your first or last chance – depending on which direction you're heading – to get an "I survived the Alaska Highway" T-shirt. A surprising amount of the town's economy depends upon the sale of "official" highway merchandise.

Two and a half miles south, on Highway 2, is the **Walter Wright Pioneer Village** (☎ 250-782-9595), open May to August; entrance fee, CAN $5. At the village you'll find old pioneer buildings and an array of farm machinery. Tours are available from the end of May through Labor Day, from

Dawson Creek is Mile 0.

10 am to 6 pm. If you're wondering what it was like to live here a hundred years ago, this will give you some idea.

Adventures on Water

 Paddling: Dawson Creek is part of the **Peace River** drainage, so there are some great hiking and boating opportunities around.

Adventures on Foot

 Hiking: For hikers, the **Bear Mountain Hike** is 7.5 fairly easy miles (12 km) – the route is used by cross-country skiers in winter. Access is 3.7 miles/six km south of town by the bypass road turnoff – the same turnoff trucks carrying hazardous cargo are supposed to use.

If you've got a day to kill, take the Hart Highway to the Heritage Highway past Tumbler Ridge; turn left (away from Chetwynd) and take the Quintette Coal Mine Exit. If all this sounds complicated, the payoff is worth it. From Quintette there are turnoffs into the **Kinuseo Falls Provincial Park**, ☎ 250-787-3407. Take the Murray River left fork (there are signs), jump on the trail and hike 21.5 miles/35 km back to the falls. It's too far to attract heavy hiker traffic, and the reward is a waterfall that's higher, at 225 feet/68 meters, than Niagara.

There are a bunch of hikes around **Tumbler Ridge**. It's best to ask around town for suggestions and detailed directions. The Info Centre does have a handout on the hikes, but it won't tell you much. Easiest to reach – although not to take on – is **Bald Spot**. The trailhead is right on the highway, just past Tumbler Ridge. It's 1.2 miles/two km straight up, but you get views that would leave you gasping, if you had any breath left. Much easier is the three-mile/five-km hike to the **Flatbed Pools**, with its trailhead a half-mile southeast of Tumbler Ridge.

There are a bunch of canyon and waterfall hikes in the area, including a six-mile/10-km hike to **Bergeron Falls**, which, at 330 feet, is the biggest fall in the area. Look for the trailhead at the gravel pit, 10 mile/16 km northeast of Tumbler Ridge.

Where to Eat

 The stop of choice for lobster, pasta, hamburgers, gourmet coffee, and a small dose of history, is the **Alaska Café**, in business since 1936, at 10209 10th St. Prices range from CAN $7 up. They've also got steak and seafood. It's really the only restaurant you need in town, but if it's full, try the **Mile Zero Café**, 1091 Alaska Ave.

Where to Stay

 The **Lodge Motor Inn and Café**, at 1317 Alaska Ave., has clean and comfortable rooms from CAN $55. ☎ 250-782-4837 or 800-935-3003. The **Inn on the Creek**, 10600 8th St., ☎ 250-782-8136, is also a good choice. Doubles start at CAN $60. **The George Dawson Inn**, 11705 8th St., ☎ 250-782-9151, has a fitness center and a restaurant. Doubles from CAN $80.

Camping

Mile 0 Campground (☎ 250-782-2590) is at Mile 1 on the highway. The 85 sites are nice and grassy, and vehicle sites run CAN $12-17. **Northern Lights RV Park** (☎ 250-782-9433) is another half-mile down the road. It has RV sites from CAN $16-23.

Dawson Creek to Fort St. John

The highway starts off as a good two-lane road, with wide shoulders on both sides. The surface is smooth and the driving is easy. But there's little of interest right along here – a lot of factories and strip malls – so you can move towards the better stuff farther north pretty quickly.

Two miles out of Dawson Creek, there's a repeater station for the Cantel telephone/telegraph lines. When this line was first put in, it stretched from Alberta to Fairbanks and was one of the world's longest open-wire circuits.

■ Kiskatinaw Provincial Park

At Mile 17, there's a turnoff for Kiskatinaw Provincial Park. The park contains a section of the original Alaska Highway, which was abandoned for a straighter, easier path. You can follow this road for 4.5 miles/7.2 km, joining today's highway again after crossing the Kiskatinaw River, over an old **wooden bridge** that offers dramatic views. The bridge was the first of its kind built in Canada and is the only wooden bridge still on the highway today. It's a three-span trestle bridge, and it curves nine degrees over its length. You've really got to wonder just what the engineers were thinking. Just before the river is a nice campground with 28 graveled sites for CAN $12 each, some overlooking the river. Water is available – boil it before you drink – and there are outhouses that adhere to the spotless BC standards. The road is rather tight inside the campground, so larger RVs should use caution. You can fish for grayling on the river, but prepare to be eaten alive by mosquitoes.

The **Kiskatinaw River** is popular with canoeists, but only experienced paddlers should try it during high water levels. The river hasn't been graded, but we figure it to be at least a Class III. Not a bad place for some practice with your rodeo kayak.

■ Peace Island Regional Park

The road enters the **Peace River Valley**, with sweeping views to the northeast. More camping is available at Mile 34, in the Peace Island Regional Park, on an island in the middle of the river. The island is connected to the shore by a causeway. There are 20 sites, open from May to September. There is no room for RVs, and you'll have to supply your own firewood. Every year in August, they hold the World Gold Panning Championship here. Contact Park HQ for details, ☎ 250-789-9295.

> **WARNING:** *There are two dams on the river, and the water levels can change dramatically, so use caution.*

■ Taylor

The town of Taylor is at Mile 35. Before the highway was built, Taylor was a ferry town for travelers crossing the Peace River. During WWII, the Alcan Ferry was used here to help transport the Army while the bridge was under construction; it was the main transport link connecting the north and south. The original Peace River suspension bridge, the longest bridge on the highway, collapsed in 1957. From this piece of road, you can see a long suspension bridge used to carry a gas pipeline. **Taylor Visitor Information** is on the north side of the highway in a small log cabin (☎ 250-789-9015). Taylor is the official town sponsor for the World Individual Gold Panning Championships in August, held back down the road at Peace River. Novices are welcome, but if you're planning to come for the event, remember the town overflows and you'll probably have to commute from a distant campground. Because of the river and its rich soil deposits, there are excellent **market gardens** around town. In summer, Taylor is a great place to stock up on vegetables. Its only other claim to fame is the "world's largest golf ball," an old fuel tank that's been painted. Hey, winters can be long up here.

Taylor is a good pullout point if you want to put a canoe into the Peace River. You can put in at Hudson's Hope, at the old ferry landing, and then take out at Taylor, the Halfway Bridge or Clayhurst. It's a one- to four-day trip, with little water above Class II. You can set up your tent on river islands.

■ The Peace River Area

The Peace River is one of the first shots you get at wild Northern territory, although there is a tourist association for it. You can contact them at Box 6850-AG, Fort St. John, BC V1J 4J3 (☎ 888-785-4424). The Peace River runs on a slight arc, one that is followed by roads roughly from beyond Taylor to Hudson's Hope. Farther west, the river runs into Dinosaur Lake, which eventually flows into the huge Williston Lake. If you've got a canoe or kayak, you can happily spend weeks out here without seeing anybody; and when you get tired of paddling, you can hunt for fossils on shore. There is an endless chain of rivers and parks to explore. Get topo maps in Fort St. John at BC Maps (10600 100th St.), stock up on freeze-dried chow and head out. It's mostly Class II paddling, with some nastier stretches.

An outstanding brochure, *Peace River Alaska Highway Canoeing*, is available in local tourist spots. Highlights include the Heather-Dina Lakes circuit, outside of Mackenzie. There's a loop of six lakes with only small portages required. See the Mackenzie section (below) for full details.

There's also great hiking along the rivers. We've listed hikes from the towns closest to the trailhead.

■ Fort St. John

History

 One of the oldest non-Native settlements in mainland BC, Fort St. John has been bounced from pillar to post along the Peace River, as the fortunes of the Hudson's Bay Company rose and fell. It was a headquarters for the fur trade from its establishment in 1794 into the early 1800s, and then became a full-fledged city with the influx of workers for the highway, when it was one of the two biggest camps and the field headquarters for the eastern sector of construction. Before the highway, the only way north from here was on dog and pack trails. The area, which was described by early surveyors as "one big morass," became completely impassable with spring thaw.

Today, Fort St. John calls itself the "Energy Capital of British Columbia," due to the large oil and natural gas fields in the area.

Attractions

As in Dawson Creek, it's better if you don't ask the locals what to do. One answer we got was, "work and go to bars." For the visitor who isn't working or drinking, most of the attractions are in one place: at the **Infocentre**, which is easy to spot since it's behind a 140-foot oil derrick at 9323 100th St. (☎ 250-785-3030). Hours are 8 am to 8 pm. The building houses a museum (admission, CAN $4) with an excellent display of artifacts from the Hudson's Bay Company and an interesting case of objects the Army issued to highway workers. It has all the usual items of area history and prehistory, and is better arranged than most local museums, with reconstructed rooms of early homesteaders and the first store in Fort St. John. There's also a nice little museum shop.

For good views of the Peace River Valley, drive south on 100th St. to the end of the road, at **Lookout Park**. There are good mountain biking trails in the park.

Canadian Forest Products offers a tour of how they reforest after clearing timber. It's free, but you need to call for a reservation (☎ 250-785-8906). If you're tired of looking at deforestation, you can see what comes next here. There's also the Fish Creek Community Forest just north of town, beside the Northern Lights College. Self-guided tours offer a look at the local flora and fauna.

Backcountry Adventure Tours (☎ 250-787-5359) in Fort St. John does jet boat trips up the Peace River or the Pine River; they also guide canoe and backpacking trips.

Seasonal Activities

There's a huge annual fair at the end of July, with all the events state fairs back home have led you to expect. In early July, there's a rodeo. Call ☎ 250-785-3033 for details.

Where to Eat

Jade's Garden, at 10108 101st Ave., offers Chinese specialties and a quiet atmosphere. Take-out is available. Dinners range from CAN $4 to $15. **Wilson's Pizza**, 10503 100th Ave., has Italian dishes in the same price range.

Where to Stay

The town is unusual because it's actually just as full in winter – when the oil and gas surveyors appear – as it is in summer. Most hotels in the area are at the cheap end of things, CAN $50

to $75 per room. There's rarely a shortage of places to stay, even in summer.

Northwoods Inn, ☎ 250-787-1616, 10627 Alaska Rd., has a coffee shop, lounge, cabaret and pub. Rooms run CAN $60 for a double or triple. **Four Seasons Motor Inn,** ☎ 250-785-6706, downtown, is simple, but cheap. Doubles go from CAN $60.

For something a little more luxurious and corporate, there's a **Best Western** in town, ☎ 888-388-9408, with rooms from CAN $80, and a **Ramada,** ☎ 250-785-9255, with rooms from CAN $90.

The Alexander Mackenzie Inn offers about the same standards, with rooms from CAN $65. ☎ 250-785-8364.

Camping

The most convenient – though far from scenic – place to camp is **Fort St. John Centennial RV Park**. It's right behind the Infocentre and is open May to September. The 31 sites (with hookups) go for CAN $12 to $20. There's lots of grass, but no trees, and if you're looking to camp, it's nicer six miles north at Charlie Lake (see below).

Fort St. John to Fort Nelson

■ Along Charlie Lake

Camping is available at Mile 49.5, **Beatton Provincial Park,** ☎ 800-689-9025 or 604-689-9025, on the east end of Charlie Lake. It's one of the oldest provincial parks, and the lake has good fishing for walleye and pike. In winter, there's excellent cross-country skiing and ice fishing. The park has a boat launch, a playground, and swimming. There are 37 sites, going for CAN $12. The campground is open May to October.

If you need hookups, try **Ron's RV Park** at Mile 52, ☎ 250-787-1569. Open from May to September. All services are available here.

Still on Charlie Lake, there's **Charlie Lake Provincial Park,** ☎ 800-689-9025 or 604-689-9025, with 58 sites. It's a very quiet, beautifully treed area right on the edge of the lake. It has water, a kitchen shelter and a picnic area, plus a .7-mile/one-km hiking trail. There are also lots of mosquitoes, and some of the spaces are very tight; if you're in an RV, be prepared to back up. The park campground is a popular end point for mountain bikers, so watch out as you walk.

For canoeists, Charlie Lake is excellent flatwater paddling. There are quite a few spots around the lake where you can get out of the boat and explore. Although there's some heavy algae in late summer, you'll find good fishing for walleye, Northern pike and perch.

Charlie Lake is the site of some of the oldest settlements in BC. It was on the migration trail, and the animals headed through the valley. According to archeologists, this was the place to be even before the ice age.

Along the highway, the area is pastureland punctuated by forests. It was all combed for gold, but the miners came up empty and headed farther north. As the highway does the same thing, the road conditions improve slightly.

Just past Mile 72 is what was once the **Beatton River Flight Strip**, one of the four gravel airstrips built during highway construction to provide emergency services for the military.

■ Wonowon & Moose Territory

Wonowon, at Mile 102, is not much more than a gas and rest stop. The Husky gas station/hotel/restaurant complex has single and double rooms starting in the CAN $55 range. ☎ 250-772-3288. It also offers campsites.

During WWII, Wonowon was a control station, a military checkpoint set up to make sure no Japanese were trying to head north along the road.

You'll find a different kind of danger along Mile 110. There are a lot of natural gasworks in the area, and signs are posted: "Dangerous Gas Area – No Parking or Camping." Check in Wonowon for the latest details.

More gas – the safe kind for your car – is available at Mile 143, at **Pink Mountain Campsite & RV Park**, ☎ 250-774-5133. RV sites and tent sites are available for CAN $16, and there are basic cabins for CAN $30. There's good fishing in the Halfway River in August and September. Rig your lures for lake trout and Dolly Varden. Paddlers should take the turnoff at Mile 147 to the bridge (about 10 miles/16 km). The upper portion of the river is Class III; the lower, Class II, suitable for intermediate paddlers.

From here to the end of the Trutch Mountain stretch – about the next 40 miles – you're in serious moose territory.

Mile 148 is what was called **Suicide Hill** when the highway went in, as it was the most treacherous hill on the road. Travelers found this greeting posted at the beginning of the hill: "Prepare to meet thy maker."

At Mile 168.5 a rutted turnoff road leads to **Sikanni River Falls**. Where the roads starts to widen (10.5 miles/16 km in) a trail takes you down a short hike to steep cliffs and some lovely waterfalls. Plenty of hiking trails thread around the falls and canyon, and you have a chance to see goats or bears. It's worth a quick side-trip.

There's camping at **Buckinghorse Provincial Park**, ☎ 250-787-3407, at Mile 173. The park offers quiet sites along the river for CAN $12.

At Mile 176 is the beginning of the **Trutch Mountain bypass**, where a part of the original highway is visible to the east. The original road climbed to a pass of over 4,100 feet, the second-highest pass along the route first laid down. As soon as the engineers had time (well, about 40 years later), they found a more level route, which is what you travel on today.

The **Prophet River Provincial Park**, no phone, at Mile 217, has a hike from the campground to the river, but it's in a bear area, so be sure to make some noise as you walk. Gas, food and lodging are available at the tiny settlement of **Prophet River**, at Mile 233.

Camp at Mile 265 in the **Andy Bailey Provincial Park**, ☎ 250-787-3407, seven miles off the highway, which has 35 campsites, a boat launch, swimming and fishing for pike. The park is set deep in a lovely spruce forest, but the road is narrow, and there is only one place wide enough to turn around an RV.

The highway crosses the Muskwa River (the name means "bear" in Slave Indian) at Mile 281. This is the lowest point on the highway, at 1,000 feet.

■ Fort Nelson

History

 Named for the famous British Admiral Lord Nelson, Fort Nelson was established in 1805 as a fur trading post. The word "fort" in the town name – and in Fort St. John and many other small towns – is appropriate. The fur trading posts were truly forts, designed to hold off the enemy in a siege. Depending on the area, Indian attacks on the trading posts were common. A more serious danger, though, were attacks from a rival trading company. In the historical annals of the Hudson's Bay Company are countless stories of attacks by rival companies, such as the North-West Company, and by independent traders (called peddlers), who took advantage of HBC's policy of letting the furs come to them. While the HBC cowered behind walls, the independent traders were opening up Western Canada.

With a population of 4,000, Fort Nelson is the biggest city between Fort St. John and Whitehorse. Once fur trading halted, the city depended for years upon the world's largest chopstick manufacturing company for its economic survival. The chopsticks were made from the huge poplar forests that surround the city; they were sent to the Orient, where each set was used once and thrown away. Take a good, long look at the trees while you drive around. These are the survivors of years of government-subsidized deforestation. Once the subsidy was gone, the factory packed up, leaving the town's economy a shambles until somebody else started to buy the trees.

If you don't have your own car, about the only ways to Fort Nelson are by hitching or on a **Greyhound Bus** (☎ 250-774-6322).

Attractions

 The **Infocentre** is on the highway, at the north edge of town, in the rec center. It's small, but helpful. The staff can often arrange tours of local businesses; check with them if you see a place that interests you. The center is open 8 am to 8 pm in summer.

Fort Nelson Heritage Museum, ☎ 250-774-3536, is next to the Infocentre, and it's open from 10 am to 9 pm daily. Admission is CAN $5 for adults, CAN $3 for kids and seniors. Inside, they show the Trail of '42 video, an excellent work compiled from government films on the construction of the highway. It's the best look at just how difficult it was to put the road through: vehicles swallowed by mud, workers freezing, mosquitoes as thick as clouds. The soldiers – more than 2,000 of them were here at the peak of construction – felt incredibly isolated, and it shows on their faces.

Another interesting exhibit explains the steps used to build a birch bark canoe – a necessary skill for a Native or a trapper (if it whets your appetite, get a copy of John McPhee's book, *Survival of the Birch Bark Canoe*). Out behind the museum is a reconstruction of a trapper's cabin and some old shop fronts. In the front and side yards there are vintage cars and construction vehicles restored by the museum's curator, Marl Brown. Each one is in running condition.

If you're missing an essential piece of camping gear, try the **Army Surplus Store**, in the center of town, south side.

Seasonal Activities

 During the summer months, Fort Nelson presents a **Welcome Visitor** program at Town Square, just east of the Infocentre. These free programs involve slides and discussions of the Northern lifestyle, including the interesting quirk of grass burning – you burn the grass so it will grow back greener. Unfortunately, this activity also tends to take a few barns and garages with it, keeping the local fire department jumping. The programs are run from May 15 to August 15, at 6:45 pm, Monday through Thursday. ☎ 250-774-6400.

Where to Eat

Dan's Neighborhood Pub, at Mile 300 on the highway, is the most popular place with the locals. It's got a lively pub and the best food and drinks in town. Steaks, seafood, even vegetarian fare, from CAN $6 to $20.

Inside the **Provincial Motel** there's a restaurant with good stir-fry and other Chinese and Western dishes. Prices range from CAN $6 to $25. **The Northern Deli**, downtown, is the place for cheap food; also the place to pack up on cheeses for the road ahead.

Where to Stay

Fort Nelson Hotel, ☎ 250-774-6971 or 800-663-5225, at Mile 300 on the highway, has 135 rooms, a restaurant, coffee shop and lounge. Rates start around CAN $60.

Bluebell Inn, ☎ 250-774-6961, has rooms for CAN $80; some have kitchenettes. Another choice is the somewhat fancier **Woodlands Inn**, ☎ 250-774-6669, 888-966-3466, which has basic rooms from CAN $80, working up towards suites at twice the price.

Camping

Near the museum is the **Westend Campground**, ☎ 250-774-2340, with 110 camping spaces in a nicely wooded lot. Showers, laundromat and ice are available. Cost is CAN $17 to $23 per vehicle. The spaces are small and it feels crowded, but it's the only campground with full services in the area.

Fort Nelson to Muncho Lake

The road worsens noticeably in this section of the highway, but the scenery is beautiful enough to take your mind off any troubles. The old Alcan is visible in some spots to the north. The old road, even more curved than the new one, is being eaten up by vegetation.

Allow some extra time for driving this section; although the narrow turns and gravel patches will slow you down, the photo opportunities will slow you down even more.

Leaving Fort Nelson, you pass through large groves of poplars. Early in the summer, the road is also lined with wildflowers. Off in the distance, to the south, the Rockies are visible, snowcapped year-round.

At Mile 320, the road begins a long, steep climb to the top of **Steamboat Mountain** (3,500 feet/1,000 meters). This piece of road seems to be under construction almost every summer. Grades through the area reach 10%, and the higher you get, the better the views. This is especially true around Miles 348 to 350, just before you start heading down the mountain at Mile 352.

Take the pullout at Mile 350 for a lovely view down through the Muskwa River Valley and over to the Rockies.

The down side of the mountain is in worse shape than the up side. The road gets worse, the turns get sharper. There are glimpses of the river valley through the thick forest, and at Mile 361 you can see **Indian Head Mountain** dead ahead, its profile formed by erosion caused by receding glaciers. Another erosion feature, **Teetering Rock**, is on the horizon to the north, at Mile 363.

> **AUTHOR NOTE:** If it's late in the afternoon or looking like it might storm, consider pulling off to camp for the night around the Tetsa River. Farther ahead, at Stone Mountain and Muncho Lake, the weather can turn mean very quickly. Especially for tenters, if there are dark clouds in the sky, stop down here.

Tetsa River Provincial Park, ☎ 250-787-3407, is at Mile 365. It's a pleasant spot, with some sites having good river views. It's also pretty quiet and rarely crowded. Pitch the tent or park the camper and go for a walk along the river banks. This is an undiscovered treasure along the highway. There's good fishing for grayling and Dolly Varden, and sites are only CAN $12.

You enter **Stone Mountain Provincial Park**, ☎ 250-787-3407, at Mile 371.5. The next section of road is one of the most hazardous on the entire highway. For the next 100 miles/160 km, the road travels through the habitat of the stone sheep. The sheep themselves are only an occasional hazard. They come down near the road to look for salt. The true danger is people stopping their vehicles on blind curves to take pictures.

When you spot sheep, get your car completely off the road before stopping. No animal-viewing opportunity is worth an accident, and there are many accidents in this stretch of road every year. A park ranger told us that she never drives this section of road faster than 35 mph; she also said that, if she could tell all travelers just one thing, it would be, "Don't stop in the middle of the road for the sheep." In our conversation, she came back to this point over and over.

The government is trying to solve the problem by putting in artificial salt licks, with overlook points, but so far their efforts to move both the sheep and the road hazards have not been successful.

STONE SHEEP

Stone sheep are considered to be a geographical variation on the better known Dall's sheep, their northern cousins. Stone sheep are brown, with white patches around the muzzle and rump; Dall's sheep are a creamy-white color, except for a few dark hairs occasionally found along the spine and tail. A full-grown stone sheep male averages just over three feet at the shoulder and weighs 200 pounds; a Dall's male is about the same height, but as much as 40 pounds lighter. Both varieties live on grasses and sedge, and are preyed upon by lynx, wolverine, wolves and grizzly bears. The sheep prefer to live in high, rocky areas, where they have a good view of anything coming up at them.

The sheep in this area are very used to cars; they will not bolt when you stop. Sometimes, they even come closer – this is a good time to drive away. They are not usually being aggressive, just curious. But curiosity draws them into the middle of the road. There are frequent pullouts in the area. For everyone's safety, get to one before stopping your vehicle.

From here, the road narrows a bit, but it is in good condition as it follows the rocky-bottomed Tetsa River. The banks of the river are lined with forest.

The road climbs to **Summit Lake**, and at Mile 392 is the **Summit Lake Lodge**, offering gas, food and lodging. The lodge is known for its enormous, delicious cinnamon rolls, and it also has good burgers. ☎ 250-232-7531.

The view from here is of the barren Stone Mountain Range, with a few peeks of the peaks of the Rockies behind. **Summit Lake** lies at an altitude of 2,680 feet/814 meters; the mountains around it climb to over 7,000 feet/2,128 meters. The most dramatic of these is **Mt. St. George**, at 7,419 feet/2,255 meters. On a very still day, it is reflected in the blue-green waters of the lake with dramatic effect. For those wondering, the lake's color is caused by copper-oxide leaching into the water from the limestone bedrock. It's worth spending a day here just to watch the water's color change as the light hits it from different angles.

Summit Lake Campground, no phone, right on the edge of the lake, offers 28 sites in a clean, graveled area. The campground itself isn't exciting – in fact, considering the location, it's pretty bleak, just a gravel pad jammed in between the road and the mountains – but the scenery around it can't be beat. Watch for sudden weather changes. If the wind kicks up, you could easily find your tent in the lake. Sites here are CAN $12, and

Northern BC

there's a boat launch in the campground – no boats with motors allowed. Fish for lake trout, grayling, whitefish and rainbow trout.

There are quite a few hiking trails in the area; two of them begin right at the campground. A 2.5-mile/four-km round-trip hike goes to **Summit Peak**, where there are good alpine views. Plan for up to five hours to make it there and back. The 3.5-mile/six-km hike to **Flower Springs** offers alpine lakes, flowers and waterfalls.

For the more ambitious, there's hiking along the **MacDonald Creek Valley**. Pick up the trail near Rocky Mountian Lodge, five miles/eight km west of Summit Lake. This one- to three-day hike takes you through prime moose, caribou and sheep country. Watch the weather; this is a flash flood area. Another option is through the pristine **Wokkpash Valley, Forlorn Gorge** and the **Stepped Lakes**. Access to the trail is at Mile 400, on Churchill Mine Rd. It's 12 miles/20 km back from the road, and only four-wheel-drive vehicles will make it past the river.

Check at the Fort St. John park office, ☎ 250-787-3407, before you take on a long hike in the Wokkpash. It's a 15.5-mile/25-km trail, with an elevation change of nearly 4,000 feet/1,200 meters. Figure on at least two days to hike it. There's also a longer option, 43.5 miles/71 km, which takes you from MacDonald Creek along the valley, then back to the creek and the highway. Don't go without a topo map. The astounding hoodoos are what makes these hikes popular.

HOODOOS

Hoodoos are created by rain wash. During a storm, each droplet of rain impacts at about 20 mph. The hoodoos are eroded out of glacial debris, soft stone left behind by the receding glaciers. As the rain hits this, the softest stone erodes, revealing boulders beneath. The boulder then provides a cap for the pillar, protecting the softer rock underneath. The ground around the boulder continues to erode. When looking at a group of hoodoos, you can see some with the cap, and some that have not yet found the cap and so are less defined. Generally, hoodoos are found in semi-arid regions, at the edges of steep slopes. Hoodoos are easily seen at Mile 394, where there's a very short viewing hike.

The **Wokkpash Protected Area**, just south of Stone Mountain Provincial Park, covers 68,000 acres of pure wilderness: no road, no nothing. If you hike into it, know what you're doing, and be sure to take all proper bear precautions.

Just 112 miles from the lowest point of the highway is its highest point: Mile 392, altitude 4,250 feet/1,290 meters at the summit. Engineers had to blast through rock to make this pass.

Camp at **One Fifteen Creek Provincial Park**, where there's fishing for Dolly Varden and a close-up look at beaver dams and lodges. It's on the south side of the highway, 11 miles/18 km past Summit Lake.

Mile 422 has the **Toad River Lodge**, ☎ 250-232-5401, with gas, a café and motel offering doubles from CAN $65, camping sites from CAN $10 to $20. They've also got a collection of more than 6,000 hats hanging from the ceiling. It's a good place to stop for lunch, and the store has a small assortment of CDs, their biggest sellers. "You know how often we get told drivers are sick and tired of listening to the same dozen records?"

■ Muncho Lake

Muncho Lake Provincial Park, ☎ 250-787-3407, which covers nearly 162,000 acres, begins at Mile 427; at 428, there is a view of Folded Mountain, an interesting combination of erosion and plate tectonics.

For the next 37 miles, a "watch for wildlife" warning is in effect on the road. The warning is primarily for stone sheep, but there are also a lot of moose in the area, as well as caribou, elk, black bear, mountain goat, mule deer and the very occasional grizzly bear. The road narrows, and in many places there is no shoulder; do not stop on the road. Also, watch for landslides. The mountains are steep and treeless, and can come down without warning.

The river running alongside the road is the Toad, headed north. In June, this is an excellent area for wildflower viewing, especially wild roses, sweet pea and yellow daisies. You'll also see yellow lady's slipper and bog orchids, one of the northern species of orchid.

Muncho Lake itself comes into view at Mile 454. The lake is 7.5 miles/ 12 km long and has virtually no shore; it just drops off, as deep as 650 feet/200 meters in places. Highway crews were practically standing in the water trying to cut the road. Like Summit Lake, Muncho Lake's brilliant color is caused by copper-oxide leaching in from the bedrock. But at Muncho Lake, the color is deeper, more arresting. Staring into it is one of the highlights of a trip on the highway. Best photo ops are at the viewpoint at the north end of the lake. Along the way, you'll pass several alluvial fans, evidence of the great forces of water and ice that formed the lake.

"Muncho" means "big lake" in the Tagish language. It's the longest lake in the Northern Rockies – technically in the Terminal Range of the Rockies, which end near here (or begin, depending upon your point of view), 1,850 miles/3,000 km from their other end in New Mexico. The next range of mountains north, the Mackenzies, are geologically quite different, and also have much longer lakes – Teslin Lake is about 80 miles long.

Northern BC

Adventures on Water

 Boating: The best activities at Muncho Lake are on the water. Canoe and boat rentals are available at the hotels, as are boat excursions. The lake offers good fishing, too. You can catch trout, grayling, Dolly Varden and whitefish. In July, try your luck at the annual **Muncho Lake Fishing Derby**, ☎ 250-787-3407. The lake has Class I paddling, suitable for a novice, but be careful of sudden strong winds.

Liard Air Co., ☎ 800-663-5269, 776-3481, has charters and fly-in fishing deals.

Adventures on Foot

 Hiking: There's abundant hiking in the area; ask at the hotels or restaurants for a trip to fit your ambition. Remember the bears, and be sure to make some noise. A couple of trails right off the highway lead back and pretty much straight up.

There are a couple of good, easy, short hikes, too. **Strawberry Flats** starts at the campground of the same name located 26.6 miles/43 km north if Muncho Lake, right off the highway. The hike goes 1.8 miles/ three km (one way) along the old Alaska Highway, for views of the lake. **Sheep Flats** is a 2.5-mile/four-km round-trip that follows an alluvial fan to a salt lick popular with stone sheep. If you didn't see any standing in the middle of the road, this may be your chance. The same goes for the **Trout River Mineral Lick Trail**, a .9-mile/1.5-km circuit right off the road that takes you to another favorite lick spot.

Where to Stay

 There are three motels in town, each of them offering camp- sites, too. There are also places for campers only. All of these fill up early. Make reservations at least a day ahead.

Our top pick is the **Northern Rockies Lodge**, at Mile 462. They've got beautiful cabins on the water's edge, with rates from CAN $60. There are also rooms in the lodge – the largest log building in BC – from CAN $85. There are also 30 camping sites that go for CAN $16 to $25 per vehicle. They have electricity, water and sewer. Also here is a small store, a fan- tastic restaurant, a gas station and a laundromat. The lodge rents canoes and boats (CAN $20 to $40 for five hours), runs long tours into the moun- tains, fly-in fishing excursions and flightseeing trips. ☎ 250-776-3482 or 800-663-5269. One caveat: this place gets heavy European traffic, and it's really geared towards German tourists. This means it's a great place to buy a schnitzel lunch, but it may also be full up with package tourists.

J and H Wilderness Resort is 1.5 miles/2.4 km farther down the road, at Mile 463. The motel is small (doubles go for CAN $60), but the campground has 60 good sites by the lake for CAN $22-25 per vehicle, hookups included. There's a laundromat, showers and a licensed dining room. Boat rental is available at CAN $10 an hour. ☎ 250-776-3453.

Finally, there is **Muncho Lake Lodge** at Mile 463. It's open May to October. Doubles and triples go for CAN $55. Campsites start at CAN $14 per vehicle, with hookups and showers available. Tenters can pitch pretty much anywhere on this huge chunk of lakefront property with great views. There's also a restaurant, laundromat and gas station. ☎ 250-776-3456.

There are two camping-only sites at Muncho Lake: the **Provincial Park Campground** at Strawberry Flats (Mile 457) and the **MacDonald Campground** (Mile 462.5). The two provide only 30 sites in one of the most beautiful spots in Canada. Sites in either place run CAN $12. Both campgrounds have boat launches. MacDonald fills up faster, but you can't get any closer to the lake. ☎ 250-787-3407 for both.

Muncho Lake to Watson Lake

After briefly following the lake, the highway begins to climb and the landscape gets a little greener as the road heads off along Trout River. Behind the front range of mountains you'll get glimpses of higher, rocky and snow-covered peaks.

At Mile 473 is a turnoff for a mineral lick. From the turnoff parking lot, there is a short, uneven trail leading to an overlook. If you haven't seen any sheep or other beasts so far, try here, especially in the early morning. It's a little less than a mile loop. But around here, animals are much more often in the road than they are at the lick. Still, this is a good place to get out and stretch your legs while looking at the limestone, dolomite and shale formations.

At Mile 490, the road begins to follow Liard River. This river can be taken in a canoe, from Muncho Lake all the way to Liard Hot Springs. The highway hugs the river for the simple reason that it made laying out the lines a lot easier for the highway engineers. Liard River itself drains into the Mackenzie River, which ultimately drains into the Arctic Ocean. The **Liard River Bridge** is the last suspension bridge on the highway. It's a local favorite spot to fish for grayling, and if you look a hundred yards or so upstream of the bridge, you'll see some ruins of old squatter cabins.

> **AUTHOR NOTE:** The area code in this area is 250, but when you cross the Yukon border around Mile 590 at Contact Creek, it changes to 867.

■ Liard Hot Springs

Located at Mile 496, **Liard Hot Springs Provincial Park**, ☎ 800-689-9025 or 250-787-3407, is a great place to soak out some of your sore driving muscles. There are two pools for a bath. The first, Alpha (up to 127°F), is about a quarter-mile from the parking lot. The second pool, Beta (a cooler 104°F – good hot bath temperature), is about the same distance from Alpha. Both pools are accessed by wooden walkways. The Beta pool is used more for swimming than soaking. Both pools offer changing rooms and bathing platforms. Park rules require that all bathers wear something, but they don't say what. If you didn't pack a bathing suit, just jump in with your clothes on.

During peak summer months, a ranger is on constant duty near the path to the pools. He or she will answer your questions about the area, or just fill you in on details about the wildlife. Moose, bear and deer also like the pools, although they'll stay away when people are around. Nature walks are given daily, and they're worth taking. The flora around the hot springs are like nowhere else on the highway; it's almost tropical. Look for ferns and orchids, as well as a few carnivorous plants, including sundew and butterwort. The hot springs have caused a microclimate, the warm air allowing plants and animals to thrive that would otherwise freeze this far north. More than 250 species of plant are found around the springs, at least 14 of them much farther north than their normal range. There have been sightings of 28 mammal species and more than 100 species of bird here. A short path leads back from the pools to the hanging gardens, where a cascading spring has made a beautiful tiered area.

The hot springs have been a popular stopping point since the first French trappers came through looking for fur. The word "liard" is French for poplar, a nod to the trees that surround the area. In the days of the gold rush, miners would pause here to gather strength. During construction of the highway, being posted here was a prime assignment, since it was the only warm area during the winter. Workers bathed daily here, and once a week the springs were cleared for women to use.

Where to Stay

Just past the springs is **Trapper Ray's Liard Hotsprings Lodge**, ☎ 250-776-7349, which is open year-round. Doubles go from CAN $75, campsites from CAN $10. This new log cabin-style lodge is very clean and comfortable. There's also the **Liard River Lodge**, ☎ 250-776-7341. Doubles here rent from CAN $65, tent sites from CAN $10. No RV hookups.

There is a **campground**, ☎ 800-689-9025, near the entrance to the springs with 53 sites that fill up early.

Onward from Liard

 Leaving Liard, the road is narrow and there is a lot of broken pavement. This area is frequently under construction, but the wild roses offer a distraction from the gravel, which is mostly hard-packed; there is quite a lot of washboarding in some places. The road climbs and drops, with some very steep hills.

At Mile 514 there's a turnoff for a hike down to **Smith Falls**. You can get a look at the two-tiered falls from the road.

Mile 543 has the **Coal River Bridge**, where the Coal meets the Liard. There was a forest fire here not long ago, and it's interesting to see how the woods are regenerating.

There's a turnoff for "do it yourself camping" here – a few fire rings and a clearing – and you can hike around the rapids of the Liard. The river, which is really moving at this point, has thrown trees as far as 75 feet from the normal flow level. You can climb around on the rocks, which is dangerous but a lot of fun.

Contact Creek Bridge, at Mile 588, is one of the points where the highway construction crews met up, connecting two sections of the road. They met here on September 25, 1942, and there's a turnout with an informational plaque on the spot.

Food, gas and lodging are available at Mile 590; gas is two or three cents a gallon cheaper here than it is farther up the road at Watson Lake.

A SMALL CHUNK OF THE YUKON

By this point, you've already crossed into the Yukon several times; there's no official notice of that fact, other than a lone sign telling you that it's the law to drive with your headlights on.

This is indeed a guidebook to BC; however, if you're doing the Cassiar-Alaska Highway BC loop, you're going to drive a small chunk of the Yukon, so we're including that here.

> **HIGHWAY TIP:** Driving with your headlights on is a good idea on most of the roads in the North; a dark car is almost invisible against a background of forest.

Altogether, the road crosses back and forth over the Yukon/BC border seven times. The road is poor overall, with a lot of dirt, gravel, washboarding, and construction to Watson Lake.

A **Yukon Government Campground** at Mile 615 has 55 sites, some by the lake, where you can fish for grayling, trout

Northern BC

and pike. Sites go for CAN $12, and there's a boat launch and good swimming in the lake.

There's a turnoff for **Lower Post**, an old Hudson's Bay Company trading post, at Mile 626. It offers no services today. By the turnoff is the **Lucky Lake picnic area**, which has water slides into the lake. Leading from the area is a two-mile trail, an easy walk heading up Liard Canyon. Across the river is a cabin dedicated to Robert Campbell, said to be the first white man to enter the Yukon.

■ Watson Lake

Watson Lake is in the Yukon, but a lot of BC travelers end up here.

Before the advent of the white traders and trappers, this was the home of the Kaska Indians. The lake was originally known as Fish Lake, and it's still a great place for fishing.

History

The first settlement was **Sylvester's Landing**, part of a series of trading posts. By the 1870s, with the discovery of gold, the area was booming, and the city got its new name from Frank Watson, a hopeful miner from Yorkshire, England. He was on his way to the goldfields, but stopped here, became a trader and married a native.

In the 1930s, mail planes began to land on Watson Lake, which grew as a fueling stop, but the real boom came when the Alaska Highway construction began and Watson Lake became a supply center. The airfield was upgraded to handle fighter traffic headed for Russia along the Northwest Staging Route.

Today, Watson Lake, at Mile 621 on the Alaska Highway, thrives on logging and tourism; its population of 2,000 makes it the third-largest city in the Yukon.

Attractions

The big attraction in town is the **Alaska Highway Interpretive Centre**. Just look for the signs and the RVs at the junction of the Alcan and the Robert Campbell Highway. The center is open from 8 am to 8 pm, mid-May to mid-September (☎ 867-536-7469). It has tourist information, a photo mural showing construction of the highway and a real Army tent, set up the way it was for the workers. A three-projector slide show on the history of the highway is played at regular intervals. The show is unique to this center, and well worth watching. The center also broadcasts a visitor radio show on 96.1 FM.

Outside the center is the famous **Signpost Forest**, which now boasts more signs than any sane person wants to keep track of, and is growing at a rate of a couple of thousand a year. It was started in 1942 by a homesick GI named Carl Lindley, from Danville, Illinois, who put up a sign pointing to his hometown. Other workers followed suit. Maintaining the tradition, anyone with a hammer and nail can put up a sign today. A part of the forest was taken down and displayed at Expo 86, in Vancouver, at the Yukon Pavilion.

The signpost forest was started in 1942.

Heritage House Wildlife and Historic Museum, across from the Watson Lake Hotel, is free and is open from 9 am to 9 pm, June 1 to August 31, and from 9 am to 5 pm, September 1 to October 15. The collection is in the oldest house in Watson Lake (built in 1948). There is a variety of taxidermied animals, including one that is billed as the second-largest stone sheep ever shot.

The Northern Lights Centre is a sort of planetarium devoted to the *Aurora borealis*. It has a 110-seat theater, interactive exhibits and several different shows running about every hour during the day. If you're traveling in the summer, you're not likely to see the aurora – it's never dark enough – so this is a good substitute. CAN $10 admission.

Adventures on Foot

 If you want to get out of town, you can **pan for gold**. Be sure to stay away from regions between white stakes with silver heads; those mark off claims, and people get very touchy about them. There are a number of hiking trails around, but your time is probably better spent elsewhere.

Adventures in the Air

 You could charter a helicopter from here to **Coal River Springs Territorial Park**, a weird landscape of limestone and calcium carbonate formations.

Where to Eat

 Other than hotel restaurants, there are only a few places to eat in Watson Lake. **The Pizza Palace**, at the corner of the Sign-post Forest, has good chicken and pizza dishes, from CAN $5 to $20. In the same building is a gas station and a laundromat.

For something a little fancier, the **Nugget Restaurant** has Western and Chinese food, and serves breakfast all day (CAN $2 to $10), lunch (CAN $7 to $12), and dinner (CAN $8 to $20).

Where to Stay

 Watson Lake is seriously pricey. It's better to stay north or south of it, but if you don't have that option, there are a couple of choices.

Watson Lake Hotel, ☎ 867-536-7781, next to the Visitors Centre, is the most popular place in town. Doubles start at around CAN $100. There's a good dining room, with breakfasts and lunches starting at CAN $5, dinners at CAN $11. Book your room early. **Gateway Motor Inn**, ☎ 867-536-7744, also right on the highway, is comparable, but a couple of dollars more expensive. **The Big Horn Hotel**, ☎ 867-536-2020, keeps you in the same price range, perhaps a bit lower. While Watson Lake Hotel gets more business, the rooms are nicer here. There's even a Jacuzzi suite available.

Much more basic is the **Cedar Lodge Motel**, ☎ 867-536-7406. Doubles start at CAN $75; some rooms have kitchenettes. The motel also rents bikes. The **Belvedere Motor Hotel**, ☎ 867-536-7712, is open year-round. It has rooms ranging from CAN $100 for a double in the hotel to CAN $85 in the motel.

The cheapest rooms are at the **Air Force Lodge**, just west of town. Rooms are clean and simple – bed and table, that's it. They run only CAN $55, with a shared bath. ☎ 867-536-2890.

As soon as you're out of Watson Lake, prices begin to drop. **Liard River Resort** is only a few minutes out of town, but can save you CAN $25 over in-town rates. It's not as swank as the places in town, but if you're on a budget, it's a lot more reasonable. ☎ 867-536-2271.

Upper Liard Village, at Mile 643, and **Junction 37 Services** at Mile 648, where the Alaska Highway meets the Cassiar Highway, have other, cheaper options.

Camping

For camping, the best spot is the **Gateway to Yukon RV Park**, ☎ 867-536-7448, at Mile 635. Full hookups are CAN $16; unserviced sites are CAN $10. There's a Husky gas station, a large store and a restaurant. This is much better than most of the private RV parks.

Campground Services, ☎ 867-536-7448, has 140 spaces on the southeast side of town, running from CAN $10 to $16, depending on hookups. **Green Valley RV Park** (☎ 867-536-2276), Mile 641, has grassy tent sites for CAN $7.50 and hookups for CAN $16.

Even Farther North: Atlin & Roads to Alaska

There's part of BC that you can only get to if you go into Alaska or the Yukon first: the small, beautiful town of Atlin, and two of the north's glory roads, the highway into Skagway and the even better Haines Highway.

■ Atlin

Get to Atlin off the Alaska Highway, taking Highway 7 south from Jake's Corner. It will take you most of the day to get to Atlin from Watson Lake (see page 312).

Atlin is the most northwestern town in British Columbia. In 1899, at the height of its boom days, Atlin was called the Little Switzerland of the North, and it was supposed to be a lovely town, very advanced for the day. It was on the phone and telegraph lines quite early and, after the gold petered out, there was a tourist boom that lasted into the 1930s. It was actually the second-richest goldfield found, surpassed only by the Cariboo, with more than CAN $23 million of gold taken out. Upwards of 8,000 people lived here at one time, all looking for the glimmer of gold.

Today it's just a tiny town overlooking the huge (85-mile/137-km) Atlin Lake.

Attractions

 The **Tourist Infocentre** is at the museum on 3rd St., in the old school building. It houses great historical photos of Atlin's salad days and documents the history of the local Tlingits. There's a walking tour that takes in some good historical buildings, and you can look at the MV *Tarahne*, a 1916 luxury lake boat built by the White Pass Company to handle the people and cargo that came with the mining.

The *Tarahne* has a pretty interesting history. She started off at 79 feet/24 meters long and was the first gas-driven boat the White Pass Company used. In 1928, there was so much traffic to Atlin that the White Pass Company lengthened the boat – on April Fool's Day that year, they cut the boat in half and put in a new middle section, bringing its total length to 119 feet/36 meters. New engines and propellers were installed and the boat could cruise at 12 knots. Being bigger and better made her more expensive, too: the refurbishment added about 5¢ a mile to the running cost.

The Depression brought an end to the heyday of the ship. In 1936, she was beached.

Atlin Historical Society (☎ 250-651-7522) now owns the ship, and they've worked hard to restore her. They're not done yet. There are regular special events held on the ship, and it's well worth looking at, as the last remnant of Atlin's glory days.

Adventures on Foot

 Hiking: To get the best views of the town and lake, try the **Monarch Mountain Trail**; two hours of walking gets you great panoramic views. The trailhead is off Warm Bay Road. If you're a birder, you can add a few of the 200 species of bird that call the area home. The prize sighting would be an oldsquaw, quite rare in this area. There are also the scarce white-winged scoters, and Atlin Lake was the first place in British Columbia where a nest for the Arctic loon was found.

In Atlin Provincial Park, the **Telegraph Trail** leads from the lake along the Pike River, uphill to Kuthoi Lake and beyond. This is the route the telegraph originally followed, but it's mostly overgrown now. Still, if you've got time and you're ambitious, it's lovely.

Adventures on Water

 Paddling: Take the highway to its end at Atlin Provincial Park. The park is remote enough – and more than beautiful enough – that it was used as the setting for much of the movie *Never Cry Wolf*, the best movie ever made about wolves. If you've seen the movie, you've probably already pointed the car down the road, just to get a look at this place.

The best thing you can do in the park probably is paddle Atlin Lake. There are some beautiful, remote campsites on Sloko and Griffith islands, and at Lake Inlet. There's enough lake here to wear out a set of paddles.

At the southwest tip of the lake, if you're in the mood for a long paddle, is the gigantic **Llewellyn Glacier**, which extends almost to the coast at Juneau. The glacier is in one corner of Atlin Provincial Park; in fact, about one-third of the park's total area is glacier.

If paddling doesn't do it for you, but you want to get out on the lake, rent a boat from **Norseman Adventures**, ☎ 250-651-7535. The lake is big and makes its own weather, so it's not really a place for you if you're not comfortable with running boats. Another outfitter is **Atlin Quest**, ☎ 250-651-7659, 800-651-8882, www.atlinquest.com. They run jet boat tours on the lake and the Yukon River, and also have guided walks on Llewellyn Glacier.

Where to Stay

 To overnight in the town, stay at the **Atlin Inn**, ☎ 250-651-7546, which has a good café downstairs. Doubles run about CAN $120.

Camping

Camp at **Pine Creek**, no phone, south of town on Warm Bay Rd.

■ The Tagish Road

The second road leading out of Jake's Corner is the Tagish Road, a shortcut to Carcross and the road to Skagway. It's gravel as far as Tagish, then paved from Tagish to Carcross. Camp at Mile 13, Six Mile River, just before the town of Tagish (the word means "fish trap" in the local language).

Two miles south of town is **Tagish Post**, originally Ft. Sifton, a Mounties checkpoint where they kept track of stampeders headed to the Klondike. The Canadian government used the checkpoint to collect duty and make sure the miners were properly prepared and not going to drop dead on Canadian soil.

Northern BC

The road ends at Mile 34, the junction with the South Klondike Highway. Turn left for Carcross and Skagway, right for Whitehorse.

The South Klondike Highway

Miles are read from Skagway – but most of the road is still in British Columbia. The junction of the South Klondike and the Alaska Highway is at Mile 905 on the Alcan. The South Klondike Highway essentially follows the same path the would-be miners used to get up to the Klondike goldfields. It goes along the tracks of the White Pass and Yukon Route Railway, which was built on top of rocks worn smooth by the footsteps of the miners.

There's an old **White Pass and Yukon Route Railway shed** at Mile 86.7, and the remains of the old **Robinson Roadhouse**. At Mile 73, you'll see the stunning **Emerald Lake**. There is no way to describe the color of this piece of water – "emerald" doesn't do it justice.

In contrast to the beautiful water, at Mile 66.9 is the **Carcross Desert**, the smallest desert in the world, at about 644 acres. The area was originally covered by a glacial lake, but as the glaciers pulled back, this sandy "desert" bottom was left behind. Strong winds kept the plant life to a minimum.

The junction with the Tagish Road is at Mile 66.1, and the town of Carcross, population 400, is a tenth of a mile farther.

■ Carcross

Carcross was a depot town for the White Pass and Yukon Route Railway; it later served as a supply center for the Conrad Mine, on Tagish Lake, and as a transfer point for cargo headed to Atlin. The town was originally called Caribou Crossing because of the regular caribou migration in the area.

The **Tourist Infocentre** is at the old White Pass and Yukon Route Railway depot. It's open daily in summer from 8 am to 8 pm. For a small town, it's a better-than-average center.

There's a stern-wheeler dry-docked next to the center. This kind of boat was used to move people and freight on the area lakes – notably Lake Bennett, where miners switched from walking to floating. The people who started it all, Skookum Jim and Tagish Charlie, are buried in the Carcross Cemetery, half a mile south of town.

As you head out of Carcross, watch for sections of the old wagon road, visible from the highway.

Mile 59 has a pullout with overlooks of the **Windy Arm** of Tagish Lake, and at Mile 52 you can see the remains of the **Venus Mill**, an old gold and silver mine.

> **AUTHOR NOTE:** Canadian Customs is at Mile 22.4, open 24 hours a day in summer. All traffic must stop. The border is at Mile 14.9. US Customs is also open 24 hours a day.

The summit of White Pass, 3,290 feet, is at Mile 14.4. Look across the canyon for the White Pass and Yukon Route Railway tracks. The road drops here, twisting and corkscrewing its way down to US Customs at Mile 6.8.

At Mile 2.3 is the junction of the Dyea Road (see below for details), and then you're in the historic town of Skagway.

■ Skagway

Skagway isn't really the point of this book, but if you've come this far, you're going to end up in town, so here it is. **Note that all prices for Skagway are given in US dollars.**

A "ton of gold" was carried off the docks into the small town of Seattle in July 1897. A full year had passed since the stuff of dreams had been discovered in the Klondike, on Rabbit Creek, a tributary of the Yukon River; but it was only when the ship hit Seattle, wallowing gold-heavy in the light swells of Puget Sound, that the rest of the world had its first news of the gold strike.

The very next ship heading north from Seattle was overflowing with hopeful prospectors. The rush was on, and it all channeled through Skagway, the northern port for the would-be rich.

History

 Skagway became one of the most famous cities in the world in 1897. There was hardly a newspaper printed in the continental US that year that didn't have an article on the gold rush and the trip north. It was from Skagway that thousands headed up the murderous Chilkoot Trail, bound for the goldfields of the Yukon, 600 miles/966 km to the north. The Chilkoot actually started in nearby Dyea, which would have been the boomtown if ships could have gotten to it more easily, but a huge mud flat meant ships stayed well away. Miners would disembark from their ships in Skagway and head over to the trailhead as quickly as possible, getting ready for the arduous climb over the mountains.

CAPT. WILLIAM MOORE

Captain William Moore, anticipating the gold rush by almost a decade, had staked claim to 160 acres at the mouth of the Skagway River nine years before the first strike and begun construction of a wharf. When the first load of miners arrived in his would-be village of Mooresville, a group including surveyor Frank Reid forced Moore and his claim aside, drew up a new town plan, and renamed the town Skaguay, after the Tlingit "Skagua," or windy place. Moore never did make his fortune, though after years of court battles he finally received a small part of the value of the land.

Skagway was the largest Alaskan town during the gold rush years, with a population between 10,000 and 20,000. It also had a reputation as lawless and dangerous. Many stampeders never reached the goldfields but instead lost everything to one of the myriad of conmen waiting at the docks. Many more lost everything in the mud, on the trail, or they simply came to their senses – not many in this last category – and headed back home. One estimate is that a grand total of 100,000 people started off for the goldfields. Half made it to Alaska. Maybe fewer than 50 actually got rich.

During the first year of the gold rush alone, about 20,000 to 30,000 gold seekers headed up the Chilkoot Trail from Dyea. After starting from the port in Skagway, the trip took an average of three months. As the Canadian government required that each person carry a year's supply of food and necessities – the Canadians weren't that interested in finding dead hopefuls on their land – a lot of hiking back and forth between Skagway and the top of the pass was required.

Figuring that a miner's gear – 350 pounds of flour, 150 pounds of bacon, 100 pounds of sugar, another 100 pounds of beans, 70 pounds of coffee and tea, plus clothes (all wool, remember, in these pre-synthetic days), bedding, shovels, picks, etc. – cost a total of roughly US $500-2,000, you know there were plenty of people waiting and hoping to sell stuff. It was the only sure way to get rich off the gold rush (one estimate says that within two weeks of the first ship of gold docking in Seattle, local merchants sold US $325,000 worth of mining gear). Along the way, boomtowns sprang up, some considerably bigger than modern Skagway. Atop the pass, miners built rough boats on the lakes and floated the Yukon River up to the goldfields.

Later in the rush, an alternative route at the White Pass, first charted by Frank Moore, came into its own. The trailhead for this route was practically in the center of Skagway. Nicknamed "Dead Horse Trail" for the 3,000 or so animals that died (according to Jack London, "like mosquitoes at the first frost") hauling packs along its length, the White Pass was considerably less steep but longer than the Chilkoot. There was no shortage of miners who took a look at the steep slopes of the Chilkoot and then decided the slow route might be the better one to take, and so the White Pass saw more than its share of stampeders trying to get their gear up to where it could be approved by Canadian Customs. Within two months, the trail had become almost impassable from overuse.

In 1898, construction began on the White Pass and Yukon Route Railway (WP&YR), which still operates today. The line didn't get finished until June 8, 1900, after the bulk of the rush was past. All those pictures you see of miners hiking straight up a hill – the "Golden Stairs" – in the snow come from the winter of '98-'99; and remember, they probably each went up and down that hill close to 50 times. Getting the line through meant the trip to the goldfields was cut from six months to six days, but the traffic was already thinning.

After the gold rush the railroad was leased by the US War Department in 1942 for the duration of World War II and used to transport supplies and men for the construction of the Alaska Highway. Everything arrived by barge, was transported to the army's base camp in Whitehorse, and then moved out to the work sites along the highway. During the months of construction, the line moved 15 tons of freight every two weeks – more than it had moved in the 40 years previous. There were up to 17 trains a day running through the pass. It was on this railroad that the idea of container shipping was first tried. Truck trailers came off barges, were loaded onto the train, then transported north to the road. Now used worldwide, the idea started right here.

 There are two excellent books on the gold rush and the White Pass, detailing the early history of Skagway and the trials of the miners: ***The Klondike Fever***, by Pierre Berton, covers the gold rush; ***The White Pass***, by Roy Minter, is a fascinating history of the WP&YR railway.

Skagway Today

 Except when the cruise ships are in, Skagway is considerably calmer than it once was (and even then, as one long-time resident put it, "In the gold rush days, we had 20,000 people walking the streets with guns; now we just have six or seven thousand tourists"). This sleepy town of 850 year-round residents faces more tourist jams than guns now. From 9 am to 9 pm, there can be as many as 7,000 cruise ship passengers on Skagway's one street, all of them come to see a town that's being restored to its full 1898 glory.

Don't let the numbers put you off. Skagway is a beautiful city in one of the most dramatic settings you'll ever find. During ship hours, head for the mountains; when the ships are out, come in and walk around the beautiful town.

Basics

 The **Information Center** is right downtown, in the old AB Building. You'll recognize it by the herd of tourists out front taking pictures of its beautiful driftwood exterior. It has the usual assortment of stuff and a map of the Skagway walking tour – Skagway is a great walking town. If you're doing the tour, though, take a good look at the map first and check for shortcuts to the places you're really interested in. Nothing is very far away in Skagway. The Info Center is open daily 8-5 in the summer, 8-12 and 1-5 the rest of the year. ☎ 907-983-2855.

The **National Park Service Visitor Center** is in the old WP&YR offices, right in the center of downtown. They're open daily 8-7 in summer, 8-6 in May and September, and 8-6 Monday through Friday the rest of the year. ☎ 907-983-2921. See below for more details.

Internet access is available at **Skagway Cyber Café**, next door to the Great North Hotel, on Broadway.

Sockeye Cycle rents mountain bikes. ☎ 907-983-2851.

Charter a helicopter from **Temsco**, ☎ 907-983-2900, which also has heli-flightseeing tours of the local glacier area. **LAB**, ☎ 907- 983-2471, **Wings of Alaska**, ☎ 907-789-0790, and **Skagway Air**, ☎ 907-983-2218, charter and run similar tours in fixed-wing planes, as well has having regularly scheduled runs to nearby towns.

Haines-Skagway Water Taxi, ☎ 888-766-3395, offers a good way to take a day-trip to Haines, get some views of the Lynn Canal and some wildlife, and still be back in Skagway in time for dinner. The trip takes roughly an hour each way; the taxi makes two round-trips per day. Fare is US $35 round-trip. US $90 puts you on the fast boat to Juneau.

The Fjord Express, ☎ 800-320-0146, also runs fast ferries to Juneau, for US $99 round-trip.

> **CUSTOMS ALERT:** If you're heading back into BC or coming down the road to Skagway, the Canadian border is open from 8 am to midnight from November 1 to March 31, and 24 hours a day the rest of the year. If you're traveling in winter, remember that these are Canadian times – an hour ahead of Alaska. You'll need a passport to cross the border. A driver's license doesn't cut it anymore.

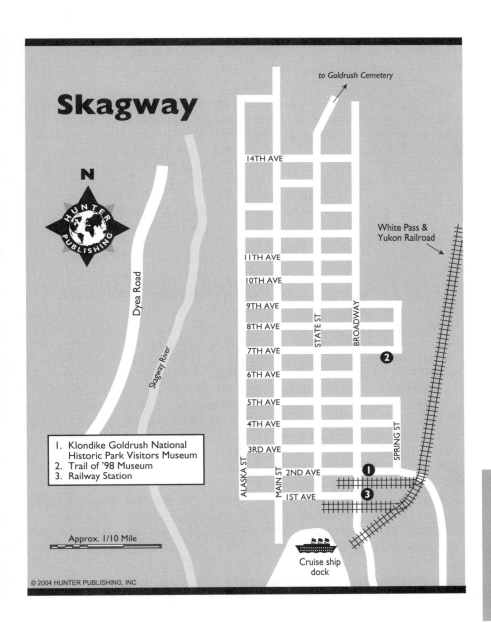

Skagway

N

to Goldrush Cemetery

White Pass & Yukon Railroad

Dyea Road

Skagway River

14TH AVE

11TH AVE

10TH AVE

9TH AVE

8TH AVE

7TH AVE

6TH AVE

5TH AVE

4TH AVE

3RD AVE

2ND AVE

1ST AVE

STATE ST

BROADWAY

SPRING ST

ALASKA ST

MAIN ST

1. Klondike Goldrush National
   Historic Park Visitors Museum
2. Trail of '98 Museum
3. Railway Station

❷

❶

❸

Approx. 1/10 Mile

Cruise ship
dock

© 2004 HUNTER PUBLISHING, INC

Northern BC

Attractions

Skagway's attractions are all pretty close together; you can walk to everything. It's a great town for walking, too, because ocean and mountain views come out and surprise you around the edges of Victorian houses everywhere you turn. Despite the madding crowd, Skagway is a fun place to hang out. Even if the ships sometimes make downtown look like an old fraternity gag – how many people can you stuff into a VW Bug? – don't let it get you down. There's no way around it, the town is still a blast, and on the off-chance there's no ship in, most of the attractions will be closed anyway.

Klondike Gold Rush National Historical Park, Broadway and 2nd, is open 8 am to 8 pm, ☎ 907-983-2921, June through August, 8 to 6 in May and September. Once the depot for the WP&YR, it's now the forest service and park headquarters and marks the beginning of a seven-block corridor that houses many restored buildings dating to gold rush days. The center has daily film shows, and it's the starting point for free guided walking tours of the town. The tours take about an hour and are well worth joining. The film, 30 minutes long and shown on the hour, is way above average for this kind of thing, and really worth your time. There are daily ranger talks at 10 am and 3 pm, as well. They've also got some great displays of old mining items. Finally, this is the place to begin planning your hike up the Chilkoot.

Be sure to pick up a copy of the ***Skaguay Alaskan***. The Skagway Trail Map is also invaluable if you plan to do any hiking.

The **White Pass & Yukon Railroad** is next door to the old depot; the new depot becomes a hive of activity when the train pulls in to start the trip up the White Pass. All the publicity shots show a steam train on this run; sorry, it's not gonna happen. They use the steam train only for special occasions, and odds are high all you'll see moving is a diesel. Still, the carriages are either originals or beautifully made replicas, the scenery is simply astounding – there's no feeling quite like looking out the train at places where miners wore paths down into bedrock as they hauled their gear – and it's a must-do for train buffs (everybody loves a choo-choo train, right?). The four-hour trip up to the summit and back is a great way to spend the afternoon. Everybody comes off this ride with a smile on their face. Tickets are US $82 for adults, US $41 for kids age three through 12. There's also connecting service to Whitehorse. For more information, ☎ 907- 983-2217 or 800-343-7373. The train does have wheelchair access.

The railway climbs more than 2,800 feet/850 meters in only 20 miles and, because the line follows the curves of the mountain, there are some great chances to lean out the windows and catch pictures of the train even when you're on it. If you want to shoot pictures of the train as it goes by, stand along Spring Street. Back in the old days, the tracks actually ran down the center of State Street; the train yards are still there, to the north of town.

Train fans might want to check out the **Train Shoppe**, inside the depot. It's got a large selection of train stuff, from whistles and books to videos and models.

Tatshenshini-Alsek Wilderness Provincial Park. (© Vivien Lougheed)

Athabasca Falls, Jasper National Park. (© Vivien Lougheed)

Above: Mt. Robson. (© Readicker-Henderson)

Below: A home in Dease Lake. (© Vivien Lougheed)

Along the Icefields Parkway. (© Vivien Lougheed)

Above: Columbia Icefields, Jasper National Park. (© Vivien Lougheed)

Below: Outdoor sports abound in the parks of BC. (© Vivien Lougheed)

Mistaya Canyon, Banff National Park. (© Vivien Lougheed)

Railroad bridge over the Stikine River. (© Vivien Lougheed)

Lake Louise. (© Readicker-Henderson)

Other White Pass excursions include the Chilkoot Trail Hiker's Service – the train picks you up at Lake Bennett – for US $30. There's also a long ride up to Carcross in Yukon for US $90 round-trip, including lunch.

Coming out of either the Park Service building or the WP&YR station, you'll see the **Red Onion Saloon**, ☎ 907-983-2222, right across the street. It's a lively place, with music and crowds until late in the evening. Once a brothel, it's now a restaurant with the best food in town and a very interesting atmosphere. There are also (somewhat dubious) rumors of a ghost.

The Trail of '98 Museum, in the old City Hall (see below), ☎ 907-983-2420, displays artifacts pertaining strictly to Skagway and its history and the gold rush. Among the attractions is a display of early gambling equipment from the time when Skagway was at the very edge of the Wild West. Open daily in the summer; admission is US $3. The **old City Hall** is on 7th Street; turn east off Broadway. It was the first granite building in Alaska, and it's worth a look even if you're not interested in the museum. It was recently renovated, and over the next few years it will be fascinating to watch the new stone blend in with the old.

The **Corrington Museum**, ☎ 907-983-2580, is inside a gift shop, but that's not what's important. This museum has a decent collection of Aleutian baskets and ivory, with good model displays. It also has some of the best scrimshaw you're going to find. The museum is open daily in the summer, at 5th and Broadway. Well worth stopping in.

The **Gold Rush Cemetery** is the final resting place for, among others, two people who made Skagway history: Soapy Smith, a gang leader who held the town under his thumb for years, and Frank Reid, the man who killed Soapy on July 8, 1898. Soapy had just enough time to shoot back, and Reid died 12 days later. It's two miles/3.2 km north of town, near the WP&YR lines. Sadly, they've put up replica stones next to the real ones – mostly too worn to read – and it ruins a lot of the effect.

Klondike Gold Dredge Tours, ☎ 877-983-3175, let you see just how far people would go in their search for gold. They've taken a huge dredge – one of those machines that ate rivers whole – and opened it up for tours. For US $25, you get a movie (try to stay awake if you can), a tour of the dredge and you get to try some gold panning yourself. Best for those who like big machinery, but the gold panning is always a hit.

Eight miles on a bumpy gravel turnoff leads to the ghost town of **Dyea**. Once almost as big a boomtown as Skagway, living off the miners headed north, the town collapsed when the WP&YR was completed. All that remains are the skeletons of buildings, a wharf and Slide Cemetery. However, the drive out is lovely, there's a good chance of seeing seals in the bay, and Dyea is the trailhead for the Chilkoot Trail, detailed below.

Northern BC

Dyea had been the end of a trading trail for centuries, part of the extensive trade network the Tlingit operated in Southeast Alaska, connecting them with the interior. The first trading post was built in 1880 and, seven years later, there were nearly 200 people in town. Right after the news of gold got out, though, the town boomed to nearly 8,000 people. As with any boomtown, it didn't last long. As a port, Dyea sucked. Literally. The mud flats exposed at low tide swallowed more than one miner's gear, and ships couldn't get anywhere near the town. If the trail hadn't been there, nobody would have come near the place and, after an avalanche in April 1898 killed more than 60 wannabe miners, even more of the traffic moved over to Skagway and the White Pass Trail. By 1900, only two years after the gold strike, the town was back down to 250 people. By 1903, there were all of three people rattling around what had once been one of the largest towns in Alaska.

The site is now a National Historical Park, with all the protection thereof. There's lots of stuff under the brush and grass, but leave it there. The Park Service has daily walks of the townsite at 2 pm in the summer. Meet at the parking lot in Dyea.

For more than half a century, the Fraternal Order of the Eagles has been putting on the **Days of '98 Show** in the Eagle's Hall at 6th and Broadway. The show gives a good, entertaining history of Skagway – complete with the fight between Soapy Smith and Frank Reid, plus a few chorus girls. Daytime shows are at 10:30 am and 2 pm; the evening session has gambling, starting at 7:30, with the actual performance beginning at 8:30. It's a good way to spend the evening. ☎ 907-983-2545.

Adventures on Water

 Kayaking: If you are an experienced kayaker and have your own boat, you can easily paddle the 15 miles/24 km to Haines, getting a good look at both the Lynn Canal and the Taiya Inlet. You can rent a kayak from the **Mountain Shop**, at 5th near Broadway.

> **AUTHOR TIP:** The best paddle is probably over to Haines, or turn up the Lutak Inlet and paddle for the old town of Chilkoot.

Klondike Water Adventures, ☎ 907-983-3769, has introductory paddles on Lake Bernard. Prices vary widely, depending on trip duration.

Floats: Skagway Float Tours, ☎ 907-983-3688, has a great combination hike/float for US $75. You hike a bit under two miles/3.2 km on the Chilkoot Trail (not the steep part, but there is a pretty good uphill portion), and then load into rafts for a relaxing float back downstream on the Taiya River. The trip takes about four hours, and it's a lot of fun – plus you get to claim that you've hiked at least part of the Chilkoot Trail. If the hike is more than you're up for, just the float runs US $65.

Adventures with Dogs

 Sledding: Alaska Sled Dog Adventures, ☎ 907-983-3392, has dog demos, where you get to ride around on a wheeled cart. Sled dogs are as much – more – a part of Alaskan history than the greed for gold. There's nothing quite like watching a half-dozen huskies blast off. The ride, demo and getting to play with puppies runs US $78.

Adventures on Foot

 Hiking: Packer Expeditions has a great trip that gives you the best of Skagway. You travel by helicopter up over the Juneau Icefields to Glacier Station; once there, you hike five miles/ eight km along the Skagway River over to Laughton Glacier. Finally, you return to town on the WP&YR train. The trip runs CAN $299. They've also got a cheaper full-day hike up the Denver Trail; you take the train six miles/10 km to the trailhead, then hike back to the head of the valley, past waterfalls and into the old growth forest. You're going to need to be in shape for these hikes, but you'll have the time of your life. ☎ 907-983-2544, or stop in at the Mountain Shop, on 4th Ave. just west of Broadway.

The best hiking is obviously on the Chilkoot (see below), but there are a lot of other options that aren't quite so strenuous.

There's a quick viewpoint hike out to **Yakutani Point**, a good place for a picnic. Take the footbridge past the airport and head left.

The easiest hike is along the **Lower Dewey Lake Trail**, only .7 miles/ 1.1 km. You go from 2nd Ave. and head east. There's no way to miss the signs. From Dewey Lake, you can hook up with the Northern Bench Trail, another mile that takes you back toward town. The trailhead is at the northwest corner of the lake. If you want to see Upper Dewey Lake, it's only another 2.3 miles/3.7 km. It's pretty steep at first, but levels out, ending up in a muskeg meadow.

The more ambitious should try the **Denver Glacier Hike**, a bit more than three miles/five km from the trailhead at Mile 6 on the WP&YR, or seven miles from the Gold Rush Cemetery. You go through spruce and hemlock forests typical of Southeast Alaska's mid-latitudes rainforest, then climb up the mountain along the banks of the East Fork Skagway River, through an area covered with alder and devil's club.

A hike up **AB Mountain** will kill a full day. It's 10 miles/16 km, round-trip, and it has an elevation gain of around 5,000 feet/1,500 meters, so you'll be hurting by the top. Pick up the trail on the Dyea Road, and make sure you don't lose it once you get above the treeline.

The **Lost Lake Trail** leaves from Dyea, climbing 1,400 feet/426 feet over its 2.9-mile/4.7-km route. You can camp up at Lost Lake, most of the way up the mountain.

Pick up a Skagway Trail Map at the Infocenter or at the Forest Service Office.

The Chilkoot Trail

Not to be attempted lightly, the Chilkoot is still open for hikers. It takes three to five days to hike this historic 33-mile/53-km route, and it can be a bit crowded in the summer. About 3,000 people hike the trail each year. At the end of the trail, you'll be given a certificate by the Canadian Park Service documenting your accomplishment.

Before setting out, stop by the National Park Visitors Center (in the old train depot) for mandatory registration, and for their useful handouts on the trail. Ask here for the latest trail conditions.

Parks Canada now requires CAN $40 (Canadian dollars) for a permit to hike the trail; only 50 people a day are allowed on the trail. Call well in advance of your planned trip for reservations: ☎ 800-661-0486.

Go fully prepared, taking all necessary camping gear, food and personal items, keeping in mind that the weather can change dramatically and quickly. There are no shelters on the trail. Bring your own tent.

There are 10 designated camping areas along the way; Canyon City, Sheep Camp, Deep Lake and Lindeman are especially nice.

None of the water is safe for drinking, so be sure to boil it first. All camps are in bear country, so keep the camp clean.

 There's a good guidebook specific to the trail, *A Hiker's Guide to the Chilkoot Trail*. You can pick it up in town or order it from the Alaska Natural History Association, ☎ 907-274-8440, www.alaskanha.org.

ARTIFACT ETIQUETTE

Along the way are many artifacts dropped by the tired miners: Do not touch these. Nearly a century of being exposed to the elements has left them extremely fragile, and they are part of a living museum protected only by state law and your courtesy. Take photographs and leave the objects untouched for other hikers and the researchers, who are putting together a picture of life on the trail.

Shopping

It's a small town designed for handling masses of cruise ship passengers in a very short time. You're not going to have any trouble finding the stores.

The Mountain Shop, on 4th Ave. just west of Broadway, has a full line of outdoor gear, a lot of it at prices cheaper than you're going to find back in Canada. ☎ 907-983-2544.

Gold Vein Designs, on Broadway near 6th, has beautiful trade beads – one of the best selections in the state.

Corrington's Alaskan Ivory, at 5th and Broadway, is worth stopping in for the free museum; they've also got the standard tourist fare, but with some interesting twists.

The Miner's Cache, at 6th and Broadway, has some really nice prints, lithographs, sketches and more, as well as good knives.

Skaguay News Depot, on Broadway between 2nd and 3rd, can take care of your reading needs for books on the town's history.

Where to Eat

You can eat very, very well in Skagway.

The Skagway Fish Company and the **Stowaway Café**, both on the east side of the boat harbor, are the places to go for the best food in town. Try the halibut and brie at the Fish Company, or one of the Cajun specialties at the Stowaway. You're not going to be sorry. Entrées start around US $15.

The **Red Onion Saloon**, mentioned above, has burgers and steaks priced under US $12. Lots of atmosphere. ☎ 907-983-2222.

The Corner Café, 4th and State, has great lunches and big breakfasts, and is quite cheap. Ten bucks or so fills you up.

There are two places for Italian: the **Portobello**, ☎ 907-983-3459, 1st and Broadway; **Northern Lights Pizzeria**, ☎ 907-983-2225, 5th and Broadway.

The Sweet Tooth, Broadway and 3rd, is a converted saloon that now serves up a great breakfast of eggs, sausage and excellent hash browns for only US $5. It gets crowded here around 7:30 in the morning.

The restaurant in the **Golden North Hotel** has a good selection, reasonable prices and a microbrewery. Plus, there's always the chance of spotting the hotel ghost.

Where to Stay

There are no bargains in Skagway. Early reservations are a must. The **Golden North Hotel**, ☎ 907-983-2451 or 907-983-2294, at 3rd and Broadway, is the town's oldest hotel. Doubles run around US $100. **Sgt. Preston's Lodge**, ☎ 907-983-2521, is also a good bet. It's centrally located on 6th, a block west of Broadway, and has rooms from US $85. They've got a courtesy van, too. It's off Broadway, so a little quieter.

Gold Rush Lodge, ☎ 907-983-2831, 6th and Alaska, has 12 rooms from US $75. Good and comfortable.

Smaller but still okay is the **Skagway Inn B&B**, 7th and Broadway, ☎ 907-983-2289. Doubles in this 1897 Victorian house start at about US $80.

Mile Zero B&B is one of those lovingly run places that just amaze you when you stay. Rates start at US $80, and all rooms have private entrances and, rarity of rarities, soundproof walls. At 9th and Main, ☎ 907-983-3045.

If everything else is full, try the **Westmark**, which has more rooms than the rest of the town combined. Be aware it's often filled with package tourists. ☎ 907-983-2291.

The Forest Service runs one of the best places to stay: a converted **caboose**, five miles up the train line. You have to bring your own gear. Reservations can be made online at www.reserveusa.com.

Camping

Skagway has recently increased its camping facilities, so your chance of finding a spot is much greater than it used to be. Still, things can get really busy when a ferry arrives, full of people who don't want to start the drive into Canada for another day. So check in early. **Pullen Creek RV Park**, ☎ 907-983-2768, is down by the ferry terminal. Full hookups are available for US $20; dry sites are US $10.

More scenic are the RV and tent sites at Broadway and 14th, in **Hanousek Park**. This is also the best place for watching the steam engine of the WP&YR go by. Phone for reservations, ☎ 907-983-2768. Hookups, CAN $16; dry sites, CAN $8, but the place is often full of summer workers.

Garden City RV Park, ☎ 907-983-23RV, 15th and State, has full hookups for CAN $16, dry sites for CAN $8.

If you want to get out of town, drive to Dyea and stay at the **National Park Service Campground** there. Camping is free. The road to Dyea is not recommended for RVs, and this makes the campground a haven for tenters. There are 22 sites, and you just need to show up and see if there are any spots available.

■ Onwards

From Skagway, you can drive back out the way you came, or hop on an Alaska Marine Highways ferry to Haines – which lets you drive the Haines Highway so you catch the final corner of British Columbia – or south to points in Southeast Alaska and back down to British Columbia at Prince Rupert. Contact the AMH at ☎ 800-642-0066, or go online www.alaska.gov/ferry.

 For more on the Alaska Marine Highway, see our *Adventure Guide to the Inside Passage and Coastal Alaska.*

 If you want to keep driving into the Yukon and Alaska from here, we've got you covered on that, too: get a copy of our *Adventure Guide to the Alaska Highway*.

The Haines Highway

Stay in the Yukon as far as Haines Junction and you can drop down through one more tiny corner of British Columbia, via the Haines Highway. Haines junction is at the edge of Kluane National Park, which, together with the Tatshenshini-Alsek Park and Alaska's Wrangell-St. Elias Park, form the largest protected wilderness in the world. Haines Highway is one of the most beautiful roads in the world. Once you're on it, you run out of superlatives pretty quickly.

The road leaves from the Yukon town of Haines Junction, starts to climb, passes Kathleen Lake, and ends up high between mountain ridges, with glacial melt ponds lining the wide, smooth road, snow-covered peaks everywhere, and rainbows chasing the traffic, jumping from pond to stream. You have to keep stopping the car so you can gawk. If all that wasn't enough, the road then drops down off the ridge and the Chilkat Pass – once crowded with miners headed north – and catches up to the Chilkat River, running alongside the banks for the last stretch into town. It's probably the most beautiful drive in the North. And almost no one does it, so the road is wide open.

Camp along the way at **Kathleen Lake**, Mile 134 (where you can pick up the trailhead of the 53-mile/85-km loop Cottonwood Trail – allow four days to finish it, with much of the hike along old mining roads); **Dezadeash Lake**, Mile 119; **Dalton Post**, Mile 99; or the truly marvelous **Million Dollar Falls**, Mile 96.2. Million Dollar Falls has a lovely board walkway down to the river and the steep falls beyond. You also stand a good chance of moose nosing around your campsite. Watch for mountain goats on the peaks.

> **CUSTOMS CONTROL:** Canadian Customs is closed between 11 pm and 7 am, but you can go through after-hours if you stand in front of the camera and follow the directions. Check with your embassy about current ID requirements. You must have proof of insurance for your car at Customs . Officers can also ask about your finances: You must have CAN $50 for 48 hours in Canada, CAN $200 for longer. Plastic is okay. The Customs station is at Mile 42 on the Haines Highway. US Customs is at Mile 40.4.

The last stretch of road is along the banks of the Chilkat. The Chilkat – wide and tree-lined to one side of the road, while the other side is mountains heading straight up – is home to as many as 3,000 bald eagles, and the last nine miles of road are in the Chilkat Bald Eagle Preserve. Here there are eagles, good fishing spots, and the river is great for rafting, too.

■ Tatshenshini-Alsek Wilderness

The west side of the Haines Highway, from the Yukon border to Customs, travels along the edge of the **Tatshenshini-Alsek Wilderness Provincial Park**. This British Columbia park, which is contiguous with Kluane and Wrangell-St. Elias parks, forms part of the largest protected wilderness area in the world.

The Tatshenshini-Alsek Wilderness was set aside in 1993 in response to a particularly stupid mining plan. The proposed mine would have dumped tailings and poisons into the Alsek River. The mining company said that all poisons would be contained behind an earthen dam and wouldn't have hurt anything. Yeah, right.

There was a huge public outcry – part of the issue being that the mine was going to be in Canada, with most of the damage downstream in Alaska – and this beautiful park was the result. For once, the good guys won.

Adventures on Water

 Whitewater Rafting: Because it is a wilderness area, no motorized vehicles are allowed. Experienced rafters who have been on the waiting list for several years and whose number has finally come up can shoot the Tatshenshini or the Alsek, both of which have Class III-IV whitewater and both of which are increasingly popular. But you'd better know what you're doing. The currents in the canyons are very tricky, and the water is cold enough to give you hypothermia in a matter of moments. If you're in a hurry, you can do the Alsek in five days, but it's kind of pointless. Better to take 10 and enjoy yourself. This is one of the best river trips in the world, a marvel of scenery.

Permits are required for most river trips on the Alsek or the Tatshenshini. Check at the **Kluane Park headquarters**, ☎ 867-634-2345. Only one launch a day is allowed on the upper Alsek, and half of those permits are reserved for commercial companies. If your trip is going all the way down to Glacier Bay, you'll need a permit from **Glacier Bay National Park**, ☎ 907-697-3341 – and it'll cost you US $25 just to get on the waiting list. Be prepared to wait a very long time.

If you've got to go this year, book with **Alaska Discovery**, 5449 Shaun Drive #4, Juneau, ☎ 907-780-6226 or 800-586-1911. They have 10-day trips on the Tat, which includes Class III water through the Tatshenshini Gorge. A trip will run you around US $2,500. Twelve days on the Alsek – rougher, more remote than the Tat, water up to Class IV – runs about US $2,750, including an airlift past the unrunnable Turnback Canyon.

Chilkat Guides, in Haines, ☎ 907-766-2491, www.raftalaska.com, has 10-day trips on the Tat for US $1,975, and 13-day jaunts on the Alsek for US $2,400. They've got a video of their Tat trip available for US $15, which gives you a pretty good idea what you'd be in for.

> **WARNING:** *If you do get a permit and decide to take the river on your own, make sure you know what you're doing. You'll also be as deep in the wild as you have ever been in your life, which means help is a long, long way away. This is not a solo trip for the novice.*

Campgrounds surrounded by 20 glaciers become old hat after a few days. People who have run both the Tat/Alsek and the Stikine can rarely make a choice as to which they prefer – either trip is the trip of a lifetime. You need to make your choice on available access.

Trips on the Tat usually cover about 140 miles/225 km; on the Alsek, you go closer to 200 miles/322 km. About half of each trip is run below the confluence, where the rivers meet. Higher up, though, they have rather different characters. If you're after bear, take the Alsek; that's also the choice for those looking to get as remote as possible and who aren't as worried about fast water. The Alsek is like traveling through the last ice age: this is what the world looked like right after the ice pulled back. The

Tat has much more lush scenery – the land has had more time to recover from the last round of glaciers – and lots of moose, but not so many bears.

Adventures on Wheels

 Mountain Biking: Old mining roads in the park make for good mountain biking. Try the trailhead at Parton River, Stanley Creek, or about a mile and a half above the Selat Viewpint, where you can ride on the original Haines road.

> **WEATHER:** *Remember, weather conditions change quickly in the park. Go prepared.*

■ Haines

Again, like Skagway, Haines isn't really the point of this book, but if you've come this far by driving the westernmost road in British Columbia, this is where you end up.

History

 Haines was almost always a way to get somewhere else. The Chilkoot and Chilkat Indians lived in the Haines area, using it as a trading base. Its position on the coast gave them access to groups in the interior, as well as to the riches of the coast and the islands. The modern Haines airport is on the site of the old village of Yendestakyeh. Other major Native settlements were along the Chilkat River (Klukwan survives today) and on Chilkoot Lake.

The Russians passed Haines by and it wasn't until 1881 that Hall Young, a missionary who had first seen the region two years before when traveling with John Muir, established a mission in the area. Although the locals called the mission Dtehshah, or "end of the trail," the new settlers chose the name Haines, after Mrs. F.E. Haines. Although she was never actually in the city that bears her name, Mrs. Haines was an important fundraiser for the mission.

The mission settlement grew quickly. With the base population stable, canneries were built and, during the years of the gold rush, Haines was an alternative to the more popular (and crowded and lawless) Skagway. When the gold petered out, the military moved in. In 1902, construction began on Fort Seward. During World War II, the presence of the base and the large contingent of soldiers made Haines an important point on the planned supply route to the Aleutians and the interior, in case of Japanese attack. The Haines Highway was built to connect the coast with the Alaska Highway and the interior, to further ease transport of supplies.

Haines Today

Since the war, things have calmed down. The town survives on tourism, lumber and fishing, and on its convenience as a middle point between other destinations. It thrives on its beautiful location. Haines is one of the most attractive towns in Alaska and also the fastest growing – *Outside* magazine named it the place to live if you've just won the lottery and don't have to worry about making a living. The next few years will reveal how growth and beauty mix in this spectacular setting.

Basics

The **Tourist Infocenter** is at Second Ave. and Willard. It's open 8-8 daily, except for Sunday (11-6) and Wednesday (8-11). ☎ 907-766-2234.

Haines-Skagway Water Taxi offers an alternative to the ferry. The taxi makes two daily round-trips between the towns and takes no vehicles (except for bikes; an extra US $5 charge). A one-way trip takes a little over an hour. Reservations are strongly recommended – call at least a day in advance. Fare is US $35 round-trip, US $18 one-way. ☎ 907-766-3395 or 888-766-3395 for schedules and information.

Skagway Air, ☎ 907-766-3233, **LAB Flying Service**, ☎ 907-766-2222, and **Wings of Alaska**, ☎ 907-766-2030, all fly out of Haines, and offer charter flights as well.

Internet access is available at **Northern Lights Internet Lounge**, 715 Main St., ☎ 907-766-2337.

Attractions

In summer months, many of the shops and attractions may be closed if there isn't a cruise ship in town. If there is a cruise ship, the whole place can be too crowded to deal with and, unless you're after something in a specific gift shop, cruise time is a good time to go hiking.

Sheldon Museum & Cultural Center, on Main Street near the boat harbor, is a good first stopping point in town. The museum is open Monday through Friday in the summer, 8:30-5, and admission is US $3. Check for other opening times, which can be slightly irregular. The small but excellent museum shop has a good selection of Alaskana books. Haines was a center for the Tlingit Indians, and you can see their local history illustrated beautifully here. Don't miss the blankets on the second floor. Make sure to pick up any of the free historical sheets on topics that interest you. ☎ 907-766-2366.

The **Alaska Indian Arts Workshop**, ☎ 907-766-2160, downtown by the totem village, lets you see native carvers and artists at work making totem poles, masks, and blankets. It's open 9-5 weekdays. The workshop is housed in what used to be the recreation hall for the old **Fort William H. Seward**. The fort was built just after the turn of the century, after the Protestant mission deeded 100 acres of land to the government to establish a base. Fort Seward was used as a training base in World Wars I and II. After World War II, the fort was decommissioned, and it lay vacant until it was purchased by five World War II veterans in 1970 and declared a National Historic Landmark. Pick up a walking tour map of the fort at the visitors center and explore the old barracks and other areas. Most of the buildings have been taken over by private concerns and are now shops or hotels. There are also quite a few private residences among the fort buildings. If in doubt, ask.

Next to the Parade Ground at the fort is **Chilkoot Sled Dog Adventures**. Demonstrations are held nightly for US $3; they also have a drawing for a dog sled ride. ☎ 907-766-3242.

Nightlife in Haines is not as eventful as it was in the early gold rush days, but there are still a few things going on. At the **Chilkat Center for the Arts** are the incomparable Chilkat Dancers, who offer a rare chance to see traditional dancing as well as Chilkat blankets. Shows on Monday, Wednesday and Saturday nights; admission is US $8. There's also a dinner deal with a salmon bake. ☎ 907-766-2000. Look for it in Ft. William Seward.

Tsirku Canning Company has tours of a small-scale salmon canning operation. The good thing here is that they've still got the can-maker working – probably your only chance to see one of these, as most canneries order their cans from down south. The tours (US $10) are held daily at 1 pm, and are well worth it to see what fueled the Alaska economy for so long. And, oh, yeah, you get a chance to buy fish at the end. They're at 5th and Main, ☎ 907-766-3474.

Adventure Outfitters

There's enough stuff to do around Haines to keep you busy for months. The trick is narrowing down the list.

Portage Cove Adventure Center, ☎ 907-766-3800 or 877-766-2800, www.portage.klukwan.com, on the street at 142 Beach Road, is a central booking service for a lot of expeditions around town. Some good packages include a round-trip to Skagway on the water taxi, with a ride on the White Pass & Yukon Route Railway for CAN $109. They also book Glacier Bay trips, and lots of fishing and boating on the Chilkoot.

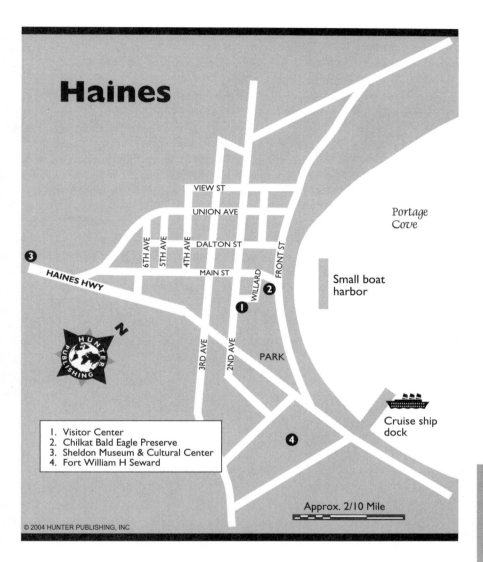

Haines

VIEW ST
UNION AVE
DALTON ST
MAIN ST
6TH AVE
5TH AVE
4TH AVE
WILLARD
FRONT ST
HAINES HWY
3RD AVE
2ND AVE
PARK

Portage Cove

Small boat harbor

Cruise ship dock

Approx. 2/10 Mile

1. Visitor Center
2. Chilkat Bald Eagle Preserve
3. Sheldon Museum & Cultural Center
4. Fort William H Seward

© 2004 HUNTER PUBLISHING, INC

Northern BC

Adventures in Nature

Birding: The highlight of Haines is the 48,000-acre **Chilkat Bald Eagle Preserve**, which each winter hosts the largest gathering of eagles in the world. The birds generally come here from November through February to feast on the late chum salmon run. There can be almost 4,000 eagles along the river at peak times. There are few sights as impressive as a bald eagle swooping down for a fish (it's also a lot of fun to watch them miss).

Take a good camera, fast film and warm clothes; the sun is up only from about 10 am to 2 pm in December and January, and there's likely to be rain or snow. About 200 eagles live in the area year-round. Haines has started an annual **Bald Eagle Festival**, held in November, with educational talks, films, tours, native dances and more. ☎ 800-246-6268.

There are a few rules to obey when you're looking for eagles. First, remember the birds have better civil rights protections than you do. Hassling the birds can get you a CAN $10,000 fine. When you're in the preserve, stay off the flats – that's where the birds are, so it's where you shouldn't be. The parks people want you between the river and the highway, which gives the birds a nice buffer zone. This does not mean stop your car on the roadway. There are turnouts. Use them, or keep your insurance company phone number handy. The best views are usually somewhere between Miles 18 and 21 on the highway.

Keet Gushi Tours, ☎ 907-766-2168, does a tour of the eagle preserve, along with a visit to Klukwan, where you can see the totems and the fine screen that separates the main part of the clan house from the area reserved for the head of the clan. These are always highly decorated with clan images. The 2½-hour trip runs CAN $65.

Adventures on Foot

Hiking: Alaska Nature Tours, ☎ 907-766-2876, has guided hikes along the Chilkat Valley for CAN $50.

Haines has some pretty good hikes. The **Mt. Ripinsky Trail** is a 4.5-mile/7.2-km hike up the mountain. From the top you can walk along the ridge before heading back down. If you do the ridge walk, figure on overnight camping. The trailhead is off Young St. – keep left when the road forks. The first 1,600 feet/486 meters are relatively easy, but it gets steeper at the end, peaking out at 3,650 feet/1,110 meters, where you've got killer views of Haines, the Lynn Canal and more snow-covered mountains than you can imagine. Obviously, with the elevation gain, this is not an easy hike, so go prepared and allow up to 10 hours, round-trip.

There are other trails up the mountain at Piedad Road and Seven Mile, on the Haines Highway. At Seven Mile, the trail leads up to the Seven-Mile Saddle, a 2,400-foot/730-meter mountain pass below the peak of Ripinsky. Go prepared for mud. This isn't a hike for beginners; figure five hours just to get to the saddle.

Mt. Riley is a little easier. Pick up the trail on Mud Bay Road and hike just over two miles/3.2 km to the summit. Figure three hours or so. This hike offers good views of the river and the canal. There are alternate ways up the mountain via Lily Lake – 2.8 miles/4.5 km each way. The trailhead is off the FAA Road behind Officer's Row in Ft. Seward. The trail is more gradual than the Mud Bay alternate, plus you get a lake along the way. Finally, you can get up from Portage Cove on a four-mile/

6.5-km hike, one-way. There's only one steep section on this trail, which leads you to a muskeg meadow a few hundred yards below the summit.

Seduction Point is 6.8 miles/11 km from where the Chilkoot and Chilkat inlets meet. Allow 10 hours or so for this fairly easy forest and beach walk. Along the way, you'll get good views of Davidson Glacier and a great chance to look at both inlets. The trailhead is at Chilkat State Park Campground.

Adventures on Water

 Canoeing, Kayaking: If you've got your own canoe or kayak (or have rented one), head to the **Chilkat River**. It's a relatively sedate Class I, with excellent animal-watching; look especially for eagles and bears. The best place to put in is at Mile 19 on the Haines Highway. Then you can paddle back to town.

All through the gold rush, the goal for the miners was to get up the river. They were missing the point; it's a whole lot more fun to come down.

The Chilkat is not a whitewater river; what you're in for is an incredibly beautiful float, with mountains ranging above both sides of the river. On the wide flats there are almost always eagles and you stand a really good chance of seeing moose and, maybe, bear. There are few sights quite as beautiful as a mother moose and calf walking across the flats.

Deishu Expeditions, ☎ 907-766-2427 or 800-552-9257, has an introductory paddle on a lake near town. A half-day costs CAN $485; full days are CAN $120. They're also the people to call if you want to rent a kayak.

Chilkat Guides, ☎ 907-766-2491, www.raftalaska.com, takes you out to Klukwan, then brings you back to town in a raft, for CAN $82. The trip takes about four hours.

Eco Orca, ☎ 907-766-3933, www.alaskafloattrips.com, has a similar program for CAN $62.

Shopping

 Form and Function Gallery, 209 Willard, ☎ 907-766-2539, has beaders and carvers working in the shop, plus a great selection of nice pieces – particularly masks and boxes.

The Far North, just around the corner on 2nd Ave., has lovely ivory works, walrus whiskers and other items from Inuit lands.

Buy some fish for the road ahead at either the **Tsirku Canning Company** at 5th and Main, or at **Dejon Delights** in Ft. Seward. Pick up some wine to go with your fish at **Great Land Wines**, ☎ 907-766-2698. They're a ways out of town, but the grocery stores will have their local wines, made from, among other things, rhubarb, onion, "porcupine carrot gold," and a wide variety of berries.

Finally, just because you can, check out the **Lost Coast Surf Shop**. It's a block up from the fast ferry dock. Really. We're not making this up. It's really a surf shop.

Where to Eat

Some of the best places to eat in Haines are a way out of town. **The Thirty-Three Mile Roadhouse**, ☎ 907-767-5510, is out past the Chilkat Bald Eagle Preserve, nearly to Klukwan. Try it for steaks, seafood and the view. Dinners start at CAN $14. True gourmands should try **Weeping Trout's** Saturday night dinner. For CAN $47.50, you get an astonishing meal at the resort, which is located on the edge of a lake well outside Haines – it takes two boat rides to get there. The basic price includes transport from the first boat landing; if you need a ride all the way from town, it's CAN $74 for the trip and the meal. Go early and play a round of golf at the resort before dining.

Local choice downtown is the **Bamboo Room**, open all day. It has burgers from CAN $6, steak for CAN $21.

Fort Seward Lodge, ☎ 907-766-2009, makes a good night-out dinner. It offers steak and seafood from CAN $9 and all-you-can-eat crab dinners for CAN $25.

The **Port Chilkoot Potlatch Salmon Bake** is open from 5 to 8 pm (except Thursday). It has an all-you-can-eat deal for CAN $21.75, and you dine in a replica of a native house.

Chilkat Restaurant and Bakery, at 5th and Dalton, has the town's best baked goods, as well as soups, sandwiches and salads.

The **Mountain Market**, at 3rd and the Haines Highway, is the town's health food store. There's a deli inside.

Finally, **Howsers Supermarket**, on Main St., has a deli next to the groceries that offers sandwiches, chicken and ribs, cheap.

Where to Stay

In Haines, much of the lodging is located in or around Fort Seward, and thus many of the buildings are historic sites. Nothing is really cheap.

Try the picturesque **Hotel Halsingland** for historic accommodations; you may get a room with a claw-foot tub. Doubles from CAN $85. There are also some cheaper rooms with shared baths. ☎ 907-766-2000 or 800-542-6363.

Another lovely old house turned into a hotel is **Fort Seward B&B**. On the National Register of Historic Places (it used to be the surgeon's living quarters), it's very small, so book early. Doubles from CAN $85. They'll pick you up at the airport or ferry terminal in a vintage Lincoln Towncar. ☎ 907-766-2856.

Fort Seward Condos offer one- and two-bedroom apartments complete with full kitchens year-round, from CAN $85 a night. There's a two-day minimum, and longer-term stays receive extra deals: a free night with a week stay, or a monthly rate of only CAN $850. ☎ 907-766-2425.

Downtown there is slightly more generic lodging. Nicest is **Captain's Choice Motel**, ☎ 800-247-7153, 800-478-2345 (in Alaska), 800-247-7153 (outside Alaska), with rooms from CAN $85 to $175. Nearby are the comfortable **Thunderbird**, ☎ 907-766-2131 or 800-327-2556, with doubles from CAN $70, and **Mountain View**, ☎ 907-766-2131, with rooms from CAN $70 (plus a few bucks more for a room with a kitchenette).

A lovely option out of town is the **Weeping Trout Sports Resort**. It's about 90 minutes from town, on Chilkat Lake and is accessible only by boat. Packages, including boat use, start around CAN $200 a day. It's rustic – no hot water in the very comfortable cabins – but how many other places have you been where you can play a round of golf and fish without going more than a hundred yards from where you slept? ☎ 907-766-2827, www.weepingtrout.com.

The cheapest place to stay in town is the **Bear Creek Camp & Hostel**, Box 1158. They offer cabins from CAN $40, as well as tent (CAN $8) and dorm (CAN $14) space. ☎ 907-766-2259. It's really quite pleasant, and they'll pick you up.

Camping

There are four lovely state park campgrounds in Haines: **Chilkat State Park**, seven miles south of town on Mud Bay Rd.; **Chilkoot Lake**, 10 miles north of town off Lutak Rd.; **Portage Cove** on Beach Road, just under a mile out of town; and **Mosquito Lake**, at Mile 27 on the Haines Highway. All of them have water and toilets, along with good fishing. Sites cost CAN $6 to $8 a night. There are no phones at the above sites.

If you require hookups, there are several choices: **Alaskan Eagle RV Park**, on Union Street, ☎ 907-766-2335, and **Haines Hitch-up RV Park**, at Main and Haines Highway, ☎ 907-766-2882.

Leaving Haines

 From Haines, you can drive back out the way you came or hop on an Alaska Marine Highway ferry to Skagway and take a loop back into BC that way. Or catch the AMH south to points in Southeast Alaska and back down to British Columbia at Prince Rupert. Contact the AMH at ☎ 800-642-0066 or www.alaska.gov/ferry.

For more on the Alaska Marine Highway, see our ***Adventure Guide to the Inside Passage and Coastal Alaska***.

 If you want to keep driving into the Yukon and Alaska from here, we've got you covered on that, too: get a copy of our ***Adventure Guide to the Alaska Highway.***

The Parks

Warning: Follow this chapter, and you're going to hurt your neck from gawking. This is scenery like you've never seen before, beauty carried to the umpteenth degree. This is, flat out, one of the prettiest, most dramatic, interesting, fun places in the world.

Although this is a British Columbia guidebook, we're moving east into Alberta, the next province over for most of this chapter. If you let the historical quirk of a snaking boundary line stop you from seeing the parks – Jasper, Banff, Kootenay, Yoho – you're doing yourself a serious disservice.

This whole region has been declared a World Heritage Site by the United Nations. It's one of the largest protected wilderness areas in the world, and there's a good reason for it: mirror-still lakes, roadsides with mountain goats, towering peaks that are part of the most dramatic mountain landscape we've ever seen anywhere in the world.

There is one disadvantage to all this startling beauty, and that's the continual presence of the many bus tours – plus the hordes of other tourists – going through the same area. Either make your reservations well in advance if you're planning to stay in an inn or motel, or plan on camping – and you'll need to reserve your campsite or stop very early in the day.

But, as in most heavily traveled areas anywhere in the world, it's surprisingly easy to get away from the crowds. Many people never leave the roads. Get onto a trail, look at the backcountry, go out later in the evening and, any time of year, you're likely to have this glorious place all to yourself.

One note, right up front. This area is worth a guidebook all to itself. All we can do here is give you a good listing of the highlights and make some suggestions of where you might look for more. Once you're in the park system, the possibilities are truly endless.

■ Rules

To get into the park system, you've got to pay. There are fee gates, where you pay CAN $5 per day; the pass gets you all the way from here to the other end of the park system, beyond Jasper. Keep your ticket on the windshield; these things are regularly checked.

The Parks

Mt Robson Park

Jasper

Kinbasket
Lake

Jasper

5

National

93

Park

40

22

Mica Creek

Rocky Mtn
House

Donald

Mt Revelstoke
N.P.

Rogers Pass

Field

Banff N.P.

Lake Louise

Sundre

Golden

Glacier N.P.

Revelstoke

Yoho N.P.

1A

22

Banff

Kootenay N.P.

Beaton

Canmore

Cochrane

Upper Arrow Lake

95

93

Calgary

23

31

Radium
Hot Springs

Duncan Lake

Invermere

Turner
Valley

Naksup

Purcell
Wilderness
Conservancy

95

93

40

Fauquier

Elkford

Kaslo

31

BRITISH COLUMBIA

ALBERTA

43

22

Nelson

Kimberley

Sparwood

Cranbrook

Crowsnest Pass

NOT TO SCALE

The parks are open year-round, but some of the roads get snowed under during winter. Obviously, Japser and Banff both depend heavily upon winter traffic for their livelihood. You can check current conditions, rules, etc., at www.parkscanada.ca. Contact **Parks Canada** National Office at 25 Eddy Street, Hull, Québec K1A 0M5, ☎ 888-773-8888.

Kootenay National Park

Kootenay is the only national park in Canada with both glaciers and cactus. For the most part, the park is rugged limestone cliffs and red rock country dotted with hot springs. While the scenery is much the same as in the other parks – Kootenay is drier and sometimes hotter – Kootenay is considerably less crowded than Jasper or Banff, which gives you a better chance to see the stunning assortment of wildlife: elk, bear, moose, mountain goats, several varieties of wild sheep and more. It also means that you'll have the place more as you want – all to yourself.

Kootenay has fewer services and hiking trails than the other parks. Really, most people never do more than drive through here on their way to Banff. It's good that way. It means there's lots out there for anybody who wants to get off the road.

Kootenay has maybe the most dramatic entryway of any of the parks. From Radium Hot Springs, you enter a cleft into the mountains, just like a scene from a fairy tale. Get through the narrow defile, and it's as if you're in a completely different world.

The region has always been part of a major north-south route, first used by the Kootenai First Nations people. Now it's still an active migration route for animals. When you're driving through the park, watch for mountain sheep in the southern cliffs and mountain goats in the Mt. Wordle area. The mountain goat is the symbol of Kootenay and is an amazing animal to watch, especially when one runs straight up what looks like a perfectly smooth cliff.

■ Adventures on Foot

For a quick hike, there's the very short **Marble Canyon Trail** – it takes about 20 minutes, round-trip – which crosses over narrow gorges more than 100 feet/30 meters deep in places, filled with blue-gray glacial runoff. The trail ends at a lovely, roaring waterfall.

Another pleasant stroll is to see the **Paint Pots**, three ponds of different colors created by different oxides in the water. There's a red, an orange and a yellow pool. Of course, something this good was extremely important to the First Nations people, who used these pigments for their art. It's a .6-mile/one-km walk from the hiking area back to the pots.

If you're just getting warmed up after that, take the 10-mile/15-km trail from the pots back to **Helmet Creek**, which ends at a waterfall. Along the way you get glacier views. It's a tough hike; figure five hours each way, but there is a campground at the end of it.

Another good hike out of the paint pots is to **Tumbling Creek**, six miles/ 10.5 km, with an altitude gain of about 2,470 feet/750 meters. It offers good creek views. If you don't feel like doing the full vertical hike, there's a good turnaround place at Rockwall Pass.

The **Stanley Glacier Hike** is 5.5 miles/nine km round-trip, with not too much elevation gain – about 1,150 feet/350 meters. The trailhead is just west of the Continental Divide, and that's the point of the hike: to get views of where the waters part and the Stanley Glacier, where the water got frozen and now is melting back.

There are some longer, multi-day hikes in the park. To do the full **Rockwall Hike**, which covers upwards of 31 miles/50 km, will take you four or five days – more, depending on how much the mountains slow you down.

 The Canadian Rockies Trail Guide, by Brad Patton and Bart Robinson, is the book you need to get farther into the boonies.

Before you head for the backcountry, be sure to check in at a ranger station to get the latest conditions.

■ Camping

 Camp in **Marble Canyon** or **McLeod Meadows**, if you have a tent (beautiful sites, no services), or **Redstreak**, near the West Gate, if you need a hookup. They don't take reservations at any of these parks, so show up early to claim your spot.

■ Onward to Banff

 Highway 93, the main road through Kootenay, crosses Vermillion Pass and then joins the Icefield Parkway about half-way between the towns of Banff and Lake Louise in Banff Park, so when you leave Kootenay, there's plenty more scenery to come.

We're going to head south, then turn back north.

Banff & Banff National Park

Banff was Canada's first national park and, today, if you asked most people to name a park in Canada, Banff is what they'd come up with. It's the quintessential resort town, world-famous for skiing, hiking and the huge numbers of Japanese tourists who descend upon it each year. Tourists do, however, stick to the roads. Because of the sheer volume of traffic, regulations on using designated areas for camping, picnics and such are much more tightly enforced than in other parks. However, if you head out into the backcountry (remember, permit and registration are required), you're going to be all alone.

The City

Stop at the **Tourist Infocentre** in Banff, Lake Louise or Jasper to pick up a copy of the *Backcountry Visitor's Guide* or *Drives and Walks*.

The town of Banff can be a little overwhelming. Why is it inevitable that as soon as a place becomes known for its beauty, developers come along and screw it all up? It's not as frightening as, say, Whistler, from a strictly aesthetic point of view, but it's as if the architects were intimidated by the stunning natural scenery, and so decided all their buildings should be as mediocre and uninteresting as they possibly could be. Add in serious parking problems and tons of people walking the streets every day of the year. The result is that you may well want to leave as soon as you get there.

But take a deep breath and look around. There's some good stuff in town, and it's worth the stop.

■ Attractions

 Start at **Banff Visitors Centre**, 224 Banff Ave., ☎ 403-762-0270; there's a Parks Canada office in the same building, ☎ 604-762-1550. If you come into town in high season without a hotel reservation and you're hoping to spend the night, come here first. They'll help you out as best they can – there's a board listing hotels that still have rooms, and they'll call around. They also have all the usual useful stuff on the town and what you can do nearby. Get your backcountry permit from the Parks Canada side of the room.

Take a walk on **Banff Ave.**, the main shopping street in town. There's a lot of generic merchandise for sale, with some better-than-average stuff mixed in, but it's the main drag and, even if you're not interested in buying from the Gap, it's worth hanging out for a while to people-watch.

For the best selection of books on the parks, stop in at **Banff Book & Art Den**, 94 Banff Ave., ☎ 403-762-3919.

To get an overview of the town, hit the **Banff Gondola**, a tramway that takes you 2,200 feet/670 meters up to an observation deck at 7,486 feet/2,281 meters. From the top, you get absolutely killer views of the Rockies, a good chance of seeing big horn sheep and maybe some marmots (think of a weasel on steroids) and, of course, there's a restaurant and gift shop too. Rides are CAN $20.

■ Adventures on Water

Boating: The best adventures here are the mountain hikes but, if you're looking for water, you have a few good options. **Wild Water Adventures**, ☎ 888-647-6444, and **Kootenay River Runners**, ☎ 800-599-4399, both take trips out of Banff to the Kicking Horse, one of the best whitewater rivers around. A day of Class I-IV water, including transport from Banff, runs about CAN $100.

Hot Springs: Nearby are the Upper Hot Springs, part of the heavy geothermal activity in the Rockies. If you didn't take a dip at Radium, try it here. It's CAN $7.50 for a day pass, and they're open year round.

■ Where to Eat

Most of the town's restaurants are right in downtown, along Banff Avenue. Try **Guido's**, 116 Banff Ave., for Italian dishes from CAN $12. Nearby is the **Maple Leaf Grill**, 137 Banff Ave., which is maybe the best place for a cheap lunch, serving fish and chips or burgers for under CAN $10. A half-block off Banff Ave. is **Bruno's**, 304 Caribou St.. A local favorite, Bruno's is laid back and cheap. Finally, try **Melissa's**, 218 Lynx St., one of the oldest eateries in town. It's open for all meals and, on a nice summer day, there are few better places to hang out than on the patio here. For dessert, hit **Rogers' Chocolates**, 133 Banff Ave.

■ Where to Stay

Banff is a busy, busy place, and finding a hotel room can be an issue. If you're showing up in town without a reservation, check at the Info Centre and try calling **Banff Central Reservations**, ☎ 877-542-2633. It's not a bad idea to come into town with a backup plan.

Prices are high because hotels are full most of the time. You really don't have a lot of choice except to shell out.

There is a hostel in town, **Banff Alpine Centre**, ☎ 403-762-4122, about two miles/three km from downtown. Even here, just a dorm bed is going to run close to CAN $30 a night.

The Arrow Motel, ☎ 403-762-2207, on the grounds of the Ptarmigan Inn, 337 Banff Ave., is a reasonable budget choice. CAN $130 gets you a double that will serve nicely as a place to crash. If you want a few more amenities, the **Ptarmigan**, at the same address and phone number, runs about CAN $220 for a double – standard Banff rates – and has some good rooms with balconies and fireplaces.

Banff Voyager Inn, 555 Banff Ave., ☎ 403-762-3301, is another good budget choice, with rooms from CAN $120. There's a pool and a sauna. **Spruce Grove Inn** shares the sauna and pool with the Voyager. Spruce Grove, 545 Banff Ave., ☎ 403-762-3301, has doubles starting at CAN $155. It's a new property, still pretty shiny and clean.

Just a bit more expensive is the **Red Carpet Inn**, 425 Banff Ave., ☎ 403-762-4184, with doubles starting at CAN $150. It has some Jacuzzi rooms and some balconies so you can watch the world go by.

If you're willing to go over CAN $200 a night, your options get a little wider. **The Banff Traveller's Inn**, 401 Banff Ave., ☎ 403-762-4401, has a steam room, balconies and a good ambience. In the same price range is the **Dynasty Inn**, 501 Banff Ave., ☎ 403-762-8844, which has some rooms with fireplaces and balconies.

Brewster's Mountain Lodge, 208 Caribou St., ☎ 888-762-2900, keeps you downtown but gets you off Banff Ave. It's a kicky old-fashioned sort of place with log furniture. Rooms cost around CAN $200.

Move up some, to the CAN $300 neighborhood, and you can try the **Mount Royal Hotel**, 138 Banff Ave., ☎ 403-762-3331, which has some rooms with fireplaces and fridges, as well as Jacuzzis. It's a great place to spend the night, if you can pay the price.

Finally, to really blow the budget, there's the **Fairmont**. You've seen pictures of it all your life: the quintessential mountain castle-style hotel. CAN $500 a night should see you through.

Camping

There's lots of good camping in Banff. Problem is, you can't make reservations, so show up early in high season to claim your spot. Once you've registered, you're safe, so you can head right back out without worrying about claim jumpers. Most sites run around CAN $25.

Closest to town is **Tunnel Mountain Village**, a trio of campgrounds; only Tunnel Mountain Village 1, open in summer, allows tents.

North of town are the pair of **Two Jack** campgrounds – main and lakeside. These are better than the Tunnel Mountain sites, and a whole lot better if you've got a tent or don't want to spend the evening looking into the windows of the vehicle parked next to you.

The huge **Lake Louise Campground** is right outside Banff. It's quite pleasant, and has interpretive programs, full hookups and showers. One caveat is that it's right next to the railroad, which can be distracting.

The Park

Once you're settled in the town, it's time to head out. Go along **Johnston Canyon** (off the Bow Valley Parkway; it runs parallel to the Icefields Parkway for about 50 miles/80 km), an eight-mile/13-km trip through alpine scenery with clear, startlingly blue lakes, waterfalls and meadows full of wildflowers.

Of course, **Lake Louise** is the main draw. Nobody comes to the park without coming here. Because the very tiny lake acts as a perfect mirror, Lake Louise is one of the most photographed spots in all of the park system, and the lodge on its shores is justifiably famous. (It's also bigger than the lake itself, which is really more pond-sized than lake.) Unless you've got a wide-angle lens, it's very difficult to get good photographs of the lake – it's simply too small and too jammed in.

■ Adventures for the Eyes

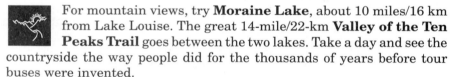

For mountain views, try **Moraine Lake**, about 10 miles/16 km from Lake Louise. The great 14-mile/22-km **Valley of the Ten Peaks Trail** goes between the two lakes. Take a day and see the countryside the way people did for the thousands of years before tour buses were invented.

Another good water view is of **Lake Minnewanka**, the biggest lake in the park. It was formed by a dam built back in the early years of the last century. It's northeast of town. Once there, **Lake Minnewanka Boat Tours**, ☎ 403-762-3473, has 90-minute cruises (CAN $30) that get you mountain views.

Driving through the park, you can get off the main highway and onto **Bow Valley Parkway**, which runs parallel. This is the back way between Banff and Lake Louise, a narrow, twisty road, but there are lots of places to get off the pavement and take a look around. It's also, of course, a lot prettier than the main highway, since you're running back in closer to the trees. The best things along the parkway are the wetlands areas, **Backswamp** and **Muleshoe**, which are birder paradises.

■ Adventures on Foot

 Hiking: You'll find some good hikes right off the parkway. Try **Cory Pass**, four miles/six km one-way, for great views of Mt. Louis. It tops out with a very long, steep ascent, and the gasping is worth it. The trailhead is at the Fireside Picnic Area.

If that's too much climbing, try **Edith Pass**, which is a forest walk leading out of the same picnic area. It doesn't have the great views, but is a good leg-stretch walk, just under three miles/five km.

In **Johnston Canyon** (take the Johnston Canyon road where Bow Valley meets the Trans-Canada), you can walk the edge of the canyon – not the biggest around, but pretty nonetheless. Or head out to the **Ink Pots**, a batch of cold mineral springs. It's 1.6 miles/2.7 km from the trailhead at the Johnston Canyon Lodge back to the Upper Canyon falls, which drop about 100 feet/30 meters. From there, it's another 1.8 miles/three km back to the Ink Pots.

■ Onward to Yoho

 From Lake Louise, where the Bow Valley meets the Johnston Canyon Road, you have a couple of choices on which way to go. The Trans-Canada down to Yoho is one good option.

Yoho National Park

If you're coming into the parks system from Golden, this is where you'll start off; it's easy access to central British Columbia.

Yoho is, like Kootenay, is underutilized. People drive through it, but they don't think about stopping. If you can't find a campsite in Jasper or Banff, this isn't a bad place to try. Yoho has the same stunning scenery as the other parks, but it rains more, and cloudy days are more frequent on the western side of the Rockies.

■ Attractions

 From Lake Louise it's a dramatic downhill run to the small town of **Field**. Along the way, you'll pass the **Spiral Tunnel Viewpoint**, which lets you see just how determined they were when they built the first transcontinental railway in Canada. They tried laying a regular line but, because the grade was so steep, the result was a lot of dead trains. The solution, then, was to build two spiral tunnels through the mountains. The tunnels, 1.2 miles/two km long, brought an end to the train crashes, although they did perturb people who didn't like running circles in the dark.

Just for fun, remember that the main highway you're driving on follows the original rail route, the one that caused so many train crashes.

A little farther downhill is a viewpoint that overlooks the merging point of the Yoho and Kicking Horse rivers. As we've said before, the Kicking Horse is some of the finest whitewater in BC.

■ Adventures for the Eyes

 There's a turnoff from the main highway to Yoho Valley Road. Follow this nine miles/14 km to **Takakkaw Falls**, more than 820 feet/250 meters high, rumbling out of a glacial river. This is well worth the side trip. There's an easy walk that gets you better views than you'll have from the parking lot.

The main highway flattens out at the small town of Field, where there's the **Visitor Information Centre** (open 8 am to 8 pm). You need to stop here to see what the fossils from the Burgess Shale (below) really look like. Quite frankly, most people walk away wondering what kind of drugs the paleontologists were on to get those creatures out of those fossils, but this is going to be your best view of some of the most important fossils ever found.

■ Adventures on Foot

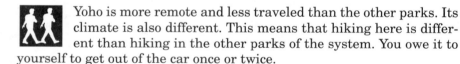 Yoho is more remote and less traveled than the other parks. Its climate is also different. This means that hiking here is different than hiking in the other parks of the system. You owe it to yourself to get out of the car once or twice.

The most popular hike is probably the **Emerald Lake Loop**, just over three miles/five km along the lakeshore. This is an easy walk with lots of scenery, a perfect after-dinner stroll.

Back in Yoho Valley, from the Takakkaw Falls parking lot, try the **Twin Falls Hike**, five miles/eight km that takes you past more waterfalls than you're going to want to count. At the end, there's the Twin Falls Chalet, where you can pick up a snack or drink before heading back.

For the more ambitious, the overnighter to **Lake O'Hara** offers alpine scenery at its best.

■ The Burgess Shale

The best reason to visit Yoho is to see firsthand why we're driving cars and not sludging around in the mud at the bottom of the ocean somewhere. Inside the park boundaries is the Burgess Shale, one of the most interesting fossil finds in the world. The shale was formed about 530 million years ago. It's only 10 feet/three meters thick and 100 yards long, but more different types of life have been found here than in any other spot on the planet. Life, essentially, has narrowed its choices since the shale was formed, keeping only a few species. In the Burgess there is evidence of the processes of life going on a wild experimental binge, producing incredible shapes of animals – beasts that looked like walking tinker toys, with five eyes, what paleontologist Stephen Jay Gould called animals "whose mouth was a circular nutcracker."

Although some paleontologists argue with his theories, Gould's book *Wonderful Life* is a great history of the find and the implications of the incredible variety of animals in it.

Perfectly fossilized in the shale formations are 20 to 30 kinds of arthropods (spiders and lobsters are modern arthropods) that don't fit into any modern group. In other words, entirely new kinds of life developed and disappeared.

The fossils here were discovered by Charles Walcott in 1909. Walcott was the head of the Smithsonian Institution, and today you can tour the quarry that has been named after him for CAN $45. It's an all-day, 12.5-mile/20-km hike that will take you to the best part of the formation. If that's a bit more than you have in mind, there's a shorter hike to the **Mt. Stephens Fossil Beds**, where mostly trilobites have been found, for CAN $25 per person. It's a 3.7-mile/six-km round-trip hike. While both hikes are considered moderately difficult, the shorter one actually has the steeper grades.

Tours run from July to September or October, depending on weather conditions. Reservations are required. Phone the **Yoho Burgess Shale Research Foundation** at ☎ 800-343-3006 for details. However, they're notorious for not bothering to answer their phone, so be persistent. Once you do get through, bring your own lunch and prepare to be amazed. Why sit through a video of computer-generated dinosaurs when the real miracle of prehistoric life is right here?

If you can't get in on the tour, stop by the **Yoho Visitor Centre**, which has some of the fossils on display. Looking at them, you're going to be struck most strongly by wondering what kind of freaks scientists are. Compare the fossils to the drawings of the animal the way they think it looked before it got flattened out. There are things the specialist's eye catches that you and I will never see. Check out the hyoliths, which look like octopus who got bred with crossbows; or the chelicerata, distant relations to scorpions and spiders, and something you wouldn't want to see crawling at you. In all, about 170 species have been found at the Burgess Shale.

 The gift shop has good trilobite postcards as well as copies of *The Fossils of the Burgess Shale*, by Derek Briggs, Douglas Erwin and Frederick Collier. This is a serious book – it runs upwards of CAN $40 for the paperback – but well worth it for the dino-inclined.

■ Where to Eat

The choices are minimal in Yoho. It's a good place to plan a picnic. Try the **Truffle Pigs' Café**, downtown, for a huge menu and crowds of locals not in the mood to cook. A good place.

■ Where to Stay

 Hotels are a little cheaper here than in Banff or Jasper, but not by a whole lot. **Emerald Lake Lodge**, ☎ 250-343-6321, has rooms in chalets, with fireplaces, a hot tub and a sauna. Doubles from CAN $140. **Kicking Horse Lodge**, ☎ 250-343-6303, is outside of town in a beautiful, quiet location. Some of the rooms have kitchenettes, and there is a restaurant on the grounds. Doubles from CAN $98.

Cathedral Mountain Lodge & Chalets, ☎ 250-343-6442, is out towards Takakkaw Falls. Here you can stay in a log cabin and walk along the Kicking Horse River before dinner. Doubles from CAN $195.

Camping

On the road to Takakkaw Falls is **Kicking Horse Campground**, the park's biggest. If you have a tent, though, keep going back to **Takakkaw Falls Campground**, a walk-in only facility. **Hoodoo Creek** is also a good choice, southwest of Field. It has trees and flush toilets.

The Icefields Parkway: Lake Louise to Jasper

The Icefields Parkway leaves Lake Louise, heading for Jasper. Traffic can be slow, especially in the long, narrow valley along the Continental Divide. You'll want to drive slowly anyway to take in the view. Watch for wildlife along the entire route: goats and sheep in the south, more elk and deer toward Jasper.

It's 141 miles/230 km from Lake Louise to Jasper, but it's best to figure on a full day to do the trip. There's plenty to see, and always a good chance of wildlife along the road – elk, mountain goats, maybe bear – and there are plenty of places to get out and walk around.

> **AUTHOR NOTE:** A lot of people can be on this road in summer. Drive carefully. Because it's such a good road – wide, with generous shoulders – there can also be a lot of bike traffic on the road. Any time you're coming around a blind corner, slow down. There's no telling what's on the other side of it, be it an animal, a bunch of people stopped for an animal, or somebody on a bike.

The road is open year-round, although it can sometimes be closed for a little while in winter due to avalanches.

All that said, it's one of the prettiest stretches of road you'll ever be on. Get the camera ready.

Distances we list here are from Lake Louise.

The **Crowfoot Glacier** viewpoint is 20 miles/33 km north of Lake Louise. Crowfoot is shrinking fast, so you'd better see it now. The name comes from what looked like three toes coming down off the main glacial face; one toe is gone, the other two won't be around much longer.

Another 2.4 miles/four km up the road is **Bow Lake**, the source of the Bow River, and

Along the Icefields Parkway.

it's all fed by the Bow Icefield and Bow Glacier. The water can be mirror-still – if you didn't get the mountain reflections you wanted at Lake Louise, try here.

The Parks

The road heads uphill from here, to the **Bow Summit**, just over 6,500 feet/2,000 meters high. From here, it's all downhill to Jasper – which is why most people on bikes are going north, not south.

Peyto Lake, 25 miles/40 km from Lake Louise, is just behind the Bow Summit parking lot. It's an easy walk back to the lake, one that you really shouldn't miss. Take all the pictures you can, because it's going to take proof when you get back home and tell your friends about the colors of the water. Depending on how the sun is hitting it, you can get anything from emerald green to a dark blue; the color changes seasonally, as well, depending on glacial melt. You don't want to miss this.

Pretty much everybody stops at the **Columbia Icefield Visitor Information Centre**, almost halfway between Jasper (64 miles/105 km north) and Lake Louise (81 miles/132 km south). The center is huge, with a cafeteria, dining room and an impressive interactive glaciation display. That's reason enough to come in, but while you're here, if you've never walked on a glacier before, now's your chance. The center is just across the highway from the Athabasca Glacier (part of the immense Columbia Icefields, the largest in the Rockies), and there are regular trips that take you out onto the glacier itself. Buy tickets from the booth upstairs in the center; they'll tell you when the next bus is leaving. From the center, you load onto a bus, drive across the road, along a glacial moraine, and then load into snowcats, buses with huge treaded tires, that take you down the moraine and onto the ice of the glacier. These things move very slowly – they top out around four mph – but you're probably not in a hurry, as you can get terrific ice and mountain views. The end of the ride comes at a large, cleared area. Okay, it's a parking lot carved into the glacier. If you've been on glaciers before, this is going to come as a bit of a disappointment, as you can't get any farther onto the ice. If you've never been on a glacier, this is a good introduction. It's also easily accessible for people with limited mobility. Tickets are CAN $29.95.

You can book a glacier hike at the center. They take only small groups and you need to be pretty fit. Three-hour walks (CAN $45) leave at 11 am. On Sundays and Thursdays, there's the more ambitious "icewalk deluxe," which runs CAN $50 for five hours on the ice. ☎ 800-565-7547.

The Columbia Icefield is melting fast, but in places the ice is still over 1,000 feet/300 meters thick. Meltwater from the icefield feeds the North Saskatchewan, Columbia, Fraser, Athabasca and Mackenzie rivers.

> **AUTHOR NOTE:** Mt. Snow Dome is the "hydrographic apex" of North America. What this means is that a drop of water balanced at the absolute top of the mountain stands an equal chance of ending up in the Atlantic, Pacific or Arctic ocean. It's a three-way continental divide.

Drive away from the center and the mountain views are, to use a cliché, breathtaking. Any direction you look on a nice day, you'll see steep slopes, thick forest and ice-capped mountain peaks. The tallest mountains top out at over 10,000 feet/3,000 meters; the tallest in the park is Mt. Forbes, 11,975 feet/3,630 meters tall, which you can see on the way to **Sunwapta Pass**.

The pass is the border between Jasper and Banff, but the scenery doesn't change any. However, at this point, we're going to switch and give you distances to Jasper from here. Stop at **Sunwapta Falls**, 34 miles/55 km south of Jasper, if you haven't had your fill of waterfalls yet.

The last miles into Jasper are tree-lined, pretty, perhaps a little less dramatic than farther south. Jasper makes you work just a little harder to be dazzled, but there's no shortage of the spectacular. Actually, we like it best of the whole system.

Jasper & Jasper National Park

The Town

Jasper bills itself as the "Gem of the Canadian Rockies," and that's no joke. With probably the prettiest scenery of the four parks (although it's hard to compare superlatives), Jasper has the usual mountains, gorges, lakes and streams, but somehow they're put together even better here. Whereas the other parks are a little more sedate, Jasper is where people come for serious, hard-core outdoor action. If you're packing a canoe or planning some rock climbing, you'll want to spend your time here.

If you thought Banff town was a little hurried, the town of Jasper is much more laid back. It doesn't have the shopping or the fine dining that Banff does, but it has families sunning themselves on the lawn in front of the Visitor Centre and a slower, more laid-back feel to it. It's a mountain town that hasn't been ruined yet by its proximity to the mountains.

There's no way to miss the **Info Centre**: it's right downtown in a beautiful old stone building. ☎ 780-582-6176. There's also a Parks Canada office in the same building, if you want a permit for access into backcountry areas.

Everything you need in town is within walking distance of the Info Centre. Along the main stretch of road are plenty of restaurants and souvenir shops. There's nothing outstanding, but you won't have any trouble here if you've got money burning a hole in your pocket.

The Parks

■ Where to Eat

 Mountain Foods Café, 606 Connaught, is the place to hit for breakfast. It has fresh baked goods and, for later, you can pick up a sandwich or wrap. **Jasper's Pizza Place**, 402 Connaught, is a local favorite. Its small wood-fired pizzas will set you back about CAN $12.

One street back from Connaught is Patricia St., where **Spooner's** is upstairs at 610 Patricia. Balcony seats let you watch the people moving by as you munch on good light sandwiches and salads. A nice place for lunch.

For dinner, try **Villa Caruso**, 640 Connaught, for steak and seafood, from CAN $15. At the fancier end of things is **Andy's Bistro**, 606 Patricia, with local ingredient specialties.

■ Where to Stay

 As far as hotels go, Jasper is cheaper than Banff, and you stand a better chance of rolling up and finding a room on short notice, but it's still best to plan ahead.

Rocky Mountain Reservations, ☎ 780-852-9455, 877-902-9455, can book you into hotels anywhere in the parks. Call them if you haven't planned ahead. You can also try **Banff Accommodations**, ☎ 877-226-3348, which will book Jasper hotels.

Becker's Chalets, ☎ 780-852-3779, is just south of town in a pretty location. Some of the rooms have balconies and fridges, but none has a phone. Good, clean and comfortable doubles start at CAN $130.

The Astoria Hotel, 404 Connaught, ☎ 780-852-3351, is downtown. It is comfortable and has clean rooms, all with a fridge. Doubles from CAN $150.

The Athabasca Hotel, 510 Patricia St., takes you one street back from the main drag. Some good touches include high-speed Internet access. Doubles start at CAN $110.

Jasper Inn Alpine Resort moves you up the comfort and price scale. A lot of the rooms have real wood fireplaces. There's a heated pool on the grounds, plus a sauna and steam room. Doubles from CAN $215.

The Maligne Lodge, 925 Connaught, ☎ 780-852-3143, has rooms with balconies; some with fireplaces. Doubles from CAN $180.

The Tonquin Inn, 100 Juniper St., ☎ 800-661-1315, is another good choice around CAN $200. It's at the end of town, but still in walking distance of attractions. Some rooms have fireplaces.

Finally, at the top of the economic scale, is the **Fairmont Jasper Park Lodge**, with everything you expect from a Fairmont. It's on Highway 16, just outside town, ☎ 800-441-1414. Doubles from CAN $550.

Camping

Whistlers Campground is the biggest in the parks, just south of town. It's huge, but its layout leaves you with some feeling of privacy and being in the woods. It offers everything from tent sites to RV sites with full hookups.

Another 1.2 miles/two km south of town is the **Wapiti Campground**, which is also huge. If you're coming in winter, this is your only option.

You can't make reservations at these campgrounds; you have to show up and hope. Check out time is 11 am, so plan accordingly to claim your spot during high season.

The Park

Take Highway 93A for views of Mount Edith Cavell reflecting in a glacial melt lake. Off Highway 16 East, there are hot springs, waterfalls and frequent traffic jams caused by elk herds. One of the more popular drives is back to **Maligne Lake**. Head back on Maligne Lake Road, just outside of town. There's a stop at **Maligne Canyon**, where you can take a short, easy hike along the gorge. When you hit the end of the road – which has gorgeous mountain and river views, some of the best anywhere in the parks system – you can launch your canoe on Maligne Lake, the second-largest glacier-fed lake in the world, more than 14 miles/22.5 km long. Boat rentals are available from Maligne Lake Boathouse.

A tramway climbs **Whistler Mountain** (just south of the town of Jasper), past the Whistlers Campground. The tram climbs 3,200 vertical feet/973 vertical meters, taking you nearly 8,000 feet/2,277 meters up the mountain. Hiking trails lead the rest of the way to the summit – figure 1½ hours to get to the peak and back.

This is a really dramatic ride and, if you've got a clear day, you're going to run out of film very quickly. Watch for marmots galumphing along the trails. It's a good place to see what the high alpine landscape is really like. The round-trip is CAN $20 and cars depart every 12 minutes. Go early; it can get really crowded as the day wears on.

Other good hiking trails include the **Pyramid Lake Trail**, about 12 miles/19 km and fairly strenuous, or the truly ambitious **Saturday Night Lake Circle**, about 18 miles/29 km and running past a string of lakes. The trailhead is in town. Actually, once you take any of the trails out of town heading up the mountains to the west, you are on a huge network of interlacing trails that could keep an experienced hiker busy for weeks. A quick hike would be the 1.5-mile/2.4-km **Lake Annette Loop**. The trailhead is on Maligne Road.

From Whistlers Campground, walk up the road toward the tramway, then hit the **Whistlers Trail**, which leads off south. This is a steep, switch-back trail but, once you're at the top, you've got killer mountain views and a chance to see some of the high alpine landscape. It's 13 miles/ eight km each way – figure as much as five hours up, three hours down.

 There's a free brochure, *Summer Trails in Jasper*, that lists some good hikes. If that's not enough for you, we again suggest the marvelous *Canadian Rockies Trail Guide*, by Patton and Robinson.

■ Adventure Outfitters

 No matter what you want to do outside, you'll find an outfitter here.

For the Mountains

Peter Amann, ☎ 780-852-3237, runs mountain climbing and guiding classes. A two-day rock climbing intro runs CAN $150; two days on snow and ice is CAN $220. These are a great chance to hone up on your skills or find out if these are skills you really want to have.

Paul Valiulis, ☎ 780-852-1945, does rock climbing trips for CAN $60, canyoneering trips – think of rock climbing combined with a water slide – for CAN $65.

For the Water

Of course, with all the snowmelt, there's great whitewater rafting in the park on several rivers. **Maligne Rafting Adventures**, ☎ 866-625-4463, 780-852-3370, runs trips on the Maligne, the Athabasca and the Kakwa – from quick trips for CAN $44 to three-day runs for CAN $450 and up.

Rocky Mountain Voyageur, ☎ 780-852-5595, has trips in a classic voyageur canoe – these are the boats that opened western Canada. It's a smooth-water paddle good for all ages. Two hours on the water runs CAN $48 for adults, CAN $29 for kids.

For Hikers

Overlander Trekking and Tours, ☎ 888-SUNDOG1, leads some easy day hikes and packages hikes with other local attractions. Take in the Maligne Valley for CAN $49 (just the hike), or CAN $70 if you add on a cruise. Day hikes include the Sulfur Skyline, which will take four-six hours (CAN $55), or the half-day Cavell Meadows Hike, which gets you alpine views (CAN $55).

Edge Control Outdoors, ☎ 780-852-4994, does the Maligne Valley for CAN $45 for a three-hour-plus hike, Mt. Edith Cavell Meadows and Angel Glacier for CAN $55.

For Wildlife

Edge Control Outdoors runs morning two-hour trips for CAN $45, and they bring the spotting scope. **On-Line Sport**, ☎ 780-852-3630, has half-day trips for CAN $99, or they'll take you out on a boat to look for waterfowl and raptors for CAN $129. Some of the species you might tick off your life list include barred owls, Barrow's goldeneye, Lewis woodpeckers and ovenbirds.

Alpine Art, ☎ 780-852-3709, leads nature safaris, where you have a good chance of seeing elk, moose and maybe a bear. Half-day trips run CAN $49.

In the Air

Plenty of flightseeing options in Jasper. **Air Jasper**, ☎ 780-865-3616, does 75-minute flybys of the Columbia Icefield for CAN $135. **High Country Helicopter Tours**, ☎ 780-852-0125, has a CAN $198 flight that gives you the best mountain views, the best array of terrain. They also do helihiking: half-day, three-person minimum, CAN $415 per person. This is the best way to walk where none of your friends have ever been.

■ Transport

 If you don't have your own car, you can get back and forth between Jasper and Banff on the **Jasper-Banff Connector**, a daily bus service. It's CAN $55 one way, and they'll pick you up at your hotel. ☎ 888-786-3641.

If you're looking to move onward from Jasper, you can hop on the **Skeena**, a train which goes from Jasper to Prince George on VIA Rail. It's about six hours to Prince George, from which you can keep heading south by rail to Terrace. ☎ 888-VIA-RAIL.

If you're going from Jasper to Prince George, you'll pass through **Mt. Robson Provincial Park**, a relatively small park just west of Jasper. People come here to see the mountains and to camp in sites that are usually much less crowded than those in the nearby parks. Best views are of Mt. Robson (you can't miss it − it's the mountain view that makes you stop your car), the highest peak in the Canadian Rockies, at over 12,000 feet/3,650 meters. Rearguard Falls (about 13 miles/eight km west of the park headquarters) and Overlander Falls (a mile/1.6 km east) are worth-while stops. Hikers can take a 90-minute walk out of Overlander.

Mt. Robson.

If the campsites by the road are full, shoulder your pack and try the **Rockingham Creek** crossing site: it's 3.7 miles/six km from the trailhead (at the Yellowhead Lake boat launch). Head up 6.8 miles/11 km more and you're in beautiful alpine lakes.

If you're looking to spend a week in the backcountry, the **Berg Lake Trail** (13.6 miles/22 km long), links up with the **Moose River Trail** for a total of just over 50 miles/81 km. Along the way you pass more than a dozen glaciers. The trailhead is 1½ miles past the Visitors Centre, where you must stop and register before leaving.

The Canadian Rockies are one of the premier destinations in the world for people who love the outdoors. We have only scratched the surface here. But let's close the chapter with this statement: We go through these parks all the time. Every time, we find something new to do, something we never expected. Every time, it's the scenic highlight of the trip.

This place is amazing.

Appendix

Recommended Reading

BC has a great publishing industry all its own. There's no shortage of books on the province.

Start by picking up a free copy of **Read BC**, available at most Info Centres. This lists more than a hundred books on the province, broken down according to geographical region. It's a good place to start looking for what's available.

There are two books that are absolute must-haves as you travel BC. The **Beautiful British Columbia Travel Guide** covers almost every road in the province, with good maps, lots of interesting facts and plenty of side-trips. It's like the *Milepost* guide, only without the endless ads.

Cheryl Coull's **Traveller's Guide to Aboriginal BC** is a masterpiece of historic traveling. Over a 20-year period, she hung out with tribal elders and got their stories, as well as their takes on the land around them. This is, flat out, one of the best guidebooks to native culture and history ever written.

George Bowering's **Bowering's BC: A Swashbuckling History** is the perfect introduction to how BC became what it is. Bowering has a great grasp of the forces of history, and he makes it fun. You can read this book like a good novel and only later will you discover just how much you've learned.

Once you've got that nailed, pick up Rosemary Neering's **Traveller's Guide to Historic British Columbia**, another great one to have in the car with you.

There's no way to travel around BC without wondering just what the HBC was thinking much of the time. Peter C. Newman's **Company of Adventurers** tries to answer that question. It's a little light on BC – the book is more interested in the HBC's early days in the east – but a must for understanding the second-oldest corporation in the world (behind the Zildjian Cymbal Co.).

Robert Bringhurst won a ton of awards for his **A Story as Sharp as a Knife: The Classical Haida Mythtellers and Their World**. He deserved them all. It's a huge volume of Haida oral legend, beautifully translated and lovingly presented. You won't find a better book on the inner life of the coast First Nations groups anywhere. It's part of a series of three, so if you've got the time and the money, this is a must buy.

Now that you're loaded down on history and culture, let's offer up a few books that specialize in particular corners of the area.

The Canadian Rockies Trail Guide, by Brian Patton and Bart Robinson, is what you need if you're going to spend a couple of weeks hiking in the parks. There are other guides to the trails out there, but this is the one to own. It's skimpy on the maps – you'll need topos, but then you'd need them no matter what – but it has very detailed descriptions of the trails and something for hikers at every level.

The Southern Gulf Islands, published by Altitude, is worth picking up if you're going to be spending a lot of time in that watery space between Vancouver City and Vancouver Island.

50 Best Day Trips from Vancouver, by Jack Christie, has a spot on almost every Vancouver-ites bookshelf. The longer you're in town, the more you'll need this book.

Mary & David Macaree offer up *109 Walks in British Columbia's Lower Mainland*. This takes in the area around Vancouver, up to Whistler, and into the Fraser Valley.

Finally, *Gotta Hike BC*, by Skye and Lake Nomad, covers BC south of Route 1. It profiles more than 40 hikes, all with very detailed directions.

If you're going to be in Vancouver for any length of time, pick up a copy of *Vancouver: The Ultimate Guide*, by Judi Lees. Updated regularly, it's the city handbook.

> **AUTHOR NOTE:** You'll get the best selection of books on BC in Victoria, at **Munros** or **Chapters** (www.chapters.ca), or at the Chapters in downtown Vancouver. You won't be able to find much of what we're listing here if you look south of the border.

Index

Index